INSIDE THE ACADEMY AND OUT: LESBIAN/GAY/QUEER STUDIES AND SOCIAL ACTION

Edited by Janice L. Ristock and Catherine Taylor

There is an urgent need for effective political and social action in support of lesbian and gay rights. Writing from the field of lesbian/gay/queer studies, however, is often merely sophisticated theorizing about identity and representations, ignoring the need for action at a community level.

Inside the Academy and Out demonstrates that the pedagogical and theoretical insights offered by lesbian/gay/queer studies can have relevance to a broader social sphere. The essayists represented here come from a wide range of disciplines, including English, education, philosophy, sociology, and women's studies. Their essays are divided into two broad areas: 'Pedagogy and Research' and 'Spheres of Action.' Taken together, they explore teaching and research theory, examining their implications in areas such as AIDS education, social services, law reform, and popular culture.

JANICE L. RISTOCK is an associate professor and coordinator of women's studies at the University of Manitoba.
CATHERINE TAYLOR teaches in the Centre for Academic Writing at the University of Winnipeg and is a doctoral candidate in critical pedagogy and cultural studies at OISE/University of Toronto.

EDITED BY
JANICE L. RISTOCK AND CATHERINE G. TAYLOR

Inside the Academy and Out: Lesbian/Gay/Queer Studies and Social Action

UNIVERSITY OF TORONTO PRESS
Toronto Buffalo London

Barnard

© University of Toronto Press Incorporated 1998
Toronto Buffalo London
Printed in Canada

ISBN 0-8020-0860-7 (cloth)
ISBN 0-8020-7848-6 (paper)

Printed on acid-free paper

Canadian Cataloguing in Publication Data

Main entry under title:

Inside the academy and out : lesbian/gay/queer studies and social action

Includes bibliographical references and index.

ISBN 0-8020-0860-7 (bound)   ISBN 0-8020-7848-6 (pbk.)

1. Gay and lesbian studies.   2. Homosexuality – Research.
3. Action research.   I. Ristock, Janice L. (Janice Lynn).
II. Taylor, Catherine.

HQ76.25I574 I198   305.9′0664′07   C98-930220-2

University of Toronto Press acknowledges the financial assistance to its publishing
program of the Canada Council for the Arts and the Ontario Arts Council.

This book is dedicated to our parents,
Bob and Jan Ristock,
and Helen and the late Reg Taylor,
with thanks for their loving ways

Contents

viii   Contents

Preface

The idea for this volume emerged from conversations about our work (Catherine's on pedagogy, Janice's on research), where we saw that we were confronting similar issues despite the different contexts we were addressing. Our questions would centre around issues such as how to focus on lesbian and gay identities in research and how to teach without essentializing them; also how to take up deconstructive practices central to queer theory and postmodern writings while mobilizing our work for social action in the here and now. Both of us were involved in the steering committee that led, in 1994, to the formation of a new Learned Society, provisionally called the Canadian Lesbian and Gay Studies Association. Many of the questions we were struggling with in our own work were also playing out in the meetings of the association, particularly over the issue of settling on a name for it. Discussions were heated as we debated issues of representation, identities, and exclusionary language practices. Should it be named the Queer Studies Association as a way to exceed the limited membership suggested by the term *lesbian and gay studies*? Would this name be intelligible to our academic institutions, or would it still be heard mainly in its original pejorative sense? Should we be called the Lesbian, Gay, Bisexual, Transgendered Studies Association in a more differentiated gesture of inclusiveness? Who would we be leaving out in that gesture – who in the name of queer? Would the focus on the area of study suggested by the term *sexuality studies* be preferable to the focus on the identity conditions of membership possibly suggested by lesbian and gay studies, or would we thereby be constituting the business of the association as research on sex? The first annual general meeting (AGM), in Calgary in 1994, resulted in the name The Canadian Lesbian and Gay Studies Association, perhaps the most generally intelligible choice but in many ways the most limiting. We hoped we would be able to undo any damage our name might do by clarifying our positions during our calls for conference proposals and membership efforts.

Each AGM continues to raise the issue of naming. The issue with respect to how we want to identify ourselves is in many dimensions an issue of pedagogy (what we teach ourselves and others by how we are represented) and epistemology (what paths of knowledge production our name would promote and what paths it might discourage). When the work is conceived as part of a highly contested social movement that aims to change the way people think about sexuality and sexually categorized identities, there is much at stake in this terrain of teaching and knowing.

We attended the meetings of the association in Calgary and Montreal and heard a number of wonderful papers that addressed issues of pedagogy and research theory within a social-action framework. We solicited several of these papers for our volume and invited many other scholars not presenting at those meetings to develop papers specifically for the collection. We did most of our communicating by e–mail and snail mail as authors developed, rewrote, and revised their work (complaining only mildly about the quaint minutiae of Chicago style).

We would like to thank all of the contributors for their commitment to our project. We think this volume brings together an exciting group of papers, all of them previously unpublished. We hope others will be encouraged to develop the connections between the social-action work we do through academic research and university teaching, and the work we do outside the academy in other spheres of social action.

We would also like to thank the editors at the University of Toronto Press, Virgil Duff and Margaret Williams. The growing interest of scholarly presses in projects like ours is clearly important to the development of gay and lesbian studies in Canada. The extent of support is such that we abandoned our working title, *Sexualities and Social Action: Inside the Academy and Out* (one we had thought might avoid the thickets of identity-specification on the book jacket, at least), when the executive editor of UTP instructed us to 'get lesbian, gay, and queer studies into your title.'

Our thanks to Lois Grieger, a research assistant who helped in the preparation of the manuscript. Thanks also to friends with whom we have discussed pedagogy and research, including colleagues in Winnipeg (Doug Arrell, Karen Busby, Rhonda Chorney, Keith Louise Fulton, Pauline Greenhill, Susan Heald), the members of the steering committee for the CLGSA (Jane Aronson, Doug Arrell, Roy Cain, Steven Maynard, David Rayside), members of the first executive of the CLGSA (Irene Demczuk, Gloria Filax, Monica Kendel, Rick

Lee, Debra Shogan, and, again, Doug Arrell, who finally suggested that we call ourselves the Canadian Judith Butler Studies Association and be done with it).

We would also like to acknowledge the work of some of the first Canadian scholars to publish in the area of gay and lesbian studies. Some are featured in this volume; others are Barry Adams, Mary Louise Adams, Dick Delamora, Gary Kinsman, Kathleen Martindale, Steven Maynard, Henry Minton, Becki Ross, Mikeda Silvera, George Smith, Sharon Stone, Mariana Valverde, and Jeri Dawn Wine. Their work has made important contributions to the social, cultural, and historical study of the production and regulation of sexuality. Of course they have been involved as well in activist work: teaching and developing courses on lesbian and gay studies, writing for queer and mainstream popular presses, and lobbying the government. All of them made early forays into Canadian academia that helped open doors for the publication of the kind of work represented here.

Finally, we dedicate this volume to everyone struggling to create queer spaces (or to queer the space, however that work is conceived) in the heteronormative world of university teaching and scholarly life.

INSIDE THE ACADEMY AND OUT:
LESBIAN/GAY/QUEER STUDIES AND
SOCIAL ACTION

Introduction

JANICE L. RISTOCK AND CATHERINE G. TAYLOR

Antiheteronormative efforts in universities go by the names Sexuality Studies, Queer Studies, and, most commonly, Lesbian and (or) Gay Studies. We use the usefully awkward term *lesbian/gay/queer* to describe the areas covered in this volume. Our choice reflects the differences among contributors, some of whom focus on lesbian and gay cultures, some on ways of queering people's perspectives on dominant cultures; many attempt both. These areas fall more often into the scholarly publishing category than into the academic structure, more often emblazoning book catalogues than departmental letterhead. Although they show up across the university curriculum, they usually occur either as separate courses of study at the margins of mainstream disciplines, or as incorporations into or 'queerings' of mainstream courses. As recently as 1993 only a few courses were described in Canadian university calendars as including some kind of lesbian and gay or sexuality content.[1] These areas have since enjoyed a boom period, particularly in the United States but in Canada as well. A primary focus on lesbian/gay/queer content has become quite common: *Centre/fold*, a newsletter of the Toronto Centre for Lesbian and Gay Studies, now publishes an annual list of courses being offered across the country in various institutions of higher education;[2] and the Canadian Lesbian and Gay Studies Association has grown to several hundred members in only three years. Some of us see our work only reluctantly as political, others as crucially and wholeheartedly so. But whatever the institutional form in which they occur, teaching and research in the area of lesbian/gay/queer studies – against tremendous resistance from dominant cultures, inside the university and out – are attempts to change the way people think about sexuality.

No wonder, then, that pedagogy and research theory are taken so seriously by scholars of lesbian/gay/queer studies as forms of social action where much is at stake in our mistakes and successes. Questions of research theory – What can we know? What good can knowing do? – and pedagogical questions – How can we teach? What can we learn? – are connected through a social action project concerned with transforming the systems of domination that keep understandings of sexualities stuck within an oppressive homo/hetero divide.

Though none has focused on research and teaching and their connection to social action, writings on the topic of lesbian/gay/queer studies can be found in a variety of publications across a range of disciplines. One of the first was Henry Minton's *Gay and Lesbian Studies* (1992), in which contributors offer strategic analyses of the institutional emergence of this area of study in Europe and North America, rather than methods of teaching and research. Appearing the same year was John d'Emilio's *Making Trouble: Essays on Gay History, Politics, and the University* (1992), which includes a section on institutional issues in gay and lesbian studies and campus life. Contributors to Linda Garber's *Tilting the Tower: Lesbians Teaching Queer Subjects* (1994) cover both pedagogical approaches in high school and university classrooms and institutional issues in lesbian life and lesbian studies. Lisa Duggan and Nan Hunter's *Sex Wars: Sexual Dissent and Political Culture* (1995) includes a selection of their papers on academic activism and the institutionalization of lesbian and gay studies. Tamsin Wilton's *Lesbian Studies: Setting an Agenda* (1995) begins with a chapter on deviant pedagogies and includes an assessment of sociological research methodologies in an attempt to develop a matrix for a theoretical analysis of sex and gender appropriate to lesbian studies. *Professions of Desire: Lesbian and Gay Studies in Literature*, an MLA volume edited by George Haggerty and Bonnie Zimmerman (1995), includes several chapters on teaching approaches and methods. Zimmerman and Toni A.H. McNaron's *The New Lesbian Studies: Into the Twenty-First Century* (1996), an anti-elitist collection of papers on institutional emergence and classroom issues with an emphasis on teaching lesbian history and culture, includes many papers first published in the groundbreaking *Lesbian Studies: Present and Future* (1982), edited by Margaret Cruikshank. Most recently the journal *Genders* (26, 1997) published an issue called 'The Gay '90s: Disciplinary and Interdisciplinary Formations in Queer Studies,' edited by Thomas Foster, Carol Siegel, and Ellen E. Berry.

Many of the volumes that foreground the field of lesbian/gay/queer studies in their titles try to offer a range of scholarship produced within the field rather than focus on issues of scholarly practice. Interestingly, the first publication in this anticanonical field to declare itself *The Lesbian and Gay Studies Reader* (1993) is exemplary of this point, with its single offering on such an issue: Joan Scott's 'The Evidence of Experience.'[3] The focus of John Champagne's *The Ethics of Marginality: A New Approach to Gay Studies* (1995) is academic discourse rather than teaching or research. Diana Fuss does include two chapters on pedagogy (by Cindy Patton and Simon Watney)[4] in *Inside/Out: Lesbian Theories, Gay Theories* (1991). Richard Parker and John Gagnon's *Conceiving Sexuality: Approaches to Sex Research in a Postmodern World* (1995) is mainly sex theory rather than sex research theory. Papers on pedagogy and research theory can be found in the special issues on gay/lesbian/queer topics of many journals, such as the *NWSA Journal* (spring 1995); the *Harvard Educational Review*'s special issue (summer 1996) entitled 'Lesbian, Gay, Bisexual, Transgender People and Education'; *Critical Sociology* (20, 3, 1994); *Sociological Theory* (July 1994); and the 'Queer Theory, Queer Concerns' issue of the MLA journal *Concerns* (fall 1993), to name a few.

Clearly there has been a great deal of work done on gay and lesbian studies as an emergent field. Writers are concerned with pedagogical questions, and academics are interested in issues that are part of a social-action agenda. Yet there has not been a volume that shows how pedagogical and research practices in fact are parallel projects in lesbian/gay/queer studies, each conceived as a form of transformative work relevant to the larger social world. We see this effort as an important opportunity for coalitionary work that brings together the typically disparate, situated struggles we enact in (more or less) common cause.

In titling this volume *Inside the Academy and Out*, we are pointing of course to the very recent phenomenon of uncloseted academics. We are, more importantly, establishing a connection between the theorizing on research and pedagogical practices done inside universities, and the work done to change people's thinking about sexualities in other spheres of action. But we are not trying to create a false dichotomy on some such mythical line as that imagined between 'town and gown.' We are acknowledging instead the conditions of work in lesbian/gay/queer studies, where everything from departmental politics to our own pressing sense of connection to social issues turns such distinctions inside out; in Diana Fuss's words, 'most of us are both inside and outside at the same time.'[5] The papers in this collection clearly show that a classroom can be a site of social struggle (as shown in the chapters by Deborah Britzman, Margot Francis, Didi Khayatt, and Catherine Taylor, which address issues in university classrooms); a movie theatre can be a place where pedagogy is practised (as Lee Easton shows in Chapter 12); social service organizations and groups are often research sites (as Jane Aronson, Roy Cain, and Janice Ristock's chapters show); and gay/lesbian/queer-studies academics are by definition activists. Various positionings of gender, race, class, and other 'constructions of difference' intersect with sexuality to make us inside and out at the same time, both in our political understandings and in our social relations. Though this volume takes sexuality as its main focus, it does not treat that category as homogeneous, and contributors often explore the inflections of these other axes of power in their own problematizings of identity and representation.

Issues concerning how we teach and how we know are crucial inside and out because of the massive pedagogical and epistemological project implied by any antihomophobic social politic in these days of right-wing mobilization: as Foucault and others have remarked (and Suzanne de Castell and Mary Bryson's paper reminds us) homophobia remains the last socially acceptable prejudice, or form of stupidity. Certainly we have made gains with respect to legislation and in the courts; we are less subject to police raids; we see positive representations of gays and lesbians on television; and for many of us our everyday experience is radically freer than in more closeted times. Yet many people – including, it sometimes seems, entire political parties and church memberships – exhibit a stubborn refusal to budge from murderous hostility towards any less frantically heterosexist imagination. The ways of thinking available to people through dominant discourses are so thoroughly loaded in favour of heterosexuality that other sexualities are always already positioned as the problem to be solved when times are tough: witness the spectacle of the American President Bill Clinton, who proclaimed himself dedicated to gay rights in 1992, only to campaign in 1996 on his prudence in having signed the Defense of Marriage legislation after four years of homophobic attacks from the right. (In Chapter 9 Kristin Esterberg and Jeffrey Longhofer discuss the impact of the religious right, an American-based movement with cross-border aspirations to the land of REAL women, the Reform Party, and other opponents of gay and lesbian human rights.) Despite federal, provincial, and municipal laws now protecting our freedom in Canada, the vast majority of us would not dare come out at work or walk a city block holding hands with our lovers. (See Chapters 13 and 14, by Jean Noble and Diana Majury, respectively, which explore the impact of recent legislation and how sexualities are represented in the Canadian legal system.)

We have learned that if decrees can restrain the heartless, but cannot change the heart (in Martin Luther King's words), our ambitions have to reach beyond legislation against hate crimes or discrimination: we need to change people's hearts if we are to loosen the grip of heteronormativity on our lives. In our roles as university educators we try to do this work, if at all, through teaching and research. The challenge of this volume is to bring together a range of work on pedagogy and research theory done in lesbian/gay/queer studies in order to provide an occasion to consider the possible usefulness of insights from that field to social action within and beyond universities. In taking up this challenge we are giving a pedagogical/research focus to concerns for action that are evident throughout the field.

AIDS, for example, is an area that has been taken up in a number of different ways by lesbian/gay/queer studies scholars (in this volume, Britzman, Cain, Easton, Francis, Namaste, Noble, and Rehkopf). AIDS activists draw on a range of old and newer teaching and research strategies for changing people's thinking about sexualities: by sharing corrective information through safer-sex education (with disappointing results among young gay men); by appealing to the dominant culture's self-interest ('Canada has AIDS.' – a strategy which has to fight against denial and ignorance); and by hoping for empathy (which wages a similar struggle). A research and pedagogy focus looks behind strategies and techniques to ask, What is it that we are trying to teach? What are the conditions of learning? As Cindy Patton reminds us in her writings on AIDS education, 'Reimagined sexualities – sexualities imagined beyond the nation – must become embedded in everyday life, not set apart as exceptional or extraordinary. Finding and using the implicit and explicit theories that inform the personal, political, and educational approaches to preserve the lives of sexual dissidents is not just an immediate project; it is our lives.'[6]

Convictions about sexuality seem so deeply embraced that setting out to change people's minds amounts to an attempt to alter the grounds of consciousness, to change not only the content of the forms through which we think, but the very forms themselves. Thus the swift ascent of the term *queer* in the nineties, both in its street activist forms and in poststructuralist/postmodernist theorizing, is part of this move to interrupt the relentless reproduction of the heterosexist binary of straight and gay. While queer approaches such as deconstructive readings of social texts have been critiqued all along by scholars and activists as frivolous distractions from the material conditions of people's lives, people who use queer theory and methods also struggle with questions of relevance to political work. (Most contributors to this collection raise such questions in relation to work at their particular sites of social action.) As Mary Louise Adams writes, 'Theoretically, this way of mobilizing broadly defined "queerness" appeals to me very much. I'm much less clear about what it might mean in actual practice.'[7]

It seems naïve, some days, to think that heterosexist normalcy can become interested enough in undoing itself to make 'queering' a strategically sound social-action pedagogy. We can wonder whether attempts to denaturalize categories of sexual orientation can be useful anywhere, if Shane Phelan is right that 'voters in Colorado, or homophobes with baseball bats, will not be persuaded by discussions of gender ambiguity' but will see them as 'a return to the closet.'[8] To many people it seems more strategic to capitalize on the logic and truth effects of existing discourses by arguing for minority rights. And yet, as Jane Flax reminds us, 'It is far from clear what contributions knowledge or truth can make to the development of ... feelings and communities [anyway]. At its best, postmodernism invites us to engage in continual disillusionment of the grandiose fantasies that have brought us to the brink of annihilation.'[9]

Obviously, these are complicated problems for which the contributors to this book do not pretend to offer tidy solutions. Activists working to dislodge a prejudice that is everywhere supported by the institutions, practices, and discourses of our culture, and that is enmired in the most personal levels of people's lives, are in the thick of a struggle that will have to continue for many years. Our volume reflects the diversity and breadth of scholarship engaged in that effort within such diverse fields as cultural studies, education, English, law, philosophy, sociology, social work, and women's studies, all of which theorize sexuality as a major axis of power.

We have organized the book into two parts: the first brings together a set of papers on teaching and research theory that focuses on scholarly practice; the second, another set of papers concerning various spheres of social action where both strategic opportunities and problematic obstacles are explored through various levels of explicit reference to concepts of pedagogy and research theory. However, in keeping with the inside–out boundaries of queer perspectives, the chapters in Part 1 are often as much about social action as the chapters in Part 2 are about theory and practice. Our hope is that reading the second section in light of the first will help the reader further develop and mobilize insights into pedagogy and research theory by applying them to problems of social action. As Patti Lather concludes in her own work on feminist research and pedagogy, *Getting Smart* (1991), 'The best solution I have been able to come up with in these pages is to do our thinking and our investigating in and through struggle and to learn the lessons of practice, one of which is that there is no "correct line" knowable through struggle.'[10] In that spirit, what the publication of this book contributes is a space to gather together the farflung efforts of many scholars across the university curriculum who explore pedagogical and research approaches to sexualities and the struggle for social change.

Notes

1 Based on unpublished survey research reported by Catherine Taylor at the Canadian Women's Studies Association (CWSA) June 1993 and 1994.

2 *Lesbian, Gay, Bisexual, Transgender Studies in Canada: A Directory of Courses*, available from the Toronto Centre for Lesbian and Gay Studies, 2 Bloor St W., Suites 100–129, Toronto, ON M4W 3E2.

3 See Abelove, Barale, and Halperin, eds., *Lesbian and Gay Studies Reader*, 397–415.

4 Patton, 'Visualizing Safe Sex,' 373–86; Watney, 'School's Out,' 387–401.
5 Fuss, ed., *Inside/Out*, 5.
6 Patton, *Fatal Advice*, 139.
7 Adams, 'Thoughts on Heterosexism,' 39.
8 Phelan, '(Be)Coming Out,' 782.
9 Flax, *Disputed Subjects*, 147.
10 Lather, *Getting Smart*, 164.

Part I
Pedagogy and Research

THE CHAPTERS IN PART I are organized to address pedagogical concerns first, then research concerns. Yet as Chapter 4, by Margot Francis, clearly shows, research and pedagogy inform one another, particularly when we are asking strategic questions related to political action. Francis thus explores the implications of using deconstruction in historical research on sexuality and its application to activist pedagogy. However, the contributions to Part I vary in their use of feminist theory, critical theories, and postmodern/queer theory just as they vary in focus. For instance Catherine Taylor's chapter, 'Teaching for a Freer Future in Troubled Times,' focuses on marginalized students in university classrooms and questions the costs of stressing either identity-affirming or identity-troubling pedagogies to the exclusion of the other. Didi Khayatt shifts the emphasis to the teacher in the classroom and critically analyses the pedagogical assumptions and presumed political benefits behind 'coming out' in class. Deborah Britzman, in her chapter 'Queer Pedagogy and Its Strange Techniques,' focuses on education as a 'structure of authority,' and asks how a pedagogical project might 'think the unthought of normalcy.' Whereas Taylor and Khayatt focus on the effects of different approaches to identity on students and teachers, Britzman looks more at the terrain of normalcy that is embedded in the whole project of education and disrupted in the classroom.

Similarly, in the chapters on research the authors focus on different concerns and paths in the production of knowledge. Knowledge is not viewed as innocent in these explorations of methodologies; rather, social inquiry is viewed as the kind of re-searching that explores what a lesbian/gay/queer perspective has to offer the research process. Suzanne de Castell and Mary Bryson, and Ki Namaste, in their very different approaches, look at ethnography as the preferred methodology for researching sexualities. Namaste explores how a queer ethnographer can problematize monosexism using poststructuralist insights within sociological research, yet remain grounded within social theory. De Castell and Bryson (like Britzman in her work on pedagogy) suggest that strategic ethnographic research should study normalcy. For them, studying heterosexuality is a way of telling 'queer tales that work to unravel the fabric of normalcy.' Finally, the chapter by Janice Ristock on community-based research brings us back to a concern with the participants in research (just as Taylor looked at the students in a classroom), and suggests that research that both affirms and disrupts is not only strategically necessary but well within the methodological reach of a feminist, postmodernist perspective.

Many large questions underlie this section: What are education and research for? How does the classroom/research site relate to the rest of the world? Is teaching/research even possible? Is there a place for empowerment in teaching and research that aim to disrupt? Can we 'read' part of our way towards social progress? Can a private deconstructive revolt matter much? What does a research focus on the needs of marginalized people do for them? Given the oppressive effects of a heteronormative context, can such a focus even be justified? The chapters in this section reveal common problems in using or destabilizing sexual-identity categories. All are concerned with efforts to work for social change in educational contexts, where disciplinary cultures discourage disruptive thinking, though everyone involved is at least formally positioned as 'willing' by their voluntary roles as teachers, students, research participants, and researchers. This is easily imagined as quite a different dynamic from that common in other social spheres, where activists do not enjoy an institutionally conferred entitlement to attempt to alter people's thinking and behaviour. Yet these contributors explore an academic terrain bristling with eruptions of institutional discipline into punishment, together with the personal resistance, denial, misrecognition, and hurt that challenge activists everywhere, and in this they address matters of urgent and everyday concern.

1

Teaching for a Freer Future in Troubled Times

CATHERINE G. TAYLOR

Early empowerment pedagogies seemed to imagine a student in the position described by the educator and Black activist W.E.B. DuBois in 1903: burdened with a 'sense of always looking at one's self through the eyes of others, of measuring one's soul by the tape of a world that looks on in amused contempt and pity.' Not all students positioned as 'other' in the classroom are in the same stage of vulnerability to the pain that can attend the 'double consciousness' described by DuBois, where an extremely stigmatized, culturally inscribed identity feels like an accurate measure of one's soul, and 'One ever feels his [*sic*] two-ness.'[1] A range can be imagined, with some more inconsolably hurt than others; some aware of their marginalized social status but recognizing it as the world's mistake, not their defect; some already social activists – long before they meet us in transformative classrooms – who are anxious to get on with the work of changing their oppressive peers and teachers. The teacher herself, if she is not white or not male or not straight, for example, probably has some experience of it. The teacher cannot always tell who is where in this familiar continuum, and the details of feeling will differ with the social location of the individual, but we do know that the state psychologized as low self-esteem is a common one for members of oppressed groups. Virginia Uribe and Karen Harbeck's description of the painful mental states of many gay and lesbian high school students in the eighties differs from DuBois's of Black students eighty years earlier, mainly with respect to the effects of the closet:

Those who openly admit their sexual orientation ... are verbally harassed and physically abused. Those who conceal their homosexual feelings experience loneliness and alienation, a splitting of their gay, lesbian, or bisexual identity from the rest of their personality. Most conceal their sexual feelings because of internal confusion, pain, and the fear of rejection and hostility. By developing elaborate concealment strategies these young people are often able to 'pass as straight,' but at some significant, unmeasurable cost to their developmental process, self-esteem, and sense of connection.[2]

Yet we know that individualistic psychology isn't the point, that context is key. Those of us who are normally self-confident and vocal in our everyday lives can feel paralysed by our stigmatized identities in a situation where we feel positioned as other. Classrooms are one such situation, where power is at work not only in the teacher-student relationship so prolifically theorized since the development of student-centred pedagogies, but in social relations across such differences as gender, race, and sexuality, the results of which tend to be described in harrowing tales of identity politics.[3]

Beyond a basically caring stance in common, progressive pedagogical responses to the presence of students in oppressed states is divided. Having spent years fighting against the racist system of segregated schooling, DuBois became convinced of the obdurateness of racist power relations in integrated classrooms, and devoted his energies to improving segregated schools.[4] Educators working in the area of lesbian and gay studies (whether in specialized courses that draw mainly lesbian and gay students or in mainstream courses across the university curriculum) have been similarly conflicted over questions of how to teach in ways that empower, rather than further damage, students marginalized because of their sexualities. There is a long history of such struggle in all those identity-based study areas (Afro-American, Judaic, Native, women's) called 'progressive' because they push the boundaries of the liberal arts to work for liberation (or more cautiously now, social change). The division occurs in answers to these questions: Since such students have a negative sense of identity, are they in need of affirming? Or are they, and the world, in need of transforming? Do educators get to decide?

Identity-Affirming Approaches

Within the broad range of approaches taken up by educators working in the area of sexualities – feminist, critical, and postmodernist – it is feminist pedagogy that tends to be associated with affirmative moves. These moves include attempts to empower students by valuing their experiences, making room for their voices, supplying positive representations of their oppressed and neglected cultures, and providing women professors as confidence-building role models.[5] In saying this, I do not want to misrepresent the place of experience in feminist thinking, which is rarely naïve; the politically situated construction of personal experience and social identity has been analysed in feminist theory and praxis from the first consciousness-raising groups onward. The common feminist practice of critical reflection on one's own identity-based experiences in the complex dynamics of race, class, gender, sexuality, size, ability, and other power differentials checks the tendency to emerge from consciousness-raising about sexism in utterly valorized, innocent form. But insofar as the focus is nevertheless on their experiences (or even on materials by or about members of their identity groups), the effect is to 'affirm' an entitlement to voice and place that may otherwise have been actively denied marginalized people throughout their formal education.

Affirmation, then, covers the full continuum of meanings of 'representation' from its modest political sense of including members of systemically excluded groups, to its essentialist philosophical sense of claiming to be depicting some categorical truth about them. For example, most feminist educators would see themselves as role models in the limited (yet remarkable) sense of signifying to students that being a woman does not make being an educator impossible; but some would go much further, feeling a deep responsibility to behave and speak as though students are appropriately modelling their own future selves on what they see of our identities. This second meaning of role modelling is frequently trounced for social and psychoanalytic naïvete as presuming an automatically profound identification of one person with another merely on the unproblematized basis of social group membership.[6] Many feminist and other progressive educators now take issue with these more ambitious aspirations of empowerment through representation as not only inaccurate but presumptuous: the more the teacher imagines herself to be providing for the students, the more she must be imagining them to lack.

In this deficit-model of empowerment, what students are chiefly presumed to be lacking is self-esteem, and attempts are made by caring teachers to provide opportunities to acquire it. The implicit expectation that the teacher's relationship to her students ought to be a maternal and nurturing one is problematic in various ways: for example, in its splicings of parenting and teaching, of educating and comforting; in its erasure of agency among students; and in its assumptions about what education is for.[7] The approach is still common in multicultural education and not uncommon in feminist classrooms. But even without the complications of maternalism any affirmation through representation in the curriculum can be problematic in that it can reoppress those marginalized students who do not fit the affirmed categories: transgender or bisexual students, for example, who feel excluded in the 'lesbian and gay' studies classroom; or disabled students who are frustrated never to see reflections of themselves in an ostensibly inclusive curriculum. To some extent the value of representation is asserted (sometimes confoundingly) from the course title onwards in any identity-based classroom, whether it be, as in the present case, lesbian and gay studies, or Native studies, or women's studies; or more generally in any traditional discipline that has adopted an 'inclusive curriculum' to make the classroom more comfortable for marginalized students. (The same approach to social change through representation has recently been taken up by network television, which by *Entertainment Weekly*'s count had trotted out twenty-two prime time lesbian and gay characters for the fall 1996 season, with Ellen pacing at the gate until 1997.)[8]

The problem that most directly affects those 'othered' students who do answer the call of the representations on offer is that identity-affirming approaches to empowerment supply more warmth than light. While it may well be important in some sense for pedagogy to start with comfort, if it stops there it can be depoliticized. When the focus of the classroom narrows from 'lesbian (or Black, or Jewish, say) in a white, straight, Christian culture,' to 'lesbian pride,' any hope, in bell hooks's words, of working to 'radically change our relationship to self and identity, to educate for critical consciousness, to become politically engaged and committed' gives way to one of working to 'explore one's identity to affirm and assert the primacy of the self as it already exist[s].'[9] Henry Louis Gates's summary of such an approach is a bit stinging: 'for every insult there is a culture: that is, if I can be denigrated as X, I can be affirmed as an X. This mechanism of remediation is perhaps not the most sophisticated, but its intentions are good.'[10] Although the focus of remediation is an embattled social identity, empowerment in this formulation veers back towards liberal individualism and the mere 'psychological experience of feeling powerful,'[11] and away from self-fashioning for ethical relation to others within a socially transformative project.

Identity-Transforming Approaches

Feminist identity-based approaches, of course, are not monolithically affirmative. Kathleen Martindale came to reject nurturant pedagogy as classist maternalism, and, expecting discomfort, focused on it as a site of learning about the implications of difference in a feminist context.[12] Mimi Orner describes her 'high risk pedagogy' that requires students to undertake social-action projects that presume to 'interrupt business as usual,' but only after self-critically considering, 'Who are YOU in relation to THEM?'[13] Bell hooks encourages students 'to work at coming to voice in an atmosphere where they may be afraid or see themselves at risk.'[14] For hooks empowerment means finding the courage for revolutionary work, not finding psychological comfort. Her 'difficult, demanding, and very frightening' pedagogy of confrontation across identity lines at the end of the twentieth century is a far cry from DuBois's proposal for segregated education for Black students at the beginning of it, or even from Shrewsbury's terminologically similar recent description of her students as 'able to take risks' because they are in a classroom community that celebrates difference. While it is still possible to find feminist educators who experience the classroom as an harmonious community led by a 'teacher who is above all a role model,'[15] it should be noted, Gates's assessment notwithstanding, that what she teaches by example has never been merely how to feel powerful, but the leadership necessary to contribute to a feminist revolution. Still, feminists are apt now to argue that classrooms are, appropriately, places where students work out the terms of their own empowerment by struggling to negotiate and renegotiate the power dynamics of our gendered, raced, classed, and otherwise oppressive culture. This change has come about with the increased recognition that ultimately the struggle for 'individual empowerment – an important goal – depends upon a transformation in the social relations of power,'[16] and with the conviction that 'even given all the pain and suffering associated not just with being victimized, but also with being agents against that victimization ... there's also a deep joy and ecstasy in struggle.'[17]

This transformative approach to identity-based empowerment is limited politically, though, in that its greatest social potential in an untransformed culture, including the classroom culture, is identity politics. Typically, the reported results of mobilizing identity politics are that a reversed hierarchy is produced, sometimes with the oppressed culture valorized and the dominant culture demonized,[18] or rather reverse hierarch*ies*, as many as there are politicized power differentials or even hidden, individual differences in the classroom;[19] just as often with members of dominant cultures refusing self-reflection and members of oppressed cultures bitterly disappointed.[20] Ellsworth's response has been that it is best for marginalized students if pedagogy works, not directly to empower them but to change power relations in the world, beginning with that part of the world contained in the classroom: other students and the teacher. In this kind of pedagogy, classroom attention, turning away from the contents of some oppressed identity in order to get the oppressed out from under it, is redirected 'to turn the uninvited othering look back on itself.'[21] Students positioned as marginalized are potentially involved in this project of changing the grounds of sociality, since even people in the most abject combination of social locations are likely, on a few counts, to be in a position to other others: their gaze, too, is implicated in a web of power relations. Another response to the depressing results of classroom and other local identity politics is to strengthen one's identity by realizing one's links with more people who are in some way like one; thus Paul Gilroy's analysis of ethnic absolutism argues for the importance of Blacks moving from double consciousness (the state that comes with identifying as a Black American) to a new sense of 'metacultural' identity as part of a community of globally oppressed Black people.[22]

But critical theorists argue that such fortifyings of oppressed identities are provisional because, ultimately, social identity is inscribed through the very power relations that liberation aims to change: 'if being subordinate is a constitutive aspect of identity, then a liberation politics would foreclose an identity politics and vice versa.'[23] The goal of liberation makes the link between identity-based empowerment and social transformation very much at issue in the literature of progressive pedagogies. We can't, apparently, have both. Gates, who stands a little outside the regimes of critical and feminist pedagogies that he sees as Utopian, puts the critical case succinctly:

Identity politics, in its purest form, must be concerned with the survival of an identity. By contrast, the utopian agenda of liberation pursues what it takes to be the objective interests of its subjects, but it may be little concerned with its cultural continuity or integrity. More than that, the discourse of liberation often looks forward to the birth of a transformed subject, the creation of a new identity, which is, by definition, the surcease of the old.[24]

Lest Gates be thought hyperbolic in predicting the fate of current identities in a liberated future, Roger Simon identifies a crucial reciprocity in his argument for a critical approach to empowerment through transforming the grounds of identity. According to Simon we must 'open *both* character and community to revision' in 'a double ethical address: the person *and* the familial and communal forms within which people live' if we are to exercise transformative pedagogy capable of contributing to a project of securing both 'the expansion of forms to accommodate capacities and the expansion of capacities to make the realization of new forms possible.'[25] The aim, though, is to increase the range of possible identities, not to foreclose on any.

To return to the lesbian or gay student positioned as other in the classroom or in the larger culture, if the problem is experiencing one's identity as it has been inscribed by an oppressive world, the socially transformative response would be to 'attempt to alter experience'[26] by deconstructing what has been written on the body, rather than to become all the more identified with it, albeit in cleansed and/or valorized form. This means that the transformative educator asks students to seize the opportunity presented by the current 'state of emergency' of identity in the postmodern world to hasten the work of social transformation by going beyond the aim of fortifying a weak identity to one of troubling the very notion of identity itself. For her, defining oneself 'as an X' – as *any* X, whether broken-down or fortified – collaborates with social forces that protect power interests by both oppressing and dividing people. In the classroom as in the larger social world, even the most successful minority rights efforts leave the status quo largely undisturbed. Judith Butler's work is a call heeded by many lesbian and gay studies educators and scholars to take up the challenge of more 'complex and generative subject-positions as well as coalitional strategies that neither presuppose nor fix their constitutive subjects in their place.' Cultural identities are worth troubling once we understand not only the '"interests" that a cultural identity has, but, more importantly, the interests and power relations that establish that identity in its reified mode to begin with.'[27] Such work demands the courage to behave as though, as Ernst Bloch puts it, the world of 'that which is not yet'[28] has already started to emerge, thereby beginning to realize it.

And yet ... it is one of the guiding insights of postmodern thinking that our political work for social change, including our pedagogical work, had better be carefully attuned to the social, historical, geographical, institutional, and other particularities of our specific locations.[29] Situated as we are within a social ecology experienced by gay people, in Sedgwick's description, as a genocidal western project or fantasy of eradicating gay identity,[30] it is hard to imagine how any project inside or outside a classroom that is predicated on destabilizing gay identity could not be experienced as agonistic, with marginalized people occasionally digging into the foxholes of their always already-embattled identities. Among the pedagogical challenges that can arise in a classroom where the teacher sets out to trouble identity is that transformative utterances can seem insensitive to the lived experience of oppression because they are not intelligible, being part of a world which is not yet. Kader and Piontek discovered that those students in their class 'whose own sexual identities may have been fought for, struggled over, and gained only at great cost were not especially sympathetic to [their] endeavor' to refuse the comfort of sure grounds of identity.[31] (In my own classrooms I now avoid trying to open minds through speeches about judgmentalism and the fluidity of sexual identity, having inspired several students to appear in class defiantly wearing the flannel shirts and Birkenstocks I had described as 'too rigid a notion of what lesbians must look like,' their assigned identity-troubling text pointedly unread.) If students, out of pain, anger, indignation, or self-protection, refuse the provocation, pedagogy stops, and with it the possibility of the classroom becoming a place of excitation to reconsider the grounds of identity.

What ethical grounds do we tread when we set out to destabilize gay identity, knowing that at least some of our students might be desperate to affirm it, with suicidal adolescent terror at homophobia not far in their pasts?[32] It might be fair enough in a city like Toronto, with a well-developed lesbian and gay/queer culture, to respond by pointing out that learning can't be comfortable or affirmative, that other cultural spaces such as gay community centres and half-million-strong gay pride parades and gay-positive therapy sessions exist to provide comfort, but that progressive education exists to disturb oppressive identities, not to accommodate us to them. In places, though, where a single classroom is perhaps the only gay-friendly social space available to the student, the ethics of denying demands for comfort might be more complicated. As Deanne Bogdan wonders of her own feminist students, 'When is feeling sick to your stomach an indication, not of the "natural" part of coming to consciousness, but of the oppressive effects of too much consciousness at the wrong time and in the wrong circumstance? And when might it be producing what Teresa de Lauretis calls a "genuine epistemological shift"?'[33] And further, to return to the question Orner asks her students: 'Who are YOU?' we might ask ourselves as educators, 'in relation to THEM? What makes you think you are well situated to do whatever it is you plan to do with/to/for them? How have you grappled with issues of social responsibility in the planning and implementation of your project?'[34] When is troubling identity worth the pain, and when is it unproductive? Who says educators get to decide? In any case, where does a pedagogy that stops affirming identity and starts to trouble it leave the troubled student?

One way of characterizing the difference between identity-affirming pedagogies and identity-troubling ones is in the way they operate in the absence of answers to these questions: pedagogy as a process of healing that priorizes the psychic state of the student (often associated with feminist positions); and pedagogy as a lesson in courage that more aggressively priorizes political effectiveness at building a freer future for all our sakes (often associated with critical positions). But both critical and feminist pedagogies are part of a progressive, student-centred pedagogy movement to which empowerment is central. While critical pedagogies may or may not incorporate a feminist gender analysis, and feminist pedagogies may be more or less critical, totalizing generalizations about feminist versus critical pedagogies are bound to be inaccurate; most of the theorists I have cited in this chapter could be called both. The difference may be one of emphasis: both attempt to enact the aims of empowerment and social transformation. Further, despite the continued representation of both feminist and critical pedagogues as naïve opponents of a third, smarter, but ineffectual set – postmodernists – most of the educators I cite have taken up the ethical and pragmatic challenges of postmodern critiques of knowledge, identity, and liberation in their thinking.

Combining Affirmation and Transformation

Many critical and feminist approaches informed by postmodernism combine affirming and troubling pedagogies to provoke participants to develop a new form of double consciousness. Queer pedagogies, for example, are affirming of oppressed identities in that they disrupt the relentless cultural production of heterosexual normalcy by opening space for the subjugated knowledge of gay and lesbian people; but they also thoroughly trouble the identities they make room for in the ways described by Butler. Such a dual practice attempts 'to teach in ways that simultaneously construct and deconstruct knowledge claims.'[35]

Mary Bryson and Suzanne de Castell offer an unsentimental account of their attempt in a lesbian studies course to forge a 'queer praxis' that would destabilize fixed identities while enacting a commitment to making room for empowerment of lesbians. Their work is a rare example of pedagogy thoroughly informed by poststructuralist understandings of identity, yet passionately committed to a focus on representation of socially marginalized identities. They asked students to engage with texts and presentations by lesbians in a variety of media, and to collaborate on assignments designed to provide opportunities to parody, investigate, deconstruct, and otherwise consider the social construction of lesbian identities.[36]

Bryson and de Castell were disappointed to find that only the students whose identities were 'constructed within oppression' – that is, not the straight white women who constitute the dominant culture of a women's studies classroom – were able to engage with the identity-subversive opportunities afforded by the postmodernist features of the course (291). Student performance followed the identity-based lines predictable from the 'familiar pedagogic wisdom about acceptance of student identities': those who were affirmed produced wonderful, engaged work; those who were experiencing less affirmation than usual wrote 'formulaic, disengaged essays' (293). Whatever responsibility students bear for their own refusals, the outcome was that dominant-culture students were stopped in their pedagogical tracks (even though both instructors devoted considerable energy to accommodating their discomfort without validating their sense of 'automatic entitlement' [300]). Insensitive to the related issues of safety and privacy, straight white women remained voyeurs and consumers of lesbian culture, not disclosing their heterosexuality and complaining that their own rights and freedoms were violated by the instructors' admonitions to recognize the ethical context of their social locations. As hope of working across differences in class faded, students organized outside class into separate identity-based support groups.

Bryson and de Castell conclude that the double effort to affirm identities and destabilize identity, while theoretically resolvable, is insistently irresolvable in actual classroom practice, because of the 'inescapable backdrop of white heterosexual dominance' which, refusing to question itself, leaves other identities fixed, 'despite our explicit interventions, all of our discourses, all of our actions' (285). Many educators reeling from such experiences of teaching lesbian and gay studies take the route of first thoroughly deconstructing heterosexuality despite the loss of focus on same-sex cultures and issues entailed for a typical six-, or twelve-, or even twenty-five-week course.[37] Thus recasting our lesbian and gay curricular interventions as 'sexuality studies' might well seem a strategically sound move, one offering both the curricular space needed to problematize heteronormativity, and an escape route from the reifying, minoritizing effects of using marginalized identity categories in the course title.

Bryson and de Castell demur. They are prepared to accept that imperfect outcomes are necessarily the pedagogical norm, and that a safe pedagogy cannot exist. They are unprepared, however, to give up on a lesbian focus, and they look towards a 'safer pedagogy' that offers opportunities for 'both students and teachers "of difference" for the construction of, and participation in, democratic, engaging, pleasurable, interesting, generative, and nonviolent learning environments' – one lets them speak 'as lesbian' without 'instantiating profoundly unproductive essentialist notions of fixed, stable, and marginal "lesbian identities."'[38] With respect to this commitment, they are aligned with the sentiment expressed in a poster featured on the cover of Garber's *Tilting the Tower* (well aware of the agonies of contradiction accepted in being nevertheless): 'Another Queer Theorist for Lesbian and Gay Studies.'[39]

Other educators looking for ways of making room for cultural representation of marginalized identities have created more placid classrooms by backing off the principles of affirmation and empowerment, often not coming out as lesbians or any other sexuality category themselves, in keeping with their attempt to destabilize notions of identity (see Didi Khayatt's view in Chapter 2). Like Bryson and de Castell they might ask students to read texts in which identity is clearly in trouble or refuses to yield to rigid categories of sexual orientation, but they do not foreground lesbian or any other culture as a curricular focus. Some carefully conceived recent work in progressive pedagogy conjures up an alternative to the raucous provocations of identity politics in a strangely peaceful classroom of readers (interestingly, with little classroom dialogue reported), where the teacher recognizes, like Socrates and Freud, that teaching is impossible, and instead of confronting students with what she knows, provides opportunities for students to encounter themselves in a literary adventure of insight.[40] Thus Deborah Britzman and Alice Pitt describe a pedagogy 'interested in raising questions about eros in friendship and in education' but 'not interested in instructing the erotic views of our students,' a pedagogy in which texts are 'just a scene to stage particular kinds of problems rather than a content meant to cure the preconceptualized problem.' Student readings, being unhinged from compliance to the rule of planned learning objectives about the texts, range all over the map from 'evad[ing] the questions of friendship altogether' to 'consider[ing] their own identities as social relations, not predetermined educational building blocks.'[41] Ellsworth describes a pedagogy informed by psychoanalytic understandings of the impossibility of transmitting knowledge, and she likewise turns from the notion of the possibility of correct readings to the inevitability of partial, strategic, interested ones.[42] Like Britzman and Pitt she entrusts students to take control of their own educations, this time by recognizing and refining the strategic purposes for their encounters with a text, and requesting certain kinds of attention and not others in Ellsworth's feedback on their responses.

And indeed, the reading self (especially one encouraged to practise self-subversive self-reflection) enjoys as much elbow-room as life on this planet allows for attempts to exceed the self by breaking the social rules to which we are subjected by our group memberships and attendant practices of self-surveillance. Temporarily beyond the reach of identity politics, students reading troubled tales can get practice in reading themselves reading, and encounter themselves encountering others, perhaps opening up other identifications than those culturally inscribed, perhaps experiencing their grounds of consciousness shift in ways that offer glimpses of a less oppressive social compact. A world which is not yet might begin to be imagined inside a classroom of readers (or even a theatre of filmgoers?) that is very different from the one dominant outside it: a kind of sociality in which identity is not held out as a shield defending us from taking an interest in each other. Again, the liberatory possibility presented is that of self-fashioning for a freer world: a choice not between affirmation and trouble, claiming identity and refusing it, but a choice of both, choosing to refuse culturally inscribed identity and choosing to produce one's own.

Such approaches might invite all participants to develop a kind of double consciousness very different from that oppressed state described by DuBois. Instead of attempting to somehow unify the subject by replacing the world's tape with the identity-group's tape (which seems to be the semantic drift of some liberatory pedagogies that look to holistic methods for integrating the divided self), or refusing any sense of social individuation (as in some of deconstructionism's dreamier episodes), pedagogy works towards a double vision of social inscription and self-fashioning, where DuBois's ironic gift of second sight[43] can be experienced as a source of political acumen and personal autonomy, and pain has a chance of giving way to a passion for social transformation.

It is important to ask, though, if progressive education is conceived as allied with social struggle, can we afford such patient pedagogies as Britzman's and Pitt's that decline to preach, when, meanwhile, less fastidious minds with no such pedagogical misgivings about accuracy and ethics, everywhere from school boards to Parliament Hill, browbeat the public to join the historic project of 'eradicating gay identity' through disentitling, demonizing, criminalizing, and pathologizing its bearers? Might we be better to launch a reverse discourse in the classroom, perhaps fighting gay-bashing by teaching that homophobia is a sign of repressed same-sex desire? Some educators and other activists well aware of the fictive status of identity reluctantly argue that whatever our ontological views, such an onslaught demands a strong response of strategic essentialism,[44] especially in the face of claims that lesbians and gays constitute only 1 per cent of the population, and a curable 1 per cent at that. (Consider the sign, seen at the 1993 March on Washington: If we're only 1%, we're all here!) Others maintain that the alternative future towards which we need to work requires more freedom, not more propaganda; that, unfortunately, nothing short of learning will work. Susan Johnston, accepting responsibility for the ethical implications of 'without question, leading students along an analytical path,' explains why she nevertheless avoids 'instructing the erotic views' of students through antihomophobic lectures in her classrooms, and rewards deconstructive rigour rather than progressive attitudes:

I taught Sex and Identity twice during fervid antihomosexual campaigning by the OCA [Oregon Citizens Alliance]. It was tempting, given the right's pathologizing typifications of queers, to fall into 'defending' homosexuality; but to argue that homosexuality 'isn't bad' reinscribes the same heterosexual-homosexual binary that fuels heterosexism and the current attacks by the right. My occasional anxiety attacks over the political utility of the analyses provided in my course were assuaged by the very cogent analyses of my students.[45]

Leaving little room for concern about her own or her students' comfort (neither claiming nor giving credit for identity-group membership or personal experience, for example) Johnston's pedagogical efforts focus on a critical examination of the production of knowledge which she sees both as requiring intellectual freedom, and as entirely 'political and pragmatic: the political and social agenda of the right is dependent on essentialist constructions of gender, sexuality, and race.'[46]

Teaching Troubles

Ellsworth charges that the literature of critical pedagogy assumes a mythical norm as the teacher, one who employs a perfectly unoppressive-because-critically cleansed gaze; that its language of transformation is abstracted out of any connection to the lived terms of struggle; and that it assumes a united class-room front against an oppressive world, pretending the classroom is not part of the world, contrary to daily evidence of the complex interrelations among vari-ously positioned students.[47] Any such tendencies are clearly problematic. Fur-ther problems are presented by affirmative pedagogies that presume a caretaking role for the teacher, or that propose the teacher as a role model worthy of emu-lation. And all pedagogies, even scrupulously power-conscious feminist versions of them, position the teacher as the one who knows (even though she may know, and teach, that knowledge is partial, subjective, embodied, and impossible to teach), in that she is authorized to set transformation in motion,[48] and in that she remains the privileged reader (albeit a 'response-able' one)[49] of her student's work. Ethical problems have been identified throughout progressive pedagogies – feminist, critical, and postmodernist – where, despite a language of enabling, facilitating, and empowering that offers a semantic check on missionary zeal, we focus considerable pedagogical effort on fundamentally changing students' lives – altering the very grounds of experience, aiming (now directly, now obliquely, but ever-hopefully) at the psychic level of existence – and that despite ample evi-dence that some students do not want their lives changed.

The ethics of exercising transformative designs on students are taken up in Jennifer Gore's work on the important question of critical and feminist pedago-gies as new regimes of truth with new rules for self-fashioning, and new forms of restricting individual human freedom.[50] The basic rationale supplied by transformative pedagogues is that all pedagogy has politically consequential effects on students, whether to help them transform the world or adapt them to it, and critical practices at least are ultimately on the side of students' autonomy within an ethic of care. Some educators give priority in their theorizing to avoiding abuse of power; others, just as aware of the stakes, focus on different aspects of the problems of progressive pedagogies, such as managing represen-tations. When affirming the identity categories that are sites of extreme oppres-sion for some can turn out to be acutely oppressive to others, and even *queer*, a term mobilized to confound categorization, can swiftly ossify into just another homogenizing-and-thus-exclusionary label,[51] it is clear that we teach and learn in troubled times. Yet both 'Queer Theorists for Lesbian and Gay Studies' and 'lesbians teaching queer subjects' need to remember, with Foucault, that it's 'not that everything is bad, but that everything is dangerous.'[52]

In the end I find myself less worried about being stuck with the dangers of utterance, or about the guru-role adopted by progressive educators, than about a certain progressivist tendency in the literature of progressive pedagogy. We used to pay more attention than we seem to now to the emotional state of individual students in a homophobic world; we used to develop pedagogical approaches such as identity-based affirmation that experience proved to be problematic. After twenty-five years of sophisticating our notion of what it means for the personal to be political, we have our eyes on pedagogical approaches that look less explosive and more politically promising in terms of developing effective coalitionary practices. But surely nineties students are in no less danger of double consciousness than seventies students. Are we developing pedagogical sophistication that leaves the most psychically-damaged students behind? Is part of our shucking sometimes motivated by our own annually elaborated histories of identity politics rather than by the best interests of the individual student who might be stepping out of the classroom closet for the first time? If bell hooks is right that women's studies teachers are paying less attention to pedagogy than before,[53] and if progressive pedagogues have taken to blaming the oppressed for identity politics, then we have lots of work to do. At the very least, not giving students the affirmation they often crave, and that many of us fervently believed not long ago that they – and the revolution! – needed, should continue to give us pause.

But border skirmishes in attempts to exceed the self, refusals of pedagogy by students in pain, resurfacings of oppressive relations, and even the awareness of ego-investment on the part of a progressive teacher are not evidence of pedagogical collapse; they are signs that we are right to be working for social transformation, for the sake of those students struggling under the burden of double consciousness, and for all our sakes.

Notes

1 DuBois, *Souls of Black Folk*, 364.
2 Uribe and Harbeck, 'Addressing the Needs,' 11.
3 See, for example, Fuss, *Essentially Speaking*; Kader and Piontek, 'Not a Safe Place.'
4 See DuBois's writings from the 1930s advocating segregated education and businesses. Some of these are usefully collected together with examples of his earlier calls for integration in 'Segregation versus Integration: Race Solidarity and Economic Cooperation,' in Paschal, ed., *W.E.B. DuBois Reader*, 137–97.
5 See, for example, Manicom, 'Feminist Pedagogy'; Shrewsbury, 'What Is Feminist Pedagogy?'
6 See, for example, Britzman, 'Beyond Rolling Models'; Roof, *Come as You Are*; Sedgwick, *Epistemology of the Closet*; and in this volume, Khayatt.
7 See, for example, Briskin, *Feminist Pedagogy*; Martindale, 'Theorizing Autobiography.'

8 See Jacobs, 'Out?'

9 hooks, *Talking Back*, 106.

10 Gates, 'Beyond the Culture Wars,' 8.

11 Lather, *Getting Smart*, 3.

12 Martindale, 'Theorizing Autobiography.'

13 Orner, 'Teaching for the Moment,' 73.

14 hooks, *Talking Back*, 53.

15 Shrewsbury, 'What Is Feminist Pedagogy?' 9, 11, 14.

16 Briskin and Coulter, 'Feminist Pedagogy,' 259.

17 West, 'Cornel West on Heterosexism,' 363.

18 Fuss, *Essentially Speaking*.

19 Sedgwick, *Epistemology of the Closet.*

20 See Bryson and de Castell, 'Queer Pedagogy'; also hooks, *Teaching to Transgress.*

21 Ellsworth, 'Teaching to Support,' 9.

22 Gilroy, 'Cultural Studies.'

23 Gates, 'Beyond the Culture Wars,' 9.

24 Ibid., 8.

25 Simon, *Teaching against the Grain*, 29–30.

26 Giroux, 'Disturbing the Piece,' 11.

27 Judith Butler, 'Gender Trouble,' 339.

28 See Simon, *Teaching against the Grain*, 7.

29 Lather and Ellsworth, 'Introduction.'

30 Sedgwick, *Epistemology of the Closet*, 130.

31 Kader and Piontek, 'Not a Safe Place,' 27.

32 Many studies show a disproportionate representation of gay and lesbian youth among suicides and attempted suicides. According to a recent major study by Pierre Tremblay at the University of Calgary, young gay and bisexual men are at fourteen times more risk for a serious suicide attempt than their straight counterparts. See Tremblay's website at http://www.virtualcity.com/youthsuicide.

33 Bogdan, 'Singing School,' 352.

34 Orner, 'Teaching for the Moment,' 72.

35 Ibid.

36 Bryson and de Castell, 'Queer Pedagogy,' 288–90.

37 Fonow and Marty, 'Shift from Identity Politics,' 411.

38 Bryson and de Castell, 'Queer Pedagogy,' 297, 299.

39 Garber, *Tilting the Tower*, cover illustration.

40 Felman, *Jacques Lacan.*

41 Britzman and Pitt, 'Pedagogy and Transference,' 122.

42 Ellsworth, 'Situated Response-ability.'

43 DuBois, *Souls of Black Folk*, 364.

44 See Fuss, *Essentially Speaking*; Phelan, '(Be)Coming Out'; Spivak, *The Post-Colonial Critic*.

45 Johnston, 'Not for Queers Only,' 118.

46 Ibid., 120.

47 Ellsworth, 'Why Doesn't This Feel Empowering?'

48 Manicom, 'Feminist Pedagogy.'

49 Ellsworth, 'Situated Response-ability.'

50 Gore, *The Struggle for Pedagogies*.

51 de Lauretis, 'Queer Theory.'

52 Foucault, 'Genealogy of Ethics,' 343.

53 hooks, *Teaching to Transgress*.

2

Paradoxes of the Closet: Beyond the Classroom Assignment of In or Out

DIDI KHAYATT

What is the relationship between critical and dogmatic philosophies of action? By 'critical' I mean a philosophy that is aware of the limits of knowing. By 'dogmatic' I mean a philosophy that advances coherent general principles without sufficient interest in empirical details.[1]

Gayatri Chakravorty Spivak

In my view solidarity does not mean that everyone thinks in the same way; it begins when people have the confidence to disagree over issues of fundamental importance precisely because they 'care' about constructing common ground.[2]

Kobena Mercer

I currently teach a graduate course on feminist pedagogy. The course often attracts a variety of students from different racial and class backgrounds, some of whom are self-identified lesbians or gay men. On one occasion one of the students presented a seminar on some of the ways that being a lesbian influenced how she was treated as a student and perceived as a tutor. Since I have never been able to come out in any of my classes by announcing my sexual orientation in a declarative statement, I am always in awe of anybody, student or teacher, who accomplishes this feat gracefully. Coming out, though, is more than making a declarative statement about one's sexuality. So occasionally in my graduate courses I am able to speak of my research or my work, which is invariably about some aspect of sexual orientation. If I am really comfortable with the group I may speak of 'my partner ... she,' relying on ambiguity while at the same time unrelentingly challenging my students on their heterosexism and/or homophobia. Concerning those who want to know my sexual orientation, I depend on them to understand and to pick up on the innumerable cues I present during the course of my teaching.

The graduate student who presented that day, however, came out by simply stating her sexual identity. I sat there listening to her intently, my heart throbbing with a mixture of excitement, fear, pride, and tension. Should I come out to the class in a similar way, in solidarity? Was she giving me an opening to declare my sexuality? Was she merely exploring possibilities, which, for her as a graduate student, were academic? I did not speak out that day. The usual hesitations and misgivings I have about such disclosures overcame my moment of respect for my student's performance.

Several weeks after this incident my partner and I were having dinner with a couple of lesbian friends who also work in the academy, and the discussion turned inevitably to what our responsibility is, as tenured lesbian professors, to our lesbian and gay students. Should we come out? My friends were arguing adamantly that as lesbians it was our responsibility to put our bodies on the line, to declare our sexual orientation clearly in class, to force a predominently heterosexual academy to confront our queerness. This was certainly not the first time I had engaged in such a discussion concerning an issue that is constantly on my mind when I teach, one that seems to crop up periodically with students and colleagues alike, and is a concern about which I have previously written.[3] As a result of my friends' insistence that I should 'be out in class' I asked myself, What do they actually mean by coming out? Were we discussing the same closet? The degree of defensiveness on all our parts seemed to indicate that the extent to which we each come out, as well as the very closets from which we might emerge, were both in question.

In this chapter I address the assumptions often made and the reasons given for why lesbians (or gay men, bisexuals, transsexuals) who are teachers, at any level of schooling, should disclose their sexual orientation to their students. I explore the questions that arise out of what it means to come out in class, the pedagogical and political notion that such an act would challenge students' heterosexist and homophobic beliefs, that it would be supportive of lesbian and gay students, that it would unsettle the very foundations of the institutions that employ us. Finally, I examine the pressures often imposed on lesbian and gay teachers to be role models for students. Having said that, my aim is not to dissuade anyone so inclined from coming out in class, but to take up the arguments for doing so and to discuss some of the tacit assumptions underscoring the pressures to come out in class. I also examine the contradictory moments that inform our decisions, as teachers, to come out or not, depending on our particular circumstances.

Several years ago, for my book *Lesbian Teachers* (1992), I interviewed eighteen lesbian teachers in Ontario concerning how they managed their sexuality when teaching at the secondary or elementary levels. All interviews were completed prior to 1986, the year the Human Rights Code in Ontario passed Bill 7, which made it illegal to deny anyone employment, housing, or services on the basis of sexual orientation. As a result, when I asked each one of these teachers at that time whether she would think of coming out to her students, the responses, although varied, confirmed that each believed they would, in all probability, lose their jobs if their sexuality were to be publicly acknowledged. At the same time all were also very aware that people in their immediate social environment (friends, neighbours) unofficially knew that they were lesbians.

Almost five years later, and after the passing of Bill 7, I interviewed some of the same teachers again.[4] Some had retired, some had resigned (women who had changed professions or quit teaching to go back to school) and some had had other changes of circumstance, permitting me to reach only five of the original eighteen women. This time I questioned whether the passing of a bill that protected their jobs under the Human Rights Code made any difference to their inclinations to come out to their students. Once again their answers were complex.[5] Some pointed out that although their jobs were protected they could still be harassed with impunity by both administration and students should they come out. Others assured me that though Bill 7 provided a psychological support, it essentially had made little difference in their lives. All were relieved that legal protection existed and that it provided some relief from the consequences should they be 'found out.' In an earlier article, I had argued that it was not necessarily the private lives of lesbian teachers that were at issue because homosexuality had been legal in Canada since 1969, but that 'their public persona, their image as a teacher, as a representative of the state and all the ideological implications which that position entails,'[6] made their positions within the school system vulnerable. The most powerful example of the delicate tensions that exist between the recognition of the rights of lesbian and gay teachers to employment, and the acknowledgment of the sexual orientation of these teachers publicly by the state, was given by one teacher as follows:

I sit on an equal opportunity committee, and we have put together a proposal for recommendations for hiring and promotion procedures. As part of those recommendations we obviously stated that the Board should recognize the various aspects of the Human Rights Code. In the policy statement itself, the most important factors were listed, written down in the statement. Subsequent to drawing up the policy statement, Bill 7 was passed. At a relatively recent meeting of the Equal Opportunity Committee, when we were trying to finalize these recommendations that were to be presented to the Trustees, I suggested that sexual orientation should be included amongst the list of items under the

Human Rights Code for which one could not discriminate in terms of hiring. I suggested that the onus was on the Equal Opportunity Committee to include this as it was now law. Originally, when I suggested it, it was at the tail end of a meeting. There were no comments at the time, and it was left. At the latest meeting, I brought it up again and the shit hit the fan. The group of people who were there accepted what I was saying, I think. I'm sure that they never thought of it nor did they really know anything about Bill 7. But having brought it to their attention, they acknowledged it. But the general feeling was that it should not be written down; that if it was written down, on paper, that it would open a can of worms with our Board and that they didn't want that to happen. So, the best way around it, after much negotiation, was simply to make the statement that hiring and promotion procedures should take into consideration the Human Rights Code, but in no way would it list the items that one had to watch for when hiring. And that was after, I would guess, an hour of back and forth, back and forth.[7]

However, should anyone think the above attitudes exist only in the past, here is a news report as recent as 1995:

David Ducklow of Woodstock (Ontario), a trustee with the Oxford County Board of Education, objected to including sexual orientation in a board policy dealing with race, gender, religion and ethno cultural differences.
  'They are heterosexuals practising unnatural sex acts,' said Ducklow of gay men and lesbians. 'What they are doing is harmful and immoral.'
  The policy lays out guidelines for non discriminatory employment practices and curricula. Two weeks after his initial reaction, the board passed the policy, including sexual orientation. But not without more protests from Ducklow: 'I agree within the environment of tolerance and the protection of right of others. But I cannot support this ... on social, moral and medical grounds. There is nothing positive or beneficial about homosexuality itself. It only leads to the destruction of those individuals and often those around them.'[8]

Since my book *Lesbian Teachers* and the subsequent article 'Legalized Invisibility' were pubished a number of books and articles have appeared that discuss issues of coming out in the elementary or secondary classrooms.[9] On the one hand, some are a simple compilation of self-selected teachers' coming out stories that hardly advance our knowledge of the complexities of such a decision beyond noting the ways some individual teachers 'choose' to come out to their students; on the other hand, a number of books (for instance, Jonathan Silin's [1995] work) engage the reader in intricate, thoughtful, and critical analyses of the necessity of bringing the discussion of sexual orientation into the classroom.

I have maintained continually that elementary and secondary teachers, precisely because they teach children rather than adults, have different issues to confront in coming out to their classes than those of us who teach at college or university levels. Elementary and secondary teachers have to deal with what Silin[10] calls 'the image of the hapless, innocent child essential to the romantic imagination.' The 'innocence' of the child has to be protected at all costs, particularly from any mention of sex. Eve Sedgwick reminds us that modern understanding of 'knowledge' comes to us via the late-eighteenth-century European culture where '"knowledge" and "sex" become conceptually inseparable from one another – so that knowledge means in the first place sexual knowledge; ignorance, sexual ignorance.'[11] A teacher's coming out to students, which, by its very nature, is an allusion to sexual matters, is consequently deemed outside the realm of what is considered appropriate for children to know or discuss.

The challenge that was posed to me, however, was not as an elementary or secondary teacher, but as a tenured member of the academy, a teacher of students who are considered adults. Since my job is not in jeopardy I was asked, Why do you not come out?

There are a number of issues involved in that question, not the least of which is the whole notion of what is considered coming out. Where once the expression referred primarily to the closet of sexuality, the notion of coming out has been appropriated by the mainstream media with the consequence than one can now come out in many different ways: for instance, as a beef-loving vegetarian, as an environmentalist who saves trees and wastes paper, as an animal rights proponent who loves to fish or hunt, and any or all of those myriad contradictions we each entertain within or without our political convictions. I had to think deeply about the ways I do come out to my students, and whether I inform them about my different social identities. Do I mention that I am a woman of colour? Do I advise them regarding my gender? My age? My class? What details do I actually make public about myself? It occured to me that, as it is with my sexuality, for the most part I might mention any one specific aspect of my life within the context of an anecdote, but cannot remember ever having to declare my race, class, gender, or sexuality by making a declarative statement. Conversely, I am more likely in my lectures to reveal my political positions to my students.[12]

One might argue, however, that my age, gender, race, or class are not contentious issues, that they do not need declaring, that they are obvious, and that one's sexual identity has to be proclaimed and reaffirmed because of the overwhelming presumption of heterosexuality. Yet I would contend that, for instance, I am presumed to be white as often as I am presumed to be straight. As with my race, age, gender, and class, I assume that, as a teacher, my sexuality is read by my students in complex and multifaceted ways, depending on certain contexts, cues, and cognizance. But for the sake of argument, am I not already out as a lesbian? And if I am not perceived to be out, while I think I am, how is it that this contradiction exists? 'There is not one but many silences,' Foucault reminds us.[13] And as Diana Fuss enquires, 'How does one know when one is on the inside and when one is not. How does one know when and if one is out of the closet?'[14] Eve Sedgwick maintains that '"Closetedness" itself is a performance initiated as such by the speech act of silence – not a particular silence, but a silence that accrues particularity by fits and starts, in relation to the discourse that surrounds and differentially constitutes it.'[15] Therefore, I have to ask myself, How do I play out the silences? If coming out is the opposite of being 'closeted,' then the answer is simple. I am out. I write about my sexuality, I think about it, I constantly assign articles and books on the topic in any of the classes I teach, and I put my own work in the bibliographies I hand students who enrol in my classes. But coming out is not simply the opposite of being in the closet. For those who ask about the degree of my 'outness,' only a declarative statement (in the order of 'I am a lesbian.') to each of my classes seems to count.

Here, I am not only offering an analysis of some of the more prevalent reasons for coming out, I am also attempting to present alternative ways of thinking about the assumptions underlying the political reasons for coming out, and in particular the responsibility towards students. I am making a distinction between, on the one hand, the decision to come out for myself, to choose how and when to realize that moment, and on the other hand, the pressures imposed on me, a teacher, to come out, to 'put my body on the line' because it is my political duty as a lesbian.

To begin with, in order to come out one must know one's sexual identity, one must choose a category distinct from other categories and place oneself, even if hesitantly, in it. Having done that, one must then inform others concerning where one is placed with a declarative statement in the order of, 'I am a lesbian (gay, bisexual, transsexual).' This initial step of recognizing and acknowledging one's sexual identity is already problematic, not least because the categories in which we attempt to place ourselves are socially constituted and acquire meaning in space and time. A sexual category is not a static formulation, and neither is our relationship to that category. Each sexual category has a history of its own, located in western historical accounts of how each term was coined, how it developed, when it was first used, and so on. Also, one's relationship to current uses of sexual categories is relational in that our particular sexual history develops through time. Is one a lesbian if one has had a history of having sex with men and now has a woman as a lover? Is one a lesbian if one has had women lovers but now is interested in men? Is one a lesbian if one has never had sex with a woman but assumes the category for political reasons, or if one chooses not to have sex at all? And so on. To embrace a sexual category as an identity further complicates the issue because the meanings given to any identity are negotiated.

Underlying discussions of coming out, however, are assumptions that identity is stable and fixed, because for a statement such as 'I am a lesbian' to have any coherence, there has to be an understanding of the term *identity* as stable and unchanging or a recognition that the statement is momentary. Likewise, the sexual category *lesbian* must appear stable and unchanging. This piece is precisely framed around the concept of identity as *unstable* and *ambivalent*. This instability and ambivalence signals identity as a concept that has an historical, political, and social context, and that any attempt to define it without considering that context would render the term problematic.

Therefore, in order to come out it is not enough to state one's sexual identity unproblematically, any more than one can speak of sexual categories in general unproblematically. Diana Fuss suggests that 'Sexual identity may be less a function of knowledge than performance, or, in Foucauldian terms, less a matter of final discovery than perpetual reinvention.'[16] If identity is performative, if it is reinvented perpetually, it cannot be stable. And if we acknowledge that it is not stable, that it is a 'leaky' concept, then the boundaries and fissures dissolve. Finally, if identity is problematic and performative, the question of coming out performs its own set of assumptions, including the one within current political refrain that maintains that coming out is tied to political practice.

The question of coming out in class stems from a number of assumptions. The first is that students who are lesbian or gay would be gratified and reinforced to see a lesbian or a gay man as a professor. Secondly, there is the perennial question of being a role model: by being out, a lesbian or gay teacher becomes a role model for students. Third, being an 'out' professor unsettles the heterosexism of an institution. Fourth, not to come out is to institutionalize homophobia. Finally, coming out is putting one's body on the line, a prerequisite for political action. There are, of course, such reasons as honesty and personal integrity, issues that I discuss in the process of dealing with the above. There may be other reasons given for coming out. I now deal with each in turn.

To Reinforce and Support Students

One of the reasons given for the importance of coming out to each class is that the disclosure itself will act as a means of support to those students who are struggling with their sexual identity. The logic of this presumption is that (potentially) lesbian and gay students would recognize the gesture of coming out as one of strength, pride in the identity, honesty, and integrity. By saying 'I am a lesbian' to a class I am also telling them that I am not ashamed of my sexual orientation, that I am comfortable in my sexuality, that here I am, a tenured professor and yet a lesbian. Amy Blumenthal, in a written dialogue with Mary Mittler, captures the intention: 'As an educator, I want to be a positive role model for all my students and a special support for lesbian and gay students.'[17] But what does that proclamation reveal and how do we know the way it is read? How does a teacher's revealing her sexual orientation provide support? What if the race or gender or class of this teacher gets in the way?[18] What if the gay or lesbian student does not want to be out in class? What if the professor's gayness threatens students, straight or gay, for whatever reason?

Recently, at the university where I teach, a panel on homophobia was organized and I was one of the presenters. During the question period a young man asked the members of the panel what to do in a situation such as the one he experienced: he was a doctoral student who agreed to teach a course in his field. On the first day of class he no sooner began talking than, in his words, he 'locked eyes' with a woman who was sitting opposite him. He described the incident: 'From that first moment, it was obvious to both of us that she was [lesbian] and that I am [gay]. Suddenly, as she realized our mutual connection, an incredible look of horror came into her eyes. She left the class in a hurry and never came back. I know she was traumatized.'[19] The question that was put to the panel was, What had gone wrong? I do not remember the responses given on that day, but his question is very pertinent to my current project.

Although this account, like all accounts, can only be partially analysed, there are important questions to be asked. We know little, for instance about his age and hers. Did they differ in class, or religion, or race? Was there truly a moment of reciprocal recognition? How was that moment between teacher and student constituted and understood by each? How was his look read by the student? How is this situation different from a Jewish student or a Black student acknowledging a shared particularity of history or location with a teacher? Eve Sedgwick answers: 'The double edged potential for injury in the scene of gay coming out, by contrast, results partly from the fact that the erotic identity of the person who receives the disclosure is apt also to be implicated in, hence perturbed by it.'[20] Whereas for a Jewish or Black student to acknowledge a moment of shared history with a teacher may be important for making an academic connection; in this case the woman's terror was based on a recognition which, for her, may have posed a threat of disclosure. Disclosures often assume a reciprocal gesture as well. Was the student afraid of being outed? Was she fearful of the threat of contagion (if I am gay and you are seen with me, you will be thought to be gay as well)? Or was she simply apprehensive at being recognized?

Conversely, the potential terror or discomfort of students may be perceived as precisely a reason for coming out to them. The disclosure in itself poses a challenge for all students to examine their relationship to sexuality in general and to homophobia and heterosexism in particular. But as Mary Mittler contends in her response to a point made by Amy Blumenthal, 'Students come into your class with a set of expectations, almost all rooted in course content, not the content that is you [the teacher]'[21] Mittler makes an interesting distinction between the body of the teacher as a site of disclosure and the content of the course as a location for critical readings and potential intellectual shifts. Furthermore, the power of the teacher must be considered. Is the teacher imposing personal information on students? What happens when the teacher's disclosure gets in the way of the content she is teaching? Of what pedagogical importance is this instance of coming out? Clearly, the question must always be posed as well within the context of what is being taught.

Another argument against coming out with a declarative statement could be that the ambiguity of the teacher's sexual orientation could prove to be more pedagogically challenging for students. The uncertainty itself, if we can assume that the students care to read the cues, is a challenge for critical thinking. For instance it invites them to review their stereotypes; it may even demand that they seriously reassess the simplicity of binary sexual categories. Furthermore, by putting the subject of sexuality on the table a teacher can problematize heterosexuality as well as insist on an understanding that lesbian/gay/bisexual sexualities are not only sites of discrimination but of resistance, survival, and celebration. Also, as I argued above, the *meanings* of each of the sexual categories with which one may choose to identify, is, to borrow from Judith Butler, 'not always constituted coherently or consistently in different historical contexts,' and (to continue Butler's thought) because sexuality intersects with race, class, gender, 'ethnic and regional modalities of discursively constituted identities,'[22] the terms of signification such as *lesbian*, *gay*, or *transsexual* are rendered troublesome. Therefore, by saying in a classroom that 'I am a lesbian' I can be assured neither that the connotations of my intended message are understood, nor that the declaration is complex enough to inform listeners about who I am.[23] Furthermore, a declarative statement about my sexuality may separate me as a subject from my knowledge, and may make an irrelevant distinction between what I am teaching from who I am as a teacher. In other words, by making the declarative statement 'I am a lesbian' I run the risk of becoming the text for my students.

To Provide a Role Model

The second most urgent reason given for a teacher to come out in class is that as a tenured professor I could be perceived as a role model for my students. There is something to be said for the needs of some students to see a person of a similar sexual (racial, gender, or class) identity for the student to feel included and represented; that is not the same, however, as the teacher being a role model. I am making a distinction between issues of representation (which are in themselves problematic – representing whom?) and being a role model. The role model concept makes an interesting pedagogical assumption: by coming out to my class I am teaching them something; I am standing as an ideal of some behaviour, identity, or possibility.

Deborah Britzman has written eloquently about this topic:

According to this approach positive self image is fashioned by encountering positive role models and by valuing individual differences as something 'unique' and 'special.' This formula fails to address the disruptive question of whether it is even possible for persons to imitate a role – that is, to take on the characteristics of the dominant group – given the fact that role models themselves are the result of social standards and conventions.[24]

Britzman goes on: 'Role models arrive preassembled. They are not only larger than life; they are rolled out precisely because they have rolled over all that stood in their way.'[25] Role models, for those who drag out the concept (and in education it is certainly used often), rely on several uncritical presumptions: (1) that roles can be imitated (this assumes that we can identify the role itself); (2) that we can recognize its message and perhaps separate it from the subject who performs it; and (3) that in accepting it we are at once accepting the value(s) embedded in and underlying the performance, as well as taking refuge in its 'rightness, clarity, completeness, and stability.'[26] But as Britzman argues, 'Neglected in this simple version is the fact that idealized identities do not lend insight into the mobile and shifting conditions that make identity such a contradictory place to live.'[27]

The assumption that coming out to students provides them with a role model is therefore pedagogically suspect because, as we may ask, What kind of theory of learning makes the body of the teacher so central to her pedagogy? A better set of questions might be: What can be gained by coming out? What do we want the students to know? How can we ensure that students are reading the meaning of the messages as we intend them to be read? What is the intention of these messages?

Those who advocate coming out in class to provide students with a role model make the point that seeing a person who is a lesbian (or gay, bisexual, transsexual) and out reaffirms the student's sense of self as a lesbian (or gay, bisexual, transsexual) student. It is likened to the Black student who is validated by seeing a Black teacher or professor at the front of the class. But one cannot decide to be a role model for anyone. This is a notion of representation that suggests that the very teacher's race (or sex) is somehow tied to the self-concept of the student. Students look for someone to admire in that process of identification, but a sexual (racial, gender, or class) identity is not in itself grounds for identification. Identification, like learning itself, is a process.

The assumptions underlying these notions of identification can be contested. Theorists[28] have shown that identifications are often partial, complicated, and unpredictable. Using a psychoanalytic framework Diana Fuss distinguishes between the terms *identity* and *identification*. At the same time as she differentiates between the two words, she shows how they relate and depend on each other for coherence:

Identifications are erotic, intellectual, and emotional. They delight, fascinate, puzzle, confuse, unnerve, and sometimes terrify. They form the most intimate and yet the most elusive part of our public personas – the most exposed part of our self's surface collisions with a world of other selves – we experience our identifications as more private, guarded, evasive. I would not wish to remain long, however, with a too simplistic differentiation between public identity and private identification; such a specious distinction disguises how every identity is actually an identification come to light.[29]

Fuss reminds us that identifications have an astonishing capacity to reverse, to disappear, and to reappear years later, characteristics that render identities profoundly unstable and perpetually open to change. How then can we know with which part of the perceived or declared identity they are identifying? Is it the race/class/gender/sexuality of the teacher? Is it the kindness and warmth? Is it perhaps the brilliance or the pedagogy? There is no denying that students have crushes on teachers; there is no reason to suppose, however, that this happens precisely because we have chosen to come out. Students choose to have crushes on those teachers they admire and not necessarily on those teachers who stand for a particular identity.

To Unsettle the Dominance of Heterosexuality

There are two parts to the assumption that by coming out in class a teacher is unsettling the normativity of heterosexuality. The first concerns a notion of normalizing 'homosexuality.'[30] By this I mean the belief that the collectivities have a certain power to persuade the social order to include them. The special logic of this assumption is that if many people, particularly respectable professionals (including teachers), identify themselves as lesbian (or gay, bisexual, transsexual) the more likely 'we' will be tolerated and accepted. The second aspect of this assumption is that the very act of coming out in class challenges heterosexism, as well as the notion that everyone is heterosexual. And by unsettling heterosexuality we are also unsettling sexuality.

The process of coming out in class takes for granted several assumptions: that we are admired in our roles as professionals; that our status (as professors) will lend credibility to homosexuality; that we (lesbian, gay, bisexual, transsexual) are representative of an invisible sociality (that is, that sexual identity is represented, and by extension stabilized); that perhaps our very presence in the academy automates advocacy for the plight of lesbian (gay, bisexual, transsexual) students. And, finally, that as a consequence of this coming out, people's attitudes will change. Blumenthal represents the position well:

I don't think this [lack of tolerance] will change unless more people begin to see – and get to know – teachers, doctors, lawyers, secretaries, librarians, marketing reps, carpenters, accountants who are gay. That's what I mean by modelling: letting students, faculty, administrators, and the community at large know that I am a hard working, conscientious educator who is good at her job, caring of her students and current in her field, and some of that may be even because and not in spite of the fact that I am a lesbian.[31]

There are many leaps of faith in the above quotation, not the least of which is the view that students will recognize Blumenthal as a conscientious and caring individual, not in spite of but rather because she is a lesbian. Why, however, do we equate sensitivity to issues of being out? Silin makes an interesting distinction between 'the right to privacy – to be protected from invasive prying into what is accomplished out of sight – versus the right to secrecy,'[32] where privacy is a decision about disclosure, while secrecy is a need to hide. Therefore, one can exercise her right to privacy and still be sensitive and supportive of those students who suffer any form of discrimination. Furthermore, how do sheer numbers of people coming out produce change? Sheer numbers of African Americans or African Canadians have not eliminated racism in either the United States or Canada. The point is that it is political activism and not sheer numbers that will, in the long run, make a difference.

Another issue that is glossed over is that the teacher's sexuality might be itself a potential site of change for the population at large. How can being Black, or female, or lesbian in themselves produce a reduction in racism, sexism, or homophobia? But that is not what Blumenthal is saying. Her point is argued from one who wants to be recognized as a conscientious worker and a lesbian, with an additional understanding that it might be because she is a lesbian that she is caring. There is a resultant gloss in the notion that a sexual identity incorporates a quality such as hard work and care.

There is still the question of how our coming out as lesbian (gay, bisexual, transsexual) ensures representation. This is so particularly because race, gender, social class, generation, religion, and ethnicity complicate sexuality. So what precisely can be represented? Also, how do we conclude that the very act of coming out in class implies a certain commitment to advocacy for students when 'identity' is so incomplete? Indeed, how can we even know how our words, cues, or behaviours will be interpreted or understood in the way we intend them?

A graduate student told of an incident that happened to him as an undergraduate don of a residence. In order to announce his sexual identity he plastered his room with gay-related posters and wore a T-shirt that said 'Nobody knows I'm gay' and a pink triangle to ensure everyone knew he was gay. He was challenging the heterosexist norm. Nothing much happened, until one day a male student stopped him in the hallway with the warning: 'You know, Blaine, you really should be careful about what you wear because people are going to think you are gay or something.'[33] Another example came from a self-identified white lesbian graduate student in my course who began her seminar presentation with the words: 'I approach this topic as an identifiable [i.e., recognizable] lesbian.' Another young woman sitting beside me at the other end of the table whispered, 'Well, *that's* news to me.' Evidently the 'identifiable' lesbian was not as clearly recognizable as she assumed, despite her close-cropped hair and her 'butch' attire. The woman beside me was Black, and the cues she was looking for were concerned with the raciality of the speaker. What is more interesting is that the lesbian student assumed that her very appearance spoke for her.[34] But what *did* her appearance articulate for the students? And once she had identified her sexual orientation, what did the student(s) understand from that pronouncement? If her dress/appearance was not intelligible to some of the students, can one assume that her statement was any clearer in indicating her 'identity'?

Audre Lorde, in her autobiographical *Zami: A New Spelling of My Name*, describes a scene from 1950s New York that is pertinent to my point:

On the last day before I finally moved away from the Lower East Side after I got my master's degree from library school, I went in for my last English muffin and coffee and to say goodbye to Sol and Jimmy [the two coffee shop owners] in some unemotional and acceptable way. I told them both I'd miss them and the old neighbourhood, and they said they were sorry and why did I have to go? I told them I had to work out of the city, because I had a fellowship for Negro students. Sol raised his eyebrows in utter amazement, and said, 'Oh? I didn't know you was cullud!'

I went around telling that story for a while, although a lot of my friends couldn't see why I thought it was funny. But this is all about how very difficult it is at times for people to see who or what they are looking at, particularly when they don't want to.

Or maybe it takes one to know one.[35]

Even the most 'obvious' cues can be misunderstood or remain unintelligible to some people. 'Not knowing,' in this case, can be a process of overlooking or not recognizing, or even politely ignoring. The reasons may be cultural, sheer ignorance, or a wish to avoid the discomfort of having to confront the 'unmentionable.' The question then becomes, By stating the 'obvious,' what can be gained?

To Avoid Institutionalizing Homophobia

One of the reasons why the declarative statement is perceived to be the *only* suitable, clear, and politically efficacious means of coming out is precisely because of the power of its supposedly unambiguous message. 'I am a lesbian' is a statement presumed to be clear, an assertion of an unambiguous identity, a reaffirmation of the difference between 'I' the lesbian, and 'them' the non-lesbians. There are several ways, however, to think about the term *identity*, ranging from a psychoanalytic analysis to a political one, none of which are mutually exclusive. Some of the properties of the term that I have been examining include, on the one hand, making a difference between the position of claiming an identity for activism, where identity becomes the locus of a shared vision for political struggle, and on the other hand, asserting one's identity as a moment of defining one's self. Where the first conceptualization of the term *identity* provides space for continual redefinition and reflexivity, the second seems to freeze the self within a circumscribed framework that separates the 'I' from the 'them.' But how can one understand the intention behind the declaration 'I am a lesbian'? Am I saying that I am part of a movement that is concerned with political struggle or am I saying that 'I' am merely different from 'you'? To come out is not simply to inform others of one's sexuality; it is a process whereby the speaker reiterates a certain relation, and perhaps a commitment, to an identity, even if momentarily, and always in context. Because a sweeping declarative statement in a general moment within a classroom has no context, intention is blurred, and hence its pedagogical or political effectiveness is essentially abrogated. Another complication of the declarative statement is that such a statement tends to suggest that I also stand in for every lesbian.

Furthermore, the very declarative statement 'I am a lesbian,' used for its supposed unambiguity, is itself a restatement of heterosexism. Since heterosexuals make no equivalent declarative statement, when lesbians (or gay men, bisexuals, transsexuals) come out, they are effectively reinforcing the hegemony of heterosexuality by announcing their difference. But how is it possible for a statement to perform its opposite?

Jonathan Silin argues that 'the closet is a function not of homosexuality but of compulsory heterosexuality.'[36] He explains: 'Coming out brings with it the destabilizing potential of the erotic even as it reproduces the oppressive social categories from which we seek liberation.'[37] Silin's point is well taken in that he puts the responsibility for the closet on the power of heteronormativity. Or, to quote Eve Sedgwick, 'gay identity is a convoluted and off centring possession if it is a possession at all; even to come out does not end anyone's relation to the closet, including turbulently the closet of the other.'[38]

To Put Our Bodies on the Line

I am assuming that those lesbian or gay teachers who advocate putting one's body on the line intend it for political purposes. One of my copanellists and colleagues at the workshop on antihomophobia mentioned earlier made the point that he always expects to be insulted, called a 'faggot,' and generally be given a hard time whenever he comes out to his large classes. He expects people to walk out of his lecture or to drop his course. His declarations are meant to provoke. Once again I have to ask, What are the pedagogical implications of putting one's body on the line? What are the transformative gains, the intellectual benefits?

To begin with, do verbal declarations alone count as putting one's body on the line? Is only the declarative statement deemed significant? What if a teacher uses dress to challenge notions of gender and sexuality? What if her body is read as lesbian when she is not?

Almost three years ago a friend of mine was walking with a gay male graduate student at about eleven o'clock at night in the French Quarter of New Orleans. Both were trying to relax from a day of presenting at a conference they were attending in that city. My friend is a woman over five foot nine who sports a short haircut. The young man accompanying her was shorter than she, and slighter. Suddenly a car stopped and two men got out and started to beat both my friend and her student. There was no attempt to rob either one of them, but they were beaten quite badly. Just as suddenly, the two men jumped back into the car and took off. Almost without exception people who heard the story and knew the individuals involved read the incident as gay bashing, presuming that the woman was misidentified as a gay man. The irony is that my friend was straight. Nevertheless, her body was as much on the line as her student's, precisely because her body was mistaken for a gay body. Thus, perhaps a teacher need not *be* a lesbian; perhaps she need only *be perceived* as a lesbian for her body to be on the line.

The question, therefore, concerning what it means to put one's body on the line, becomes somewhat rhetorical. Are we speaking metaphorically of political action or literally of putting ourselves in danger as activists? Is danger the only way of achieving equity? How do we come to equate danger with potential transformation towards social justice? Can we each not strive to find the most appropriate strategies of which we are capable in order to achieve our political ends?

Conclusion

The decision whether to come out in class and how to come out must remain within the jurisdiction of the individual teacher. In this chapter I have often argued against the notion of coming out in a declarative way ('I am a lesbian') because I believe that there are significant pedagogical reasons why a teacher may choose not to declare her sexual orientation in that way.

On a personal level, experience with coming out as a feminist to my classes has shown me that from the moment of my declaration, students filter all information or discussion of texts that occurs in the classroom through their knowledge of my political bent. Would coming out in class encourage students to filter my performance in class through their (often limited) understanding of my sexuality? Conversely, as a teacher I prefer not to stand in as a sexual category.

Finally, I have attempted here to discuss some of the prevalent assumptions concerning coming out in class. I have tried to offer alternatives to these assumptions. But this is only a beginning, an opening up of questions of pedagogy and issues of coming out, of assumptions about learning, and of the complicated ways in which we as teachers learn to cope in the classroom.

Notes

This chapter first appeared as an article in the *Harvard Educational Review*. The current version has been revised significantly for this collection; eralier versions were read in Halifax, NS (February 1996) and in Kelowna, B.C. (May 1996) at the 34th meeting of the Western Association of Sociology and the Anthropology Association.

I am indebted to Celia Haig Brown, Deborah Britzman, Alice Pitt, Katherine Arnup, Eve Zaremba, and Linda Briskin for agreeing to read the various versions of this chapter. I of course take responsibility for all positions expressed herein.

1 Spivak, *Outside in the Teaching Machine*, 25.
2 Mercer, *Welcome to the Jungle*, 284.
3 Khayatt, 'In and Out,' 210–17.
4 Khayatt, 'Legalized Invisibility.'
5 Ibid. A detailed analysis is undertaken in the original article.
6 Khayatt, 'Legalized Invisibility,' 191.
7 Ibid.
8 Money, 'Oxford, London School Board Bigots?' 17.
9 See, for example, Jennings, ed., *One Teacher in 10*; Frank, 'Queer Selves,' 44–59; Silin, *Sex, Death*; Diane Williams, 'Who's That Teacher?' 65–9; Woog, School's Out, to name a few.
10 Silin, *Sex, Death* 120.
11 Sedgwick, *Epistemology of the Closet*, 73.
12 In my lectures and in the syllabus I hand to students at the beginning of each course – which includes assigned and suggested reading, assignments, and films to be shown – I make sure my students understand that I am teaching from a feminist perspective.
13 Foucault, *The History of Sexuality*, 27.
14 Fuss, *Inside/Out*, 6.
15 Sedgwick, *Epistemology of the Closet*, 3.
16 Fuss, *Inside/Out*, 6–7.
17 Mittler and Blumenthal, 'Being a Change Agent,' 4.
18 An experience a few years ago illustrates how issues of sex are threatening in some circumstances: I was compiling a bibliography for a special issue on Canadian immigrant women for a journal, and had spent months cross-referencing and searching indexes for any work on what it meant to be both a lesbian and an immigrant woman. To no avail. The year was 1982 and nothing yet had been written in Canada about the topic. Since I was in touch with several women from that community loosely termed *immigrant* I asked a number of them for an explanation. I knew many who were lesbian; how was it that none had written of their experiences? One woman claimed that immigrant women often relied on their national (ethnic) communities for support, and that their need as lesbians were secondary to their needs to belong to their respective ethnic communities.
19 Many thanks to Blaine Rehkopf for allowing me to write about his experience here.
20 Sedgwick, *Epistemology of the Closet*, 81.
21 Mittler and Blumenthal, 'Being a Change Agent,' 5.
22 Judith Butler, *Gender Trouble*, 3.
23 Although I realize that the following argument stabilizes gender identity, another

48   Didi Khayatt

point to be made concerns bringing the erotic into the classroom. Brodkey and Fine, in 'Presence of Mind,' while analysing sexual harassment narratives of women students at the University of Pennsylvania, realized that the accounts suggest that women 'understand their own survival may depend on the ability to cleave their minds from their bodies (88).' The authors explain that while such a position is problematic in many ways, 'there is overwhelming evidence in theory, research and practice that mind, body, gender, and sexuality are not facts we must live with but social constructions we have learned to live by (88).' I quote Brodkey and Fine in order to highlight a potential gender difference in the face of introducing the erotic in class. Women may choose to avoid introducing the subject of sex into the classroom because in this culture sexuality has often been turned against women in instances such as sexual harassment, violence, or sexual objectification.

24 Britzman, 'Beyond Rolling Models,' 25.
25 Ibid.
26 Ibid.
27 Ibid.
28 For instance, see the work of Laplanche and Pontalis, *Language of Psycho-Analysis*, 205–8. More recently, see Fuss, *Identification Papers*.
29 Fuss, Identification Papers, 2.
30 I am using terms such as homosexuality and heterosexuality for expediency, and am well aware of the dangers of constituting those two concepts as binary opposites.
31 Mittler and Blumenthal, 'Being a Change Agent' 6–7.
32 Silin, *Sex, Death*, 167.
33 I am grateful to Blaine Rehkopf for the account of this incident.
34 I am grateful to Diane Naugler for allowing me to use this incident.
35 Lorde, *Zami*, 183
36 Silin, *Sex, Death*, 166.
37 Ibid.
38 Sedgwick, *Epistemology of the Closet*, 81.

3

Queer Pedagogy and Its Strange Techniques

DEBORAH P. BRITZMAN

In an essay that rethinks the historicity of identity politics and the situated question of what is at stake (and for whom) when identities are at stake, Gayatri Chakravorty Spivak worries about education. She asks repeatedly, 'What is it to learn and to unlearn?' The call is to think about what institutional education as a set of discourses and practices has to do with the self-determination *as well as* the subordination of global subaltern populations. Spivak is not asking that 'identity' be restored to a nice ontology, a site of uniqueness or comfort, a font of self-esteem, or a celebration of individuality. In fact, by centring the question of learning and unlearning, it is precisely the unthought of these sorts of regulatory declarations that she takes as a problem. What does learning and unlearning mean when one considers both 'cases of exorbitant normality rather than disease [and] cases of confounding the instituted laws?'[1] Can the project of education become the gathering ground for 'deconstructive revolts?' Can pedagogy provoke ethical responses that can bear to refuse the normalizing terms of origin and of fundamentalism, those that refuse subjection?

The concern for 'cases of exorbitant normality' and how such 'cases' are produced in education is not new.[2] Near the end of *Civilization and Its Discontents* Freud addresses a footnote to educators. Having already deemed education as one of the impossible professions, he notes one of its fault lines: 'In sending the young out into life with ... a false psychological orientation, education is behaving as though one were to equip young people starting on a polar expedition with summer clothing and maps to the Italian Lakes.'[3] The phrasing 'false psychological orientation' can be read as a critique of the way education disavows the complexities and treacherous conflicts of 'civilization': of education's repetitious offer of tidy stories of happiness, resolution, and certainty as if life were something to be overcome and mastered with as little disturbance as possible. Freud's concern is with how education came to conduct itself without a theory of conflict and otherness, and how education might think about making selves interested in life as a state of emergency. As with Spivak's call one might read Freud as saying that there is a problem with narratives that promise the normalcy of life, that presume a life without difference, without a divided self.

What makes normalcy so thinkable in education? How might pedagogy think the unthought of normalcy? To allow such questions, three different forms of practice will be set in tension: those of queer theory, those of pedagogy, and those of psychoanalytic reading practices. Queer theory transgresses the stabilities of the representational; pedagogy situates the problem of normalcy in classroom sites and worries about the social production of the learning self; and psychoanalytic theories of reading refuse knowledge as certainty in order to call into question three forms of subjection: the subject-presumed-to-know, the capacity of the subject's response to be unencumbered by that which it cannot tolerate: and the subject's own 'passion for ignorance.'[4] Taken together, these practices make one curious about the means by which normalcy becomes the great unmarked within classroom sites and the means by which pedagogy itself might intervene to agitate the limits and fault lines of normalcy. Once normalcy is constructed as an historical problem of pedagogy and marked as a production of pedagogy itself, a further question is raised: Can the reading of normalcy be a queer reading practice?

Each part of this chapter depends upon the assumption that education is a structure of authority even as it structures the very grounds of authority required for its own recognition. As a practice and as a discourse, education intimately disciplines the conceptual needs of students and teachers. Some of these needs concern a desire for a transparent truth, for stable communities and identities, and for a pedagogy that ignores contradictions. And even those needs that desire an oppositional or critical practice bear the traces of these first demands. At the same time, all these contradictions compete with the ways discourses of affectivity and intellect are organized and differentially lived. In bringing into dialogue queer theory, psychoanalytic reading practices, and pedagogy, and by using these three terms to consider the problem of how knowledge of bodies and bodies of knowledge become a site of normalization, this chapter is an attempt to practice the kinds of deconstructive revolts raised earlier by Spivak: to take apart the conceptual orderings that conceal the very difficult question of what difference difference makes. If, then, every learning is an unlearning, 'what is it to learn and unlearn?'

My attention to these tensions is part of an attempt to imagine a queer pedagogy (as opposed to a queer pedagogue), a pedagogy that worries about and unsettles normalcy's immanent exclusions, or, as many now pose the problem, normalcy's passions for ignorance.[5] It is a pedagogy that attempts to provoke what Gary Wickham and William Haver term 'the very proliferation of alternative sites of identification and critique' necessary if thought is to think the limits of its own dominant conceptual orders, and if new desires are to be made. This means thinking a pedagogy whose grounds of possibility require risk, uncertainty, and implication in traumatic times. It means imagining a pedagogy prepared to exceed the doubled Foucauldian subject: 'subject to someone else by control and dependence; and tied to his own identity by a conscience or self knowledge.'[6] And while it may be difficult to conceive of self knowledge as a site of subjection, much of my argument is meant to unsettle old centerings of the self in education: to unsettle the myth of normalcy as an originary state and to unsettle the unitary subject of pedagogy. However, rather than offer a 'how to' manual of pedagogy, I am trying to imagine a queer pedagogy along the lines of what Sue Golding calls 'technique,' 'a route, a mapping, an impossible geography – impossible not because it does not exist, but because *it exists and does not exist exactly at the same time.*'[7]

In thinking a queer pedagogy, I wonder if the terms of queerness can exceed and still hold onto its first referent, namely transgression and an economy of affection and practices of desire, that, in its hesitations, both speaks and departs from its relational name. And by holding to this tension can a queer pedagogy implicate everyone involved to consider the grounds of their own possibility, their own intelligibility, and the work of proliferating their own identifications and critiques that can exceed identity as essence, explanation, causality, or transcendence? The shift, then, of a queer pedagogy is one that becomes curious about identifications and how identifications constitute desires.[8] The move is meant to pose a question concerning how it is that one decides the desirability and relevancy of representation itself. It is a movement, akin to Lee Edelman's curiosity, towards 'the way in which identity turns out to be a trope of representation.'[9]

Whether one looks for one's own image in the other and hence invests in knowledge as self-reflection and affirmation, or whether, in the process of coming to know, one invests in the rethinking of the self as an effect of and condition for encountering the other as an equal, is the problem this chapter engages. And in claiming as desirable the proliferation of identifications and critiques necessary to imagine sociality differently, can a queer pedagogy wander, along with Samuel Delany, 'the margin[s] between claims of truth and the claims of texuality'[10] between what is taken to be real and what is constituted as experience, between the immediacies of expectation and the afterthought of (mis)-recognition? Can pedagogy move beyond producing essentialist subject positions and ponder the fashioning of the self that occurs when attention is given to the performativity of the subject in queer relationality?

I

Queer Theory proposes to think identities in terms that place as a problem the production of normalcy, and in terms that confound the intelligibility of the apparatuses that produce identity as repetition. As deconstructive revolts, queer theories acknowledge the intrusion of exorbitant normalcy and the ways such normalcy ignores the everydayness of queer identifications, pleasures, practices, and bodies. The concern here is in thinking the cost of narrating identities and the cost of identities itself.[11] Queer theory is not an affirmation but an implication. Its bothersome and unapologetic imperatives are explicitly transgressive, perverse, and political: transgressive because it questions the regulations and effects of binary categorical conditions such as the public and the private, the inside and the outside, the normal and the queer, and the ordinary and the disruptive; perverse because it turns away from utility even as it claims deviancy as a site of interest;[12] and political because it attempts to confound instituted laws and practices by putting into place queer representations on their own everyday terms.[13]

Queer theory, then, becomes queer when, as Teresa de Lauretis notes, it 'conveys a double emphasis on the conceptual and speculative work involved in discourse production, and on the necessary critical work of deconstructing our own discourses and their constructed silences.'[14] Queer theory takes up that queer space of simultaneously questioning and asserting representations and in outing the unthought of normalcy. The attempt is to provoke yet-to-be-made constructions of subjects interested in confronting what Peggy Phelan terms as 'the not all' of representation.[15] As an unruly collection of discursive strategies of reading and of narrating bodies and histories, and as performative street politics that refuse to think straight, queer theory engages what Alexander Duttman terms 'a supplement of impertinence,'[16] or the dissimilitude within representation: what cannot be recuperated, said, or managed; what becomes undone despite a promise of certainty.

Where queer theory meets pedagogy is in how it conceptualizes normalcy as negation.[17] It constitutes normalcy as a conceptual order that refuses to imagine the very possibility of the other precisely because the production of otherness as an outside is central to its own self-recognition. This orientation to normalcy as the pernicious production of such binaries as the self/other and the inside/outside may be quite significant to the conceptualization and transformation of the education of education.[18] This is so because within contexts of education the pointing to normalcy as exorbitant production allows one to consider simultaneously the relations between and within those who transgress and undress the normal and those whose labour is to be recognized as normal. When pedagogy meets queer theory and thus becomes concerned with its own structure of intelligibility – with the education of education – and when pedagogy engages its own impertinence, the very project of knowledge and its accompanying subject-presumed-to-know become interminable despite the institutional press for closure, tidiness, and certainty.

And yet, to get to the space where difference and not similitude is the space of pedagogy, a detour into the question of identity is necessary. To notice that 'identity' has become what Michel Foucault has termed 'an incitement to discourse,'[19] perhaps slides too easily over the very problem articulated within the field of queer theories. As an incitement the concept of identity seems to mobilize and regulate whole sets of epistemic anxieties over such agitated relations as identity and politics, narrations and practices, history and representation, identity and identifications. What seems common to queer theory is an insistence on understanding identity as both a social and historical production and as a relational ethic: identity as neither transcendence nor equivalence.

In queer theory, talk about identity has moved well beyond old formulas of accepting experience as telling and transparent and as supposing that role models are the transitional object to self-esteem. Something far less comforting is being put into place: namely, identity is examined as a discursive effect of the social and as being constituted through identifications. The self becomes a problem of desiring a self and hence in need of a social. It is identification that allows the self-recognition and misrecognition. And it is through identification that desire is made. But because identification is a partial, contradictory, and ambivalent relation with aspects or dynamics of others, it may be thought of as a means to make and direct desire. Many positionings are possible: identification of, identification with, identification against, over-identification, and so on.[20] Diana Fuss's working definition suggests the tensions of identificatory relations: 'Identification inhabits, organizes and instantiates identity ... [It can be considered] as the play of difference and similitude in self-other relations [and] does not, strictly speaking, stand against identity but structurally aids and abets it.'[21] To shift from an insistence upon identity to an exploration of identifications allows pedagogy to consider the problem of how the self reads itself.

In discussing the debate between identities and politics Douglas Crimp poses the problem of relationality:

Identification is, of course, identification with an other, which means that identity is never identical to itself. This alienation from the self it constructs ... does not mean simply that any proclamation of identity will only be partial, that it will be exceeded by other *aspects* of identity, but rather that identity is always a relation, never simply a positivity ... perhaps we can begin to rethink identity politics as politics of relational identities formed through political identifications that constantly remake those identities.[22]

If identity is not identical to itself, but only a possibility in relation to another, and if such a relation is one of difference within as well as difference between identities, what might it mean for pedagogy to think about identity as a problem of making identifications in difference? Such a question is *not* one that requires a naïve empathy. For, as Freud reminds educators, the project of empathy is actually a projection of the self into the conditions of the other.[23] This projection becomes forgotten with the hope that it is possible, in Freud's words, 'to feel our way into people.' And yet, because feelings are contradictory, historical, ambivalent, and a statement of need, feelings are a response to something and hence are already constitutive of relations. To feel one's way into someone else, then, cannot be an originary moment, and to act as if it were means one must shut out both the infinite variations and slippages of affect and the fact that feelings are also contradictory and ambivalent forms of thought or structures of intelligibility that depend upon historically specific spheres.[24] In other words, feelings are not capable of transcending history and the relations already supposed. As Freud remarks, 'We shall always tend to consider [we can imagine] people's distress objectively – that is, to place ourselves, with our own wants and sensibilities, in their conditions, and then to examine what occasions we should find in them for experiencing happiness or unhappiness.'[25] Yet, even in this very imagined moment, one can only imagine the self.

   If one cannot feel one's way into people without, in actuality, representing the self as the arbitrator and judge of the other's actions and possibilities, perhaps it is time to question what one wants from empathy and whether the educational insistence that feelings are the royal road to attitudinal change is how identificatory structures actually work. Instead, one might consider feelings as constituting ignorances, ambivalences, and knowledge, and thus as that which cannot exist without narrative conventions and their own structures of intelligibility and unintelligibility. The argument here is not that feelings do not or should not matter, or that one should not work with perspectives and conditions that are not own's own. It is to suggest that feelings are symptomatic of more than the individual's intentionality. Indeed, precisely because feelings are matters of history, of location, and of bodies, one might consider feelings as symptomatic of contradictory pushes and pulls of relationality and need. In the context of a queer pedagogy, a more useful way to think about feelings requires attention to what it is that structures the ways in which feelings are imagined and read. This means constituting feelings for another as a curious reading practice, as a problem of ethical conduct, and as a symptom of identificatory engagement. That is, pedagogy might provoke the strange study of where feelings break down, take a detour, reverse their content, betray understanding, and hence study where affective meanings become anxious, ambivalent, and aggressive. Rather than invoking a discourse of empathy that cannot explain itself, pedagogy might become curious about what conceptual orders have to do with affectivity, and with what reading practices have to do with proliferating one's identificatory possibilities and modes of critique.

II

In questioning the question of reading practices, linking reading practices to forms of sociality, and hence to the very structuring of intelligibility, identifications, modes of address, and civic life, I mean to signal not just how one comes to recognize, imagine, and contain signs. Rather, in education the problem becomes how one comes to think, along with others, the very structures of signification in avowing and disavowing forms of sociality and their grounds of possibility; to question, along with others, one's form of thinking, one's form of practice. Reading practices, then, are socially performative. And part of the performance might well be the production of normalcy – itself a hegemonic sociality – if techniques of reading begin from a standpoint of refusing the unassimilability of difference and the otherness of the reader. This case of 'exorbitant normality,' or passion for ignorance, occurs when 'the other' is rendered as either unintelligible or intelligible only as a special event, and hence as never entitled to an everyday. Exorbitant normality is built when the other is situated as a site of deviancy and disease, and hence, as if in need of containment. Such cruel reading practices, all too common, may well be a symptom of what Michael Warner calls heteronormativity.[26]

Reading practices might well perform something interesting, and this has to do with producing social selves whose thinking about their own structures of intelligibility recognizes and refuses the confinement of sameness and the seduction of affirmation that has as its cost the expulsion of otherness. Reading practices might be educated to attend to the proliferation of one's own identificatory possibilities and to make allowance for the unruly terms of undecidability and unknowability. One might think about the proliferation of identifications as a means to exceed – as opposed to return to – the self. What if one thought about reading practices as problems of opening identifications, of working the capacity to imagine oneself differently precisely with respect to how one encounters another, and in how one encounters the self? What if how one reads the world turned upon the interest in thinking against one's thoughts, of creating a queer space where old certainties made no sense?

In naming reading practices as having the capacity to be queered, I am offering not so much a remedy for the ways reading practices can construct normalcy. The production of normalcy, as Foucault points out, is not 'a history of mentalities,' or one of meaning, but rather 'a history of bodies' and is hence a problem of how sociality can be lived and how politics can be imagined.[27] To focus the question of reading practices as activities central to classroom pedagogies one might consider reading practices as social effects of something larger than the one who reads – a different order of time than the moment of reading might suggest. My concern is with constituting reading practices as symptomatic of relations of power, as capable of both expressing a desire that exceeds subjectivity and as provoking deconstructive revolts: reading practices as a technique for exceeding auto-affectivity and the accompanying investment in pinning down meanings, in getting identities 'straight.' My interest is in thinking of reading practices as possibly unhinging the normal from the self in order to prepare the self to encounter its own conditions of alterity: reading practices as an imaginary site for multiplying alternative forms of identifications and pleasures not so closely affixed to – but nonetheless transforming – what one imagines their identity imperatives to be. Then pedagogy may be conceived within two simultaneous terms: as an imaginative way to think about and to perform reading practices that still manage, however precariously, to be overconcerned with practices of identification and sociality; *and* as a technique for acknowledging difference *as the only condition of possibility for community.*

The problem I am trying to get at is something different than a plea for inclusion, or merely adding 'marginalized voices' to an overpopulated curriculum. Inclusion, or the belief that one discourse can make room for those it must exclude, can only produce, as Judith Butler puts it: 'that theoretical gesture of pathos in which exclusions are simply affirmed as sad necessities of signification.'[28] The case of how gay and lesbian studies has been 'treated' in a sentimental education that attempts to be antihomophobic serves as my example of where arguments for inclusion produce the very exclusions they are meant to cure. Part of the tension is that there tends to be only two pedagogical strategies: providing information and techniques of attitude change.[29] The normal view is that one should attempt to 'recover' authentic images of gays and lesbians and stick them into the curriculum with the hope that representations – in the form of tidy role models – can serve as a double remedy for hostility towards social difference for those who cannot imagine difference, and for the lack of self-esteem for those who are imagined as having no self. However, the question that cannot be uttered is, Just how different can these different folks be and still be recognized as just like everyone else? Or, put differently, given the tendency of the curriculum to pass knowledge through discourses of factuality and morality, how can difference be different? And, different from what?

The liberal desire for recovery and authenticity that takes the form of inclusion in the curriculum, perhaps as an add-on, certainly in the form of a special event, attempts two contradictory yet similar manoeuvres. On the one hand, the strategy constructs an innocently ignorant general public. Here, I want to signal how the normal of the normative order produces itself as unmarked sameness, and as if synonymous with the everyday even as it must produce otherness as a condition for its own recognition. For those who cannot imagine what difference difference makes in the field of curriculum, the hope is that the truth of the subaltern might persuade these normative folks to welcome the diversity of others and maybe feel their way into people in order to transform, at the level of these very transferable feelings, their racist, sexist, heterosexist attitudes. But how, exactly, is it possible to feel one's way into what can only be imagined as difference without producing, in that very act, the same? On the other hand, this strangely estranged story of difference requires the presence of those already deemed subaltern. Here, the recovery being referenced is the recovery of what the norm supposes these different folk lack, namely the self-esteem of the same. The originary myth of self-esteem, or a self-knowledge that assumes the self as lack, actually works to shut out the very conflictive operations that produce the self as lack and incapable of desire.

These liberal hopes, these various narratives of affirmation that are lived, however differently, as conceptual needs – and oddly, as one-way instances of empathy – are, however, really about the production of sameness. Certain subalterns might be invited into the curriculum, but not because they have anything to say to those already there. Indeed, if these textualized folks began to talk to one another, what would they actually say? Could they even make sense? The problem is that the lived effects of 'inclusion' are a more obdurate version of sameness and a more polite version of otherness. David Theo Goldberg puts it this way: 'The commitment to tolerance turns only on modernity's "natural inclination" to *in*tolerance; acceptance of otherness presupposes as it at once necessitates delegitimation of the other.'[30] Pedagogies of inclusion, then, and the tolerance that supposedly follows, may in actuality produce the grounds of normalization. Lived at the level of conceptual needs, such hopes are only able to offer the stingy subject positions of the tolerant normal and the tolerated subaltern. Put differently, the subject positions of US and THEM become recycled as empathy.

Returning to the double subject of Foucault, what does this subject precisely know about itself in talk about the other? Is there a form of self-knowledge that can untie the self from gender, racial, and sexual centrings? How is it that talk about queerness might refuse such binary oppositions like the public and the private, or refuse to produce a chain of signification that Toni Morrison calls 'the economy of stereotypes,' and instead, in the words of Peggy Phelan, make talk that 'upset[s] representational economies.'[31] How might pedagogy address what Eve Sedgwick terms the great divide of homo/hetero, and thus begin to confront the question of everydayness: 'In whose lives is homo/heterosexual definition an issue of continuing centrality and difficulty?'[32] Can pedagogy admit, as Judith Butler advises, 'the different routes by which the unthinkability of homosexuality is being constituted time and again?'[33] Or put a bit differently, can pedagogy admit to the unthinkability of normalcy and how normalcy 'is being constituted again and again?'

These questions might provoke a different take on discourses of information in terms of their centrality to the intelligibility of educational design and in terms of addressing the trauma it invokes. Along with cultural activists such as Cindy Patton doing AIDS education work, I assume the failure of the old information discourses of education: knowledge of 'facts' does *not* provide a direct line to the real, to the truth, and to righteous conduct.[34] As a discourse of knowledge, 'information' cannot account for things like affective investments as recalcitrant and as conflictively fashioned within particular narratives. It has nothing to say about how such information produces a hierarchy of addressees and therefore constitutes authority and modes of passions for ignorance. The information model is not capable of thinking how authorization is imagined and lived in classrooms. Nor can reliance upon the evidence of information account for the confusion when one's own sense of cohesiveness becomes a site of misrecognition, or the trauma unleashed when the discourses borrowed to work upon and perform the fictions of subjectivity stop making sense. Indeed, the reliance upon facts as the transitional object to attitude change provides no pedagogical theory of negation, or the way ideas and facts can become unattached from and even work against emotional ties.

There are at least two regulating fictions about information as the direct line to knowledge that need to be deconstructed. The first is that receiving information, acquiring 'just the facts' is no problem for the learner. The myth is that information neutralizes ignorance and that learners and their teachers will rationally accept new thoughts without having to grapple with unlearning the old ones. The second fiction is that information is a mirror of the real and hence an antidote for ignorance. The reasoning goes something like this: If people had the real facts, they might rationally decide to act better towards the 'victims' of ignorance or view their own ignorance as self-victimization. This view safely positions the knower within the normative, as a sort of volunteer who collects knowledge not because one's social identity is at stake, or even only made possible through the subjection of others, but rather because such information might protect one from the unintelligibility of others. Thus this discourse called information purports to construct compassion and tolerance as the correct subject position but in actuality performs the originary binary opposition of US/ THEM in more elaborate and normalizing terms.

At this point, it is helpful to ask whether discourses of information and discourse of feelings discussed earlier are actually different from each other. Information models of education assumes that facts are an objective corrective to ignorant feelings. Feeling models of education attempt a subjective corrective to the distancing mechanisms of objectified knowledge. But as a corrective, what must be ignored is that feelings are not rational techniques of self-adjustment nor is knowledge 'un-implicated' in its own sets of ignorances. However, to maintain itself each discourse depends upon the very inside/outside distinctions that provoke new forms of US/THEM. These discourses might be understood best as two kinds of social effects that spring from positioning classroom subjects as lack: as either lacking the proper feelings, whether these feelings be those of toleration or self-esteem, or as lacking knowledge, either the knowledge of the other or the intelligence of information. What cannot be considered however, is the question of cathexis and negation: where affect either meets the idea or becomes untied from the idea. The problem here is not one of abolishing either affectivity or intellect from the classroom. The problem is one where the valorization of either diminishes the very possibility of thinking about what happens when affectivity is imagined as constitutive of conflictive identificatory strategies and when conflictive discourses are imagined as mapping neatly onto desire. The problem is for pedagogy to insist upon affectivity and intellection as dialogic, as desire, and as implication.

Exploring how experiences of those deemed subaltern are imagined, then, means taking a second look at the everyday normative and rethinking the normative as producing the grounds of estrangement and new forms of ignorance. For some, such a second look means embodying the fear that these queer terms may well decentre the very terms of their own identity and hence the grounds of intelligibility upon which the self is supposed, coalesced, and recognized. At the same time, when the normative order is already lived as a site of estrangement, as it is for those always already positioned as subaltern, something different happens when listening to how one's identity gets pinned to estrangement: this has to do with not recognizing oneself in the discourses of otherness, of not living one's life as a stereotype, and of having to uncouple oneself from the regulations of stereotypes as the only condition of talk. Can pedagogy unleash new terms, new subject positions that move beyond voyeurism, social realism, spectatorship, and the metaphysics of presence, and onto ones that take into account the historicity – as opposed to the psychology – of social difference?

III

If, as suggested early on, the only condition of community is difference, which forms of sociality are allowed (and which prohibited) when difference is, however contradictorily, imagined? Consider how two different stories of ignorance are produced when pedagogy stalls within the humanistic faith that representation can deliver what it promises: unmediated access to the real. And consider how everyone involved gets caught 'in the margin[s] between claims of truth and claims of textuality.'[35] The first instance is drawn from the work of Cindy Patton. Patton analyses how U.S. governmental discourses of information both construct and exhaust subjects. The specific crisis of education Patton addresses is how AIDS education becomes organized when there is no direct relation between acquiring the facts about viral transmission and fashioning safer sex practices.

Patton examines how purportedly inclusive governmental campaigns of information as a discourse actually work to produce the basis of exclusion, discrimination, and social policing. The addressee of these 'facts' are actually two: the 'general public,' who might get the virus, and 'risky communities' who spread the virus. She argues that the general public is positioned as having *the right to know*, whereas communities placed at risk have *the obligation to know* not to spread the virus and to confess their relation to HIV. Precisely because such discourse claims are tied to varying contexts of self-knowledge, or identity, all that can be produced are identities that are either suspected or innocent. The limits of this campaign stall in the argument over the right to know as opposed to a universalizing of safer practices of the body. The general public is thus constructed as composed of innocent bystanders, who, with facts in hand, might be able to protect themselves, and this officially inclusive discourse, in and of itself, is anti-discriminatory: if safety can be constituted as if outside the epidemic, then there is nothing to fear. Thus, with nothing to fear the general public has no 'reason' to discriminate and is safely positioned within the realm of rationality.

This dynamic of subjection becomes even more elaborate in the recent AIDS information discourses of 'No One Is Safe.' While ostensibly producing inclusivity, at the level of social effects, new forms of exclusivity are being performed. In Cindy Patton's words: 'Far from breaking down the sharp dichotomy between "risk groups" and the "general public," the rhetoric of "no one is safe" produced a policing of identity borders as well as community borders: "no one is safe" because you can't tell who is queer.'[36]

The No One Is Safe campaign supposes queerness as the social virus and heteronormativity as being at risk, in that heteronormativity can become a site of misrecognition, however vehemently it is performed. What can happen to anyone is that anyone can be queer. Two kinds of social policing, then, are provoked: (1) the normal must suspect both the self and the other; and (2) in a queer turn, one might consider that far from being an originary state, the normal, too, requires a pedagogy. In such a campaign Foucault's doubled subject is alive and anxious: to be normal is to be tied to self-knowledge and subject to dependence upon others for recognition. But while, as Patton suggests, the No One Is Safe campaign works to set in motion a policing of identity borders, something anxious is also produced in that the campaign unleashed, in part, the unthinkable: no place of safety, no stable comparisons, and the struggle with the fear of being mistaken, of not knowing or being known. Sometimes something queer happens when the categories of US/THEM scramble for articulation even as they are disrupted.

But the disruption of identity, in its anxious attempts to coalesce, can take a different form. In the second story of the passion for ignorance, even when identities are asserted, however one imagines their emancipatory possibilities there is no guarantee that representation can instantiate its desires to know and be known. Eve Sedgwick describes the flip side of No One Is Safe as it is lived in education.[37] In this case a graduate seminar composed of men and women attempt to read gay and lesbian literature. Sedgwick reports her own discomfort in the course: originally, she and the women of the seminar situated the discomfort '... to some obliquity in the classroom relations between [women] and the men. But by the end of the semester it seemed clear that we were in the grip of some much more intimate dissonance.'[38] And this had to do with the differences between and within women. In discussing gay and lesbian literature, readers – from whatever position – were confronted with their own self-knowledge. They were, at the same time, subjected to someone else's control even while they scrambled to become tied down to their own identity. In Sedgwick's words:

Through a process that began, but *only* began, with the perception of some differences among our mostly explicitly, often somewhat uncrystallized sexual self-definition, it appeared that each woman in the class possessed (or might, rather, feel we were possessed by) an ability to make one or more of the other women radically doubt the authority of her own self-definition as a woman; as a feminist; as a positional subject of a particular sexuality.[39]

Here, the problem is not that no one was safe, because in this case one could tell who was queer. Rather, telling queerness in the context of identity politics seemed to set up new forms of authority and new hierarchies of knowledge and identity that called into question old forms of authority, namely categories such as woman, feminist, and sex. At the same time newly inverted forms of US and THEM emerged from reading gay and lesbian texts, and consequently the boundaries of the inside and the outside were maintained. These positions were neither implicitly pedagogical nor emancipatory in that, in this case, identification remained tied to self-knowledge, to identity. Evidently, and perhaps in spite of the curriculum, gay and lesbian literature was read as a special event – perhaps a vicarious means to learn something about the other, perhaps a vicarious means for 'others' to affirm their otherness and berate those who are imagined as the same. So even when the course material has gestured to difference, there still remains the question of how difference is to be read and ethically engaged. The 'facts' of gay and lesbian literature were not telling, and acquiring the 'facts' was a problem for all involved. No one is safe, not just because anyone can be called queer but because something queer can happen to anyone when one attempts to fix and unfix identity.

As Sedgwick reminds us, this 'intimate dissonance' should not be read as a social effect of bad pedagogy but rather as the beginning of pedagogy. If hierarchies must first be inverted, rendered as already estranged, in order to draw attention to themselves, this first move is a tricky beginning. Any inversion, after all, is what should provoke pedagogy to do something more: to engage its own impertinence and imagine what it might mean to be a social subject in a place called the classroom. But if pedagogy is to do something more with inverted hierarchies, it must not fall into the cul-de-sac of merely reversing the place of expertise, shutting down identifications with epistemological privilege, and providing a stage for what Foucault calls the 'speaker's benefit,' or the pleasure that is made from fleeing power.[40] Instead, pedagogy might consider the problem of engaging its own alterity, of staying in that space of difference described by Samuel Delany as within 'the margin[s] between claims of truth and the claims of textuality.' Within these margins everybody might begin to consider the fact that representations and the identities they assume to serve, however emancipatory, cannot provide access to an unmediated real, or even invoke, in and of themselves, thought that can think against itself.

Now Patton's reading of governmental AIDS information discourses shows how the normal subject-presumed-to-know and the deviant subject-obligated-to-confess are both discursively produced. Both positions require boundary policing although such policing does not work in the same way and each demands different degrees of subjection. But these networks of power – discursively lived at the level of bodies and disciplined by normative educational practices – depend upon an insistence of stable and hence predictable identities that can then be contained. This, of course, is the authorship of normalization. Then we have Sedgwick's description of her seminar, where differences within, say, the category 'woman' disrupt the impossible promise of sameness, the promise of a community whose very basis depends upon subjects who presume but cannot know the same. In Sedgwick's seminar the identity hierarchy is upset, although epistemological privilege is still dependent upon the fashioning of bodies into stable identities whose knowledge is thought to spring from an unambivalent identity. In both instances, then, although in different ways, identity disciplines bodies and cannot articulate its own identificatory structures. The cost of 'difference' is thus the very acknowledgment necessary for political practices, for what Giorgio Agamben names as 'the idea of an inessential commonality, a solidarity that in no way concerns an essence.'[41]

The two examples, however singular, point out two divergent directions provoked by the same problem: namely, the social effects of identity when identity claims take on an aura of verisimilitude and hence are taken as if they can exist outside of the very historicity that provokes such claims, and their attendant feelings in the first place. What is left unthought, then, is the very reading practices that structure intelligibility and that make identity possible even as these practices perform impossible identities. If a pedagogical project is to move beyond the repetition of identity and the only two subject positions allowed when identity is understood as one of self versus others, then pedagogy itself must become a problem of reading practices, a problem of social relations, and a problem of the means to refuse to think straight.

IV

Shoshana Felman's exploration of the pedagogical practices of Lacan's return to (and rereading of) Freud offers a way to rethink reading practices beyond the impulse to instantiate identity as the repetition of sameness. Her concern is psychoanalytic: to consider techniques of thinking 'beyond one's means,' to consider the possibility of exceeding the self by becoming interested in questioning the impulse to normalize. Felman notes three analytic practices of critical interpretation: those having to do with alterity; those having to do with dialogue; and those having to do with theory. Taken together these three techniques may allow one to create new strategies for reading. While I will briefly outline Felman's practices, they will be elaborated by rereading some of the issues raised earlier by Patton and by Sedgwick.

Reading for alterity begins with acknowledgment of difference as the precondition for the self. One begins not by constructing resemblances with another, but the reading necessarily passes through the other, and in the other reads not identity (other or same) but difference and self difference.'[42] Reading as an interpretive performance, then, may become an imagined means to untie self-knowledge from itself if the self can be encountered as split between recognition and misrecognition. In this way no category is sufficient, final, or total, and no category can be mastered or known as sheer positivity.

A second reading practice is provoked in dialogue. Here Felman borrows Freud's recognition of dialogue as a 'structuring condition of possibility.' To read is automatically to construct a dialogic relation with a self and with a text to allow for something more. But in making such a dialogue the reader is asked to consider what she or he wants from the text. Both the text and a self perform differential replies, perhaps in the form of a question, perhaps an argument, perhaps a misunderstanding. Reading thus begins with a supposition of difference, division, and negotiation. When reading practices are privileged over the intentions of the author or reader, the concern becomes one of thinking through the structures of textuality as opposed to the attributes of biography. This makes possible the disruption of the interpreter/interpreted hierarchy. And so the insistence of such a dialogue is implication not application.

Finally, as a practice, reading provokes a theory of reading not just a reworking of meaning. How one reads matters. In Felman's words, 'There is a constitutive belatedness of the theory over the practice, the theory always trying to catch up with what it was that the practice, or the reading, was really doing.'[43] Such belatedness, where the recognition of how one reads in terms of what one wants drags behind the investment in the immediacy of gathering meanings, marks uncertainty as a condition of possibility. And in the marking of one's theory of reading one can then begin to study where one's reading breaks down. What might become a problem is the study of one's own theoretical limits.

How, then, does one get to a place where identity is not the primal scene of reading as a repetition, but instead a discursive practice, a practice of the self that can exceed the self? In considering the reading practices of Lacan, Felman sketches what she terms 'a new mode of reflexivity.'[44] She argues that for interpretations to be critical and hence exceed the impulse to normalize and contain meaning, reading must begin with an acknowledgment of difference within identity and not reduce interpretation to a confirmation or negation of identity. This is a question of reading as alterity through the consideration of the fault lines of identity. The exploration becomes one of analysis of the signifier, not the signified, and hence an analysis of where meaning breaks down for the reader. The problem is to think of reading practices as a means for disrupting inside/outside hierarchies – beginning with a self that reads as a means to exceed that very self. And within such excess one might consider the belatedness of theory. In this way Felman suggests how one might begin to depart from the self in order to think the self as always already divided from itself, as embodying difference and division.

If the problem were posed as how subjection is made from any body and what makes normalcy thinkable in education, then the information campaigns of AIDS education that Patton describes and the hierarchy of identities that Sedgwick worries about might be encountered or produced differently. There might be a decision on the part of those positioned as outside the AIDS pandemic to refuse the proffered grounds of innocence and rationality and hence refuse to identify with the general public. What might become suspect are the categorical imperatives and attendant inequalities produced with this campaign. Then, no one is safe from the governmental campaigns. As for Sedgwick's seminar, where the grounds of identity are still confined to mastery and certitude, there might be a decision to refuse these very grounds. Reading might then be one of theorizing reading as always about risking the self, about confronting one's own theory of reading, and about engaging one's own alterity and desire. Then, thinking itself, in classroom spaces, might take the risk of refusing to secure thought and of exposing the danger in the curious insistence on positing foundational claims at all costs.[45] Then no one is safe because the very construct of safety places at risk difference as uncertainty, as indeterminacy, as incompatibility. The problem, then, becomes one of working through ethical relations.

As Felman suggests, if reading practices could begin to read the real as constructed, as necessarily mediated by a self that is always already divided from itself, identity might be encountered as 'never identical to itself,' and hence located, however partially and provincially, in that queer space between what is taken as real and the afterthought of (mis)recognition. Thus a queer pedagogy is not concerned with getting identities right or even having them represented as an end in themselves. The point is to read – in radical ways – the insufficiencies of identity as positivity and to examine and to refuse 'cases of exorbitant normality,' whether such cases take the form of heteronormativity, racisms, gender centrings, ability hierarchies, and so on. And thus one might read identity as a political relation, whether that reading concerns the reader or the read.

These insights into reading practices are impertinent because they begin with an insistence on alterity, the irrevocability of difference within identity, which is to say the unthought of the thought of identity. As a pedagogical practice, reading becomes a practice of constituting the criteria that make the self and that make another both intelligible and unintelligible, an occasion for thought to think against itself. At the same time, reading practices need to be understood as constituting the dialogic, thus requiring something more than the self in order to think the self differently. And because reading practices also produce a theory of reading practices, the act of reading might become more complicated. It might return the subject to the problem of one's own subjection, rethinking the way that self-knowledge becomes, as Foucault explains it, being subject to someone else's control.

V

Now, much of my argument is predicated upon the belief that to recognize difference outside the imperatives of normalcy – that is, beyond the need to render difference through the lens of the same, either through discourses of feelings or discourses of information – requires attention to how one's reading practices as historically, socially, and psychically configured produce particular conceptual needs. My thinking has been influenced by queer theories that mark as a site of subjection the production and valorization of normalcy, and by the psychoanalytic attention to the split and desirous subject. Whether cases of exorbitant normality take big forms such as various racisms, heteronormativities, nationalisms, ethnocentricities, Eurocentrism, and colonization, or take little forms such as empathy, tolerance, self-esteem, safety, and so on, these cases should become a central problem of educational thought and practice, a central problem of pedagogy. And I raise these dynamics as a question of reading practices, because at the level of the everyday, structures of intelligibility are sustained not only by hegemonic and punishing chains of signification but also, just as significantly, in the way education closes down how the everyday might be imagined and lived, and hence how one becomes a social subject in a place called the classroom.

If reading practices partially structure one's capacity to do something more, to become something otherwise, is there a way for pedagogy to rethink how reading practices are practiced and educated in classroom sites? Are there ways of thinking about proliferating one's identificatory possibilities so that the interest becomes one of theorizing why reading is always about risking oneself, of confronting one's own theory of reading, of signification, and of difference, and of refusing to be the same? What if 'difference' made a difference in how the self encountered the self and in how one encounters one?

In my work on pedagogy, what I want to call my queer pedagogy, I am attempting to exceed such binary oppositions as the tolerant and the tolerated and the oppressed and the oppressor, yet still hold onto an analysis of social difference that can account for how dynamics of subordination and subjection work at the level of the historical, the structural, the epistemological, the conceptual, the social, and the psychic. But such an interest is also one of thinking through an implication that can tolerate a curiosity about one's own otherness, one's own unconscious desires and wishes, one's own negations. My interest is in provoking conditions that might allow for an exploration of unsettling the sediments of what one imagines when one imagines normalcy, what one imagines when one images difference. So I wonder whether identity categories will be helpful in this work if identity depends upon the production of sameness and otherness, dynamics that anchor modes of subjection. And I am thinking that maybe, given the desire for knowledge of difference to make a difference in how social subjects conduct themselves and in how sociality might be imagined and lived, the new questions that must be addressed concern what education, knowledge, identity, and desire have to do with the fashioning of structures of intelligibility and unintelligibility; with what education has to do with the possibilities of proliferating identifications and critiques that exceed identity, yet still hold onto the understanding of identity as a state of emergency. This I take as the beginnings of a queer pedagogy, one that refuses normal practices and practices of normalcy, one that begins with an ethical concern for one's *own* reading practices and what these have to do with the imagining of sociality as more than an effect of the dominant conceptual order. In the queer pedagogy I am attempting, 'the inessentially common' is built from the possibility that reading the world is always already about risking the self, about attempting, on the one hand, to exceed cases of exorbitant normality, and on the other, developing an interest in confounding instituted law.

Notes

1 Spivak, 'Acting Bits/Identity Talk,' 776.
2 McLaren's study of the eugenics movement in Canada details the historical shift from defining and containing 'deviancy' to the movement leaders' preoccupation with the fashioning of normalcy through such progressive measures as the introduction of school nursing, hygiene, sex education, and pedagogies directed at white racial improvement. From a different vantage point Foucault's first volume on sexuality traces this shift, whereby constituting normalcy becomes the central strategy of knowledge/power/pleasure.
3 Freud, *Civilization and Its Discontents*, 71.
4 The notion of 'the-subject-presumed-to know' and 'a passion for ignorance' is discussed in the work of Jacques Lacan. The subject-presumed-to-know desires an omnipotent knowledge. Paradoxically, such a subject is propped up by a passion for ignorance. Lacan theorizes ignorance as a residue of knowledge, not its constitutive outside. Statements of dismissal and dis-implication, such as 'I don't want

68   Deborah P. Britzman

to know about it' or 'That has nothing to do with me,' support the work of ignorance.

The work of ignorance also takes a different turn. Jessica Benjamin discusses the
traces ignorance bears in the following observation from *Like Subjects, Love
Objects*: '(O)ne is in theory more likely to be determined by a prior body of thought
precisely when one thinks it can be overcome simply by rejecting its postulates. The
act of rejection shapes one's starting point, and one adopts an oppositional stance
that unconsciously reverses the original coordinates of thought.'

5 See, for example: Felman, *Jacques Lacan and the Adventure of Insight*; Silen, *Sex,
   Death and the Education of Children*; Sedgwick, *Epistemology of the Closet*.
6 Foucault, *History of Sexuality*, vol. 1 (New York: Vintage Books, 1990), 420.
7 Golding, 'Sexual Manners,' 166.
8 See Borch-Jacobsen, *The Freudian Subject*.
9 Edelman, *Homographesis*, 16
10 Delany, 'Street Talk/Straight Talk,' 28.
11 The cost of narrating identities is not, in queer theory, a problem of getting identities
   right. Rather, there is a significant moment in queer theory that agonizes the conceptualization of identity: how it 'works' as history, how it is narrated as synecdoche, or
   as a part capable of standing in for the whole; and how its exclusions permit its categorical claims. (See, for example, Sedgwick, *Epistemology of the Closet*.) This mode
   of questioning owes much to the work of Michel Foucault.

   Judith Butler raises a significant tension in considering Foucault's work: 'The
   political challenge Foucault poses ... is whether a resistance to the diagnostic category of identity can be effected that does not reduplicate the very mechanism of subjection, this time – painfully, paradoxically – under the sign of liberation.' ('Sexual
   Inversions,' 355), Foucault's last sentence in his introductory volume on sexuality
   says as much: 'The irony of [the deployment of sexuality] is having us believe that
   our 'liberation' is in the balance.' (159)
12 The claim of 'perversity' as a marker of identification is quite contradictory in queer
   theories. Foundationally, the claim draws from the Freudian notion of all sexuality as
   perverse, as in polymorphous perversity (see Laplanche). But two kinds of claims
   about perversity are made in queer theories. On the one hand, perversity works as a
   means to dispute dominant chains of signification, or what D.A. Miller calls 'not a
   name but the continual elision of one [that disrupts] a system of connotation' (24–5).
   On the other hand, Eve Sedgwick ('White Glasses') and Mandy Merck take up perverse reading practices meant to disassemble the temples of gay and lesbian mythology. Both challenge the essentialist feminist and lesbian claims of identification as
   issuing from identity. For a debate on the question of whether claims of perversity
   are political claims, see 'Perversity,' *New Formations: A Journal of Culture/Theory/
   Politics* 19 (spring 1993).

13 My use of the term *everyday* has been influenced by the work of Gary Wickham and William Haver. Specifically, I am trying to theorize along with their insight that 'violence against queers is installed not merely in a legal apparatus, but in "daily life" itself, as well as in the objectification, thematization, and valorization of everydayness (as in "family values," for example)' (5). Essentially, such a formulation opens the question of how it becomes conceivable for some folks to have an everyday while other folks become either a special event or a disruption of the everyday.

14 de Lauretis, 'Queer Theory,' iv. The use of the term *queer* works quite differently in community/street politics. In discussing the discursive deployment of this term in AIDS activist groups and in gay, lesbian, and bisexual forms of militancy, Michael Warner argues that the term queer is 'thoroughly embedded in modern Anglo-American culture and does not translate easily. ... As a politically unstable term ... queer dates from the Bush-Thatcher-Mulroney era' (Warner, 'Something Queer,' 14). This historical conservatism and the refusal of the state to redress civil rights produced a performative politics meant to disturb the seemingly seamless construct of the normal from its modes of materiality.

15 Phelan, *Unmarked*, 32.

16 Duttman, 'about AIDS,' 112.

17 The concept of negation, according to Freud, is a means by which the individual can acknowledge an idea while disclaiming its emotional value or its structuring principle. In Freud's words: 'Negation is a way of taking cognizance of what it repressed; indeed it is already a lifting of the repression, though not, of course, an acceptance of what is repressed. We can see how in this the intellectual function is separated from the affective process' (*SE*, Vol. 12, 235–6). The recognition of repression does not guarantee a removal of repression. Thus one can happily claim normalcy without considering its affective costs.

18 The paradoxical phrasing – the education of education – is meant to signal education not as if it were simply an originary network of institutions, policies, learning theories, curricular moves, and a social network of subjects. Rather, such a phrasing approaches education as an effect of knowledge/power/pleasure, and thus as caught in larger historical apparatuses to which education responds.

19 Foucault, *History of Sexuality*.

20 Sedgwick, 'White Glasses.'

21 Fuss, *Identification Papers*, 2.

22 Crimp, 'Hey, Girlfriend!' 12.

23 Freud, *Civilization and Its Discontents*.

24 In Joan Copjec's terms, happiness is both objective and subjective. She clarifies Freud's views of empathy with the following observation: 'If we cannot judge immediately what measure of pain or pleasure belonged to a historical individual, this is not because happiness is subjectivity and we cannot project ourselves into her private

mental sphere, but rather because we cannot so easily project ourselves into her objective *social* sphere in order to disarm the categories of thought that constructed her expectations, narcotized her against disappointment, made her obtuse to her own suffering.' (228)

25 Freud, *Civilization and Its Discontents*, 26.

26 Warner, 'Introduction,' *Fear of a Queer Planet*, xxi. I find the term *heteronormativity* more interesting than the familiar and often misused *homophobia* because debates about gay and lesbian oppression and desire must move beyond the humanist psychological discourse of individual fear of homosexuality as contagion (and not, coincidentally, the centring of heterosexuality as the normal). The term homophobia rarely ventures into political critiques of how normalcy becomes produced and sexualized as heterosexuality. That is, how sex becomes inserted into normalcy and how normalcy becomes inserted into sex is not an area accessible to the naming of homophobia because the term is centrally given over to the correction of individuated attitude. The term heteronormativity begins to get at how the production of deviancy is intimately tied to the very possibility of normalcy. That is, normalcy can only be intelligible through the construction of its other: the deviant. In such a relation, normalcy must always make itself normal, must always normalize itself. Recent writing in queer theory suggests the problem is not fear of queerness but obsession with normalizing and containing queerness, and, not coincidently, otherness. The odd story is that such mechanisms in actuality, are, about the production of normalcy. (See, for example: Judith Butler, *Bodies That Matter*; Jonathan Dollimore, *Sexual Dissidence: Augustine to Wilde, Freud to Foucault*. New York: Oxford, 1991; Fuss *Inside/Out*; Sedgwick, *Epistemology of the Closet*; and, Warner 'Introduction').

27 Foucault, *History of Sexuality* (1990), 152.

28 Judith Butler, *Bodies That Matter*, 53.

29 Britzman, 'The Ordeal of Knowledge'; and Patton, *Inventing AIDS*.

30 Goldberg, *Racist Culture*.

31 Phelan, *Unmarked*, 26.

32 Sedgwick, 'White Glasses,' 40.

33 Judith Butler, 'Imitation and Gender Insubordination,' 20.

34 Cindy Patton's groundbreaking study traces how discourses of information produce the grounds of estrangement in that one might 'know' the facts but not how to relate 'facts' as relevant to the self. In Patton's words: 'Several studies suggest that teenagers and young adults believe that other people acquire HIV infection or develop AIDS through specific and known sets of acts while they perceive their *own* susceptibility to HIV or AIDS to be a matter of chance' (109). Such a formulation crystallizes two subject positions discussed throughout this chapter: the subject-presumed-to-know and its passion for ignorance. Moreover, if every learning is an unlearning,

discourses of information negate this complexity with a naïve theory of ignorance as lack to be filled by information.

35 Delany, 'Street Talk/Straight Talk,' 28.
36 Patton, 'No One Is Safe,' 101.
37 Sedgwick, 'White Glasses.'
38 Ibid., 61.
39 Ibid.
40 Agamben, *The Coming Community*, 189.
41 Felman, *Jacques Lacan*, 23.
42 Ibid., 24.
43 Ibid., 60.
44 Haver, 'Thinking the Thought.'
45 Benjamin, *Like Subjects, Love Objects*, 47.

4

On the Myth of Sexual Orientation: Field Notes from the Personal, Pedagogical, and Historical Discourses of Identity

MARGOT FRANCIS

In *The History of Sexuality*, volume 1, Michel Foucault argues that the notion of 'sexual identities' as constitutive of the 'truth' of our being is one influential means by which modern subjectivities are managed. However, he also suggests that this same notion has made possible a 'reverse discourse,' through which homosexual subjects have spoken back against the terms of a medico-scientific project which has relied on our existence to establish its own legitimacy.[1] While the development of this reverse discourse has been of critical importance in the lobby for lesbian and gay civil rights and the right to an everyday not organized by violence and erasure, it has *not* typically called into question the grounds of the very heterosexual/homosexual binary itself. In fact, the pedagogy of much liberal antihomophobia discourse has reinforced static notions of sexuality as identity.[2] In addition, this discourse has often failed to address sexuality as a socially and historically constituted set of relations, which may not be as settled as is generally presumed. It is precisely the possibilities inherent in this unsettling of sexual binaries that provides the axis around which this project will turn.

This chapter attempts to ground an argument regarding the instability of sexual categories in an investigation of the shifting borders of sexuality as this is mapped in three different sites: the personal, the pedagogical, and the historical. The argument will proceed in several stages.

In the first I use field notes from the personal and pedagogical as a method of reflecting on my three years of work as an antiheterosexism educator in secondary schools and in community settings. Here I investigate the construction of sexuality *not* as a discovery regarding the 'truth of one's being,' but as that which requires explanation and about which knowledge might be produced. This methodology is rooted in historian Joan Scott's analysis that 'it is not individuals who have experience, but subjects who are constituted through experience.'[3] Thus I use field notes as a self-reflexive method of drawing attention to the contradictory ways in which individual subjects and educational practices are formed, in, and through, resistance to heteronormative ideals.

The second stage uses the theoretical frameworks suggested by Jennifer Terry and Gayatri Spivak to explore one avenue through which historical research can be used to shift the grounds for political activism. I will argue that the first large-scale, empirical study of women's sexuality in America, titled *Factors in the Sex Life of Twenty-Two Hundred Women* (Davis [1929]),[4] suggests that textual representations of women's sexual *practice* were remarkably dissimilar from the *discourses* about white, middle-class women's sexuality which were emerging during this same period. Thus while empirical research indicated a remarkable complexity and fluidity in women's sexual choices, the discourses *about* women posited same-sex attractions as the result of congenital, biologically based, and binary sexual identities.[5] To explain this disjuncture I will argue that the practice of labelling sexuality as identity served a range of strategic and contradictory purposes for *both* the emerging medico-scientific *and* homosexual communities.

In the postscript to this chapter I suggest that a deconstructive approach such as the one suggested here can contribute to the project of developing a pedagogy which recognizes that the homo/hetero binary is far from pure; and can, in addition, challenge the limitations inherent in an identity-based politic. However, as my field notes from the personal and pedagogical will suggest, and as Janet E. Halley notes in her essay 'The Construction of Heterosexuality,' deconstruction itself cannot accomplish the work of politics. As she observes, 'An analysis of the definitional knots (exposed by the deconstruction of the binarism hetero/homosexuality), however necessary, is not at all sufficient to disable them. Quite the opposite: I would suggest that an understanding of their irresolvable instability has been continually available, and has continually lent discursive authority, to antigay as well as to gay cultural forces of this century.'[6]

Indeed, from the use of electric shock therapy to reprogram gay patients, to the mobilization of groups to 'cure' gay students, the knowledge of the 'irresolvable instability' of the hetero/homo binary continues to be used against queer communities. But then the protection of essentialism is no protection either, as knowledge about the supposed 'gay' gene is as likely to be used to allow parents to select *not* to have gay children as it is to further the project of establishing that homosexuality is inborn, and thus not deserving of moral condemnation. But perhaps deconstruction can take yet another turn. Perhaps the instability of the term *queer* can pose the production of *normalization* as the problem. In this context the interrogation of binaries themselves – normal/deviant, biological/social, straight/gay – can open up quite a different approach. As Deborah Britzman suggests, 'in its positivity, Queer Theory offers methods of imagining difference on its own terms: as eros, as desire, and as the grounds of politicality. It is a particular articulation that returns us to practices of bodies and bodies of practices.'[7]

This project then, examines how practices of deconstruction might be used more effectively to further the project of thinking ethically about discourses of difference and visibility in our bodies, in history, and in pedagogy – and in the risking of the self that is the grounds of all political action.

Field Notes from the 'Personal'

Work which 'rashly jettisons' essentialism takes away an interventionary strategy of the oppressed who can use it in an Irigarayian move 'to undo by overdoing,' a 'displacement and redeployment of essentialism' which thinks through the body.[8]

Thinking through the body is no simple project. For twelve years of my life I was primarily attracted to men, and for eleven years after my sustained attractions and relationships have been with women. While this shift was neither sudden nor complete, desire, as I have experienced it, has been far from coherent. 'Go the way your blood beats,' writes James Baldwin.[9] And I do. Yet a discourse which locates desire, agency, and personal truth solely within the body or the blood, fails the task.

The story of my coming out was at first a coming into my 'No.' This involved a body knowledge that I *could not* continue in heterosexual relationships, not for lack of sexual pleasure but because I could not (again) involve myself in a partnership where I was not *seen*. This is not a coming out story I will tell in a classroom, because the popular culture's discourse of sexuality as the essential ground of one's being has been too widely dispersed for this story not to reinforce stereotypes about lesbians as 'women who are bitter about men, and therefore turn to other women and deny the "true" nature of their desire.'

But what about my 'Yes?' This story is about intense intimacy and lust, and for better or worse it is about the most profoundly affecting relationships of my life. It is also about connections which have been lived in a context of growing possibilities for autonomy and fierce desires for equity. While my attraction to masculinity has been consistent I now prefer my boys to be girls.[10] Throughout, my curiosity, hunger, and courage have been stoked by queer intellectual and cultural communities, and by the unapologetic material on sexuality produced by queer and straight cultural workers. However, this also is not a story easily told within the constraints of a secondary school classroom.

Thus both the terms *lesbian* and *bisexual* are an incomplete description of the desire in my blood. They are a historical construction of identity I have both claimed and resisted; and in the end they comprise provisional strategies embraced for the possibilities they have created in resistance to heteronormative and misogynist norms. Clearly, straightforward notions of identity fail in the extraordinarily complex tasks of intimacy and desire. How then to construct a language which 'names the self' in less unitary and restrictive ways? How did the concept develop that anyone is really anything? Does the fact that the question can be asked at all attest to the instability of this category we call essential: the scent of desire?

Field Notes from an Antiheterosexism Educator

What sort of difference would it make for everyone in a classroom if gay and lesbian writing were set loose from confirmations of homophobia, the afterthoughts of inclusion, or the special event?[11]

In a classroom I survey the sea of faces in front of me and struggle with the binary which constructs this pedagogical moment – even before I step into it. We are the queers, here to educate about heterosexism and challenge the 'othering' which always and already confounds this encounter. I often wonder at the shoals that frame anti-oppression work for all of us who do antisexism, antiracism and antihomophobia education. How is it that the structure of the questions may undermine the very project we engage in? As James Baldwin suggests, when talking about racism: 'as long as I protest my case on evidence or assumptions held by others, I'm simply reinforcing those assumptions. As long as I complain about being oppressed, the oppressor is in consolation of knowing that I know my place, so to speak.'[12]

How then to proceed? In the context of the heteronormative assumptions of the classroom, where we are the *queers* come to educate the *straights*, constructing a pedagogy which disrupts and challenges these objectifying paradigms is a troubling and difficult task.

Between 1993 and 1996 I served as the coordinator for a diverse team of youth called TEACH – Teens Educating and Confronting Homophobia.[13] Over the years youth involved with TEACH have identified in a range of ways, including queer, gay, lesbian, bisexual, undecided, and heterosexual; also lesbians who are occasionally attracted to men and those who refuse identification. In our work, tactics of critical analysis, storytelling, and subversion all had their use. The pedagogies we employed explored the effects of heterosexism on gay youth, and examined how the stigma of the epithets *faggot* and *dyke* are used to police all our performance of gender – masculinity and femininity – in addition to policing desire.

Most antiheterosexism educational work in North America, including my own, has relied to some degree on the narrative of the coming out story.[14] The invisibility imposed by a heteronormative culture ensures that storytelling can often disrupt and problematize the objectifying label, gay. In addition, the youth with whom I have worked have *performed* antiheterosexism educational work as an act of resistance, generosity, anger, and pride. However, a host of significant problems remains. Even where the 'traditional' coming out story is unsettled by descriptions of a range of sexualities, the assumption of sexuality itself as an essential and individualizable truth of one's being is nevertheless reinforced. Thus I ask: Does this work participate in re/forming subjectivities through the very labelling process which makes stories of *identity* possible? How then do human beings become simultaneously turned as they turn themselves into subjects? And how might this process of naming end up re/producing the very essentialist categories I want clearly to avoid?

In their article 'Queer Pedagogy: Praxis Makes Im/Perfect,' Mary Bryson and Suzanne de Castell engage a similar issue in their analysis of a lesbian studies course they co-taught in 1991:

we attempted to reflect on what it might mean ... (to) re-think, or *queer<y>* normatively sanctioned pedagogies – to insist on the 'right to speak as one,' to make pedagogical spaces where the hitherto unsayable could be uttered ... within the oppressive confines of the always-already heterosexualized classroom. How to accomplish some of this while, concurrently, resisting the incredible pressures to instantiate and reify essentialized representations of queer sexuality ... [15]

These are questions I have felt in my body; they have also engaged my curiosity as an educator and a scholar. However, after three years of working with youth to facilitate workshops I found myself falling silent. My body refused the lack of complexity as I asked, like Denise Riley, 'Am I That Name?'[16]

These are the problems with identity, yet how might one engage in a political practice without it? The very act of pedagogy has kept me cognizant of just how important visibility is, as it has brought us face to face with the heterosexist erasure that is always and everywhere present. While individual student responses to TEACH were overwhelmingly positive, myriad restrictions confounded the possibility of real change. As Deborah Britzman suggests, so long as consideration of sexualities is confined to the 'afterthoughts of inclusion, or the special event,' only the most superficial changes are possible, leaving the structure of curriculum and everyday heteronormative practices unchallenged. TEACH workshops were considered disruptive, or marginal, or both, and often ended up sandwiched into the least amount of time possible. In addition, the pervasive subtext of threat rooted in cultural taboos about sex, as well as homo-sex, continues to keep the vast majority of queer students and teachers silent about the complex realities of their lives.

And then there was the hate. Or was it desire?

At a workshop in Toronto in 1995 several young men engaged in escalating heckling and harassment of the team of presenters, and one announced that 'if he ever had a gay son, he would kill him.' Our team refused to come back to the class unless the young men were asked to leave. Their parents, fundamentalist Christians, forbade them to come back in any case.

The follow-up workshop was conducted without similar disruption and with significantly more space for other students to speak. However, as this second workshop ended, the young men who had attended the first appeared at the classroom door, anxious to speak with us. Fascinated and repelled in the same moment, they could not leave us, or the issue, alone.

On reading through the evaluation forms, which include the request that students list 'some things they learned about themselves,' five of the twenty forms contained the following comments: 'Nothing, I'm not a fag'; 'I'm not gay'; 'I don't like you, and I glad I'm strait' [sic]; 'Im not gay' [sic]; 'I'm a heterosexual and I will respect others, to an extent.' In response to the question 'What were the most helpful aspects of the workshop?' one student responded, 'When you left the building.' Heterosexual panic – and obsession – indeed.

Judith Butler suggests that sexuality and gender are embodied, but not essentialist, social practices. Encounters like the one detailed above, and the palpable discomfort evidenced by some young men when we challenged heteronormative *gender* as well as *sexual* roles, illustrates the panic felt when this embodied 'self' is unsettled. Butler continues: 'that heterosexuality is always in the act of elaborating itself is evidence that it is perpetually at risk, that is, that it "knows" its own possibility of becoming undone ... '[17] Thus while there is no underestimating the importance of being 'out,' the terms of the discourse may nevertheless reinforce notions of sexuality that undermine the very space one seeks to create. How to unsettle this pedagogical, and crucially political, dilemma?

For the task of pushing the boundaries of what is thinkable in resistance to hegemonic norms I can find no better tool than history. I turn, then, to research from turn-of-the-century America to examine possibilities for looking at the connections between gender, sex, and hegemonic notions of identity in more complex and thoughtful ways.

Sources and the History of the Subaltern

As Joan Scott has suggested, the proliferation of historical narratives occasioned by feminist, antiracist, and queer scholarship has generated a crisis for orthodox history and pushed debates about 'objectivity' to a new and critical juncture. The new histories generated in this context have multiplied not only stories, but also subjects, and insisted that histories are written from fundamentally different and sometimes irreconcilable standpoints, none of which may be completely true.[18] Current historiographic research has increasingly turned to considering how multiple social positionings – shaped by race, gender, class, and sexuality, among other things – form the diverse fields of power regulating agency and resistance in local sites.

For historians of sexuality one of the central dilemmas is the problem of sources. Most of the documents which provide information about same-gender relationships have been destroyed through heterosexist vandalism, effacement, and suppression. The remaining historical materials are most often made up of elite accounts which focus on the sin, criminality, or pathology inherent in a deviant sexuality.

In her article 'Theorizing Deviant Historiography' Jennifer Terry suggests that historians face the task of searching for a subaltern presence and consciousness, and yet must 'rely on the dominant account, not only for source material but also for tracing how these sources constructed the very conditions of subalternity.'[19] Terry emphasizes the necessity for historians to read against the grain of these largely hostile accounts. Using the deconstructive work of Gayatri Spivak, she suggests that 'instead of looking for another *identity* (the subaltern) the reader should watch for *difference* within textual operations of elite accounts.'[20]

Spivak's suggestions are particularly useful in deconstructing the development of the notion of identities, as these were applied to the homosexual or the 'sex pervert' by the medico-scientific discourse at the turn of the century. As Terry elaborates:

For Spivak, the notion of a coherent and autonomous subaltern subject whose history can be disentangled from colonial accounts is preposterous; similarly, a lesbian and gay history which hopes to find homosexuals totally free of the influences of pathologizing discourses would be an historiographic optical illusion. At best, we can map the techniques by which homosexuality has been marked as different and pathological, and then locate subjective resistances to this homophobia.[21]

Thus, the next part of this chapter is an attempt to provide a set of historiographic field notes that chart the cartography of regulation, agency, resistance, and desire evident in textual accounts of women's sexuality in turn-of-the-century America.

Sex Lives and Archives

In 1918 Katherine Bement Davis embarked on the first major survey of women's sexual behaviour to be undertaken in America. Sponsored by the John D. Rockefeller Jr. Bureau of Social Hygiene, the research was first published in 1929 under the title *Factors in the Sex Life of Twenty-Two Hundred Women*, and represents women's sexuality *across* the homosexual-heterosexual divide. The only other empirically based accounts of women's sexual behaviour during this period can be found in two smaller surveys representing case studies of fewer than fifty women.[22]

Davis solicited information from women who were graduates of women's colleges and coeducational universities and members of women's clubs, to ensure that her study would be perceived as legitimate. These groups, which were likely to be almost exclusively white and middle or upper class, were considered to be a 'respectable class of women.' Thus Davis's research methods both reflected and re-produced racialized and classed assumptions about Black, Chicana, Asian, Native American, and working-class white women who were, in different ways, always/already sexualized and seen as deviant and marginal from the norms of respectability.

Two other historians, Rosalind Rosenberg (1982) and Lillian Faderman (1981, 1991), have examined this study and both have provided only a cursory analysis of the data relating to same-sex relationships between women. As Rosenberg notes, the social discourses which legitimated the Rockefeller investigation can be found in the relatively conservative operations of maternal feminism and moral reform, while the specific impetus for this research came from the foundation's commitment to the abolition of prostitution and the eradication of venereal disease. Ironically, the actual results of the study cast doubt on white middle-class women's ability to fit within the norms of respectability – a consequence which was precisely the reverse of what the sponsors of the study had intended.[23]

The final sample for the Davis survey was composed of the first 1,000 married and 1,200 unmarried women who replied to the 20,000 surveys distributed to women's club members and alumnae from colleges and universities across the country. The majority of respondents were born about 1880 and had completed their degree at the turn of the century; the average age was thirty-seven years. College women made up almost 70 per cent of the married group, and 100 per cent of the unmarried group.

Women Resisting Sexual Normalcy

The results of Davis's study challenged several then-common notions about women's sexuality. While many middle-class commentators and medico-scientific experts at the beginning of the twentieth century considered white, bourgeois women to be passionless, the Davis study demonstrated that they were far more sexual than most people believed. Of particular interest for our purposes are the results relating to same-sex relationships. As Davis reports, 'Slightly over 50% of a group of [single] women ... state that they have experienced intense emotional relations with other women, and that in slightly more than half these cases, or 26% of the entire group, the experience has been accompanied by overt physical practices' [identified in the questionnaire as 'mutual masturbation, contact of the genital organs, or other physical expressions generally recognized as sexual in character'].[24] In the group of 1,000 married women, 30 per cent had had intense emotional relations with other women, and in half of this group, that is 15 per cent of the total, these relations were accompanied by 'physical practices' (298).

Davis had to contend with extensive criticisms for these findings, but chose to stand by the veracity of her figures. Commenting on the controversy in her introduction she notes that 'others have felt that college women are being slandered and that those who replied are not representative of college women as a whole, but are, to an extent at least, those whose experiences are abnormal ... Our own judgement would be that the figures given ... may be taken as a minimum for the group studied ... (xiv).

As the reaction to these figures suggests, they alone are significant enough to disrupt binary assumptions about the exclusive and contradictory nature of hetero- and homosexualities among this group, at least in turn-of-the-century America. Given this, it is troubling that earlier historians of women's sexuality devoted little attention to the Davis survey. For example, in *Surpassing the Love of Men: Romantic Friendships and Love between Women from the Renaissance to the Present*, Lillian Faderman accords just one page to Davis's findings, despite the fact that the report is the *sole* empirical study of romantic friendships in existence. While the study provides a remarkable store of data indicating that women's romantic friendships *were* often sexual, Faderman leaves this material unexamined.

Faderman has explained what some have seen as her desexualization of women's relationships by arguing that her central purpose was to establish that women who had romantic friendships in this earlier period could be claimed as foremothers to the more recent lesbian feminist movement. For this connection to work it was neither possible or necessary to prove that women's relations were explicitly sexual. Other critics have argued that the definition of nonsexual relationships between women as lesbian may also have suited the larger goal of promoting solidarity between feminists and lesbians – during a period when feminist organizing was often split along these lines.

While there are indeed significant connections between turn-of-the-century romantic friendships and current lesbian practices, there are also significant differences, as the wealth of newer local and historical studies attest.[25] However, of more interest for our purposes here is the observation that not only did Faderman suggest that early romantic friendships need not have been sexual, her analysis downplayed textual evidence that indeed *many were*. These elisions reflect a continuing fault line within lesbian and gay historical research,[26] and a debate to which I hope the present study will contribute. For, as Eve Sedgwick argues, sexuality does transform other languages and relations through which we know. Thus I would argue that the project of mapping the conditions that made these explicitly sexual relationships possible is an important one.

Constructing a Study, Constructing Identity

Despite the fact that same-sex desires cut a broad swath across all the participants in the Davis study, the report nevertheless seems to reflect the researchers' interests in reproducing and stabilizing heteronormative categories. Thus the fundamental axis around which the participants' responses were organized was women's status as married or unmarried.

Introducing the chapter 'Homosexuality: The Unmarried College Woman,' Davis classifies her responses into two categories. Out of a sample of 1,200 unmarried women, 605 of whom had had relationships with women, Davis categorizes the 293 who had 'intense emotional relationships with women' into Group H 1. and the 312 women who had intense emotional relationships which were accompanied by sexual expression into Group H 2.[27]

The Davis researchers were relentless in their inquiries about the 'single' women's 'failure to marry.' Similarly, the unmarried group are asked about homosexual experiences and nervous breakdowns while at no point are the married women asked to speculate about whether their heterosexuality or their married life have provoked a 'breakdown.'

In the unmarried category Davis's selection of case studies highlights those whom she characterizes as 'naturally' homosexual, which meant they rarely experienced attractions to men. Consequently the relatively uncomplicated narratives provided in the case studies fail to reflect the complexity suggested in her actual figures. However, the two case studies Davis presents of single women who had relationships with both women and men provide an ironic and amusing commentary. One reads, 'I have met so few eligible men that I could count them. Homosexualism has interfered. So have my brains' (291). The second case study presents a woman who has had three sexual relationships with women and more than one encounter with men. As Davis comments, 'She does not regret not having married, as she says that since leaving college 'my emotional life has been fed on the sex side ... I do not need the financial help of a husband. The many husbands I observe possessed by other women do not seem to me to have developed much of a genius for companionship with their wives' (293).

In eight out of the nine 'naturally homosexual' case studies Davis conducted the women characterize their experiences in remarkably positive terms. For example, in case number four, a thirty-six-year-old music teacher asserts that she has been aware of strong attractions towards girls and women since she was a child. Claiming the right to judge her own choices and engage in sensual pleasure, she writes, 'It has arisen as an expression of love, which is the only way I have experienced it, and I am qualified to judge. It has proved helpful and has made my life inexpressibly richer and deeper. I would not have been without the experience for worlds (283).

However, the possibility of finding subaltern subjects 'totally free of the influences of pathologizing discourses would be a historiographic optical illusion.'[28] This woman did not come to her sense of the legitimacy of her relationship alone, but in relation not only to the discourses of pathology but also to those in resistance. Earlier in Davis's case history she tells us: 'I realized that my emotional experiences were more or less out of the ordinary. For a while this worried me frightfully. After six months or more of great mental anxiety in this regard I finally went to a woman physician and made a clean breast of everything. She was most wonderfully wise with me, explained that this was quite natural with some people, and gave me further help and information that has stood by me ever since.'[29] Clearly not all of those who participated in the medical hierarchy accepted the pathologizing discourse of the sexologists.

In case number one a nurse who had received honours for distinguished service suggests that she has 'never met a man [she has] had the slightest desire to marry.' She continues:

I have come to think that certain women, many, in fact, possibly most of those who are unmarried, are more attracted to women than to men, through no fault of their own, but inherent in their nature; and I am somewhat inclined to think that to mate with one woman is as natural and as healthful and helpful for them as are marital relations between husband and wife. In my own case it has had a decidedly softening and sweetening effect on my temper and general attitude (280).

However, for each of these subjects pathologizing discourses are never far from view. But where the Davis study tries to obscure this with individualizing questions about 'present sex problems,' this participant replies by contextualizing the 'problem' in relation to these larger discursive practices. In response to the question about 'present sex problems' she replies that the conflict between the moral code of the church and her choice of a sexual relationship with another woman disturb her. However, she continues, 'I cannot believe that large numbers of women must forgo full development because they are attracted to a woman rather than to a man ... It seems very prevalent among humans and I feel cannot be wholly bad (280).'

Thus, despite powerful discourses mobilized to deter women's same-sex intimacy, over one-quarter of the single women in this study had sexual relationships with other women, and resisting the condemnation meted out to them, put pen to paper to document the power of connections they 'would not have been without for the world.'

In her section 'Homosexuality: The Married Woman' Davis suggests that the questionnaires for this (assumed heterosexual) group made less detailed enquiries about same-sex experiences, no doubt because they did not expect to find many. However, the problems with notions of sexual identity based on an exclusive heterosexual/homosexual binary are even more evident in Davis's research on married women's same-sex relationships. Out of a total of 1,000 women, 306 (30 per cent) said they had had 'intense emotional relations with other women,' and 157 (15 per cent) had engaged in physical practices (298).

Countering the now popular assumption that sexuality can be described as an individualizable 'orientation,' this section suggests that external factors may have had a significant effect on women's opportunity to have a choice of relationships. In this study married women who had also had same-sex relationships tended to have more education and were more often employed than their counterparts (308).

Of the 157 married women who had same-sex relationships, Davis presents the reader with eight case studies. Here she tells us her selection was based on her desire to 'illustrate several different points of homosexual experiences or raise important questions' (Davis, 313). Thus some case studies characterize same-sex experiences as 'helpful' and 'a very perfect form of love,' and others are saturated in moral admonitions about the 'menace' of a 'particular kind of girl.' However, these women certainly did *not* see their same-sex relationships as any less compelling or passionate than their heterosexual relationships. Indeed, those who condemned same-sex relationships seemed particularly aware that the 'danger' related precisely to their extraordinary intensity and thus to the intense pain of ending them or to the possibility of betrayal. For example, as case number five explains:

this girl was my grand passion. She was a boyish girl [and] we had the most radiant and spotless of comradeships. I have never before nor since, felt for any man the rapture and ecstasy and self-immolating devotion that I felt towards that girl. When, after a long time it began to dawn on me that she was not on the square with me; that there were half a dozen girls who felt toward her as I did; and that she liked to receive what we gave and to give nothing of value to any of us in return I quit. The process of disillusionment was long and painful. It left a scar on me that none of my relations with men have ever left. (321)

Case number six provides another example of this theme: 'In college several older women approached me with what, owing to an affair at the time I knew to be perverted sex appeal. It repelled me unspeakably. About six years later I experienced the strongest love of my life for a much older woman who had had at least three such passions before. My whole life was deranged ...' (323).

None of these case studies describes a relationship that was entered into lightly. On the contrary, each narrates a passionately felt emotional and sexual connection, all of which existed either prior to or alongside these women's relationships with men.

It is precisely *this* terrain of passion and contradiction – evident in both the single and married women's accounts – that historians have often glossed over or failed to explore. A variety of historians are culpable, both those who assume an always/already straight universe, and sometimes also those investigating lesbian and gay history. Thus, in so far as the either/or of identity politics shapes our investigation, we fail to allow history's real challenge: to go beyond categories into the messy contradictions which have made up women's daily lives.

There are no large-scale empirical studies to provide a textual indication of whether or not large numbers of working-class white, Black, Asian, Latina, or Native American women also engaged in same-sex relationships. Indeed, the rationale for seeking out predominately white, middle-class participants for the Davis study was that this group could be considered a 'respectable class of women.' Ironically, the notion that 'respectable' women were passionless, and the belief that 'real' sex was procreative, may have provided the protective cover which allowed this group to engage in same-sex relationships with relative impunity. While working-class women, especially those of colour, were always/already sexualized, white middle-class women, precisely because they were assumed *not* to be sexual, may have had sufficient discursive protection *to* be sexual.

Men, Gender, and Sex

Interestingly, new research on male same-sex relationships during the same period indicates a similar complexity. However, for men it was more often working-class surroundings which provided the setting for the 'bachelor subcultures' which nourished these connections. In *Gay New York* George Chauncey argues that between 1850 and 1940 an all-male culture played a significant role in the lives of urban Italian, Irish, African-American, and Anglo-American men. Although many would go on to marry, about 40 per cent of men over fifteen years of age were unmarried at any given time.[30]

Marshalling a wide range of discursive and material indicators, Chauncey argues that 'in important respects the hetero-homosexual binarism, the sexual regime now hegemonic in American culture, is a stunningly recent creation (13).' At the turn of the century differing conceptions of gender played a pivotal role in the sexual activities considered permissible for 'normal' men. Particularly in working class cultures, he asserts, normal men could and did engage in sexual activity with other men without regarding themselves, or being regarded by others, as gay, so long as they did not take the 'feminine' position in the sex act. Chauncey describes the working man's culture as one in which men could both confirm their gendered status as men, and demonstrate their sexual virility, by playing the 'man's part' in sexual encounters. Thus 'in a world in which "every woman is just another place to enter," as one Italian teenager described the attitude of men at his neighbourhood pool hall in 1930, the body to enter did not necessarily have to be a woman's (84).

In middle-class male culture, however, the hetero- homo-sexual binary became hegemonic somewhat earlier, as the late nineteenth century saw bourgeois men utilizing sexual self-control as one crucial element in the attempt to distinguish themselves from the working classes. However, only a few decades earlier, in the first two-thirds of the nineteenth century, romantic friendships between men had been both common and accepted. Anthony Rotundo, who has studied the diaries of dozens of nineteenth-century men, argues that young men frequently slept together and felt free to express passionate love for each other. Drawing on Rotundo, Chauncey writes:

these ardent relationships were 'common' and 'socially acceptable.' Devoted male friends opened letters to each other with greetings like 'Lovely Boy' and 'Dearly Beloved'; they kissed and caressed one another; and, as in the case of Joshua Stead and the bachelor lawyer Abraham Lincoln, they sometimes shared the same bed for years. Some men explicitly commented that they felt the same sort of love for both men and women. 'All I know,' wrote one man quoted by Rotundo, 'is that there are three persons in this world whom I have loved, and those are, Julia, John, and Anthony. Dear beloved trio.' It was only in the late nineteenth century that such love for other men became suspect, as men began to worry that it contained an unwholesome, distinctly homosexual element. (120)

While Rotundo argues, correctly, that these men cannot be classified as 'homosexual,' as no such concept existed in their culture, he nevertheless persists in calling them 'heterosexual.' However, one side of this binary relies on the other. As Jonathan Katz has argued in *The Invention of Heterosexuality*, *normal* men and women only began to become *heterosexual* in the late nineteenth and early twentieth century, when they started to make their normalcy contingent on renouncing such intimacies. This process proceeded at a different pace in different contexts and was dependent, as we have seen, on gender, class, and race, among other things.

While it is impossible to determine just how widespread the sexual practices documented in Davis and Chauncey's research actually were, Alfred Kinsey's studies, published in 1948 but compiled in the 1930s and 1940s, do provide a fuller picture. Kinsey himself intended his work to be used to demonstrate the extent of various kinds of sexual behaviour, rather than the incidence of particular kinds of 'identity.' In his research, fully one-quarter of his male respondents acknowledged having had 'more than incidental homosexual experience or reactions' for at least three years between the ages of sixteen and fifty-five.[31]

In addition, Kinsey's own remarks 'indicate that many of the men he interviewed believed their sexual activity with other men did not mean they were homosexual so long as they restricted that behaviour to the "masculine role."[32] In women Kinsey found that 19 per cent of the women he interviewed had had 'overt lesbian relationships.'[33]

What are we to make of the instability evident in these accounts? I would argue that twentieth-century notions of sexuality as identity provide little of the nuance and complexity necessary for understanding the notions of sexuality, gender, power, experimentation, friendship, and intimacy evident here. Both the Davis study and the research by Chauncey and Ronaldo suggest a rich mine of historical investigation, indicating both the range of women's and men's sexual practices and the process by which identities were inscribed, embraced, and resisted. However, the larger question of this research consists in investigating the rationale for the binary notion of identities in the first place. It is to this issue that we must next turn.

Unstable Relations

In 'Imitation and Gender Insubordination,' Judith Butler argues that both sexuality and gender are sites of 'necessary trouble,' where the dominant patterns of relationships are reinscribed through a compulsive repetition, designed to produce the effect of naturalness, originality, and authenticity. She asserts:

if the category were to offer no trouble, it would cease to be interesting to me: it is precisely the *pleasure* produced by the instability of those categories which sustains the various erotic practices that make me a candidate for the category to begin with. To install myself within the terms of an identity category would be to turn against the sexuality that the category purports to describe; and this might be true for any identity category which seeks to control the very eroticism that it claims to describe and authorize, much less 'liberate.'[34]

Building on Butler's argument I would argue that rigid and binary notions of identity have served both to *acknowledge* sexual differences, and, paradoxically, have operated to *contain, regulate, and polarize* this instability.

How then do we understand the implications of this notion for the construction of sexual categories in history? Postmodern theorists have characterized modernist discourse as a grand narrative consisting in a steady movement towards increased freedom and tolerance. Foucault, however, suggests that we must develop a strategic awareness of the possibilities existing in particular historical moments and discourses, and argues that '"effective history" exposes not the events and actors elided by traditional history, but instead lays bare the *processes* and *operations* by which these elisions occurred.'[35] Through what operations, then, did the idea of binary sexual identities come to take prominence over eighteenth-century notions of a procreative sexuality or a sensuality legitimized by 'true love'?

As noted above, a complex range of material and economic factors, all of which threatened the traditional family unit, affected this shift. Key elements included changes in the wage labour system, which allowed a larger number of men and some women to live independent of the family;[36] increasing rates of urbanization; challenges to gender relations through women's involvement in the paid work force; the influence of first wave feminism; and an increased flexibility in sexual relationships occasioned by the dancehalls and speakeasies that developed in urban areas, particularly during Prohibition.

However, among the most contradictory and influential of the forces shaping the new idea of sexual identity was the emerging medico-scientific discipline of sexology. Michel Foucault has argued that this discourse constituted a new technology of power used by the bourgeoisie to extend their influence through ever more elaborate definitions of *normalcy* and *perversion*.[37] However, as Jeffrey Weeks has countered, the language of sexuality is often a metaphor for larger and more intractable battles. With rapidly changing social and economic conditions, and major shifts in gendered relations, sexuality became a symbolic battleground.[38] Carroll Smith-Rosenberg agrees:

Social, not sexual, disorder lies at the heart of this discourse. The control of literal sexual behaviour at all times constitutes a secondary goal. Male sexologists were obsessed not with sex but with imposing order through the elaboration of categories of the normal and the perverted. Perverted behaviour did not have to cease. Quite the contrary. A proxy, it existed to be railed against and thus to give the sexologists a sense of power over chaos and reaffirm their faith in their ability to restore order.[39]

In this drive for control sexology moved with, not against, the grain of other nineteenth-century 'reform' movements such as social purity and eugenics.[40]

However, sexology itself was not a monolithic or unified movement. Some, like Edward Carpenter and Havelock Ellis, took strong stands in support of the decriminalization of male homosexual relationships in Britain. However, many sexologists also spoke out against the emerging influence of the New Woman. For Ellis, like Freud, the instability of sexual identities was explicitly acknowledged. However, this perspective served not as the basis for affirming a plurality of sexual choices; instead, it occasioned his lobby for the reverse. Ellis believed, above all, in the complementarity of the genders, and in the supremacy of men. The social changes occasioning women's independence profoundly threatened these values. The sexological discourse on women's same-sex relationships was profoundly different from that developing about male homosexuals, and was used largely to discredit the influence of the New Woman. Thus Smith-Rosenberg concludes:

And so Havelock Ellis transformed the New Woman into a sexual anomaly and a political pariah. Citing Ellis as an unimpeachable scientific expert, American physicians and educators launched a political campaign against the New Woman, the institutions that nurtured her, and her feminist and reform programs. 'Female boarding schools and colleges are the great breeding grounds of artificial (acquired) homosexuality,' R.N. Shufeldt wrote in the Pacific Medica Journal in 1902.[41]

However, the history is yet more complex, as homosexual activists themselves also took a role in this debate. While some spoke under the protective cover of professional identities as sexologists (Edward Carpenter, Karl Heinrich Ulrichs), others, like Radclyffe Hall, entered the public discourse in a more direct manner. With the publication of her widely read *The Well of Loneliness*, Hall initiated a literary 'reverse discourse' of homosexual women speaking for themselves. For Hall, as for some sexologists, a binary and biologically determined sexual identity allowed her to argue that homosexuality was inborn, and thus should not be subject to moral condemnation.[42]

Thus the discourse of sexuality as identity, and of a binary juxtaposition of homo- and heterosexualities served a range of strategic purposes, for *both* the emerging sexological and homosexual communities. When the instability of sexual categories *was* acknowledged, this perspective served primarily to fuel the antifeminist campaigns then taking shape in response to women's increased social and political power.

Postscript

This chapter has attempted to ground an argument regarding the instability of sexual categories in a personal, pedagogical, and historical study that explores the shifting and porous borders between homosexual and heterosexual definitions and desires within the past century. In addition I have highlighted the conflicted uses to which the notion of sexuality *as constitutive* of identity has been put, both by the medico-scientific establishment and by homosexual communities themselves. The thrust of this text is towards challenging biological determinists – straight and gay, establishment and activist – who have attempted to convince us that sexual and relational feelings must be physiologically located and fixed in order to be considered natural and normal. This argument is in substantial agreement with the poststructuralist turn to questioning the possibility of a unified or homogenizing 'self.' However, the implications of this analysis for pedagogy and activism remain unclear. As Steven Seidman suggests, poststructuralist approaches, as they have been articulated to date, have serious limitations:

As disciplining forces, identities are not only self limiting and productive of hierarchies but are enabling or productive of social collectivities, moral bonds, and political agency. Although the post-structural problematization of identity is a welcome critique of the essentialist celebration of a unitary subject and tribal politic, post-structuralism's own troubled relation to identity edges toward an empty politics of gesture or disruptive performance that forfeits an integrative, transgressive politic ... Whereas identity politics offers a strong politics on a weak, exclusionary basis, post-structuralism offers a thin politics as it problematizes the very notion of a collective in whose name a movement acts.[43]

Thus we end where we began. Deconstruction cannot do the work of politics, yet how can we do the work of politics within oppressively naturalized notions of identity?

Despite the intractability of this dilemma I would argue that deconstruction *does* provide a starting place for a different kind of discussion. The possibilities inherent in an activist historiography proceed not from the abandonment of notions of a collectivity, but from a commitment to illuminating the possibilities *and* contradictions inherent in notions of identity *within our pedagogy*. To this end, the research by Davis and Chauncey might be mobilized to serve as an example, not of coming out as *something/someone*, but as puzzles and unsettlings for the ways we can think about and represent sexuality, gender, and the self.[44] Can we then use this analysis to illustrate how particular historical moments, including our own, may make certain forms of desire, friendship, exploration, and intimacy possible, *at the same time* as they preclude others?

Social construction theory argues that the 'fact' that a certain percentage of the population engages in same-sex practices in the 1990s does not mean that the same percentage did so fifty years ago when Kinsey conducted his research, or seventy years ago when the Davis survey was completed, or one hundred and seventy years ago when Abraham Lincoln and Joshua Stead shared their bed. One of the considerable ironies implied in this research is that the post-gay liberation, identity-based culture of the 1980s and 1990s may well constitute a context in which it is *more* difficult for some individuals to explore same-sex desires than in the turn-of-the-century period documented by Davis and Chauncey. As Davis implies and Chauncey concludes, if sexuality is culturally organized and subject to change, then the prewar sexual culture may have made it easier for some women and men to engage in casual same-sex relationships when these did not ineluctably mark them as a homosexual.[45]

Thus the historical tension evident in this data is indicative of that hesitant and scary movement from *sexual practice* to *deviant sexual identity*.[46] Does the current historical moment suggest a reverse discursive strategy might be in order, in which we begin to shift the emphasis from identities to practices? As Cindy Patton argues, one indication of the utility of such an approach can be found in the cultural politics surrounding HIV and AIDS. In this context the discourse of 'risk groups' instead of 'risk behaviours' has already had life and death implications. While most heterosexuals continue not to employ safer sex practices with their partners, the definition of the category heterosexual remains problematic. As data collected in a 1990 study of HIV-positive male blood donors suggests, of the 129 men who reported having sex with both men and women since 1978, 30 per cent self-identified as homosexual, 34 per cent as bisexual, and 36 per cent as heterosexual. Further, behaviourally bisexual white men were more likely to identify as homosexual, whereas Black and Latino men were more likely to identify as bisexual and heterosexual, respectively.[47] Once again, we see the problems with identity. While in most parts of Canada and the United States young adults demonstrate sufficient knowledge about HIV and AIDS, few actually practise safer sex.[48] It is 'other people' who develop AIDS, and those others are associated not with the performance of specific acts, but with specific identities or subcultures.

However, the utility of a pedagogy which deconstructs notions of identity can be seen not just in relationship to AIDS, but must also be recognized in the broader discourse about sex. I would argue that a shift in emphasis from identities to practices may open up options for desire, intimacy, friendship, and exploration beyond those which are possible within a unitary conception of the self. In addition, this starting point is better suited to acknowledging that sexuality is constructed in profoundly different ways in different cultural and geographic sites. Two stories from more recent pedagogical experiences will help to illustrate this point.

From 1994 until 1997 I was employed as a teaching assistant for the Introduction to Women's Studies course at the University of Toronto. During the fall of 1996, in the week when we were to talk about lesbianism and bisexuality, I told my students a story from Dutch sociologist Ingrid Foeken in order to illustrate how very different meanings can be attached to similar acts:

Benin, West Africa. The year is 1976. Two women get to chatting on a bus. One is a local woman, the other a European. Towards the end of their journey the African invites the other to stay with her large family. That night they sleep together in one bed.

They talk for a while, then, responding to each other's gestures, they make love. The next morning the European woman asks her new friend whether she often has such experiences with other women, and how she feels about being a lesbian.

Astonished, the African woman answers that it is quite usual for her to let a friend comfort her in this way.[49]

In the discussion that followed a student who had recently immigrated to Canada from Nigeria commented that indeed women and men in Nigeria do comfort each other this way, but few would identify these activities with the terms lesbian or gay.

Also in the fall of 1996, Lynne Fernie, the director of the National Film Board's recent coproduction about lesbian and gay youth, *School's Out*, previewed the video with a Toronto secondary school audience. In the discussion following the screening a student who was originally from India and had come to Canada after several years stay in the Middle East, suggested that films such as *School's Out* should also talk about non-western notions of sexuality. The student suggested that in some areas of the Middle East the bride price made it difficult for men who were poor to get married.[50] In his view this situation resulted in some men choosing to have relationships with each other. However, the lens through which these same-sex relationships were understood was fundamentally different from western notions of identity implied in the terms lesbian or gay.[51]

In the multiracial context of most large North American cities these stories are far from uncommon. Yet the pedagogical strategies used by anti-heterosexism educators usually seem to assume a mythical and homogeneously Western context, untouched by colonial and imperial legacies. As Didi Khayatt has argued, our failure to theorize these contradictions can lead to the erasure of new (to some) epistemological frameworks for thinking about sexuality, gender, and the self:

> The West's global intellectual hegemony leads us to suppose that everyone everywhere understands exactly what we mean by the sexual categories that identify homoerotic behaviour, as evidenced by the number of books and articles which attempt to discuss 'homosexuality' on an international level, and in doing so, subsume all homoerotic activities under one rubric. This tendency renders different notions of same-sex activities invisible. However, it is important to recognize that it is not merely a difference in words that we are discussing, nor is it just particular meanings of corresponding terms. It is a distinctive conceptualization, different in theory as well as in substance, and thus could be said to refer to a different reality ... Not only do such sexual categories exclude the experiences of men and women of the 'Third World,' but the terms seem to be insufficient to capture the myriad differences in sexual expression.[52]

Thus I would argue that while educational strategies may include the language of identity they must, at the same time, extend an invitation to examine the problematics inherent in this process. For it is only through making the messy contradictions of 'our' various histories and movements visible that we will have constructed a pedagogy that does justice to any of our sexualities.

I am suggesting here that the task of understanding the discursive processes by which identities are ascribed, resisted, or embraced is fraught with contradictions. Nevertheless I would assert that 'queerying' these usually unremarked operations which 'indeed achieve their effect because they aren't noticed'[53] can be a critical function of an activist pedagogy and historiography.

If sexual categories are both inevitable, and inevitably troubling, I would argue that we must *wear* these notions of identity lightly, so they do not contain us, or contain the work of understanding desire. To do this we must not erase the profound differences and contradictions found in historical texts or in community and classroom settings, but instead mine them. For it is only in so doing that our pedagogy can re-construct the passions which have made up both our movements and our lives.

Notes

This chapter is based on the work of a great many people and it is a great pleasure to thank them. First, Kathleen Rockhill and Barbara Williams for their imaginative intellectual work which helped launch me on this project, and to Ruth Roach Pierson for inspiring me to investigate the pleasures and dangers of historiography. All three also provided critical comments and support. Secondly, my thanks to all the youth who have participated in Teen's Educating and Confronting Homophobia (TEACH) for their fierce, smart, and generous energy; to Vanessa Russell, Joanne Bacon, and Dawn Sheppard each for their substantial contributions to the continued life of the program, and to Lynne Fernie for her wonderful movie *School's Out*, which features some of the youth involved with TEACH. Many others involved in queer intellectual work and equity work have moved my thinking forward. I hope they will recognize themselves here.

This chapter is dedicated to my parents, each for their very different courage.

1 Foucault, *History of Sexuality*, 101.
2 See, for example, the pedagogy workshop section of Blumenfeld, *Homophobia*.
3 Scott, 'Experience,' 26.
4 Two other, smaller studies of women's sexuality pre-date the Davis report. The first, titled *The Single Woman* by Robert Latou Dickinson and Laura Beam (Baltimore, 1934), and was reviewed by Rosalind Rosenberg in *Beyond Separate Spheres* (New Haven: Yale University Press, 1982). Dickinson's report is based on forty-six case studies of the sexual life of working women in the 1890s. In Rosenberg's brief review of this study she suggests that Dickinson found that 'among his single patients, homosexuality, which he at first failed to notice, even among patients who were living together, represented, he gradually realized, a widespread practice' (202).

The second study, titled 'Statistical Study of the Marriage of Forty-seven Women,' by Celia Duel Mosher is contained in volume 10 of her unpublished work, 'Hygiene and Physiology of Women,' compiled from 1892 to 1920. It has been examined by Carl Degler in 'What Ought to Be and What Was: Women's Sexuality in the Nineteenth Century' and by Rosalind Rosenberg (as above); however, there is no indication that Mosher inquired about same-sex experiences in her survey.

There was, of course, considerable diversity and conflict within the medico-scientific literature of the period regarding the etiology of same-sex relations. The binarist model of sexuality, however, was supported by two of sexology's most influential voices. Richard von Krafft-Ebing described same sex relations as a biologically-based disease in *Psychopathia Sexualis* (New York: Stein and Day,

1978), and Havelock Ellis characterized them as a congenital condition in 'Sexual Inversion with an Analysis of Thirty-three New Cases,' in *Medico-Legal Journal* 13 (1895–1896). The major opposing view was championed by Sigmund Freud, who characterized same-sex attraction as originating in an arrested form of childhood sexual development. For a summary of Freud's position see C. Standford, M.D., 'Homosexuality' in *Journal of Mental Science*, vol. 67 (London, 1921). Havelock Ellis and others did acknowledge some instability in women's same-sex desire – however, as I will argue later, he deployed this perspective in specific, and for women, damaging ways.

6 Halley, 'The Construction of Heterosexuality,' 98.
7 Britzman, 'Queer Pedagogy'? 152–3.
8 Lather, *Getting Smart*, 30–1, referring to a point made by Diana Fuss.
9 Goldstein, 'Go the Way,' 173.
10 For a discussion of one stream of thought about the pleasures and contradictions of en-gendered desire, see Pratt, *S/HE*; also Feinberg, *Stone Butch Blues*.
11 Britzman, 'Queer Pedagogy?,' 11.
12 Goldstein, 'Go the Way,' 184.
13 TEACH was sponsored by the East End Community Health Centre and the Department of Public Health in Toronto. For a visual representation of the work of TEACH see the video *School's Out* (1996), a Great Jane Production distributed by the National Film Board and directed by Fernie (of *Forbidden Love* fame).
14 Information is from 'Taking Risks: Anti-Homophobia education in America,' an unpublished paper completed for Dr Didi Khayatt in 1994, in which I surveyed numerous organizations doing anti-homophobic work in the United States and Canada.
15 Bryson and de Castell, 'Queer Pedagogy,' 296.
16 Riley, *Am I That Name?*
17 Judith Butler, 'Imitation and Gender Insubordination,' 23.
18 Scott, 'Experience,' 24.
19 Terry, 'Theorizing Deviant Historiography,' 58.
20 Ibid.
21 Ibid.
22 See note 4 above.
23 Rosenberg, *Beyond Separate Spheres*, 200.
24 Davis, *Factors in Sex Life*, 27.
25 For just two examples of published work in this steadily growing field see Kennedy and Davis, *Boots of Leather*; and Becki Ross, *House That Jill Built*.
26 See for example Jeffreys, 'Does It Matter.'
27 Davis, *Factors in sex Life*, 247.

28 Terry, 'Theorizing Deviant Historiography,' 58, referring to a point made by Spivak.

29 Davis, *Factors in Sex Life*, 283.

30 Chauncey, *Gay New York*, 76.

31 Ibid., 70.

32 Ibid., 71.

33 Irvine, *Disorders of Desire*, 54.

34 Butler, 'Imitation and Gender Insubordination,' 14.

35 Terry, 'Theorizing Deviant Historiography,' 56.

36 Although low wages made marriage a financial necessity for most women, for a small group in the upper and middle classes, their newly won right to education brought options for professionalized employment and for shaping an independent life. These 'New Women,' as they were called, represented over one-third of the students of higher education in America. (See Faderman, *Odd Girls and Twilight Lovers*, 14) During this period the actual numbers of women receiving advanced degrees and entering the professions reached a peak not to be equalled again until the late 1970s (Smith-Rosenberg, *Disorderly Conduct*, 43). In addition, up until 1910 the majority of the graduates of women's colleges remained unmarried, and by 1920, 75 per cent of female professionals were single (Rapp and Ross, 'The Twenties Backlash,' 94).

37 Smith-Rosenberg, *Disorderly Conduct*, 268.

38 Weeks, *Sexuality and Its Discontents*, 74.

39 Smith-Rosenberg, *Disorderly Conduct*, 268.

40 Weeks, *Sexuality and Its Discontents*, 76.

41 Smith-Rosenberg, *Disorderly Conduct*, 280.

42 Newton, 'The Mythic Mannish Lesbian,' 281–93.

43 Seidman, 'Identity and Politics,' 134–5.

44 I want to acknowledge Barbara Williams, who suggested this way of thinking about using the historical material (OISE, 1995).

45 Chauncey, *Gay New York*, 71.

46 I am indebted to Kathleen Rockhill for suggesting this insight (OISE, 1995).

47 Tielman, Carballo, and Hendriks, eds., *Bisexuality and HIV/AIDS*, 28.

48 For Canadian figures see Michael Ornstein, *AIDS in Canada*, 50. For information on the United States see Cindy Patton, *Inventing AIDS*, 109.

49 This story was told by Dutch sociologist Ingrid Foeken at the 'Which Homosexuality?' International Conference on Lesbian and Gay Studies in Amsterdam, Holland, in 1987. It is documented by Vanessa Baird in her article 'Pride and Prejudice' in *The New Internationalist*, no. 201 (November 1989), 4.

50 Unfortunately I have not been able to speak to the student personally, and do not have the information which would specify which country in the Middle East he is

referring to. I realize this phrasing may reproduce stereotypes about the Middle East as one homogeneous region, and that it fails to specify the extraordinary historical, ethnic, and cultural differences which exist in different regions.

51 Personal communication from Lynne Fernie to the author.

52 Khayatt, 'The Place of Desire: The Exclusion of Women in the Third World in Theorizing Sexual Orientation' (May 1993), 10–11. Work in progress, quoted with permission of the author.

53 Scott, 'Experience,' 33.

5

Queer Ethnography: Identity, Authority, Narrativity, and a Geopolitics of Text

SUZANNE DE CASTELL AND MARY BRYSON

People are strange
When you're a stranger
Faces look ugly
When you're alone

When you're strange
Faces come out of the rain
When you're strange
No one remembers your name
When you're strange
When you're strange
When you're stra–ange

The Doors, 'People Are Strange'

The universe is not only queerer than we imagine, but queerer than we can imagine.

J.S. Haldane, in Oliver Sacks's *An Anthropologist on Mars*

A heavy cloak of wilful silence continues to shroud sexualities as important sites for the production and reification of difference/s in the textually constructed subjects of ethnographic research. Texts, including scholarly texts, are 'virtual space' locations we occupy – or don't – as a function, largely, of our relational positioning on the uneven and slippery sociohistorical landscape upon which a range of marginal identities are invented, measured and weighed, adopted, negotiated, and contested: girl, Fag!, Black, dyke, queer, and countless other 'others.' Ethnographic texts, to the extent that they have 'dared to speak Its Name' have so far largely constructed 'queerness' as, at best, the *object* of study. In pursuit of an explicitly 'queer ethnography' – a repositioning from a hegemonic to a queer-centred frame, our interest is in the *inversions* effected when queerness occupies a *subject*-position in ethnographic accounts and accounting practices.

Queer ethnography, we will try to show, radically inverts ethnography proper, and this across the broad scope of concerns raised particularly in rhetorically oriented critical ethnographic scholarship.[1] This work asks us to (re)consider axiomatic assumptions of ethnographic practice/s: Who is the ethnographer?' What is field-work experience? What kinds of stories count as ethnographic accounts? How are they to be written and read? and, finally and most importantly, Why are ethnographic stories told, how are they told, and to whom? This chapter attempts to make a start towards saying something useful about some difference queering ethnography might make in relation to identity, authority, and narratology, and concludes by reviving an old standard for theory and research capable of taking a measure of *différance* – the Lesbian Rule.

This chapter proposes that critical, ethical, and representational 'aporias' confronting ethnography today – fundamental conceptual and methodological roadblocks which have at times appeared capable of delegitimating ethnography altogether, both as a fruitful strategy for empirical analysis and as a politically alert research practice – can be significantly reconfigured by queering ethnography 'proper.' By mapping out what, typically, are uncharted constitutive positions within ethnographic practice, the subject-specificity of these obstacles is exposed, with the result that new resources for a rearticulation of ethnography are able to be considered. There is in this project a temptation to imagine that perhaps only a queer ethnography offers hope for the salvage and reclamation of ethnography: ethnography '*im*-proper.'

Considering Identity in Ethnography: Who Is the Ethnographer?

Disciplinary practices denying queers' presence as speaking subjects in ethnographic theory and research secure thereby the centrality of hegemonic heterosexist voices in the academic world. This is a subject-positioning which becomes visible only as it is challenged by queers researching and writing *as* queers, and not *about* them.

James Clifford, quoting Barthes's pronouncement that 'a text's unity lies not in its origin but in its destination,' argues that 'The ability of a text to make sense in a coherent way depends less on the willed intentions of an originating author than on the creative activity of a reader.' And Clifford goes on to suggest that 'It is intrinsic to the breakup of monological authority' (a breakup that comes with the realization that ethnography can no longer be seen as the monopoly of 'certain western cultures and social classes' that 'ethnographers no longer address a single general type of reader.'[2] Clifford's important point here is that subject-specific political and epistemological practices are built into ways of writing, and that these subject-specific practices constitute presuppositional acts ethnographers may ignore no longer.

But even these strong exhortations to 'radical' inclusion aren't enough to rescue ethnography proper from its failure to establish human cultural diversity at the center of concern – what Rose has called its 'crippling weakness.'[3] It is no longer plausible (if it ever was) to 'move over' and 'make room' for the participation of ethnography's traditional 'others.' The problem isn't a lack of space, it is the *kind* of space, the kind of *place* ethnography is, which shapes it ethos and its conditions of occupancy. This is a problem which can only be addressed by interrogating ethnography about its politics of location: the situatedness of its truth claims and its opportunities for voice.

One way to begin to interrogate these problematics is to ask (as indeed many people have asked) 'Who is the ethnographer?' Dan Rose, in *Living the Ethnographic Life*, even as he urges a kind of responsibly postcolonial ethnographic standpoint, is nonetheless able to ask, 'What relationships should ethnographers take up with peoples of other cultures or classes? Can *we* not move beyond abstract relations with *them*?'[4] [emphases ours]. In such articulations, despite his clear intention to subvert, reverse, and open up ethnography by asking, 'What new cultural formations and identities may suddenly arise?'[5] by so doing Rose makes abundantly, if inadvertently, clear to readers just who 'us' and 'them' are. So that despite the excellent critical discussion in his text, ultimately unredeemable are exhortations such as 'Do radical ethnography, one that gets you closer to those you study at the risk of going native and never returning ...' This 'going native' tactic seems to fall a bit short of the radical reversals Rose is seeking. Just consider what ethnographies of PWAs would look like in Rose's regime? What would going native mean for the 'we' who are presumed embodiments of 'the ethnographic life?' Why must accounts of cultural interiority be conducted by dissimulators in order to count as 'accounts'? What would it do to ethnography proper if the following kind of account were to count?:

I look at myself in the mirror everyday and assess the spread of the KS wildfire sweeping low over my skin, my soul lets out a shriek. I collect the scattered bits and pieces of my dignity and self-image. A queen bashed by a heavy-handed destiny. I was 22 when I was diagnosed, many of my contemporaries are now dead. I have never known a different Canadian life, sexual or social. Then I reach for the Clinique beauty-AIDS.

Lately I have been forced to sublimate sex due to technical difficulties. Until recently I went to dark places, good lighting is the Martha Stewart clue to queer good living, lesions cannot be seen, my old tree noduled skin untouched, or I enjoyed myself thoroughly, but life has its way of taking away everything we cherish: erections, youth, dreams, lovers; so now I write acrid diatribes.[6]

The difference which makes a difference here is between diversity management – (the inclusion of marginal subject-positions) and radical in/version (the creation of new centres). What might the ethnographic field colonized by queer subjects, the ethnographic text written from its margins, look like? This question is rather like Dorothy Smith's question about sociology:[7] What would it look like, she asks, a sociology formulated from the standpoint of women? What key concepts and practices would change, and how? What questions would disappear, and what new ones appear?

Oops! What's So Queer about the 'Queer Ethnographer'?

An insistent and nagging problem must intrude awkwardly at this point in the text because it must inevitably fail in any attempt to define, straightforwardly, an escape route from those paralysing critiques of postmodernism on the one hand, and the obvious fiasco of the modernist critical project on the other. Queer, surely, is not simply an adjective one can add on to ethnography as if the necessary corrective here were linguistic in nature! Presumably, in some fundamental sense the very definition of ethnographer precludes the queer. The ethnographer is a certain kind of person, a certain kind of unqueer character in the Bakhtinian carnival. The proper ethnographer is like the perfect house guest, politely 'just visiting,' or like the well-meaning tourist endeavouring to go native and thereby to fit in and make as little difference as possible. That being so, it seems crucial to establish just *who* might inhabit, however precariously, the role of the *queer* ethnographer before proceeding to describe how ethnographic practices might be radically transformed thereby.

And so a logically (and perhaps ontologically) prior question looms large at this juncture: how honestly to explain something about which entire volumes need to be written – about the colonization of the domain of the queer as it has moved most recently from contagion to commodity: about queers as troublemakers, and queering as setting awry; about the motives, reasons, and causes for disruption; about why just the way we have sex is not what queer is about, and why the way we have sex is precisely what queer is about ... about the essential, fundamental, irrefutable fact of queerness as a construction, even more a confabulation; about the conceits of a subject whose motivation can only be suspect, since, after all, 'concerned colleagues,' upon hearing about homophobia as a question at all for the ethnographer, need only ask, 'Why do other people have to know?' 'Why do you need to flaunt it?' or 'How do they know that you *are* one?'

In this discursive maelstrom, the category 'queer' most surely loses its strict association with homosexual or 'deviant' sexual practices and embraces other persons 'of difference,' physically less-abled, disfigured, of colour, mentally ill – anyone who has ever had the benefits of 'passing,' of not drawing attention to one's 'difference' urged upon them. Correlatively, of course, this means that not all research and writing done by people who enact homosexual or other 'deviant' forms of sexual practice, can usefully be characterized as queer work.

These issues, only briefly noted here, are introduced to alert readers that queer in this essay marks the location of a fierce struggle both to seize and control the meanings of that sign, and also to proliferate its indeterminacy and instability. From that conceptual trajectory, then, this chapter's project is first to explore some ways in which destabilizing heteronormative ethnography radically inverts ethnography proper. The remainder of the chapter then returns to the matter of identifying further conceptual, methodological, and narratological in-versions as these illuminate projects of queer ethnography.

'A Place in the Text': Queer Politics and Narrativity

'And now, friend-reader, you must prepare your heart and your mind for the most impure tale that has ever been told since our world began ...'[8]

Consider the representation of place in textual reality. Can we speak here about a political geography of discourse? A strange notion, to be sure. But we are looking for some way of talking about *who occupies* textual space, *and in what capacity*. Who can find a place in the text and who is exiled? What kind of text might be habitable by queer subjects? Critical narratology demands attention, as well we know, not just to the telling – the production of accounts – but to the listening, and to the conditions of listening. Every telling issues from somewhere; it also goes to somewhere, and where the story goes shapes what the story can effect. Stories, of course, are never just stories. *Queer* stories, like queer identities, are always also performances.

But What Exactly Do They Do?!

The problem of *what kinds* of stories to tell seems to us a problem demanding inquiry into the ethics of professional practices. How might we construe an 'ethics of narration' in telling tales about the 'other' subjects with whom we have sought to engage in our research? Here, then, are some still very preliminary steps towards theorizing a de-centred, disruptive narrativity. To begin, 'bell hooks reports, instructively, that: 'Searching through the critical work of postcolonial critics, I found much work that bespeaks the continued fascination with the way white minds, particularly the colonial imperialist traveller, perceive blackness, and very little interest in representations of whiteness in the black imagination.'[9]

There is, we think it is safe to say, similarly little interest in accounts of straightness from the standpoint of the queer imagination. Now, of course this should come as no surprise to any of us.

The Mis-adventure Novel of Everyday Life

Bakhtin identifies the adventure novel of everyday life as the first, most basic form of 'novelistic discourse.' For Bakhtin this novel type 'fuses the course of an individual's life with his actual spatial course or road – that is, with his wanderings.'[10] 'The hero in this type of novel' (we explain this at greater length in earlier work)[11]

is an observer of everyday life, who as the result of a fortuitous transformation is positioned to enter into everyday life as a third person. The hero may have a provisional or peripheral status in society, and be setting out to build a career. An element of chance introduces the hero into the realm of private everyday life ... The hero relates to the observed private life as a nonparticipant in that life. He or she may play an extremely humble role in common life, as a subordinate to common serving people.[12]

The particular textual example Bakhtin uses to illustrate the main features of novelistic form (the adventure novel of everyday life) is *The Golden Ass*, a sixth-century Roman text by Apeulius. Bakhtin describes the social role played by its central character, Lucius thus: 'As an ass, a beast of burden, he descends to the very depths of common life, life among muleteers, hauling a millstone for the miller, serving a gardener, a soldier, a cook, a baker.'[13] It is precisely this humble role which provides the essential condition of access to the field of observation, and it is what enables the hero *unobtrusively* to observe the events:

The position of an ass is a particularly convenient one for observing the secrets of everyday life. The presence of an ass embarrasses no-one, all open up completely. [Of a *queer* ass, our point is, precisely the *opposite* must be said. But back to Apeulius ...] And in my oppressive life, only one consolation remained to me: to indulge my curiosity which is my native bent, since people never took my presence into consideration and talked and acted as freely as they wished.[14]

The remarkable access, this unobtrusiveness, a complete absence of embarrassment and a corresponding disposition to 'talk and act ... freely' which accrue to those (dumb animals, domestic servants, the lowliest of the commonfolk) who are not counted as speaking subjects, these are far from the conditions which greet queer ethnographers who speak and act as queers in 'the field.' Quite the reverse, in fact: there is wide and deep affront; the very idea is aberrant; access is prohibited; people refuse to speak or speak with extreme guardedness, and equally often seek more to conceal their actions than to reveal them. Given the extent of the inversions effected when queer subjects take up the role of the ethnographer, the paradigmatic narrative form for the expression of Queer ethnography, within this conceptual framework, can perhaps best be characterized as the '*mis*-adventure novel of everyday life.'

Interruption: A Queer Field Note

We know that one of the most common tactics of an elite group is to refuse to discuss – to label as vulgar or uninteresting – issues that are uncomfortable for them.[15]

'All I can tell you is, you get to know after as many years as I've spent in this job. A certain taste ... A certain smell ... I don't know what it is about you people ... I can't put my finger on it ... Something just isn't quite right.' Those were the words spoken by the superintendent of a large British Columbia school district in a red-faced, angrily delivered monologue about our unsuitability as researchers. That is to say, it was our *new-found* unsuitability, despite the fact that we had been granted permission already to conduct research on gender, educational equity, and uses of new technologies in a school in his district, that we had been awarded a large research grant and had been meeting with the district research committee for several months leading up to this, our final and most inauspicious meeting.

And how unexpected it all was ... unexpected and yet so familiar. During the first meeting the superintendent had asked us point-blank: 'So are you here to court us?' 'Absolutely,' we had countered with studied firmness, not really knowing, inside, *what* to say. The sheer implausibility of it all: two dykes wearing matching Gap pants, Doc Martins, and jackets 'courting' the superintendent and his henchman, the Director of Instruction. After our first meeting they were jubilant – gushing about how well we had done ... that we were in a league with IBM and a select few others who had been able to withstand their intense scrutiny and tough questioning. They 'loved' our research proposal and were ready to sign on the dotted line. We had to shake their respective hands. We had to accept (one copy each) their respective business cards. *We were in.*

Or so we had thought. Our strategy had been quite clever, or so we imagined at the time. We proposed to study 'what works' in relation to girls and new technologies by taking our cue from communities of practice where gender was being articulated with greater agency and equity than was typically the case in school contexts. We had plenty of funding, and we were set to go. But the superintendent couldn't put his finger on it, so we were out. Surprise! (Not.)

Meanwhile, Back on the Road

Now, whereas Apeulius's Golden Ass, 'our hero,' could go anywhere and hear and see everything, and tell an ethnographer's story of 'how it was in the field,'[16] in the practice of queer ethnographic fieldwork *it matters greatly 'who'* the ethnographer is. That is to say, it matters greatly what position is occupied by the ethnographer. Role occupancy as a queer subject – always and only an antihero results in precisely the opposite of the Ass's invisibility, and with precisely the opposite effect. The ethnographer 'proper' can lay claim to an account, whether more or less adequate, of 'how they really were; what happened in the field,' with the aim and assumption being that the ethnographer will alter conditions as little as possible by his (usually his) presence in the field. In contrast, the only story to which the ethnographer *im*-proper can lay claim, by virtue of the ways in which normative structures shape and articulate the basic conditions of work – the 'research practices of everyday life,' to beg from de Certeau – is inevitably about him or herself and the trouble s/he causes.

And such an account cannot be one of moving fluidly and unobtrusively through the field, permitted to hear and see everything. It must instead be a story of estrangement, refusal, disruption, ejection. The misadventure novel of everyday life will, in its most typical form, tell about what it is to get kicked from pillar to post in the conduct of daily research practice, about what is refused (access, cooperation, civility) and prohibited, about threats and backlash, and, more mundanely, about what is funded and what is not.[17] What can *not* be claimed here from such a standpoint is, epistemologically, of the greatest importance, for it is at this point that queer ethnography has everything to offer ethnography proper. For what can *not* be claimed here encompasses traditional ethnography's most troubling claims: the professional outsider's access to 'reality': the 'fly on the wall' paradigm of neutrality in the observational field.

Tsing, in her remarkably queer ethnography of the Meratus, whose 'everyday ... existence offends official ideals of order and development,'[18] makes this central point: 'Rather than characterizing any given culture, marginality becomes key to reformulating cultural theory.' Speaking of different 'ways of telling' cultural difference (13), she commends 'a world in which everyone must take responsibility for a *positioned* imagination (122).' How we can write both from and to a 'positioned imagination' so as to reconfigure cultural analysis and its reception is a guiding question for us.

Queer Measures: The Lesbian Rule

Truthfulness anywhere means a heightened complexity. But it is a movement into evolution ...[19]

There is of course much more to be said about the legitimacy, value, and significance of narrative analysis in ethnographic theory and research. The extent to which this particular postmodern turn may be seen to leave questions of truth and falsity continuously deferred, while it may only be a function of a theory of scientism that continues to cling helplessly to some notion of fundamental truth – an epistemology for which relativism appears an unconscionable and treasonous pretender to the throne – is still one to which ethnographers must respond. And so we want to take a methodological right turn in order to make a strong case for the invocation of the Lesbian Rule (a flexible carpenter's ruler for measuring irregular surfaces) as a model instrument for reconfiguring ethnographic theory and research. For in the Lesbian Rule we have a tool capable of identifying and engaging irregularities in surfaces that are not straight. The rigid regulus of normativity, an instrument ideally suited to the production of generalization and the pretence of universality, engenders situations in which, continually and on a daily basis, we have to participate in a species of 'lying game,' in which, just as in the film similarly named, the aim is not to see what is directly in front of one's face. In a classic Batesonian double bind, what openly queer researchers find is a prohibition on speaking of what one 'cannot not see.' The Lesbian Rule, by contrast, is about specificity, and particularity, about taking the measure of difference in a way that does not suppress the truth of difference, by forcing it, as it were, to straighten out. Nor – as is so often charged against any serious attempt at inclusion – does the Lesbian Rule abandon consistency altogether in an entirely 'un-ruly' pluralism which has given up on any hope of standards – such a carnivalesque pluralism being in actuality just another way of leaving things exactly as they are, as Wolff's 'critique of pure tolerance'[20] argued so long ago.

Adrienne Rich's discussion of lying as a kind of deceitful simplification draws our attention to the way in which the invocation of 'standards' can serve to legitimate lying rather than to enable more precise statements of truth: 'In speaking of lies, we come inevitably to the subject of truth. There is nothing simple or easy about this idea. There is no 'the truth,' 'a truth' – truth is not one thing, or even a system. It is an increasing complexity ... This is why the effort to speak honestly is so important. Lies are usually attempts to make everything simpler – for the liar – than it really is or ought to be.'[21]

Raymond Williams[21] observed that in any case the history of the term *standards* has more to do with flags indicating religious or national fealty than it does with quality or excellence. From this semantic standpoint, he reconsiders the contemporary idiomatic use of standards in educational debates. Keeping Williams's conceptual slant in mind, we can go on and distinguish three standards of measurement: the straight edge rule, the rule of thumb, and the Lesbian Rule.

All are types of rule, where *rule* (as defined by the Oxford English Dictionary) means 'a principle to which action or procedure conforms or is bound or intended to conform, dominant custom, canon, test, standard, normal state of things.' One good way of talking about the daily work of queer ethnographers is that it seeks always to promote, as a normal state of things, ways of thinking and acting capable of taking the measure of difference – that is, of rendering difference more visible and audible, of creating circumstances in which it is nurtured and encouraged, and making those circumstances standard, common, customary. Part of that daily struggle is making it clear, to those terrified by the mere anarchy they suppose postmodernism (in one or other of its various incarnations) to have 'loosed upon the[ir] world,' that inclusion need *not* lead us to disorder and chaos, whether intellectual, moral, or both. It need not mean incoherence, arbitrariness, or lack of standards. So the big question here is about fealty, harking back to Williams. It is about *whose* standards we will ride into battle under; about who it is, finally, that we purport to serve in our daily professional practices. What we have to make clear is that there are different kinds of standards, not only one, and that the cause of educational equity is maybe better served by one than by others.

Here, then, are three kinds of standards. The first is the familiar straight-edge ruler, which of course is a straight strip of wood, metal, or plastic material used to measure or to draw straight lines. For most of us this was the only kind of ruler we knew. Its primary uses were to inscribe margins, and for punishment.

The second, the rule of thumb, is a rule with an instructive history: it permitted a man to beat his wife, so long as he used for that purpose a stick no wider than the width of his thumb. The rule of thumb justifies approximation, and is a kind of practical measure of what 'will do' in a particular circumstance. It is a 'more or less' kind of standard, usually associated with having significant practical experience, and although in every case the stick measured by the rule of thumb is rigid and presumably reasonably straight (though for functional purposes it need not be), the actual quantity measured by the rule of thumb will vary from one case to another – a situation of thoroughgoing relativism.

The third kind of rule, discussed by one J.R. Lucas in a paper intriguingly entitled 'The Lesbian Rule,' refers to a *flexible* ruler said to have been used by the builders of Lesbos, a strip of metal which as Aristotle reported, "bends to the shape of the stone and is not fixed.'[23] In her discussion of the priority of particulars over general rules in questions of moral judgment, Martha Nussbaum remarks about the lesbian rule that 'this device is still in use, as one might expect. I have one. It is invaluable for measuring oddly shaped parts of an old Victorian house. It is also of use in measuring parts of the body, few of which are straight ... Good deliberation, like the lesbian rule, accommodates itself to the shape that it finds, responsively and with respect for complexity.'[24]

Motives, Reasons, Causes: Why Do Ethnography?

Having repopulated an hypothetical ethnographic landscape with its marginalized subjects, and equipped them with a standard capable of taking the measure of difference/s, the final inversion it may be useful to consider here is an inversion of motive.

As against the traditional philosophical ideal of the 'disinterested pursuit of knowledge,' even as against the discernibly more enlightened Habermasian thesis about the constitutive operation of human interest in the production of 'interested' knowledge (taken up gladly by those who would see their ethnographic practice/s as working on behalf of others and for their benefit), let us ask what it is to pursue inquiry and to formulate knowledge from the standpoint of *necessity*. What if the work you do is not because you're interested, or even because you have a stake in it, but because you are compelled to study it; you do it because you (feel you) *have* to? This surely puts a different twist on the worrisome ethical dilemmas concerning relevance, the validity of outsiders' perspectives, and the charge that ethnographies of 'others' are fundamentally exploitative.[24]

While bell hooks tells readers that 'there has never been any official body of black people in the United States who have gathered as anthropologists and/or ethnographers whose central critical project is the study of white people ...'[25] she is not exposing a lack, but explaining how, and how differently, what white folks call ethnography was practiced in the everyday life of hooks's Black community. Writes hooks, 'black folks have, from slavery on, shared with one another in conversations, "special" knowledge of whiteness gleaned from close scrutiny of white people ... For years black domestic servants, working in white homes, acted as informants who brought knowledge back to segregated communities – details, facts, observations, psychoanalytic readings of the white "other" (338).'

These readings of the white other, hooks advises, constitute 'special knowledge' because this is knowledge essential to assist people to 'cope and survive in a white supremacist society.' It is a species of investigation carried out, not as a matter of intellectual or exoticized interest, or out of any righteous commitment to the betterment of others, but as an inescapable prerequisite of existence in a racist society, as an essential means of survival. hooks goes on to explain:

'Living as we did – on the edge – we developed a particular way of seeing reality. We looked from the outside as well as from the inside out. We focussed our attention on the center as well as the margin. We understood both. This mode of seeing reminded us of the existence of a whole universe, a main body made up of both margin and center. Our survival depended on an ongoing public awareness of the separation between margin and center ... a mode of seeing unknown to most of our oppressors that sustained us ...' (149)

What a good deal of this ethnographic knowledge was about, hooks further explains, was 'white folks' who were, for hooks's community, 'the oppressor.' Now this kind of knowledge is not optional; you have it or you can be hurt, you can be destroyed. In the manner you better know, if you are visibly queer, all about straight people – how they dress, how they talk, which ones are violent, and in what settings they are most likely to act on that; what speech genres to invoke in particular occasions to be granted access to places, conversations, and jobs; and what speech mannerisms to avoid at all costs. But then of course there is the reverse: how to size up a potential queer who chooses conditions of ambiguity, how to engage with other visible queers in full view of the straights, without 'inviting' verbal or physical abuse for it. And most of all, how to eat, eat, eat shit, and still keep a smile on your face, cuz you know if you complain, it will be you, not the straight perp, that gets the punishment.

At Wit's End?

It is at least theoretically possible to perform an identity of normalcy on a day-to-day basis and go through life apparently as a relatively unscathed homosexual faculty member, just as it is possible to enact the role of ethnographer 'proper.' There is nothing necessarily queer about same-sex preferences in and of themselves. Queer is, *tout court*, about the deliberate enactment of an endless series of transgressions: queer shoes, queer piercings, queer hair, queer speech patterns; in short, an apparently queer set of cultural practices that define the parameters of a queer life. If queer is to signify anything stable it is a location in cultural space from which 'the normal' might suffer irreparable damage.

So while it might be tempting to propose that queer ethnography would entail telling tales about odd people living strange lives in a kind of sexual Twilight Zone, such tales, however much they might have queer contents, would still fail both to manifest queer methods and to contest the boundaries of normalcy. Queerer than these, we say, are accounts of the normal from standpoint of those who would willfully proclaim a queer identity in the face of so many opportunities to play safe, tellings from and not about the Other, strange tellings which do not describe or represent but (re)position readers in a new relation, not to ethnography's other but to themselves, so that they cannot fail to see themselves in accounts in which they must in that same moment question, rebuke, and perhaps even, *mirabile dictu*, despise themselves.

If Leslie Feinberg's[26] stories of being raped in the schoolyard are everyday events for queer subjects, who am I who does not see this? Who am I, who does nothing to change it? In stories such as these the reader is ethically (and epistemologically) challenged: the reading must make a difference, must not be able to be ignored, must in and of itself make a difference in and for its readers. Queer ethnographies, we say, seek to reveal the wires and pulleys and supports of the everyday context within which 'the normal' is invented and stage-managed, rendering its strange artifices and carefully wrought illusions evident, naming the ways in which social and cultural life are selectively re-presented to members as stable, reliable, necessary.

We have attempted to argue the value of actively queerying ethnography – queering its techniques and coloring outside the lines – going in an altogether different direction than the straight and narrow. We have identified queer ethnographies that take the risk of telling perverse and unsettling tales stories of lives lived willingly against the grain and at the cost of extraordinary hardships, extraordinary cruelty. But these will not be heroic tales featuring slain dragons and courageous characters. These queer tales will work instead to unravel the fabric of normalcy and insist on the intrusion of the monstrous other into safe spaces. No bedtime stories these, of romantic strangers adventuring in strange lands, but stories instead of the stranger lurking within the very gates of normalcy, proclaiming the fragility and permeability of its borders and the ungovernability of its citizens, insistently announcing its refusal to be ruled, and that the orderly, managed social world which is the invisible backdrop behind traditional tales of the other turns out to be far queerer than any of us dare imagine.

Notes

1 See for example Clifford, *The Predicament of Culture*; Tsing, *In the Realm*; Visweswaran, *Fictions of Feminist Ethnography*.

2　Clifford, *The Predicament of Culture*, 52.

3　Rose, *Living the Ethnographic Life*, 45.

4　Ibid., 16.

5　Ibid., 37.

6　Ibanez, Personal Communication.

7　Dorothy Smith, *The Everyday World*.

8　de Sade, *120 Days of Sodom*, 124.

9　hooks, *Yearning*, 143.

10　Bakhtin, *The Dialogic Imagination*, 120.

11　de Castell and Walker, 'Identity, Metamorphosis.'

12　Bakhtin, *The Dialogic Imagination*, 166.

13　Ibid., 121.

14　Ibid., 122.

15　Rabinow, 'Representations Are Social Facts,' 253.

16　Rose, *Ethnographic Life*; Atkinson, *The Ethnographic Imagination*; Van Maanen, *Tales of the Field*.

17　Smith, *The Everyday World*, 216; Chafetz, *Gender Equity*.

18　Tsing, *In the Realm*, 41.

19　Rich, *Lies, Secrets, and Silence*, 193.

20　Wolff, *Beyond Tolerance*.

21　Rich, *On Lies, Secrets and Silence*, 189.

22　Raymond Williams, *Keywords*.

23　Lucas, 'The Lesbian Rule,' 12.

24　Nussbaum, *Love's Knowledge*, 70.

25　Hammersley, *What's Wrong with Ethnography?*, 136.

26　hooks, *Yearning*, 338.

27　Feinberg, *Stone Butch Blues*.

6

The Everyday Bisexual as Problematic: Research Methods beyond Monosexism

KI NAMASTE

The explosive growth of lesbian and gay studies in recent years[1] has raised important methodological questions about the nature of theories on sexuality, and their political applications. A survey of the development of lesbian and gay studies in the United States and English Canada provides some useful historical insights into the resulting debates.

In the United States, early studies of sexuality emerged from lesbian and gay activism following the Stonewall riots in 1969.[2] The 1971 publication of Dennis Altman's *Homosexual: Oppression and Liberation*, for instance, was one of the first attempts to advance an analysis of the social factors responsible for gay oppression and the conditions necessary for gay liberation.[3] Jeffrey Escoffier maintains that American research on sexuality conducted in the early to mid-1970s was further committed to exploring the impact of gay liberation and feminism.[4] The contributions of historians, anthropologists, and sociologists[5] figured prominently in this field.

In the late 1980s and early 1990s, however, questions of sexuality and gender were approached in a radically different manner by scholars who are primarily located in the humanities.[6] Whereas early, social scientific studies of sexuality focused on gay politics, cultures, and communities, this new body of knowledge investigates the textual inscription of sexual and gender identities. Now grouped under the label Queer Theory, this type of knowledge draws on French poststructuralist theory[7] to make sense of how categories of sexuality are created in specific cultural sites.[8]

Critics of queer theory charge that it ignores social scientific contributions to studies of sexuality.[9] Since a specifically sociological approach to sexuality is lacking in queer theory, the relations between lesbian and gay communities and lesbian and gay scholarship are also overlooked. These questions are increasingly important given the success of queer theory in the American university.

For some critics the triumph of queer theory has occurred due to its investment in 'sophisticated' French theory, and an increasing professionalization of the field.[10] This institutional location has disregarded the organizing efforts of grass- roots lesbian and gay communities. Although queer theory emerged in the 1990s few scholars within the field provide a sustained analysis of contemporary lesbian and gay political activism.[11]

There are clear methodological differences between lesbian and gay studies as it has developed since the 1970s, and queer theory of the 1990s. Lesbian and gay studies is founded on the assumption that individuals who are lesbian and gay do exist, and that scholars are confronted with the challenge of examining different historical, cultural, and social locations in which these people live. Queer theory, in contrast, takes issue with the concept of identity as a basis for political action or theoretical knowledge. Making use of literary interpretive methods such as semiotics and deconstruction, queer theory inquires about how sexual and gender identities are written into, or outside, culture. Whereas lesbian and gay studies bases itself on lesbian and gay identities, the impetus behind queer theory is in the very suspension of identity.

Within the context of English Canada, studies of sexuality have had less institutional success than in some American humanities programs. As Steven Maynard points out, historians and sociologists have been central to the formation of lesbian and gay studies in English Canada, particular prior to 1990.[12] Given this position it is not surprising that some English-Canadian researchers have expressed discomfort with the recent project of queer theory.[13] Like American social scientists,[14] English-Canadian historians and sociologists object to the textualist nature of queer theory, and challenge the political import of suspending lesbian and gay identities at a time when they are under attack. The concerns raised by English Canadian lesbian and gay social scientists and historians have also been addressed by teachers and students of women's studies, who insist on connecting theory and everyday social relations – what is colloquially referred to as 'the real world.'[15]

The field of lesbian and gay studies and that of queer theory both revolve around objects of sexuality (or the social relations which produce these objects) and the question of politics. While both sites share an investment in sexual objects and politics, they approach these issues in unique ways. A more in-depth reading of a representative text from English-Canadian lesbian and gay studies and queer theory will clarify the fundamental differences and points of convergence of these two approaches.

Grounded and Poststructuralist Theories: Mutually Exclusive?

The development of lesbian and gay studies in English Canada, particularly in history and sociology, has forged productive relations among intellectuals and activists.[16] The generation of knowledge about sexuality which is relevant to new social movements, I suggest, emerges from such locations within the project of *social* theory, where scholars have typically rejected queer theory and indeed poststructuralism, with their mainly textual orientation, outright. In a broad sense, social theory requires that an entity called 'theory' both emerge from and be applicable to the everyday social world. Such an understanding of knowledge is reflexive: theory is not just about describing the world, it is also a way to act on it.[17]

The research program of English-Canadian sociologist Dorothy Smith exemplifies the conditions of social theory.[18] Smith is concerned with methodological and epistemological questions – issues concerning how we do research and how we come to know the things that we do. She challenges the traditional sociological methods, which devalue women's ways of knowing and which treat women as mere objects of study (if they are recognized at all). In contrast, Smith proposes that we develop ways of knowing and ways of doing research which begin from the perspective of the lived experience of the people under investigation. In such a framework women and other marginalized groups are the subjects rather than the objects of knowledge.

One of the concrete strategies Smith proposes for enacting such a research program is what she refers to as an 'institutional ethnography.'[19] Using standard qualitative data-collection techniques, such as interviewing and participant observation, institutional ethnography asks particular subjects to speak about how they understand their situation. Smith argues that the social relations which order experience are hidden. It is thus the task of the researcher to move from the standpoint of the subjects under investigation to a conceptual problematic which accounts for how people are related to their everyday worlds, through both institutions and relations of ruling. This framework is concerned with the social relations which organize how people live and experience their everyday social worlds.

The framework of institutional ethnography is particularly suited to political action, since it allows marginalized people to describe how they perceive their living conditions. Such a strategy can help illustrate the ways in which these people are located outside of a ruling apparatus.[20] Gay sociologist George Smith applies Dorothy Smith's method in his research on HIV and AIDS in Canada.[21] From his AIDS activism in Toronto, Smith appreciated that people living with AIDS (PLWAs) and the Ontario Ministry of Health held different conceptions of AIDS. While the Ministry of Health believed that AIDS was a fatal disease, PLWAs knew from personal experience and from contact with other activists that AIDS was not, at least in the short term, a fatal illness. The administration of AIDS, however, concentrated available resources on palliative care and increased support services for the dying.[22] Little information was available on experimental treatments which had proven effective in the management of HIV and AIDS. Similarly, even if people knew about various experimental treatments (through networking and correspondence with other AIDS activists around the world), they were often unable to access them in Canada.

Smith reflects on the political import of institutional ethnography. In the collection of data on AIDS in Ontario,[23] Smith learned that the Ontario Ministry of Health had no treatment infrastructure to serve the needs of seropositive people. He contends that this insight could be taken up directly by AIDS activists working outside the university. An investigation of the social relations which organize health care – the palliative care model – had immediate relevance to the Toronto-based group AIDS Action Now!: 'First, it identified a major source of the problem of access to new treatments. Second, it raised the question of what other social relations were involved in the management of the epidemic. These discoveries had the effect of focusing the politics of AIDS Action Now! very concretely on the delivery of treatment.'[24]

Smith goes on to outline the significance of institutional ethnography to his own research program. He began with the everyday living conditions of PLWAs, and developed a conceptual framework which explained how the provincial health ministry's palliative care model prevented a response to AIDS which included the needs of people living with HIV (PLWHIVs). This knowledge was then used by AIDS activists to concentrate their energies on the delivery of treatment information and services. Smith contends that the framework of institutional ethnography is especially suited to action-oriented research, since one begins with the everyday experiences of the subjects under investigation, and one's findings are subsequently (and continually) verified within this milieu. Smith comments on the development of his own research:

It would have been extraordinarily easy to move from studying the social relations of treatment to examining the social relations of public health policy. The government's public health policy was open to criticism, and for the sociologist looking at the management of the epidemic, this was what was going on – i.e., what was there to be researched. This is what a bird's-eye approach would have been like with PWAs, themselves, becoming objects of study (e.g., as 'risk groups' or 'vectors' of infection). Organizing entry to the field from the standpoint of PLWAs and PLWHIVs outside the politico-administrative *régime* meant that this was not the way my investigation developed. The examination of the social relations of public health, consequently, apart from the realization that the government's preoccupation with this issue was detrimental to PLWAs, did not become a topic of research.[25]

As the above quotation illustrates, the framework of institutional ethnography begins from the standpoint of the people under investigation, rather than creating them as mere objects of study. The knowledge generated from this approach is directly relevant to these individuals. Furthermore, institutional ethnography does not begin with a predetermined research program. The priorities of research are established as the data is collected and analysed, rather than being specified from the outset by a sociological researcher who may have no direct involvement in the communities under examination. Emerging from the everyday living conditions of people, the researcher moves to analyse the social relations which organize how these conditions are experienced. This model is also useful because it exposes the social relations of an objectivist sociology in which people become the objects of research, and in which research is generated for its own ends.

Institutional ethnography as a strategy which accounts for the social relations ordering experience requires that theory emerge from the research field. This perspective continues the sociological tradition known as 'grounded theory.'[26] A grounded theory model demands that researchers suspend their preconceived notions about the subject under investigation, and focus their initial energies on data collection. Once data collection is underway various conceptual categories will emerge, which may or may not differ from those originally anticipated at the outset of the research project. Conceptual categories are thus based on the data. Barney Glaser and Anselm Strauss underline the methodological issues involved in this type of program: 'Generating a theory from data means that most hypotheses and concepts not only come from the data, but are systematically worked out in relation to the data during the course of the research. *Generating a theory involves a process of research.*'[27]

George Smith's research on HIV/AIDS provides an excellent illustration of grounded theory. Smith began from the standpoint of people living with AIDS, outlining the problems they experienced finding treatments and information about treatments in Canada. Based on this knowledge he developed a conceptual problematic focused on questions of *access* to health care and social services. By using the conceptual category of access Smith was able to generate a theory around HIV/AIDS services which was directly relevant to PLWAs. At the same time a continued focus on this conceptual category avoided creating PLWAs as a mere object of study within the sociology of health.

The field of queer theory, like that of lesbian and gay studies, is also concerned with questions of sexuality and politics. But queer theoreticians approach these issues differently than do social scientists. In particular, queer theory draws on poststructuralist theory to formulate its framework of sexuality.[28]

The influence of poststructuralism on theories of sexuality and gender is evidenced in the work of Judith Butler.[29] Butler draws on Foucault's writing on the history of sexuality. Foucault argues that in the nineteenth century sexuality was not something which was merely forbidden and silenced by a repressive state apparatus. Rather, sexuality was something which was produced in a variety of overlapping institutional locations: e.g., medicine, law, and science. A category of people known as homosexual was thus created. Foucault argues that it is useful to understand the productive nature of power, since it can enable resistance. In the case of sexuality, the naming of homosexuals helped create the conditions for homosexuals themselves to name and understand their oppression, and to resist it. In Foucault's words,

There is no question that the appearance in nineteenth-century psychiatry, jurisprudence, and literature of a whole series of discourses on the species and subspecies of homosexuality, inversion, pederasty, and 'psychic hermaphroditism' made possible a strong advance of social controls into this area of 'perversity'; but it also made possible the formation of a 'reverse' discourse: homosexuality began to speak in its own behalf, to demand that its legitimacy or 'naturality' be acknowledged, often in the same vocabulary, using the same categories by which it was medically disqualified.[30]

Butler reflects on this notion of a reverse discourse, and inquires about some of its political implications. She notes the paradox of a sexual politics rooted in identity: when lesbians and gay men challenge heterosexism, they do so by using the names gay and lesbian. For Butler this creates a serious problem: oppositional work is always reduced to the categories established and sanctioned by the dominant order. Every time someone comes out as gay or lesbian they define themselves in opposition to that which they are not: heterosexual. In this manner the adoption of an oppositional stance reinforces the ruling regime.

Butler anticipates the response of political activists to this position:

But politically, we might argue, isn't it quite crucial to insist on lesbian and gay identities precisely because they are being threatened with erasure and obliteration from homophobic quarters?

... ought such threats of obliteration dictate the terms of the political resistance to them, and if they do, do such homophobic efforts to that extent win the battle from the start?[31]

Here Butler asks us to think about strategies for resisting heterosexism which are not premised on the identities of 'gay' and 'lesbian.' She does not mean to suggest, however, that we should *never* use the categories gay and lesbian in political activism. Rather, Butler wants us to think about what we mean by these terms; she believes that while it may be politically useful and necessary to invoke these labels now, we should also think about different strategies of social change (perhaps ones not dependent on names at all) in the future.

The questions Butler raises are representative of poststructuralist thought in the North American academy. Questions of identity are challenged in favour of difference, such that lesbians and gays only 'are' in relation to what they are not. The political implications of this position are further explored: if lesbians and gay men only exist in opposition to heterosexuals, then perhaps political action should be based on a fundamental challenge to the workings of heterosexuality, instead of a mere appeal to the names lesbian and gay.

While Butler is clearly committed to thinking about the realm of politics it is useful to reflect on how her framework is articulated. Butler uses poststructuralist theory to inform political strategy; 'theory' is an entity which is subsequently applied to another, separate entity called 'politics.' She asks her readers to consider keeping the names 'lesbian' and 'gay' open – or abandoning them entirely – but she does not offer any concrete illustration of how this could work, or why it would be useful. Nor does she provide an example of antiheterosexist activism which is not based on categories of sexual identity. Butler's program does not continue the tradition of grounded and/or social theory, since the theory she offers does not emerge from the evidence collected during a process of research. From the perspective of that tradition, at best, Butler offers a theory of sexuality which can only be verified through empirical inquiry.[32]

As previously outlined, social scientists and political activists have expressed distrust of the project of queer theory.[33] I share a concern about the ways in which many queer critics generate theory without relating it to a process of research, and I believe that social scientists need to reject this kind of research program.[34] Nevertheless, I believe that poststructuralism offers some important insights into both how we create theory, and how we go about doing research. Unfortunately Anglo-American social scientists tend to reject the applications of poststructuralism in the Anglo-American university, and extend this scholarship to poststructuralist thought *tout court*. It is useful to clarify here that poststructuralist theory and American interpretations and applications of poststructuralism are two separate, yet related, endeavours.

I agree with Anglo-American social scientists that the project of queer theory is dislocated from its social, political, and institutional contexts. I do not believe, however, that this disregard for sociological methods of inquiry is something innate in poststructuralist thought.[35] Moreover, I feel that the critique of identity categories raised by poststructuralist scholars *does* have immediate relevance for social inquiry and political action. Attention to the concerns raised by poststructuralists can help us reconsider the taken-for-granted nature of sexual identities.[36] Moreover, this type of reflection can force a reconsideration of research methods within the context of a sociological framework. Although queer theory does not succeed in offering a sustained social analysis of sexual identities in the everyday social world, it can nonetheless suggest some useful interventionist strategies for how we – as researchers, as theorists, and as activists – conceive and organize sexual identities, communities, and politics.

In the remainder of this chapter, I illustrate how activists can learn from the debates over identity and politics raised within the context of poststructuralism. More specifically, I suggest that organizing around sexual identity can actually prevent a truly broad-based, fundamental challenge to how heterosexism works.

Since I am committed to a grounded theoretical framework, I first present a case study as a way to illustrate my argument. The issue to be scrutinized is bisexuality, especially in the context of HIV/AIDS education. I begin with an overview of how bisexuality is conceptualized, and go on to examine the implications of these concepts in the context of HIV and AIDS. To conclude, I return to the theoretical and methodological debates outlined above.

Monosexist Discourse and the Erasure of Bisexuality

Any mention of bisexuality brings with it contradictory and erroneous assumptions about who bisexuals are, and how we live our lives. Common myths and stereotypes about bisexuals claim that we are confused, 'going through a phase,' politically uncommitted, afraid to come out of the lesbian/gay closet, or suburban swingers devoid of sexual politics.[37] Interestingly, all of these myths assign bisexuals to one term of a heterosexual/ homosexual dichotomy: either we are really boring heterosexual suburbanites, or we are really just too afraid to come out and deal with our lesbian/gay selves. The metaphor of the fence describes this precarious situation: bisexuals are accused of fence-sitting in an attempt to claim the best of both heterosexual and gay/lesbian lifestyles.

Individuals who call themselves bisexual, like people who name themselves gay, lesbian, or heterosexual, must negotiate this gay/straight opposition. A dualism between heterosexual and gay/lesbian identities is so tenacious that it forces bisexually identified people to align themselves with one term of this polarity.[38] Bisexuality is thus lived and experienced within gay/lesbian communities, or entirely outside of them. Carol Queen describes this dilemma well. She contends that the very strength and durability of a hetero/homo division informs how individual bisexuals come to name and live their bisexualities. For Queen this means that people who call themselves bisexual may have very little in common, depending on how they locate themselves in relation to a hetero/ homo split. Queen is eloquent on the matter:

> Nobody makes it easy; I belong to and identify with a community that, finally, could proclaim, 'Gay is good,' but that found bisexuality too difficult, too close to heterosexuality, too *confusing* to embrace. The bisexuals huddled nervously in the middle, like kids listening to their parents (the gays and the straights) fight.
>
> But utopia is not at hand; the war goes on. Many bisexually identifed people I meet now that I've moved to the big city have a limited understanding of homophobia, coming as they often do from a place of expanding on a heterosexual identity. I rarely feel at home with them. It is the bisexual people who have carved out a home within the gay world, who understand homophobia and have stood up to heterophobia, who seem to be my people.[39]

Queen underlines the profound difficulties involved in defining bisexuality. Since bisexuals are always positioned (and are forced to position themselves) on one side of a hetero/homo fence, it is impossible to articulate bisexual identity and community on their own terms.

If, as common myths and stereotypes suggest, bisexuality does not exist, scholars and activists are presented with a formidable challenge. One way to respond to this dilemma, of course, is to insist that we *do* exist. The affirmation of bisexual identity can be accomplished through the publication of bisexual magazines (e.g., *Anything That Moves*), the development of bisexual support groups and services, the writing of bisexual theory,[40] and the reclamation of public figures usually hailed to be lesbian or gay.

The assertion of bisexuality as a feasible site of erotic desires is not to be underestimated. Bisexual activists contend, however, that while we need to affirm our attraction to different kinds of bodies, we also need to focus our attention on the erasure of bisexuality as a viable possibility in our culture. Activists have coined a variety of terms to characterize the negation of sexual identities other than the sanctioned positions of 'heterosexual' and 'gay/ lesbian.' I focus on three such terms here: *monosexual, monosexuality*, and *monosexist*.[41] The word *monosexual* refers to individual heterosexuals, lesbians, and gay men – to any person who is involved with people of only one sex. (The term monosexual does not apply to transgendered and transsexual people.) Moving beyond the level of the individual, the notion of monosexuality describes the prevailing discourse on sexuality in Western culture, in which there are two, and only two, categories of sexuality available. The concept of monosexism goes one step further than monosexuality, in naming the implicit privileging of specific monosexual identities (heterosexual or gay/

lesbian) over alternative positions (bisexual, transsexual, polysexual, asexual). Like the concept heterosexism, the notion of monosexism seeks to name and challenge the social relations of sexuality. In this way activists do not wish to privilege bisexual identities over those of heterosexuals, lesbians, and/or gay men. Rather, they want to expose the conceptual framework which divides sexuality into two opposing sites. By further locating the hierarchy inherent in a gay/straight opposition, bisexual activists such as Hutchins and Ka'ahumanu link the fight for bisexual visibility to a broader struggle against heterosexism:

> Heterosexuality *needs* homosexuality, to be reassured that it is different. It also needs the illusion of dichotomy between the orientations to maintain the idea of a fence, a fence that has a right (normal, good) and a wrong (abnormal, evil) side to be on, or fall from. To the extent that we collaborate in seeing homosexuality as an opposite polarity (not part of a diverse range of human sexuality), we perpetuate this unhealthy, unrealistic, hierarchical dichotomy.[42]

Hutchins and Ka'ahumanu challenge the taken-for-granted status of monosexual identities, understanding this process as an integral part of resisting heterosexism. Their intervention should be interpreted not as an attack on individuals who choose to claim monosexual identities (e.g., lesbians and gay men), but on the social processes which only allow for two opposing categories within a hetero/homo binary. Like lesbians and gay men who challenge heterosexism while respecting the choices of individual heterosexuals, these bisexual activists ask us to reflect upon the invisible workings of monosexism. In this way Hutchins and Ka'ahumanu suggest that a radical restructuring of sexuality would involve more than the affirmation of one particular identity; for example, gay, lesbian, or even bisexual. A thorough critique of sexuality would challenge the monosexist logic which orders how sexuality is conceived, expressed, organized, and lived.

The emergence of bisexual activism provides a useful point of departure for reflecting on questions of research, methodology, identity, and politics. In the remainder of this chapter, I suggest that a critical focus on monosexism forces the development of both knowledge and action around sexuality which are markedly different from the theories and politics currently offered within lesbian and gay frameworks. Methodologically, an attention to monosexist discourse offers a view of sexuality which is located in the everyday social world (a requirement of grounded social theory), without basing that location on the name bisexual (a political strategy which thus complements and illustrates a central tenet of poststructuralist thought).

Bi-Bashing from Both Sides of the Fence: The Case of HIV

Common myths about bisexuality are especially prevalent in the context of HIV and AIDS.[43] Individuals who have sexual relations with both men and women are blamed for the transmission of HIV across the sacred boundaries of heterosexuality and homosexuality. Many of the first diagnosed cases of AIDS affected gay men living in urban American centres in the early 1980s. The demographics of AIDS and HIV clearly shifted towards the latter part of the decade: however, HIV and AIDS were increasingly recognized as realities for heterosexuals, or members of what was commonly referred to as the general population.[44] Since AIDS was initially perceived as a gay disease, heterosexuals dealing with the condition were seen to be its innocent victims.[45] This discourse relied on negative stereotypes of bisexuals for its legitimacy. Bisexuals, especially bisexual men, were regarded as the agents responsible for the transmission of HIV from gay men to heterosexuals. Jan Zita Grover explains:

In these scapegoating accounts, the bisexual is characterized as demonically *active*, the carrier, the source of spread, the sexually insatiable. At the same time, sexual desire is parceled into two exclusive realms, the homosexual and heterosexual 'communities,' with the bisexual ... acting as the secret conveyor of the diseases of the former to the healthy bodies of the latter. Such a characterization is necesary to preserve the virtue of heterosexual 'victims.'[46]

Contemporary discourse on AIDS and HIV illustrates how biphobia and heterosexism are linked. By relegating bisexuals to a mythical fence, this framework privileges the term of heterosexuality above that of homosexuality.

While normative accounts of HIV and AIDS scapegoat bisexuals, similar interpretations of AIDS can be observed in lesbian and gay communities. In their study of bisexuality, Martin Weinberg, Colin Williams, and Douglas Pryor found that many lesbians were unwilling to have sex with bisexual women, for fear of contracting HIV. The comments of several bisexual females indicate that many women still believe that AIDS only affects men:

There's a myth in the lesbian community that bi women are carrying AIDS into their community. This makes it harder to disclose [one's bisexuality].[47]

Because lesbians, as a result of the AIDS crisis, are more frightened of anyone who touches sperm, I've had some lesbian women, when I tell them I'm bisexual, just get up and walk away. They see me as a potential disease spreader.[48]

The case of AIDS illustrates how biphobia can be used differently by heterosexuals and lesbians/gay men. Whereas heterosexuals may wish to avoid contact with bisexuals because they associate them with gays, lesbians and gay men may wish to separate themselves from bisexuals because they associate them with heterosexuals. Neither of these positions recognize the possibility of a viable bisexual identity.

Although biphobia informs AIDS discourse, very little HIV/AIDS education exists for people who identify as bisexuals, and/or for people who engage in sexual practices which could be termed bisexual (i.e., having sex with both men and women). Paradoxically, bisexuals are blamed for transmitting HIV, yet are somehow not important enough a population to warrant specific AIDS education campaigns.

A complete erasure of bisexuality from AIDS education is further ironic given the organizing efforts of bisexual activists around AIDS in the early 1980s.[49] Early education programs included bisexuals – an inclusion which was quickly forgotten by the mid-1980s: 'Most of what the [early 1980s] programs stressed was incorporated in what was to become the internationally renowned "San Francisco Model" for cities and communities responding to the AIDS epidemic. But what was completely ignored by everyone was the importance of the use of "bisexual" in all AIDS education and prevention literature.'[50]

Unfortunately, bisexuals remain marginalized and excluded within AIDS education programs a decade later. Activists have sharply criticized responses to AIDS and HIV which rely on identity. The group Indigenous Queers (IQ) produced a flyer for the Bisexual Caucus of the American Association of Physicians, which was presented at the National HIV Prevention/Education Summit in Dallas, Texas, in 1994.[51] They pose a fundamental challenge to current AIDS education work, demanding the recognition of bisexual behaviours and lives:

Bisexuals blur boundaries and expose the failure of rigid category identity-based prevention and education strategies for combating HIV/AIDS. This far into this pandemic, why have not any HIV prevention and education strategies been developed for gay men who have sex with women or for bisexual men who have sex with women? Is this not reflective of our society's misogyny? ... We must not let women be put once again into the position of having to be solely responsible in this matter.[52]

Like most AIDS education, research on AIDS and HIV routinely negates the very possibility of bisexuality. Such blatant disregard is amply illustrated in a national study on HIV conducted in collaboration with the Canadian AIDS Society.[53] The study focused on the attitudes and behaviours of gay and bisexual men in the age of AIDS. Over 4,800 men responded to the survey.[54] On the question of sexual identity, 81.3 per cent of respondents across Canada described themselves as gay or homosexual. Men who identified themselves as bisexuals made up 14.6 per cent of the national respondent population, while heterosexuals comprised 1.2 per cent. A further 2.9 per cent of respondents indicated their sexual identities with other terms.

Given that the survey was primarily distributed in gay male communities,[55] these figures do not tell us a great deal about any specific population of bisexual men. But they do reveal that almost 15 per cent of men who circulate in gay male communities – bookstores, bars, baths, and community centres – label their sexual identities bisexual. One imagines that this information could be usefully applied to the development of AIDS education campaigns for men who have sex with men, but who do not associate with a gay identity (although they are involved in gay male culture). If almost 15 per cent of men in gay male communities do not call themselves gay, then perhaps the creation of safe-sex educational materials which talk about men and women's bodies are in order, and perhaps these should receive prominent distribution within gay male networks.

The mere incidence of bisexually identified men within gay male communities is missed by the researchers for this project. In an effort to distinguish between sexual identity and sexual behaviour, the authors of this study actually recode the respondents according to their sexual partners during the previous year. They propose three categories: individuals who have had sexual relations only with men in the past year (described quite simply as gay); men who have only had sexual relations with men in the past year, but who have had female partners in the past (recoded as gay men with previous heterosexual experience); and men who have had sexual relations during the past year with both men and women (listed as 'actually bisexual'). Taking these recodings into account, the percentages of respondents alter significantly: 43.9 per cent of survey respondents were classified as gay, 13.3 per cent as 'actually' [sic] bisexual; and 40.6 per cent as gay, with a previous heterosexual experience. A remaining 2.2 per cent of respondents were categorized as 'other.'[56] In combining the variables of sexual identity and sexual experience, Myers et al. discovered that 97.7 per cent of the men classified as gay in terms of sexual experience had also described their sexual identites as gay or homosexual. Among the men who had relations with men during the past year, but with a previous heterosexual experience, 88.3 per cent identified themselves as gay/homosexual and only 8.9 per cent as bisexual. Among men who had sexual experiences classified as 'actually' [sic] bisexual, 62.1 per cent described themselves as bisexual, 7.1 per cent as heterosexual or other, and 30.8 per cent as gay.[57]

I will now unpack these relations between sexual identity and sexual experience, with particular focus on the recoding of respondents' identities. I believe that in very subtle and implicit ways this framework is informed by biphobia. The distinction between identity and experience is surely worthwhile: it allows AIDS educators and community activists to recognize the fluidity of sexual behaviour, and acknowledges that many people have sexual relations with members of the same sex without calling themselves gay or bisexual. Nevertheless, monosexist assumptions underline the coding and presentation of the data. Within the study one can only 'be' bisexual if one is 'actually' having sexual relations with both men and women. Merely claiming the name is not enough. And although an actual discrepancy between sexual identity and sexual experience is small in the case of bisexual men (14.6 per cent of respondents called themselves bisexual, and 13.3 per cent were labelled bisexual), a negation of bisexual identity has deeper implications. It is curious – perplexing, even – that although the researchers use the criteria of sexual experience as the basis upon which one's sexual identity is established, they do not present data for men who claim particular sexual identities – be they gay, bisexual, or heterosexual – but who have not been sexually active in the past year. If one's sexual identity is to be scrutinized in terms of behaviour, then the issue of celibacy raises a host of methodological issues. The researchers fail to consider such issues seriously. Men who call themselves bisexual must demonstrate that they have had sexual relations with men and women in the past year in order to be classified as bisexual. Yet men who call themselves gay do not have to prove their involvement with other men in the previous twelve months. The fleeting nature of bisexual identity stands in marked contrast to the durability of gayness.

The research team suggests some concrete recommendations with respect to bisexuality and the prevention of HIV. There is a need for education campaigns directed to men who have sex with men, but who are not easily reached within gay male communities. Interestingly, these programs are referred to as special initiatives,[58] a phrase which, as Lani Ka'ahumanu and Loraine Hutchins point out,[59] implies that bisexual behaviour is not an integrated aspect of HIV prevention strategies, but merely a 'special interest.' Inadequate reflection on bisexuality is further evidenced in the other recommendations of the research team. Myers et al. maintain that more research is needed on the question of bisexuality and risk factors for HIV transmission, that in order to create such programs successfully 'it is important to understand the questions and preoccupations of the diverse sub-groups [sic] of bisexual men and to appreciate the relevance of these issues to the risks that these men take.'[60]

Although this recommendation appears to address the issue of bisexuality (or, more accurately, states the need to address bisexuality), it is contradicted by its own language. Myers et al. begin their recommendations around bisexuality and HIV by locating bisexual men as 'special interests' for AIDS educators.

Having established bisexuals as a mere subgroup of gay male communities, the researchers subsequently divide a bisexual male sample even further: people who call themselves bisexual can be grouped as one subgroup of a bisexual population; those who label themselves heterosexual comprise a different subgroup of bisexual men, and so on.

It is surely important to consider different campaign strategies for men who call themselves bisexual, for men who identify themselves as gay, and for men who label themselves heterosexual but who behave bisexually. I have no quarrels with the research team on this issue. I do think it is significant, however, that the researchers figure bisexuality as a subpopulation of gay male communities. This conception of bisexuality is further ironic given the researchers' distinction between sexual behaviour and sexual experience in the coding of the data. A meaningful 30.8 per cent of respondents who identified themselves as gay indicated that they had sexual relations with a woman during the past twelve months.[61] Such a finding illustrates the high incidence of bisexual behaviour within gay male communities. The recommendations of the research team, however, overlook this situation. There is no recommendation for HIV education programs directed to gay men who have sex with women, despite the fact that nearly a third of the sample population falls into this category!

Myers et al. only discuss bisexuality as it affects men who call themselves bisexual, heterosexual, or some other name. They are unable to account for the bisexual practices of men who identify themselves as gay. Since they work with an impoverished conception of bisexuality (bisexuals are a mere subgroup of gay male communities, and no gay men have sex with women), Myers et al. cannot address the complexity of bisexual behaviour. As the activist group Indigenous Queers makes clear, this conception of HIV *de facto* forces the women who have sexual relations with gay men to take sole responsibility for safe sexual practices.

The study conducted in collaboration with the Canadian AIDS Society ignored the realities of bisexual behaviour within gay male communities. Bisexual AIDS activists insist that we must acknowledge both bisexual behaviour and bisexual identity in our educational responses to HIV. A recognition of such realities is especially important in the development of antiracist AIDS action. Hutchins and Ka'ahumanu provide an early analysis of the limitations of an identity-based response to AIDS and HIV.[62] They cite researchers at the Fifth International Conference on AIDS, held in Montréal in 1989, who tracked the shifting demographics of AIDS and HIV in the latter part of the 1980s. Increased seropositive rates among intravenous drug users and communities of colour were in part explained due to the bisexual behaviour of some people: individuals who were having sexual relations with men and women, but without labelling themselves gay, bisexual, or lesbian. These researchers argued that such individuals and populations create 'special concerns' for AIDS education. Hutchins and Ka'ahumanu expose the assumptions which underlie this position; despite the prevalence of bisexual behaviour, bisexuality remains a peripheral interest. They ask the pointed question: 'Are we still a "special concern," not part of every planner's basic consciousness and understanding?'[63]

Recent organizing among bisexual activists has extended this work. Since many people of colour behave bisexually – without calling themselves bisexual or gay – AIDS education which continues to appeal to sexual identity is not relevant to these individuals and communities. Indigenous Queers highlights the shortcomings of AIDS education which refuses to address bisexual behaviour:

As bisexuals, we acknowledge the fact that in many of our people of colour communities and elsewhere, we live in a world of fluid constructions of sexualities, desire, and gender. There are many people out there who have sex with all genders, in varying relational configurations, but who do not necessarily identify with sexual identity politics ... We appeal to lesbian and gay organizations to combat their own biphobia... for truly creative bisexual HIV prevention/education strategies might indeed be the key to prevention for the entire population.[64]

The tract produced by Indigenous Queers offers a strong critique of identity-based responses to AIDS. Beginning with the recognition that many people are having sexual relations with both men and women without calling themselves gay or bisexual,[65] this position reconfigures the mythical fence upon which bisexuals are placed. Instead of attributing blame to individuals who are located on that fence, and instead of urging these people to adopt a name on one particular side of that fence ('heterosexual' or 'gay/lesbian'), IQ begins to seriously consider what that 'fence' actually means with regard to the transmission of HIV. In this context, the scapegoating account of HIV and bisexuality is avoided. Furthermore, IQ outlines the severe shortcomings of AIDS education created by AIDS Service Organizations. In a brilliant inversion of biphobic logic, IQ suggests that if bisexual behaviour in part contributes to the rapid transmission of HIV in heterosexual circles, then HIV prevention programs must address the social realities of this behaviour. In this instance, bisexual activists make use of a separation between identity and behaviour in order to demonstrate the profound weakness of AIDS action which is founded exclusively on categories of sexual identity. This is not just a question of sexual politics, however: groups like Indigenous Queers claim that identity-based responses to AIDS are especially narrow in terms of race and ethnicity, since they do not account for the different ways in which sexuality and gender are conceptualized and experienced in various racial, ethnic, and cultural communities.

Attention to the case of HIV and bisexuality reveals some important insights. Contemporary AIDS discourse privileges heterosexuality over homosexuality, figuring bisexuality as the vector of transmission between these two poles. Bisexuals are scapegoated, given a hierarchical relation between heterosexuality and homosexuality; in this way, biphobia and heterosexism are inextricably linked. Despite the fact that bisexuals continue to be blamed for the transmission of HIV, AIDS education programs rarely address the realities of men and women who have sexual relations with both men and women. Bisexual activists explain that such an oversight is more than a question of sexuality: a refusal to acknowledge bisexual behaviour ignores the realities of sexuality in communities of colour. This perspective also forces women to take responsibility for educating their male partners about HIV transmission. The lack of meaningful AIDS education for people who identify and/or behave as bisexuals indicates shortcomings of AIDS prevention programs which extend beyond the realm of sexuality. Issues of gender, race, and ethnicity come to the forefront once AIDS educators acknowledge the complexity of what it means to live and/or behave as bisexual.

An educational poster coproduced by two Toronto-based groups – Black CAP (Black Coalition for AIDS Prevention); and the Black Bisexual, Gay, and Lesbian AIDS Discussion Group of the AIDS Committee of Toronto – remains one of the few examples of AIDS education which acknowledges bisexual behaviour. The poster presents a Black man embracing a Black woman in the centre of the frame. The far right-hand side of the frame contains a fragment of another Black man's figure. A portion of his head is visible, and his arm (fully visible) extends towards the first man. The man in the centre of the frame, while embracing the woman, extends his arm towards the man on his right-hand side. Underneath the image the text reads, 'Somebody else in your picture?'

This poster is remarkable in light of the issues raised by bisexual AIDS activists. It acknowledges that bisexual behaviour is common within Black communities, without naming bisexuality as such. Rather than remaining at the level of sexual identity (demanding that people come out as bisexual), the representation quite astutely recognizes that most people do not label themselves bisexual, even though they may have sexual relations with both men and women. This image offers an instance of HIV prevention which not only does not appeal to identity, but which understands the profound limitations of identity-based responses to AIDS. The very omission of the term bisexual is what makes the image so successful, creating an education program which is bisexual-positive and culturally specific to African-Canadian communities. Paradoxically, Canadian AIDS education which invokes a mantra of 'gay and bisexual men' does not offer similar bisexual-positive, culturally sensitive education strategies.

Conclusion: Knowledge and Action on Sexuality

By way of conclusion, I return to the epistemological and methodological issues raised at the outset of this chapter. American interpretations of poststructuralism submit that a focus on difference, rather than identity, enables new forms of political action.[66] Anglo-American social scientists are somewhat skeptical of this claim, arguing that we need to develop 'theory' which is rooted in the everyday social world, and stating that the project of queer theory falls short of this sociological endeavour.[67] Thinking about bisexuality proves particularly useful in the midst of this debate, since activists have challenged monosexism and heterosexism without appealing to the bisexual category.

Reflection on bisexuality reveals that the term bisexual is meaningless in and of itself. This is not to say that the term does not bring with it a corresponding concept, however vague or fluid that might be. It is to state, however, that *bisexuals are always, and only, figured in relation to a heterosexual/homosexual polarity*, perhaps best illustrated by the manner in which bisexuals must align themselves primarily with gay/lesbian or heterosexual lifestyles.[68] Like it or not, bisexuals are always conceived in relation to that damned metaphorical fence!

The framework known as grounded theory proves especially useful in light of these theoretical and methodological issues. Grounded theory demands that conceptual categories emerge from the evidence collected during the research process.[69] Why is this useful for the purposes of bisexual-positive AIDS/HIV education, and what can this approach offer to contemporary sexual politics? A reflection on the research process explored in this chapter can help answer these questions.

The presentation of bisexuality offered here began with a discussion of common myths and stereotypes about who bisexuals are: sexually confused and politically uncommitted.[70] The presentation continued with a discussion of how individual bisexuals – like lesbians, gay men, and heterosexuals – must position themselves in relation to a heterosexual/homosexual binary (that recurring fence). Drawing on the work of self-defined bisexual activists,[71] I have discussed the articulation of *monosexism* as a way to both describe and move beyond this situation.

The notion of monosexism has served to frame my analysis of bisexuality and HIV/AIDS education. I have illustrated some of the contradictions and inconsistencies of monosexist discourse within contemporary HIV/AIDS sites: that although bisexuals are blamed for the transmission of HIV, there remains very little bisexual-specific HIV/AIDS education; that research on HIV makes a useful distinction between sexual identity and sexual behaviour, and subsequently fails to apply this distinction to the men who call themselves gay and who have sex with women; that identity-based responses to HIV education are especially limited in terms of race and ethnicity, since they do not account for the different configurations of gender and sexuality within various ethnic, racial, and cultural communities; and that some of the most successful, antiracist, bisexual-positive AIDS education available does not invoke the bisexual category in its discourse.

The contradictions outlined above, which become apparent upon reflection of the specificity of bisexual behaviour, highlight the value of a grounded theory analysis. Glaser and Strauss make an important distinction between a specific *fact* (which is to say, a piece of empirical data) and a conceptual *category* (an analytic tool which can help us to understand the properties facts share, and how they go together – or not, as the case may be).[72]

While the researcher may be aware of particular facts upon beginning the research, conceptual categories only emerge as the research process gets underway. We move from specific facts to how they are grouped by shared properties, to the still higher level of conceptual categories which order these properties. These categories can then be taken up by substantive theory, and subsequently articulated within the framework of formal theory.

This research method was applied using the example of bisexuality and HIV/AIDS education. The data presented clearly demonstrate that bisexual behaviour is common, although a reclamation of the name bisexual is less frequent. Furthermore, the names individuals adopt for their sexual identities do not always correspond directly to these same individuals' sexual behaviour: heterosexual men frequent gay male baths, gay men have sex with women, and some people who call themselves bisexual choose to be celibate. The terminology of grounded theory can clarify such incongruities. We can state that specific sexual behaviours (men who have sex with men, for instance), are *facts*, evidence collected during the research process. These practices, however, are understood through a naming of the sexual self. The act of calling individuals gay, lesbian, or men who have sex with men is one of the *properties* which serves to group particular sexual activities. These properties are in turn ordered by sexual *categories* (gay, lesbian, bisexual). Various sexual categories, as well as the relations among those categories, can be understood in relation to a substantive theory of sexuality.

The distinction between bisexual behaviour and identity has profound implications for a more general theory of sexuality. Researchers tend to accord more importance to sexual identity than to sexual behaviour – a difference, I have suggested, which can be comprehended in terms of facts (sexual activities), properties (the act of naming those activities), and conceptual categories (the concepts which group and order these properties). This analytic framework has been generated through a comparative analysis of various sexual identity categories, with particular attention to gay men, bisexual men, and men who have sex with men. This comparative analysis proves especially useful, because it demonstrates the importance of suspending one's preconceived notions about how sexual identities work, and instead allowing categories to emerge from the data.

Within studies on sexuality, a comparative analysis can illustrate the limitations and shortcomings of current research in the field. In the Myers et al. survey, the researchers did not allow their conceptual categories to emerge as the data was collected. Rather, they imposed their own definition of these categories onto their research subjects and their sexual activities. In this manner we can witness the ideological workings of categories within the research process. Myers et al. posit a category of gayness which is so strong as to compel the assimilation of diverse sexual behaviours to it (e.g., the recoding of self-defined bisexual men as 'gay men with a previous heterosexual experience'), and a category which ignores its internal discrepencies (e.g., gay men who have sex with women). Since they do not address the ideological nature of a gay male category, the knowledge Myers et al. produce orders the experience of the men they study. Paradoxically, they consolidate the monosexist social relations which they, in part, set out to study.

Bisexual activists have responded to this paradox, not by insisting on the reclamation of the label bisexual (as if saying to someone 'You're bisexual!' would make it so). Instead, activists have conceived the refusal of bisexual identities as a function of heterosexism. This intervention serves a variety of purposes: it illustrates the diversity of sexual behaviours; it suggests that the process of naming sexual identity organizes these activities in a meaningful way for people; and it demonstrates the ideological workings of sexual identity categories. Perhaps most importantly, activists have suggested that the denial of bisexual possibilities must be interpreted in relation to heterosexism, a social relation which privileges heterosexuality above homosexuality through an implicitly monosexist logic: 'Pick a side of the fence, and defend yourself accordingly.' By turning our attention to bisexuality, then, we can arrive at a more sophisticated and nuanced understanding of how heterosexism works.

Dorothy Smith makes a similar argument concerning the value of a comparative analysis. She contends that contrasting different groups can provide a clearer picture of how specific social relations function: 'The explication of institutional relations brings to light not only common bases of experience but also bases of experience that are not in common but are grounded in the same set of social relations. An institutional ethnography thus explicates social relations generating characteristic bases of experience in an institutional process.'[73]

As the evidence on HIV/AIDS illustrates, the specific ways in which bisexuals, heterosexuals, and lesbians/gays inhabit their sexualities can differ drastically. Likewise, many individuals can behave bisexually, without feeling the need to call themselves bisexual. In and of themselves these varied experiences may have little in common. Yet they remain part of the same set of social relations: compulsory heterosexuality, and the monosexual categories of sexual identity it dictates. The denial of bisexuality occurs due to the strength of a hetero/homo opposition, a binary juxtaposition of sexual categories which privileges the heterosexual term of the equation. So, while individual bisexuals may have little in common with lesbians and gay men (or with heterosexuals), biphobia and heterosexism are inextricably linked.

The power of the fence, symbolically and otherwise, requires that we begin our theoretical analysis and political action not with the individual experiences of bisexuals, but with how sexuality is conceptualized, formed, and organized with a hetero/homo division at its core. Given the rather vacuous nature of the term bisexual, it makes little sense to begin one's research, theory, or political action through an appeal to the 'bisexual experience,' or perhaps its postmodern variant, 'a multiplicity of bisexual experiences.' Indeed, a simple recourse to the term bisexual can function as a means for researchers and community organizers to claim that they work with a broad conception of sexualities, when in reality they privilege and describe monosexual behaviours, identities, and communities. The interventions of activists such as Indigenous Queers, as well as the efforts of Black CAP and the AIDS Committee of Toronto, are remarkable in this light. By refusing to invoke bisexual identity, experience, or names, they begin their activism with how bisexuality is lived and experienced in the everyday social world. Such a grounded perspective allows us to understand that although bisexual behaviour is common, it is named as such much less frequently. This insight can in turn be used to comprehend the intersections of heterosexism and monosexism. We thus can arrive at a sophisticated theoretical understanding of sexuality without taking for granted the identity categories which circulate in the everyday social world.[74]

Within poststructuralist queer theory it is common to make a programatic call for theorists and activists to suspend the very notion of sexual identity.[75] The comparative example of bisexuality reveals the implicit monosexist assumptions of such a queer perspective. While lesbian and gay male theorists may decide to give up their names in the interests of political intervention, bisexuals need to make sense of how our names are rendered unspeakable.[76] As Michael du Plessis remarks, we must attend to the erasure of bisexuality in order to imagine its possibility:

> We [bisexuals] may well insist on our visibility by working through the conditions of our invisibility. To insist on the social viability of our present bisexual identities, as 'blatant' rather than shady or latent, we may need to turn the tables on high- or low-brow, recondite or popular, models of sexuality that appear unthinking when it comes to bisexuality. Such models have omitted, denied, disavowed, and even appropriated bisexuality – now is the time, actively and critically, to unthink them.[77]

Du Plessis elucidates the political stakes involved in the development of antiheterosexist strategies. The bisexual category is meaningless on its own terms. This raises the immediate question of the value associated with political or theoretical work which is founded upon the (empty) name 'bisexual.' By way of conclusion I would like to suggest that instead of organizing around specific 'objects' of sexuality, we turn our attention to the social relations which constitute sexuality as we know it, in its current form. Such a model would enact a research program which is informed by poststructuralism while still remaining within a tradition of grounded/social theory.

The suspension of identity is not only sociologically possible, it is also politically efficacious. As we observed in contemporary AIDS education, it is especially important to problematize sexual identity at this historical moment, given that it remains relevant for a select few. The act of interrupting identity is much more than a detached, ungrounded exercise in high French theory. It remains a fundamental component of developing a broad-based antiheterosexist program which addresses racial, gender, and ethnic diversity. These are the relations between knowledge and action which must be confronted by antiheterosexist advocates of the 1990s. It remains to be seen whether or not we can respond to such a challenge.

Notes

1 Escoffier, 'Generations and Paradigms,' 7–26.
2 Ibid.
3 Altman, *Homosexual Oppression and Liberation*.
4 Escoffier, 'Generations and Paradigms,' 13.
5 See, for example, Katz's *Gay American History*, Newton's *Mother Camp*, Altman's *Homosexual Oppression and Liberation*, and d'Emilo's *Sexual Politics*.

6 Edelman, 'The Plague of Discourse'; Sedgwick, *Between Men*; Sedgwick, *Epistemology of the Closet*; Judith Butler, *Gender Trouble*; Fuss, *Essentially Speaking*.

7 Examples of central French poststructuralist texts include Derrida, *De la Grammatologie*; Foucault, *Histoire de la sexualité, Tome 1*.

8 For a representative sample of queer theory texts consult Fuss, ed., *Inside/Out*; Judith Butler, *Gender Trouble*; Judith Butler, *Bodies That Matter*; de Lauretis, 'Queer Theory' iii–xviii; Sedgwick, 'Queer Performativity,' 1–16.

9 Escoffier, 'Generations and Paradigms'; Warner, ed., *Queer Planet*; Morton, 'Politics of Queer Theory' 121–50; Seidman, ed., 'Queer Theory/Sociology.'

10 Escoffier, 'Generations and Paradigms'; Morton, 'Politics of Queer Theory.'

11 Warner, *Queer Planet*; Morton, 'Politics of Queer Theory.'

12 Maynard, 'In Search of Sodom North,' 117–32.

13 Maynard, 'Desperately Seeking a Discourse'; Kinsman, 'Social Constructionism.'

14 Morton, 'The Politics of Queer Theory'; Seidman, 'Queer Theory/Sociology.'

15 See, among others: Kirby and McKenna, *Experience Research, Social Change*; Reinharz, 'Feminist Methods'; Tancred-Shriff, ed., *Feminist Research*; Stone, ed., *Lesbians in Canada*.

16 Maynard, 'Desperately Seeking a Discourse'; Kinsman, 'Social Constructionism'; George Smith, 'Political Activist as Ethnographer,' 629–48.

17 The tenets of social theory are outlined in greater detail in Fay, *Social Theory*. See also Glaser and Strauss, *Discovery of Grounded Theory*.

18 Dorothy Smith, *The Everyday World*. Case studies and the application of Smith's method are collected in Campbell and Manicom, eds., *Knowledge, Experience*.

19 Dorothy Smith, *The Everyday World*, 151–79.

20 It is useful to clarify that although Dorothy Smith contends that we need to begin with the everyday experiences of women, we do so in order to understand how women perceive their social world. This approach is most useful for making sense of the social relations which organize experience. Insofar as Smith advances a theory concerned with the social organization of consciousness, her program should not be dismissed as a subjectivist appeal to ontological foundations.

21 George Smith, 'Political Activist as Ethnographer.'

22 Ibid.

23 George Smith makes a compelling case that board meetings, conversations, and events contribute to the collection of data in the field, in contrast to objectivist qualitative research methodologies such as the formal interview. These techniques are central in terms of accessing the field outside the ruling regime. See George Smith, 'Political Activist as Ethnographer,' 641–2.

24 Ibid., 639.

25 Ibid.

26 Glaser and Strauss, *Discovery of Grounded Theory*.

27 Ibid., 6. Emphasis in original.

28 An introduction to poststructuralism can be found in Rosenau, *Insights, Inroads, Intrusions*. For a rejection of poststructuralist/ postmodernist work, see Turner, *Descent into Discourse*. For a more detailed summary of how queer theory uses poststructuralism see Namaste, 'Politics of Inside/Out,' 220–31.

29 Butler, *Gender Trouble*.

30 Foucault, *Histoire de la sexualité, Tome 1*, 101.

31 Butler, 'Imitation and Gender Insubordination,' 13–31.

32 For more on the notion of verification within theory, see Glaser and Strauss, *Discovery of Grounded Theory*, 10–15.

33 Maynard, 'Desperately Seeking a Discourse'; Kinsman, 'Social Constructionism'; Morton, 'Politics of Queer Theory'; Seidman, ed., 'Queer Theory/Sociology.'

34 Namaste, 'Tragic Misreadings,' 183–203.

35 Although critics in queer theory do not generate their theories from the evidence they collect and/or examine, one could argue that both Foucault and Derrida do create conceptual categories based on their data. This argument, unfortunately, must remain the subject of another paper.

36 For more on the value of poststructuralist thought for sociology, see Valverde, 'As if Subjects Existed,' 173–87.

37 Sumpter, 'Myths/ Realities of Bisexuality,' 12–13.

38 Ibid.; Hutchins and Ka'ahumanu, eds., *Bi Any Other Name*; Queen, 'The Queer in Me,' 17–21; Udis-Kessler, 'Present Tense,' 350–8.

39 Queen, 'The Queer in Me,' 20.

40 See Hall and Pramaggiore, eds., *Representing Bisexualities*.

41 Like all social movements and political processes, bisexual activism of the 1990s is in the process of developing terminology considered appropriate to describing and resisting oppressive social relations. Readers should bear in mind that not all bisexuals may use specific terms in the same way. Within bisexual networks and activist sites, for instance, the term *monosexual* is used much more frequently that the concept *monosexism*. The distinctions I propose between monosexual, monosexuality, and monosexism should thus be interpreted as one contribution to the development of bisexual-positive, antiheterosexist theory and activism. In particular, I am interested in elaborating conceptual phrases which illustrate the intersections of monosexism and heterosexism – a conjuncture which can be too easily overlooked if activists speak of monosexuals rather than monosexism.

42 Hutchins and Ka'ahumnau, *Bi Any Other Name*, xxii.

43 Grover, 'AIDS: Keywords,' 17–30; Weinberg, Williams, and Pryor, *Dual Attraction*.

44 Grover, 'AIDS: Keywords,' 23–4.

45 Treichler, 'AIDS, Gender,' 190–266.
46 Grover, 'AIDS: Keywords,' 21.
47 Quoted in Weinberg, Williams, and Pryor, *Dual Attraction*, 274.
48 Ibid., 280.
49 Hutchins and Ka'ahumanu, *Bi Any Other Name*, 362.
50 Ibid., 362.
51 The complete text of this flyer is reprinted in the bisexual magazine *Anything That Moves* (9, no. 38).
52 Indigenous Queers, 'Preaching to the Perverted,' 38.
53 Myers, Godin et al., *L'enquête Canadienne*. In addition to the 1993 national study, readers may wish to consult Myers, Allman, Jackson, and Orr, 'Variation in Sexual Orientations,' 384–8. At the time this paper was written (spring-summer 1996), Myers was conducting a study focusing on bisexual men in the province of Ontario. A global overview of research on HIV and bisexuality is found in Tielman, ed., *Bisexuality and HIV/AIDS*.
54 Myers, Godin et al., *L'enquête Canadienne*, 25.
55 Ibid., 32
56 Ibid., 31.
57 Ibid., 32.
58 Ibid., 82.
59 Hutchins and Ka'ahamanu, *Bi Any Other Name*.
60 Myers, Godin et al., *L'enquête Canadienne*, 84 [translation mine].
61 Ibid., 32.
62 Hutchins and Ka'ahamanu, *Bi Any Other Name*, xxi.
63 Ibid., xxi.
64 Indigenous Queers, 'Preaching to the Perverted.'
65 For empirical research which illustrates the difference between sexual identity and behaviour in the context of HIV, see Boles and Elifson, 'Sexual Identity and HIV,' 39–46; Michael Ross et al., 'Differences Across Sexual Orientation,' 139–48; Earl, 'Married Men,' 251–7; and Morales, 'HIV Infection,' 212–22.
66 See, for instance, Butler, *Gender Trouble*.
67 Kinsman, 'Social Constructionism'; Maynard, 'Desperately Seeking a Discourse'; Warner, *Queer Planet*.
68 Queen, 'The Queer in Me.'
69 Glaser and Strauss, *Discovery of Grounded Theory*, 23.
70 Sumpter, 'Myths/ Realities of Bisexuality.'
71 Hutchins and Ka'ahumanu, *Bi Any Other Name*; Indigenous Queers, 'Preaching to the Perverted.'
72 See note 71 above.
73 George Smith, 'Political Activist as Ethnographer,' 176.

74 Grounded theory's emphasis on the generation of categories is especially useful for reflecting on bisexuality, since it forces us to think about how bisexuality is lived. The frequent denial of the term *bisexual* is reason enough to avoid political and theoretical arguments which appeal to 'the bisexual experience.' For these reasons I believe that grounded theory, which shows the impossibility of sustained bisexual identities, is a more productive framework than an appeal to bisexual experience, bisexual positions, and/or bisexual locations. Such a methodological difference is perhaps especially important in the context of lesbian and gay communities (and lesbian/gay studies), wherein it is currently possible for self-defined bisexual activists to claim to represent bisexuality, bisexual identities, or bisexual communities. The interventions of Black CAP/ACT are in part so successful because they address the workings of monosexism, without representing any definitive bisexual identity or essence.

75 Examples of such prescriptions can be found in Fuss, *Essentially Speaking*; Fuss, *Inside/Out*; and Butler, *Gender Trouble*.

76 Recent efforts to include bisexual and transgender categories within (predominantly) lesbian and gay organizations become extraordinarily complicated once we realize that these sexual and gender positions are constituted in very different ways from lesbian and gay identities (e.g., heterosexism denigrates homosexuality, while it attempts to undermine the very possibility of bisexuality). An invocation of the all-inclusive category 'queer' is marked by similar contradictions, if the specificity and differences of bisexuality and transgenderism are not acknowledged.

77 du Plessis, 'Blatantly Bisexual,' 19–54.

7

Community-Based Research: Lesbian Abuse and Other Telling Tales

JANICE L. RISTOCK

There are two predominant approaches to social action research on the lives of people with marginalized sexualities: one is to critically study the structures of dominance (namely heterosexuality and its relations of ruling) as a way to understand how experiences of lesbians and gays are organized;[1] the other approach is to examine the lived experiences of gays, lesbians, and transgendered people as an important source of knowledge that somehow empowers the people studied. With recent queer theory writings that trouble sexual identity categories, there has been much debate about the merits of each approach, much of it polarized. My interest is in asking, 'How much room is there for the voices of marginalized people in research that recognizes the constructedness of experience and the constitutive work of discourse? Can we develop critical queer analyses and remain accountable to the people who tell us their stories?'

Many argue that focusing on marginalized identities as a research focus can have the effect of making that identity group the object of scrutiny, pathologizing its social problems and representing identity in a way that only serves to reinforce and circumscribe binary thinking so that the hetero/homo divide remains firmly in place. To some, the more strategic research contribution to social change, given these dangers, is to focus on critiquing heterosexism and normativity, shifting away from community-based research. However, researchers like Gardner Honeychurch[2] argue that a queered perspective in research on marginalized communities, one that, by definition at least, doesn't essentialize or fix sexual identities, can help us to avoid these effects. A focus on identity as a source of privileged 'authentic' knowledge is seen as just as problematic as positivists' reliance on observation, and remains part of the empirical tradition.[3] Feminists such as Dorothy Smith, Frigga Haug, and Diana Fuss,[4] for example, have questioned the focus on women's experience in feminist theory and practice, suggesting that we must instead look at how these experiences are socially organized as a way of rejecting any universalizing, homogenizing notions about the category 'woman.' Ethnography is the methodological approach often employed to study sexualities in this way, where the emphasis is on describing the broader, cultural context that produces and governs certain experiences and constitutes subjectivities. Bringing forward voices from marginalized social identities is not the focus, and social action goals in research are directed much more at the macro level – changing the social apparatus and systems of ruling.[5] This approach is more compatible with queer theory and its emphasis on deconstructing identity so that, as de Lauretis says, 'we could then go on to recast or reinvent the terms of sexualities, to construct another discursive horizon, another way of thinking the sexual.'[6]

Many researchers who focus on identity-based issues (e.g., gay men and AIDS, lesbian caregivers, lesbian abuse) see their work as having an emancipatory or liberatory goal that seeks to empower the groups they are working with, while doing research that leads to social transformation in a more immediate way by responding to social issues or social problems.[7] They argue that focusing on the relations of ruling doesn't do enough to rectify what has been missing from research that has focused almost solely on questions and experiences that reflect the interests of white, heterosexual males.[8] Others argue that a focus on queer perspectives that challenges the limiting borders of sexual identity categories is particularly problematic for lesbians, erases our specificity,[9] and as Holly Hughes suggests, ignores the differing effects of gender: 'That "fuck you" queer identity is more easily accessible for men than for lesbians, because of sexism and just the overwhelming reality of sexual violence. Lesbians can't stop being women and dealing with that reality.'[10]

Researching the lives of people with marginalized sexual identities, without forever concentrating on queering them or deconstructing them, is an important way of mobilizing research so that it is action-oriented in ways useful to the participants. This research that focuses on marginalized people is less concerned with pushing the boundaries of identity categories (as is queer theory), and more concerned with how accurately their experiences are represented. This view is most consistent with feminist standpoint epistemology that suggests that research has to be done from multiple social locations if we are fully to understand the social world and material realities of women's lives. In other words, in the area of sexual identities research has to be done with gay and lesbian communities if we are to get a situated understanding of the terrain and work from within a social-action framework.

Recent writings also address the ethical issues involved in representing social identities, such as writing about the experiences of gays and lesbians who may not share our own social locations or experiences.[11] Joyce Trebilcot, in her essay 'Dyke Methods,' argues against speaking for others within a lesbian feminist community, saying she 'will not try to get other wimmin to accept my beliefs in place of their own on the grounds that to do so would be to practice a kind of discursive coercion and even a violence.'[12] Some suggest writing autobiography or autoethnography as perhaps the only ethical stance we are allowed; that is, writing about our own locations and understanding of our experiences. Yet bell hooks cautions against this move, which has also been prevalent in discussions on writings about racial differences: 'problems arise not when white women choose to write about the experiences of non-white people, but when such material is presented as "authoritative."'[13] For hooks, not engaging with each other's differences is a convenient way of abdicating responsibility for unlearning racism, sexism, and heterosexism.

These issues of how to do research with a social-action agenda when working in the area of sexualities have come to the forefront in work that I have been doing on abuse in lesbian relationships.[13] I have been committed to doing community-based research that is consistent with participatory and collaborative approaches often used by researchers working within social movements. These methods are most often concerned with pedagogical uses of research as a platform for social change. For instance, Patricia Maguire defines participatory action research as having three main objectives: (1) to develop the critical consciousness of both researchers and participants; (2) to improve the lives of participants in the research process; and (3) to transform fundamental societal structures and relationships.[14] Research is undertaken as a learning process. It is an interactive, critical social inquiry where researchers and participants are analysing the named problems through an educational process. This is obviously a very different research agenda when compared to the traditional one of research as a search for the truth, where the researcher is to uncover objective facts. But even alternative approaches to research that are not driven by a positivist-empirical paradigm are often more concerned with developing a critical analysis (meaning making), and less concerned with the relationship between researcher and participant and the learning processes they engage in as part of 'doing' research.

Generally, a community-based approach is consistent with my view that I must be accountable to lesbians when undertaking research in an area such as lesbian abuse where so much is at stake, and where the motive for participants is so clearly the desire to make a difference. The context is one where there are immediate needs that are real and need to be addressed. Lesbians are experiencing domestic violence, an issue that has been ignored or trivialized by social services, the legal system and other helping professionals.[15] Current knowledge about violence against women doesn't help: lesbians are not accounted for in feminist theorizing, which has developed a gendered grand narrative that only explains male perpetrators and female victims.[16]

Yet naming the issue of lesbian abuse can hurt, too, by contributing to homophobic views of lesbians as sick and unnatural. Some lesbians therefore feel this is an issue that should be addressed within the lesbian community first. They see the dangers of this knowledge being used against us, and want to control what is known and who the knowers are. Yet their notions of 'community' and 'lesbian' imply a coherent and fixed foundational reality where one could easily gather up all the lesbians for a town hall meeting and rationally discuss the problem of domestic abuse. What of the married woman having an affair with another woman in a small town, untouched by the 'lesbian community'? While I do take pains to begin every research report with a discussion of how lesbian abuse feeds into homophobic myths about lesbians, knowing that I will be read by heterosexist readers, I am unwilling to give my efforts over thoroughly to deconstructing heterosexism as the only ethical stance for my work.

Given this dangerous, divisive terrain, it makes sense for a researcher to consider participatory models where issues of accountability and responsibility are central to the social-action agenda. Claire Renzetti, a heterosexual researcher working in the area of lesbian abuse, explains her commitment to using a feminist participatory framework: 'the model simply made sense in terms of the goals of the project: to reveal many dimensions of a problem that had been hidden and ignored, that is to give voice to the experiences of battered lesbians; to identify strategies for solving this problem and, especially to empower battered lesbians who have lived the consequences of this problem in their everyday lives.'[17] Yet at the same time I am aware of the 'inescapable backdrop of heterosexism'[18] that can remain masked by a focus on empowerment so that 'our very efforts to liberate perpetuate the relations of dominance.'[19] As a researcher I constantly have to be aware of the larger social context, and continually ask: What does a focus on giving voice to battered lesbians tell us – about lesbians and about battering? As Diana Fuss asks, 'exactly what counts as experience?'[20] Further, what are we constructing in creating a category called lesbian abuse?

Joan Pennell and I have recently written about our approach to community-based research where we use features of feminism and postmodernism and still adhere to a goal of empowerment: 'Research as empowerment is an approach to research that seeks to effect empowerment through all the stages of the research process through critical analysis of power and responsible use of power.'[21] We see the value in affirming marginalized voices that have been ignored or silenced, while at the same time we see the need to disrupt any tendencies to create grand narratives about experiences. Our focus on 'feminist links' keeps the research firmly aligned with efforts to overcome gender and other intersecting forms of oppression while 'postmodern interruptions' help us remain open and responsive to culture and context in moving towards inquiry that is deconstructive (dismantling what we are studying), and deconstructing (reflecting on how we are studying). Our view of social research, then, is to see it as a strategic activity where we engage in a double play of affirming real people who are struggling with real issues while rejecting dichotomies which categorize and rank people according to supposedly essential characteristics (e.g., male/female; white/Black, heterosexual/homosexual). Nowhere has the need for this approach been more clear than in my work on abuse in lesbian relationships.

Lesbian Abuse: Telling Tales

My struggle has been to remain aware of how constructing the category of lesbian abuse can contribute to false compartmentalizing of experiences of abuse: lesbian abuse/heterosexual abuse/women of color abuse/women with disabilities abuse. In other words a subtle effect of naming lesbian abuse is that it can mean we see issues facing lesbians as a separate, special case in which race and other social differences are erased while keeping white heterosexual women's issues as the norm and at the forefront. My response to this, then, is to do research that tells troubling tales, not pretending that lesbians are unified where we are not, while at the same time providing solid information that can be acted upon to change immediate conditions for the better and respond to lesbians who have experienced abuse.

My research involves three strategic moves in this double play of affirmation and disruption that are consistent with a focus on feminist links and postmodern interruptions: (1) researching material conditions as a way to encourage social action; (2) researching discursive conditions as way to 'unfreeze' and disrupt rigidified thinking; and (3) (re)searching myself as a way of engaging reflexivity/self-reflexivity in order to be 'answerable for what we learn how to see.'[22] Like Patti Lather,[23] who has used a similar structuring tactic to write up her empirical work on students' resistance to liberatory curriculum, I use the terms *story* or *tale* to foreground the fictive dimensions of doing research and of research findings.

Listening to Voices of Experience: A Material Tale

I have been researching abuse in lesbian relationships for a number of years now, using a variety of approaches including interviews, surveys, and a training/education project with shelter workers,[24] and I feel that a primary objective has been to document the material conditions that lesbians have been experiencing. I am aware that I am constructing a story or an account in order to raise consciousness about the lives of lesbians and to encourage action.

For example, I surveyed social service organizations in Winnipeg that offer services to victims of violence. I was interested in finding out if they worked with lesbian clients and if they addressed the issue of lesbian abuse. The questionnaire contained twenty forced-choice items. Each question also asked service providers to explain their answers or provide more detail. Of the forty-one respondents 93 per cent reported that their service welcomed lesbians. In the space where they explained their response to this question most indicated that they welcomed lesbians in the following ways: by treating them no differently than other clients (18.5 per cent); by offering nondiscriminatory services (17 per cent); by not saying they're not welcome (15 per cent); by providing literature posters and other educational materials (13 per cent); and by providing programs specifically for lesbians (11 per cent). When asked if they did any outreach to abused lesbians 90 per cent answered no. When asked how many lesbians use their services 22 per cent said between 1 and 3 per cent; 17 per cent said none; and 17 per cent had no idea.

These descriptive 'findings' are not surprising, being consistent with research that has described the barriers lesbians face in trying to access services or support for their relationships.[25] I engage in this process in the hopes that the questionnaire itself can become a consciousness-raising tool that can begin to reveal the liberal discourse that permeates most social service agencies that claim they provide services to 'anyone.' The questions take service providers through a reflexive process. For example, to one question, when they answer that they do not discriminate, they are then asked to describe specifically how they make it clear that lesbians are welcome. Further, a series of questions is asked that has service providers think through their work in relation to lesbians. My hope is that this questionnaire will serve a pedagogical purpose as well as a descriptive one, where I also get a snapshot of the context in which I am doing this work. I can use the descriptive statistics, in this case, to make the claim that lesbians are not accessing services for domestic abuse.

At the same time I have been conducting interviews with lesbians who have been in abusive relationships, and I have asked them to share their stories with me.[26] In the twenty-seven interview transcripts I have analysed to date, many interesting trends have emerged that were not predictable from the current literature on domestic violence. For example, many of the participants revealed that they had been abused in one relationship and were themselves abusive in the next; others reported that their first relationship (often with an older 'out' lesbian) was the one in which they experienced abuse. This trend in particular aroused my interest. It wasn't something I expected to find, but that emerged strongly from an analysis of the transcripts. Fifteen out of the twenty-seven participants (56 per cent) described a first relationship that was abusive. Five examples (names are pseudonyms):

Melissa

I lived with two gay men and I always knew that I was a lesbian but there was no community that I was aware of. Gay men, boy there seemed like there was lots of them, but I didn't know any women and one of these guys knew this lesbian from another city. I didn't get a good impression when I met her the first time, but then she kind of won me over and I guess I was impressionable because I hadn't really met, you know, a real live lesbian. She was about four years older, a former school teacher ... I was really taken by her, you know, this was sort of the first affection that I'd gotten from a woman which I had longed for ... Knowing that I'm lesbian and not having met any lesbians, I don't think that I would have taken the first person that came along, just because I was desperate.

Jane

It's something I had never been involved in before, had never come across any abuse in my life, so I was very sheltered. I suppose the beginning of the relationship – it was the first lesbian relationship I had ever been involved in – and I think that's why I got involved in a bad relationship. I didn't know that there were a lot of lesbians out there and I didn't think that I had that much in the way of choices.

Florence

I was in one relationship that was physically, emotionally, and in every way abusive. And a relationship right after that was not physically abusive but extremely controlled. OK, so probably the physically abusive relationship was my first relationship with a woman. And I went into it with my three-year-old daughter. And we were together for almost two years and it became violent within ... well, within a really short period of time, almost right away. And for me that's the hard part, because I've been out of this relationship for three years and now looking back on it I can't understand why I stayed, even though I've read all the books ... It would have been really nice if someone at the very beginning had told me, like when I first met her, said, 'Na, na, na stay away from her.' But because I was also very new to the community, too, that's probably a big part of it. And she wasn't, I mean she was really firmly established, and a lot of people know her. Well, you know how the community is, everybody knows everybody. So she was an insider and I was an outsider and I looked straight and I had a child. Having a child in the lesbian community makes you ostracized right there.

Robyn
It was my first relationship. First long-term relationship. But you know I was, I was head over heels madly in love, and I thought this is the relationship for life. And it started out really good. This woman was nine years older than myself. It was verbally abusive to start off with and then physically. I was, quite often had black eyes and she tried – she almost killed me once, strangled me, and this went on for three years ... I was too young and insecure about the whole relationship, gay relationships, whatever. Anybody could have walked all over me. I used to have a theory that quite often if it's going to be an abusive relationship then one of them is older and the other is younger and very naïve. I don't know if you found that in your study?

Sonia
I was just out for less than a year. This was my first experience with a woman, I didn't care which woman it was.

Presenting this trend, that lesbians who are newly out and entering into a relationship may be vulnerable to entering into an abusive relationship, allows for more immediate kinds of responses or interventions. If we can show how vulnerability to violence is part of the cost of a heterosexist context where lesbians are isolated, unable to access meeting places, and often dependent on their first love for information about living as a lesbian, then maybe we can set up supportive coming out places for young lesbians.

Addressing the material conditions in this way acknowledges the experiences and responds to the needs of victims. Like the survey of supportive services, this focus on lesbians' experiences – showing how lesbians' lives are different from straight women's – can have the pedagogical effect of continuing to break through the liberal thinking that homogenizes differences. As a researcher listening to these accounts of personal experiences I find this focus also opens up new insights into the research area that I had not considered. In current interviews I now will ask questions more specifically about women's relationship histories: Did you experience abuse in your first relationship with a woman, and why might that have been? This kind of research tale troubles the seas of heteronormativity because it makes it possible to hear normally subjugated voices.[27]

Of course, tales like these also leave much undisturbed, and were the research to end there, it might well drift towards experience as foundational and fixed. As researcher, the extent of my involvement in the production of such tales is to listen attentively to the voices of the participants, and to learn from them by noticing what new insights they offer and what commonalities of experience or commentary may be found among them. I say little during the interviews, except to invite participants to tell me their stories. The interviews are open and semi-structured in that I have a framework of questions designed to elicit their experiences of abuse and relationship dynamics. Participants usually need little encouragement or direction, having arrived with stories already composed in their heads after weeks or sometimes years of working at making sense of their experiences of abuse. I have found participants to be anxious to share their experiences as almost a cathartic opportunity, believing that the story they want to tell is important and will be helpful to others in their situation. Although my role as researcher will certainly have affected the production of the 'material tale' (I have invited them to do this and identified the common themes for my analysis), my attempt is to be faithful to their stories so that they can recognize themselves when they see my rendering of their contributions.

The Politics of Naming Abuse: A Discursive Tale

Another telling tale in this research can be told, however, through a critical, deconstructive lens. In writing a material account, I am aware of the slippery slope that is being constructed through a new category: lesbian abuse. If I turned down that path in my next analytical efforts, my research would be open – rightly – to full postmodern critique as naïve essentialism. Instead, I undertake critical and deconstructive practices by considering the discursive conditions in the interview work I am doing. I do not see the discursive turn as inconsistent with the principle of respecting participants' voices. In fact, many of the women I interviewed are themselves skeptical about the concepts available for considering lesbian abuse, and quite often spoke of the limitations of a gendered, feminist analysis that did not fit their particular experiences of abuse. In other words, they found concepts such as the cycle of violence, which is often used by counselors to describe heterosexual battering relationships, to be insufficient in capturing the dynamics that they experienced. The interviewees also raise interesting questions about the limitations of our current constructions of abuse in intimate relationships. In this kind of research the participants themselves point to the need to be willing to ask, 'What assumptions about the causes and effects of violence, the perpetrators and victims of it, can be seen in the way we talk about, respond to, and research violence?' Here I once again listen to the voices of the participants and treat them as authoritative, as part of the material tale that I learn and tell.

But I also treat the interviews as accounts – constructions that reveal their subjectivities as a way of understanding the participants' sense of self, and their ways of understanding their relation to the world.[28] This is where it is important to make a critical analysis, to ask who is speaking, from what subject location, and in what historical and cultural contexts. Whereas in the material tale I ask,

'What are the participants telling me?' in the discursive tale I explore the question, 'What does the participants' language suggest about the ways in which their experiences have been produced by the available discourses and their social positioning within those discourses?' My interview transcripts become texts where I look for discursive patterns and counterpatterns (intertextually across a number of interviews, and intensively within one transcript).

For example, within the dominant discourses available to women at the beginning of their first lesbian relationships, same-sex desire seems not to exist. The logical conclusion these women drew from the overwhelming heteronormative force of the dominant discourses was that they were extremely lucky to find someone else like them. This is evident in three of the five accounts – Melissa: 'I always knew that I was a lesbian but there was no community that I was aware of'; Jane: 'I didn't know that there were a lot of lesbians out there and I didn't think that I had that much in the way of choices'; and Sonia: 'This was my first experience with a woman, I didn't care which woman it was.'

This kind of analysis of women's testimonies can help us understand the influence of dominant discourses in shaping their subjectivities at the time they were entering abusive relationships. The desperate logic produced by the dichotomies of thought which Melissa and others described as characterizing their coming out experiences would have presented a strong push towards latching onto the first 'real live lesbian' (in Melissa's words) they could find. The coming out narrative is experienced in this heteronormative world as one where the first lover is logically constituted as the conduit from the lonely, frightening side of a binary to the happier side: 'I'm the only one' → 'There's someone else'; loneliness → community; outsider → insider; 'same-sex desire' → real live lesbian. In each case the first lover presents a crucial rescue. When, added to her discursively produced advantage, the first lover exhibits extra qualities of charm known from the broader literature of heterosexual abuse to be common among abusers, the coming out woman might well be imagined as occupying a position extremely vulnerable to abusers: 'she kind of won me over ... Knowing that I'm lesbian and not having met any lesbians, I don't think that I would have taken the first person that came along, just because I was desperate' (Melissa).

These subject positions reproduce the heterosexual/homosexual divide in which gays and lesbians (but particularly lesbians, as Melissa comments) are marginalized; ergo, abuse in lesbian relationships as an effect of heterosexism, not in the way often meant by that claim (self-loathing women taking it out on their partners), but as an effect of desperateness, to use Melissa's term, arising directly from the social effects of having no nonheterosexist discourse through which to constitute oneself as other than desperate.

I continue to look at these texts with a deconstructive emphasis that also asks what isn't being said. For example, how are these subjectivities racialized? Looking at the transcripts as representing a predominantly white group of interviewees, I can explore how whiteness is assumed and constructed in the discourses available to us to describe these experiences. For example, if race is mentioned at all it is usually only when a lover is of a different race (three of the twenty-seven participants identified as having been in an interracial relationship; they were white and they described their lovers as First Nations or Black). We have to ask what isn't said by participants, to see evidence of how we are constituted partially within dominant discourses that perpetuate the asymmetry of race relations as a central organizing feature of our society.[29] Exposing the limitations of the binaries that are at work in the discourses available to us (lesbian/heterosexual; abuser/abused; white/nonwhite; male violent/female victim) is important for questioning the foundations of our knowledge. As Magdalene Ang-Lygate suggests, 'women's realities encompass a whole range of differing identities and subjectivities, all of which are enmeshed, interconnected and inseparable along shifting imaginary lines.'[30]

My critical analysis includes looking at how interviewees are socially positioned within the available discourses by their race and class locations as well as by their sexual identities and subjectivities. I use this kind of analysis not to devalue the content of what participants have told me, but to gain insights into how agency and positioning are wrapped up in these discourses in a complex way. We must include looking at silences, deflections of discourse, and not naming as part of the work of researching the power dynamics reflected in personal accounts like these.[31]

Discourse analysis is also helpful in understanding how various ideological constructions shape people's thinking. This became clearer when a committee I was working with was trying to define lesbian abuse. The committee was, for the most part, one of like-minded lesbians: we were feminists, mainly white women, who were working or had worked in social service provision or education and who wanted to start doing something about lesbian abuse (support groups, training of service providers). Two significant issues arose during a meeting to develop a shared working definition of lesbian abuse. We had accepted the common definition, one that parallels the definition of heterosexual abuse: that it is a pattern of power and control, and that abuse takes many forms, such as physical, sexual, and emotional abuse. But the committee lost members during our heated discussions of whether or not to include sadomasochism and mutual abuse in our definitions, issues that have been contentious in other lesbian communities organizing around this issue.

Some committee members felt strongly that all s/m practices must be defined as abuse, and wanted that stated in the definition we planned to include in a brochure we were developing. Some committee members also argued that our definition should state clearly that there was no such thing as mutual abuse because domestic abuse always includes a perpetrator and a victim. These strong positions led us to become entangled in a binary debate, falsely positioning people as either for or against s/m, and believing or not believing in the possibility of mutual abuse. Surrounding our discussions was the context of our positions as lesbians working within feminist understandings of violence against women.

We came to an agreement that s/m would not be included as part of our working definition of lesbian abuse, that it should be considered abuse only if a woman experiences and self-defines these practices as abusive. Experience, in this case, was seen as (or at least treated as) unassailable knowledge.[32] Yet quite contradictorily, mutual abuse was discussed by the committee as an example of false consciousness, even when one woman on the committee spoke about experiencing an abusive relationship where she felt the dynamics were different, more complex, and muddied than in the descriptions of heterosexual battering she was familiar with. Some committee members felt she was just unable to see the 'real ' pattern that was no doubt there, perhaps because she had left this abusive relationship so recently.

We seemed to be valuing experience on the one hand (which is consistent with feminist standpoint theorizing on violence), while dismissing it on the other (when it did not fit the heterosexual paradigm of a perpetrator and victim that has become dogma). As Melanie Kaye/Kantrowitz points out, in lesbian abuse we tend to focus entirely on the victim so that we can continue to ignore the abuser's gender and assert that 'abuse is abuse.'[33] (The pragmatic consequences of this ideological position are often seen in lesbian community forums and workshops on lesbian abuse. Even when the feeling is strong that the whole issue should be dealt with by lesbians only, the most common response to the question of how to deal with abusers is to ostracize them from the community, the unspoken ideo-logic being that if one is an abuser, one is not a lesbian.)

On reflection, as a committee we did not recognize the discursive dimensions of our own efforts at logic, and the politics of its construction. Rather than trying to resolve the many dilemmas surrounding our definition, we moved on and focused on barriers to service delivery, justifying this by claiming it was time to respond to some of the immediate needs of abused lesbians. While this decision allowed us to do some action work (including workshops for service providers), it effectively shut down opportunities to focus on how we were constructing lesbian abuse, opportunities that might have shifted our thinking in ways that could have led to important insights for future social action.

It is important that research include moments like these as pedagogical gestures that raise consciousness through the questioning of forms and limits of thought available to us; it keeps the work critical. The discursive tale troubles the material tale in viewing experiences as social constructions and not as explicitly transparent fact. Examining discursive conditions and deconstructing what we are creating in the research (and what is left unsaid) are important parts of the transformative agenda. We have to be willing to see what the category 'lesbian' includes and excludes when we mobilize it for social-action purposes in research like this. Will a woman who is married and has sex with other women respond to a call for interviews with lesbians? What would a transgendered person's experience of abuse at the hands of her lover add to my work? Always interesting and challenging, deconstructive thinking becomes almost a practical necessity when we are studying the lives of people who are marginalized within dominant discourses, and particularly when we are trying not to reproduce the systemic exclusions of heteronormative cultures.

Yet this critical deconstructive tale leaves out who I am in my research efforts. Ignoring the impact of my own psychic and social location can leave my voice as researcher as inappropriately authoritative, ignoring how research 'is a self-reflecting construction of others.'[34] So what the third tale troubles is my own meaning making.

(Re) Searching Myself: A Reflexive Tale

In researching lesbian abuse I am aware that I do this work as a lesbian at a time when many researchers writing about gays and lesbians remain reluctant to declare their sexual orientation even though self-description of our social location is a staple of the kind of feminist research they otherwise endorse and practise. Their reluctance is understandable, given the dangers of knowledge that mine the career tracks of lesbian and gay academics. In a study of 351 reports on homosexuality between 1974 and 1988, only two studies, both by lesbians, name the sexual identities of the researchers.[35] Many more academics identify themselves in their published work in the nineties, now that lesbian and gay studies has developed something of a presence, as do I. But in declaring my identity what am I revealing? That I have a right to do this work? That I can be trusted? So much more of my subjectivity goes into my research accounts than is displayed in the practice of showing my membership card. The reasons for not declaring may be pedagogical and personal; in any case, the gesture is hardly adequate to revealing the influence of my particular subjectivity on the research process. As I have written previously, 'Exploring the negotiations involved in the performance of our identities in our research projects is one way of seeing how power operates.'[36]

An important part my research process, therefore, is to keep a journal and to record my reflections on tape after I have conducted an interview, as a way of becoming conscious of who I am in this process and what I am constructing. For example, my reflections from a sixth interview follow here:

I thought of one other thing. When she asked me if 'I had been in abusive relationship' I did feel myself being in an awkward position. Because I knew, I really felt that she wanted to hear that I had been in an abusive relationship. And I told her on the phone, when she asked: 'I have not been in an abusive relationship.' In this interview I revealed a little bit more, something that I haven't – that I hadn't – revealed in other interviews, and that I suppose I am still working out myself, in terms of saying that I had been in one relationship where there was (pause) emotional abuse. But it felt very difficult for me to say that because I did not want to misrepresent what I had experienced, which was nowhere near the kinds of physical and emotional torment that she has gone through. So it remains a question for me in terms of defining my own experiences.

Reflecting on my own subjectivity is in some ways the most difficult component in doing social research with an action agenda. I neither want to be, nor to appear to be, self-absorbed when dealing with social problems. My reflections reveal my awareness of the sliding scale of violence in contemporary discourse. We speak of institutionalized violence and language as violence, and identify many forms and types of abuse. Though there is a pedagogical point to the many provocative usages of the term, I am concerned about seeming to trivialize abused women's experiences by employing a far-reaching, all-encompassing definition of abuse. I try to use reflexivity in the spirit of Shoshana Felman's 'self-subversive self-reflection,'[37] not to stake my claim on the problem at hand but to interrupt my own storytelling by reserving time specifically to look behind the veil at the workings of my own subjectivity. I continually ask questions: Who am I in doing this work? How am I constituted? How am I relating to the person that I am interviewing? How do these positionings change? How does my personal history show up in the trajectories of my own will to knowledge, and to ignorance? In this level of reflection, I try to understand the personal grounds of my understandings and how they might be shaping the production of knowledge.

Accounts change, our understandings change, meanings change. I use a reflexive approach to bring forward my own subjectivity for my own self-awareness, and to reveal my meaning-making process so that I can remain accountable to participants for what I am making of their stories as I produce my own. Self-reflection is not the only form of reflexivity; I think it important also to present my work for 'peer review' at lesbian workshops and meetings so that I can continue to learn from the interaction. Whatever the form or forum, a reflexive process is risky but helpful to the goal of working past personal obstacles to the production of knowledge appropriate for social action.

The three tales I have presented here are part of a project on abuse in lesbian relationships that is committed to the primacy of the individual who is in need now, as distinct from the notion of safety through silence (don't speak of lesbian abuse lest we contribute to homophobia) or presenting falsely simplified theory (keep the feminist-gendered, grand narrative of violence in place lest we open the door to masculinist attack). My approach is to question what I am doing in my work on lesbian abuse and to keep the strands of material, discursive, and reflexive analyses firmly woven into the fabric of my research. These tales are troubled, risky, and reveal the dangers of knowledge. Still, focusing on their interplay is my way of being able to respond to social issues like violence, like AIDS, in a way that is useful in the here and now, that acknowledges lesbian existence, and that is responsible. As my research assistant once said, 'there is a fire burning and someone has to put it out.'[38] Engaging in social research is not only about helping to put out fires, but about deepening our understandings and pushing at the boundaries of what we know. Gloria Anzaldua, a Chicana lesbian, has written about mestiza consciousness, 'a consciousness of the Borderlands' that she argues needs to be part of our research and theorizing. She writes:

As a mestiza I have no country, my homeland cast me out; yet all countries are mine because I am every woman's sister or potential lover. (As a lesbian I have no race, my own people disclaim me; but I am all races because there is the queer of me in all races.) I am an act of kneading, of uniting and joining that not only has produced both a creature of darkness and a creature of light, but also a creature that questions the definitions of light and dark and gives them new meanings.[38]

Doing community-based research in postmodern times calls for some such act of kneading the material, the discursive, and the reflexive, in order to produce new meanings. I find postmodern contributions to thinking about discourse, subjectivity, and the production of knowledge very useful in trying to do this. But my continued experience of listening for hours to abused lesbians, who take the risk of sharing their troubled stories with me, is more than adequate to keep me concerned, first of all, with the feminist principles of accountability and responsibility to participants. It is not a disregard for the lived experience of lesbians and gays, but a commitment to it that pushes boundaries around categories and turns them inside out, showing that 'findings' are never neat and tidy facts that we can present unproblematically. I have needed a methodology that accommodates both the lived experiences of women living our lives as lesbians and a queered analysis of the socially constructed dimensions of experience. I find in the material tale a way of recognizing participants' valuable contribution to the production of knowledge about lesbian abuse, in the discursive tale a way of pushing the limits of understandings available to us, and in the reflexive tale a much-needed check on the subjectivity behind the research.

Notes

1 Dorothy Smith, *Everyday World as Problematic*; Kitzinger, *Social Construction of Lesbianism.*
2 Kenn Gardner Honeychurch writes, 'Any claim to a queered perspective is therefore an embrace of a dynamic discursive position from which subjects of homosexualities can name themselves and impact conditions under which queer identities are constituted. Any queer position, while it may never be fully fixed, can be declared by producing visibility through that which it is, or that which it might become under its own auspicies' ('Researching dissident subjectivities,' 342–3).
3 Scott, 'Experience.'
4 Smith, *Everyday World as Problematic*; Haug, *Female Sexualization*; Fuss, *Essentially Speaking.*
5 Smith, *Everyday World as Problematic.*
6 de Lauretis, 'Queer Theory.'
7 Maguire, *Doing Participatory Research*; Lather, *Getting Smart.*
8 hooks, *Talking Back.*
9 Walters, 'From Here to Queer.'
10 Hughes, 'Identity Crisis.'
11 Roof and Wiegman, eds., *Who Can Speak?*
12 hooks, *Talking Back*, 48.
13 Ristock and Pennell, *Community Research as Empowerment*; Ristock, 'Cultural Politics of Abuse'; idem, '"And Justice for All."'
14 Maguire, 'Doing Participatory Research,' 29.
15 Ristock, '"And Justice for All."'
16 Elliot, 'Shattering Illusion.'
17 Renzetti, 'Studying Partner Abuse,' 40.
18 Bryson and de Castell, 'Queer Pedagogy.'
19 Lather, 'Critical Frames,' 16.
20 Fuss, *Essentially Speaking*, 113.
21 Ristock and Pennell, *Community Research as Empowerment*, 9; an excellent argument for merging postmodern and feminist agendas is made by Catrina Brown, 'Feminist Postmodernism.'

22 Haraway, 'Situated Knowledges,' 583.
23 Lather constructs four 'tales' to describe the empirical 'story' of her work in *Getting Smart*. The realist tale describes the research design and process and a small portion of the first level of analysis while deconstructing textual authority by using self-reflexivity. The critical and deconstructivist tales present two different readings of students' journal entries that were collected as part of the research as a way of creating a multivoiced text. Finally the self-reflexive tale presents a 'playlet.' Lather says, 'Data are used differently; rather than to support the analysis they are used demonstrably, performatively. In other words the "playlet" stands alone, without the intervention of a "researcher" who then says what the data "mean" via a theoretical analysis' (95). Her purpose is to constantly demystify and deconstruct the realities that are created by her own scientific process and in particular to deconstruct her researcher self as 'spokesperson who has privileged access to meaning' (96). My approach is similar in that I present three stories or accounts of my research that indicate multiple meanings but my emphasis is on the researcher needing to make strategic decisions in how meanings are constructed and presented when we are hoping for responses to complex social issues.
24 See Ristock and Pennell, *Community Research as Empowerment*; Ristock, 'Cultural Politics of Abuse'; Ristock, 'Beyond Ideologies'; Balan, Chorney, and Ristock, *Training and Education Project*.
25 See Renzetti, 'Building a Second Closet'; idem, *Violent Betrayal*; Ristock, '"And Justice for All"'; and Irvine, 'Lesbian Battering.'
26 This research has been supported by a grant from the American Association of Physicians for Human Rights: Lesbian Health Fund. My interview research is ongoing. I have completed transcribing and analysing twenty-seven interviews to date. The participants are mainly white, middle-class and working-class, between eighteen and sixty years of age, and reside in Manitoba or Ontario. Some interviews have been conducted by telephone, but most have been in person, lasting approximately one and a half to two hours. The interviews focus on the dynamics of their abusive relationships as well as their experiences with support services, friends, and family members. I have used pseudonyms for each of the interviewees to ensure anonymity. The work is not meant to be representative but rather illustrative of lesbians who self-define as having experienced abuse in their relationship with another woman. I have written more about the interview project in Ristock and Pennell, *Community Research as Empowerment*.
27 Foucault, *Power/Knowledge*, 82.
28 Henriques et al., *Changing the Subject*.
29 Flax, *Disputed Subjects*.
30 Ang-Lygate, 'Waking from a Dream,' 57.
31 O'Connor, 'Introduction: Discourse of Violence.'

32 Scott, 'Experience.'
33 Kaye/Kantrowitz, *The Issue Is Power.*
34 Clough, *Feminist Thought*, 161.
35 Walsh-Bowers and Parlour, 'Researcher-Participant Relationships.'
36 Ristock and Pennell, *Community Research as Empowerment*, 77.
37 Felman, *Jacques Lacan.*
38 Many thanks to my research assistant, Lois Grieger, for her insightful comments.
39 Gloria Anzaldua, 'La Conciencia de la Mestiza,' 380.

Part II
Spheres of Action

LESBIANS AND GAYS HAVE SUCH A LONG HISTORY of experiencing the oppressiveness of the closet that visibility can be imagined to constitute freedom. We express this faith through the energies we pour into gay pride parades, the hope we feel when the numbers out marching are high, the fear we can feel when the right trots out half-baked results from poorly designed studies to declare us only I per cent of the population. Yet now that we are well into the post-Stonewall era of visibility politics, we have encountered the limits of strength through public representation so often that much of our strategic theoretical work inside the academy and out is experienced as having this obdurate paradox at its core: invisibility is a sure sign of oppression, but visibility offers its own dangers to marginalized people. Representing sexualities can perpetuate oppressive social relations by reinscribing identities constituted within their dynamics; sustaining polarized thinking about us and them, insiders and outsiders, and so on. Many scholars and activists working for social change are drawn to the destabilizing, disruptive energies of queer perspectives both politically and philosophically as producing visibility without reproducing oppression. Yet many of us have major reservations about the range of 'truth effects' of queer theory possible in the context of an overwhelmingly heteronormative culture.

Building on the problems of representing identities and disrupting normalcy explored in the teaching and research papers represented in Part I, Part 2 explores various spheres of social action. Some writers engage explicitly with terms of pedagogy and research through much of their discussions, while others do not. All chapters can be read, however, as offering different strategies for social action and confrontations with pedagogical problems in different domains, though each author is concerned with teaching somebody something about sexualities. Read in another way, each chapter can be seen as an example of research where the researcher/author closely scrutinizes the production of knowledge at a particular site (for example, in a movie theatre, in a social service agency, in the radical religious right, in a law court) and develops a strategic analysis grounded in the demands of local conditions.

The first chapters in this section point to the pedagogical role of research in disrupting knowledge about sexualities. Jane Aronson is interested in disrupting dominant constructions of the family through researching lesbians and caregiving. Like Ristock in Part I, Aronson works through community-based research in which discursive conditions are seen as having significant effects on material ones. She acknowledges the problems of the category 'lesbian' as perhaps applying a fixed, unitary identity, but at the same time she wants to bring forward the voices and experiences of lesbians as a way to achieve a pedagogical goal: the creation of a discourse in which lesbian caregiving is recognized and thinkable both to mainstream policy makers and to lesbians ourselves.

The force of the ideology of the family is seen in its extreme form in Kristin Esterberg and Jeffrey Longhofer's exploration of the radical religious right (RRR). Within that ideology the RRR can easily position gays and lesbians as anti-family rather than working to make the discourse on family less oppressive. Esterberg and Longhofer's oppositional research is an example of researching heterosexuality, as Bryson and deCastell call for in their chapter on queer ethnography. Yet they are aware of the potential dangers of using the language of queer theory that seems to play into the religious right's view that sexuality is an optional behaviour rather than an integral aspect of self, and therefore not eligible for state protection. Unlike Ristock and Namaste's chapters in Part I, where researchers pay attention to the ethical demands of soliciting the voices and lived experiences of marginalized people, oppositional researchers face the ethical dilemmas of infiltration and deception as ways of expeditiously gathering information that is needed by community activists now.

Roy Cain describes his research with AIDS organizations, and, like Aronson, is concerned with the service needs of people with marginalized sexual identities. Both their chapters suggest that research within a heteronormative social welfare context, bolstered by liberal ideologies that deny difference, needs to draw on the experiences of gays and lesbians. Cain comments on the dangerous trend to 'degay' services as the discourse on AIDS education has shifted from high-risk groups to high-risk behaviours in an attempt to disrupt the equation between disease and gay identity. He points out that the contradictory truth effect of the universalizing AIDS education strategy has been that there is equal risk for all people, with the practical result that gay men are almost invisible in community services and that these services are not free to do antioppressive work. To Cain, what we need in order to meet the needs of gay men with HIV and AIDS is a stronger gay presence. Like Esterberg and Longhofer, he is well aware of the limitations of identity categories, but notes that the category-destabilizing pedagogy of queer theory seems to make matters worse for community AIDS workers grappling with identity politics. Each of the following chapters, written as reports on research, shows the ways we can use knowledge from processes of social inquiry to shape our intervention strategies.

Many chapters in this section deal with the issue of AIDS. Blaine Rehkopf argues that the separation made between who we are and what we do in AIDS education discourse is not only deadly in its ascription of moral responsibility for infection, but, finally, is also based on false ontological assumptions. Like Margot Francis he looks at the production of gay identity through the logic of scientific discourse; like Deborah Britzman, Didi Khayatt, and Jean Noble he studies the work of pedagogy in part by engaging psychoanalytic understandings of the production of identity. Rehkopf brings back a focus on subjectivity and the sociality of sex to remind us that in the here and now, identity is constituted through behaviour, that 'sex makes selves.' For him the pedagogical task of revising the discourse of AIDS and safer sex is both ethical and political: lives depend on producing a discourse in which sex is not understood paradoxically as both life and death.

While Cain and Rehkopf focus on the needs of gay men, both Lee Easton and Jean Noble look at the heteronormative student. Easton offers a close reading of another kind of AIDS education project: *Philadelphia*, a film designed to bring an antihomophobic message to a mainstream, white middle-class audience steeped in heteronormative thinking. In a move related to the work on reading practices explored by Britzman in Part I, Easton explores the conditions of learning produced through a certain kind of text, for a certain kind of 'reader': not the marginalized student who is Taylor's focus, but the mainstream audience inside and outside classrooms. He ends by considering how teachers can improve the pedagogical potential of their filmgoing students by exploring the heteronormative dimensions of such examples of antihomophobic popular culture.

Noble takes moral panic as her subject in a chapter that begins by looking at AIDS and then moves to recent developments in Canadian law. Her review of the Butler and Little Sisters cases suggests that we conceptualize the logic of epidemic as a form of psychoanalytically potent pedagogy that produces gays, and by extension lesbians, as obscene through the refractive impetus of denial and displacement. Given this dangerous discursive terrain, she examines the transcripts of the Little Sisters case for defence experiments to produce a counter-pedagogy up to the daunting task of disrupting the dominant discourse of queer obscenity within the highly regulated mind of a Supreme Court judge.

Diana Majury also studies pedagogical dimensions of law in her work on legal representations of lesbian identity. Focusing on efforts to seek human rights protections for lesbians and gay men within Canadian law, she explores the legal ramifications of the doing/being distinction at the centre of many chapters: legally, lesbian and gay sexuality is all behaviour, and only identity groups get civil rights protection. Majury also explores another key problem involved in engaging with the legal system: the law tends to demand homogeneity, effectively erasing race, class, (dis)ability, and other aspects of social identities with legal repercussions. Her pedagogical strategy is to complicate categories to make oppression more intelligible to the legal system; it is not a matter of whether to represent ourselves in legal contexts, but how. Sympathetic to queer disruptions of categories as false representations of human beings, she argues that in the important struggle for human rights protection, we nevertheless need them.

As you read about the troubled social terrain explored in the essays that follow it may be interesting to consider some of the broader implications for the work offered in Part I. Several authors in Part I explore how normalcy might become interested in undoing itself through the provocations of research and pedagogy. As they work through the problems of their own spheres of action, contributors in this section consider whether queer ideas of identity ambiguity and disrupting normalcy can offer a strategic approach to the work of social change; often, though, they conclude that it is politically preferable to stick with identity affiliations (not in any essentialist ontology, but acknowledging the importance of speaking in intelligible ways, and plugging into the dominant discourse of identity groups, with its already-established logic of minority rights).

What these chapters show is the lesson of situated politics, that there is not one path for social change, that different spheres of action call upon us to work in many ways, some of them contradictory to each other. We need both to disrupt identity categories and to understand their fluid construction. At the same time we need to find ways of connecting across social differences to work against all systems of dominance that confine and define who we are and how we get to live our lives.

8

Doing Research on Lesbians and Caregiving: Disturbing the Ideological Foundations of Family and Community Care

JANE ARONSON

In contemporary Canadian society, people needing support by virtue of illness or disability are pressed to rely on informal social ties for care. Health and social services are made available to them by the state only as a last resort, and as a result women in families – as wives, daughters, daughters-in-law, and mothers – step in to do most of the work of caring. This work involves 'the mental, emotional and physical effort involved in looking after, responding to, and supporting others' and implies a complex entanglement of labour and love.[1] Feminist analyses of 'family care' have illuminated the broad societal distribution of caring work and the patterns of inequity it reinforces, but have said little about relations of care and support among lesbians.[2] Sociological studies of social support and informal care have also tended to focus narrowly on heterosexual family ties. However, as lesbians we live much of our lives outside heterosexual kinship structures. Our care and responses to others' needs are less likely than heterosexual women's to be organized by ties based on marriage, and are more likely to be oriented to social networks of women. Compared with heterosexual women, too, lesbians may be less likely or able to turn to their families for care or support in times of need. The heterosexism of the broader culture manifests itself within families in a range of strained and stigmatizing dynamics – whether in the form of silences, social distance, and disapproval, or of complete rejection and hatred of lesbian family members. As a result the family-based model of care prominent in Canada simply does not work for many lesbians.

How, then, do we respond to lesbians who need care or assistance by virtue of illness or disability, and, needing care ourselves, how do we find support? In the absence of the prescriptions of heterosexual kin ties and familially based social solidarity, how are relations of care and need-meeting worked out and experienced among lesbians in the context of intimate relationships, friendships, and the more elusive context of lesbian communities?

Critical theorizing about family life and social ties illuminates the unsettling potential of these questions, and can point us in fruitful directions for analysis and action. Historical analyses of family and domestic arrangements reveal that they are both in constant flux. Rather than being static or politically neutral patterns of social relations – as the family care discourse implies – they are embedded in and supportive of particular social and economic orders and are, therefore, highly contested and morally charged.[3] Feminist scholars have addressed the rapidly shifting ground of interpersonal relationships and gender identity in this contested context: 'all individuals, couples, and groups ... must daily reinvent models of behaviour and reciprocal expectations, because those acquired from the past for various reasons no longer function.'[4] Arguably, lesbians and gay men are uniquely placed in this process of invention and innovation; they must exercise 'normative creativity'[5] and 'take more conscious charge'[6] of working out social relations and commitments based on choice rather than solely on prescription about gender or family obligation. Giddens describes gay men and lesbians as 'the prime everyday experimenters,' required to design social relations in relatively uncharted social spaces beyond dominant cultural constructions of support, commitment, and intimacy.[7]

My embarking on research on lesbians and caregiving stems from an interest in exploring the character and possibilities of such everyday experimenting. We know that caring rooted in conventionally defined family obligation and in limited notions of citizenship entitlements can be oppressive and coercive, both for those providing and for those needing care.[8] Understanding lesbian positioning and experience in the uncharted terrain outside the family care discourse may generate insights into other ways of supporting people deemed dependent or disabled. While feminist critiques of the societal division of caring work emphasize its exploitative potential, they also hold out visions of care that is freely given, well supported, socially valued, and responsive and respectful to those cared for.[9] That lesbians are required to design their own caregiving and its meaning may offer some glimpses at such visionary and transformative potential, and at the forces that foster or stifle its development.[10]

Making visible the positioning of lesbians affected by illness and disability in a heterosexist culture, and at a time when state services and state commitments to equity are in retreat, has some political urgency. In material terms exploration of the experiences of lesbians giving and receiving care in this context can offer some foundation from which to challenge and resist the impact of heterosexist institutions and practices. Conceptually this exploration can also clarify the complexities of being positioned outside the privileged discourse of family, and highlight suppressed images of social solidarity and connection based on, for example, friendship, community, and lesbian identity. The possibilities of friendship and community are suppressed in all women's lives, so that some of this analysis has relevance for nonlesbians.[11] The possibility of social support and survival based on being lesbian raises theoretical questions about the significance of lesbian identity as a strategic focus for action and change. In this chapter I have not pursued this line of theoretical enquiry, but focus rather on the material and political tensions embedded in caregiving for women who do identify themselves as lesbian. With this focus I do not mean to imply a fixed or static image of the category 'lesbian' (it was in fact problematized by some of the participants in the research described below), but rather want to keep in the foreground the material and nonmaterial struggles of lesbians needing and providing care in relational contexts that are marginalized and lack visibility and language. Noting the poverty of thought and language for forms of support and intimacy deemed unorthodox, Weeks emphasizes the value of focusing here on '"the subterranean social order" where diverse patterns of life are shaped and new moral communities develop. It is here, and not in the heads of theorists, that genuine "alternatives" are created.'[12]

Exploring Lesbian Caregiving Relationships

To generate a beginning description of lesbian relations of care and support in relation to illness, disability, and aging, and to consider the tensions and possibilities to which they may point, I build in this chapter on insights from the literature directly on the topic and on the accounts of lesbians participating in a study of caregiving in which I am currently engaged. Constraints rooted in the heterosexism of the broader culture are reflected in this endeavour in some particular ways. The available literature is fairly small and fairly new – signals, perhaps, of both the relatively recent politicization of issues of disability and illness among lesbians, and of the impact of heterosexism in suppressing lesbian voices. The accounts of some of the study participants have also reflected this suppression; for example, two lesbians, out in only very limited portions of their lives, explained that they had never discussed their experiences as both lesbians and caregivers before taking part in the study. In parallel, my own embarking on this project represents a coming out of sorts in the research domain in which I am established – a coming out which I would have not judged safe until relatively recently.[13]

A number of fictional, analytical, and first-person accounts give us a glimpse at lesbians facing illness, working out patterns of support with partners, friends, and families, and resisting the insults and injuries of health services and other formal institutions. Jane Rule's *Memory Board* is a fictional portrayal of two older women, partners of many years, arranging their lives to accommodate cognitive

decline and physical frailty.[14] Chris Sinding's analysis of 'The Web,' a sponta-
neous network of support that developed around a Hamilton lesbian with breast
cancer (a network in which I am involved and which was an important impetus
for this project), offers insights into the possibilities and challenges of care
between lesbians that extends beyond households and partner relationships.[15]

A number of lesbian writers are using autobiography to politicize illness, disability, and care. For example, as an instance of resistance against relentlessly
homophobic health care and legal systems, Karen Thompson documented her
long struggle for the right to care for her partner, Sharon Kowalski.[16] In another
account Kathy Rockhill articulates vividly the struggles and contradictions of
needing to be independent and to be cared for as she describes the 'fall from
privilege' that came with a car accident and her resulting physical limits.[17] Of
the painful changes wrought in the lives of herself and her partner by her injuries, Rockhill notes, 'Becky and I are not alone in this struggle with the "burden" of another's needs.'[18] Also emphasizing that other lesbians do and will
follow in their footsteps, Sandra Butler and Barbara Rosenblum chronicled the
way they faced Barbara's breast cancer and dying knowing that 'Many of my
friends will see their future in the way I handle mine. There will be others. It is
only a matter of time.'[19] And, in closing *My (Lesbian) Breast Cancer Story*,
Kathleen Martindale enjoins us to 'mourn and organize.'[20] As part of our organizing we need to become collectively more knowledgeable about lesbians' relatively uncharted journeys through caring for and depending on other lesbians,
so that we can work to change the institutional and cultural practices that make
those journeys more perilous, joyless, and isolated, and foster those practices
that ease and support them.

To complement and elaborate this literature, I am undertaking a small study
of lesbians caring for other lesbians. At the time of writing I have interviewed
eight women who have experienced either (or both) caregiving for another lesbian by virtue of her illness or disability, or needing to depend on others for
care. In this chapter I focus largely on women's experiences of providing rather
than receiving care. The care of study participants was provided in response to a
variety of health problems (breast cancer, depression, chronic fatigue, fybro-
myalgia, migraine), and consisted of different mixes of practical, emotional,
and financial help. This caregiving took place in the context of a range of different relationships: with partners, with friends, and within wider social or community networks. In unstructured one-on-one interviews women described the
care they provided and the relational contexts in which they did so. I asked
them about how they became involved in a caring relationship with another lesbian, its significance for them, how it fit into other aspects of their lives, and the
responses of others to their care.

The lesbians I interviewed responded to notices about the study placed in organizations or at events frequented by lesbians, or they were introduced to me through my own work and social networks. The resulting sample is, thus far, relatively homogeneous: all are white, employed, have middle-range incomes, live in urban areas, range in age between thirty and sixty, and identify as lesbian. As I continue with the project it will be important to seek greater diversity in the sample, so that I can explore the intersections of class, race, and generation in lesbians' experiences of caregiving. However, even with these qualifications in mind, the accounts of these first participants – rendered into taped interview transcripts – provide a basis for beginning to explore lesbian relations of care. As I integrate some of their observations into this chapter, I refer to them by first-name pseudonyms, for ease of reading and in the interests of confidentiality.

From these lesbians' accounts and from the literature I elaborate two interrelated facets of their caregiving: the social context of their care, and how they thought and felt about caregiving. The preliminary map of the external and internal structuring of lesbian caregiving generated in this way raises tensions and possibilities that require strategic attention if the transformative potential of lesbian relations of care is to be understood and realized.

The Basis of Caring between Lesbians: External and Internal Structuring

An analytical framework for thinking about the structuring of family obligations developed by Janet Finch provides a useful approach to thinking about lesbian experience.[21] Finch distinguishes between 'the proper thing to do' (142) in response to relatives' needs and how people actually 'work out' (179) what to do in the particulars of their own lives. The proper thing to do is embodied in shared understandings of 'public morality' (186) and is sustained, for example, by the ideological association of women with the home and with caring for others, the cultural prizing of the nuclear family, and the distribution of state-provided care according to the availability of women relatives. These external structures frame people's local, interpersonal worlds. They structure their sense of what they 'should' do for family members, and, while not all-determining of people's actual conduct, they represent the backdrop against which they work out their commitments to others, articulate their capacities to care, and, indeed, feel about themselves. Rachel Epstein distinguishes, in parallel, between motherhood as a social institution and as a personal experience. Just as she articulates the 'inside/outside' nature of lesbian parenting, we explore here the inside/outside character of lesbian caregiving.[22]

External Structuring of Lesbian Caregiving Relations

Within our families of origin, lesbians encounter more or less the same moral and social landscape as our heterosexual siblings. We share with them cultural knowledge of the same 'shoulds,' although our negotiation of them may be more complex or contentious. For example, limits on our siblings' availability because of commitments to spouses are likely to be taken for granted in ways that lesbians' limits because of commitments to partners may not, and the presence of their spouses at family gatherings is likely to be assumed while our partners' or friends' presence is not. However, in the portions of our lives lived outside our families – in our social and friendship networks – we occupy social spaces where the shoulds of gendered kinship do not apply, where we must work out supportive ties without the same images of public morality, and the same forms of institutional regulation and endorsement. That lesbian care relations are not regulated by the public morality of kinship or the family care discourse does not, of course, mean that they go unregulated in some sort of social vacuum. The accumulated literature on lesbian and gay social survival and activism calls attention to the host of ways in which the practices of key societal institutions (e.g., the law, health care, education, the labour market) mediate dominant cultural expectations, and thus undermine and constrain lesbian existence. In the accounts of the lesbians providing care who took part in this research, the two sites of institutional heterosexism most commonly referred to were the health care system and the workplace. From study participants' accounts and from the relevant literature, some of their practices and impacts are briefly considered.

Study participants' encounters with health care providers and with the medical enterprise were characterized by a good deal of jeopardy and anxiety. Their obvious attention to anticipating and thinking these encounters through strategically was striking. For example, two women, both caring for partners, described how they felt they needed to be constantly watchful and vigilant. Should they ask to go into the doctor's office with their partners? Should they describe themselves as partners or 'just friends'? Would either course of action jeopardize their treatment or hurt their reputations, either as worthy patients or respectable caregivers? Terry devoted tremendous energy and time to sustaining a small group caring for a mutual friend who was dying of cancer, and took her place on a twenty-four-hour hospital rota. Hospital staff and health care providers were puzzled by the constancy of Terry's care for her friend, so much so that she resorted to saying they were sisters: 'It simplified things. They knew what to do with me; each visit wasn't a hassle. Things were so bad, I didn't have the energy to take them on and educate them.' In other words, it proved simpler to fit into professionals' expectations of social support and family life and pass as a friend's blood relative.

As an extreme case of the impact of homophobic institutional practices and the absence of legitimation of a lesbian caring relationship, Karen Thompson's struggle to establish her right to care for her partner, Sharon Kowalski, stands as a blistering example.[23] After the car accident that left Kowalski physically and cognitively damaged, Thompson wanted to care for her, and proved she was, more than anyone, able to engage her and help her in her rehabilitation. However, Kowalski's father objected, and, supported by the health care and legal systems in the United States, he was able to separate the two women completely for several years, during which time Kowalski received poor care and her health deteriorated significantly. In the same register, Rockhill describes the power the medical system held over her, and in relation to the place of her partner reflects in her journal, 'When she asserts her concern as my partner, she is subjected to seething scorn ...'[24]

The lack of endorsement of lesbian caring relations stands in rather strange contrast to the experiences of heterosexual women in health and social service systems. The institutional endorsement of women's caregiving roles in heterosexual families can mean their care is coerced and that they are overburdened. The absence of alternative sources of care for those who rely on them – whether in the form of publicly provided services or of male family members' contributions – means that women are often their relatives' last resort,[25] required to engage in a paradoxical form of 'compulsory altruism.'[26] Not subject to these same family based compulsions, the absence of institutional endorsement for lesbians caring for other lesbians brings, as we have seen, quite different stresses and obstacles. On the one hand all women's provision of care to others in need is effectively put to economic and political use as public policies and prevailing ideologies exact our care. On the other hand lesbians are positioned so that we must assert our wishes and claim entitlement to provide care and to act on interpersonal commitments to other lesbians that are not granted legitimation, or, as a result, visibility or language.

Several lesbians who took part in the research found problematic the lack of endorsement in their workplaces for their caring commitments to lesbian partners or friends. Natalie observed, 'it's very isolating to be in this place – where you spend a third of your day – talking to people, and you're not out, and you do have these huge worries. It's very isolating ... It's taken me eight years. You know, if my partner were a man, it wouldn't have been like that.' It had taken Natalie eight years to develop a small number of colleagues with whom she was out and who knew about her commitment to caring for her partner. Nora also found herself in a job where she judged it unsafe to be known as a lesbian, and despite the fact that her employer had a same-sex benefits package, felt she could not risk coming out and claiming entitlements. In contrast, Gail claimed benefits for her partner and was openly out in a workplace with a reputation for being progressive. In this context she experienced her disclosure as a lesbian as much less problematic than her commitments as a caregiver. She was anxious that she lacked 'an acceptable excuse' for her unavailability for the overtime expected in her work culture, and she feared for her job security. Her experience was thus much like that of heterosexual women pressed not to intrude domestic responsibilities into the public world of work.

Study participants' accounts of negotiating heterosexism in the institutions they encountered were not all negative. Some described workplaces where they felt they could be open and were supported. Others described encounters with the health care system that were inclusive and respectful of their ties to friends and partners who were ill. Such anecdotes suggest acceptance that was undoubtedly experienced, with relief, as helpfulness. They were, however, often recounted in ways that underscored their precariousness. For example, Natalie's positive workplace relations had obviously been achieved with a sense of risk and strategy, and had taken a long time to develop. Nora noted that the instability of her workplace meant that she would soon have to begin all over again with different colleagues and superiors; she recognized that the acceptance she had achieved rested on individual relationships rather than on a more enduring institutional base of entitlement. Respectful encounters with health care providers were described, variously, with gratitude or surprise – feelings that Terry resented experiencing: 'Listen to me explaining this to you! I shouldn't *have* to be grateful, I shouldn't *have* to grovel to be recognized.'

Concern with the recognition and expectations of institutions that powerfully influence the well-being of lesbians facing illness and disability and of those who care for them, represented, unsurprisingly, a key preoccupation in participants' accounts, and a key element in the external structuring and regulation of their caregiving. Expectations or images embedded in their more immediate social worlds were also part of their accounts and represented another aspect of the moral vocabularies that shaped their caregiving relations.

Terry's family and coworkers were unable to understand why she was so committed to the care of her dying friend: 'But she's not even family!' they protested. They were, initially at least, not very supportive of her caregiving; for example, her relatives objected to her temporary withdrawal from routine family events, and her employer was reluctant to give her needed flexibility in her work hours. Effectively, their conduct reminded her that her caregiving was not considered normal or expectable.

Others described families from whom they were distant or estranged, whose disapproval of their caregiving commitments was, they felt, rooted in their dis-approval of their lesbianism. As Natalie observed, 'I didn't expect them to come in and do things for me and my partner, but I did expect they'd respect my choice and be a support in some way. And they just weren't.' Her partner's par-ents, in contrast, were very concerned and supportive. Recalling a period when she felt she perhaps could no longer sustain her caregiving or her relationship with her partner, Natalie remembered feeling that by leaving she would have been 'letting down' these parents. This memory echoes a sentiment more com-monly voiced by women in webs of heterosexual kin ties, and serves as a reminder that acknowledgment and legitimation bring with them reciprocal expectations and bonds. Natalie's situation is also a reminder of the reality that lesbians live, both inside and outside the ties of gendered kinship. Her partner's parents were themselves in poor health, and at times they required care and attention that Natalie and her partner wanted to give, despite the already consid-erable claims caregiving and illness made on their respective energies.

Reflecting on the expectations of friends, lesbians who took part in the study alluded again to a mix of responses, ranging from consistent support and encouragement to critical responses that they found undermining. Responses supportive of their caregiving resonated with their own sense that they *should* be providing needed care – a should they felt was firmly rooted in their social-ization as girls and women. Just as the gendered expectation that women care visits obligations and the potential for guilt on heterosexual women in families, so, of course, it does on lesbians.

The responses of participants' friends, who were critical of their commit-ments to care, surfaced in a competing discourse that emphasized, in contrast, the importance of independence and separateness rather than interdependence and connection. For example, Natalie recounted how friends queried her deci-sion to stay with her partner at all, and described the relief of having one friend whose partner also required some care and by whom she felt heard and under-stood: 'It's nice when you have that kind of understanding ... and I don't judge her for being in her relationship or staying in her relationship, and in the same way she doesn't judge me.' To avoid the same experience of feeling judged, Amy described how at one time she stopped telling friends and family about the demands of caring for her deeply depressed partner: 'I felt they'd be judgmental of me ... that I wasn't setting boundaries, not setting limits, not taking care of myself ... I felt I couldn't get support for what I was experiencing because peo-ple would be very judgmental.'

These reactions to Natalie and Amy highlight an opposition between auton-omy and care, such that care and connection to others is seen to limit indepen-dence and compromise self-interest. Hoagland suggests that this opposition is a false and damaging construction, rooted in the imperatives of patriarchy and capitalism.[27] I now explore some aspects of this opposition in considering how lesbians in this study actually worked out and thought about the moral basis of their caregiving.

Internal Structuring of Caregiving: Working Out the Moral and Political Basis of Caring

Lesbians caring for other lesbians must work out their commitments in a social landscape that, as we have seen, is somewhat different from that surrounding heterosexual women. While all women face injunctions to be caring and responsive to others as well as competing images of independence and self-hood, lesbian positioning outside the conventions of family obligations means that relations of care between lesbians do not conform to culturally available accounts of caring (being someone's wife, daughter, sister). In the absence of the legitimations and moral vocabularies of gendered kinship, how do lesbians understand and articulate why they care as they do? Study participants' accounts of their reasons and motivations offer a beginning of understanding with respect to these questions, and highlight different bases for caring in relations of different character and intensity.

As an instance of caregiving in response to friends or lesser-known acquaintances, Terry described how she joined a small group of other lesbians to support their mutual friend through the latter stages of cancer. She recounted that over time her family and employer became more accepting and accommodating of her actions, and came to frame their understanding of her commitment as 'sort of good Samaritan, altruistic, "Isn't she wonderful?" stuff.' Terry was appalled at this construction of her motives, feeling that it implied an offensive kind of patronage and largesse. She spoke, rather, of friendship and sisterhood as the bases for her commitment to her friend.

Social relations based on friendship are typically perceived to be less salient and enduring than ties of kinship.[28] This low social valuation effectively invalidates and trivializes bonds between friends. The dubious significance of friendship was illustrated, as we saw above, in Terry's encounters with health care providers. Janice Raymond's analysis of 'hetero-relational' culture and friendships between women illuminates powerfully how affection between women – whether lesbian or heterosexual – represents a subversion of patriarchal relations, and is, as such, suppressed.[29]

Several subjects added the notion of sisterhood to account for their commitment to responding to the needs of lesbian friends or acquaintances. Terry elaborated this explicitly: 'We'd been involved in lesbian politics and activism for a long time and had been friends for years. I wanted to stay standing beside her, in a sort of sisterhood, I suppose.' Ann, who took part in a similar concerted effort to sustain a sick community acquaintance, said: 'She's a lesbian. I wanted to do my bit with the others.' My own engagement in the Web that formed around a friend with breast cancer included this element, too. Over and above my care and concern for a friend, I knew that she and her partner could not count on the support of their families, and I imagined that they would be buffeted as well by the heterosexism within the various institutions they dealt with. However problematic the notion of community and solidarity based on sexual identity may be theoretically, the 'lesbian-ness' of my own and others' connection to them felt very central.

In these instances, then, friendships and a sense of lesbian solidarity articulated as sisterhood generated caregiving efforts that spanned households. Establishing and working out these caregiving arrangements involved a variety of tensions and challenges, as well as some clear satisfactions. Terry, for example, recalled how her small caregiving group sought the help of a therapist to work out interpersonal difficulties as they struggled to sustain their efforts. Terry felt that these difficulties were rooted partly in their particular histories, and partly in their sadness at the prospect of losing their friend, but most centrally in the dilemmas with respect to negotiating the sharing of work and responsibility in ways that all felt to be fair and not unrealistically taxing.

Sinding notes how Web members, albeit a larger group, consciously strove to ensure that people contributed by choice rather than by obligation, and that they felt entitled to ask other members for backup if they needed it.[30] Alongside such dilemmas in the working out of alternative caregiving arrangements, Sinding, Terry, and Ann all alluded as well to their satisfaction with their efforts. Ann, for example, expressed pleasure in seeing her group mobilize and 'do the right thing,' and Web members felt some pride in what they were designing and accomplishing.[31]

Lesbians describing caregiving in relationships with partners touched on some of the same tensions and rewards; they also introduced considerations in addition to the images of friendship and lesbian solidarity that underpinned other care relations. Participants caring for partners worked out the terms of their caregiving and receiving in the context of ties they regarded as primary affective and sexual relationships, the exclusivity of which mirrored the idealized form of heterosexual marriage. One partner's illness or disability thus involved the other very centrally and often, over a long period of time. The complexity of their efforts to work out caregiving and need-meeting may parallel the experiences of heterosexual spouses in some ways, but it is also distinguished by the absence of cultural legitimation for and prescription of lesbian

domestic partnerships. As discussed above, the dominant culture confronts lesbian relationships with, variously, dismissal, social sanction, or invisibility – all
of which require constant anticipation and negotiation.

Gail's thoughts about her caring, over many years, for a partner with a debil-
itating chronic illness, provides a helpful entry into exploring this complex terrain: 'When she (her partner) was sick and people would say to me, "I don't
know how you do it; I don't know how you stayed in" – not that they were den-
igrating her, but – my answer has always been, like, I never thought about it.
You don't just walk out on somebody because they're sick. I never thought of it
as a duty ... There have certainly been times when I just sort of thought "I've
had enough" ... but it's never felt like a duty or an obligation. It's just something
– life deals you these hands ... but we're still us and you pick it up from there.
Um, I can't explain it any better.' In making a distinction between caring and
duty or obligation, Gail sees her caring as something of her own design and
choice, not simply as conformity to a social template – an assertion that stands
in contrast to the sense of duty commonly invoked by wives as the basis for
their caregiving.[32] Ultimately Gail locates the basis of her sustained caregiving
for her partner in the value she attaches to their relationship. Her account is
reminiscent of Anne Opie's notion of commitment as one of four possible positions from which people provide care. Opie emphasizes that such commitment
to caring involves, at once: 'acceptance of the illness and feelings of resentment, frustration, and depression. It is not a simple process of devotion to caring in itself but first and foremost a desire to continue a valued relationship.'[33]

Reflecting back on her eight-year relationship with a chronically ill partner,
Natalie described changes in this balance between commitment and obligation.
After five years of feeling immersed in illness and caretaking and becoming
increasingly isolated, she described a period of rebellion at having 'lost my life
and my identity,' during which she detached herself and spent little time at
home. This period was followed by a time of striving to recapture their relationship, to ensure that 'the relationship comes first, instead of the illness ... Now I
can provide the things I need to and not resent them, and not feel that this is
what my life's purpose is.' Natalie's account of the changing nature of her
caregiving echoes Opie's concern that we recognize the fluidity of caregiving
relationships and the simultaneous and contradictory presence of both distress
and pleasure in caregiving.[34] Her analysis of this complexity also requires that
we recognize and better understand how caring relationships may not be
sustainable.

Describing a caregiving relationship that did end, Vera noted how, over several years, the character of her relationship to her chronically ill partner shifted
increasingly from one of commitment to one of obligation. Seeing herself as

obliged to keep caring for and supporting her partner, she struggled with resentment and guilt, feeling that the illness had taken over and 'corroded' their relationship. Her sense of obligation to care and insufficiency at not having lived up to her commitment persisted even though she and her partner had split up: 'I felt I'd abandoned her; I'd failed. I felt terribly guilty. I still do.'

This preliminary picture of the external and internal landscapes of lesbian caregiving relationships would not be complete without underscoring how often subjects had to struggle to find words for the feelings and motivations underlying their caring. Our lack of language for ties and friendships between women is a feature of their suppression. Otherwise articulate speakers, some subjects could not elaborate the basis for their commitments easily; for example: 'Well, we're friends – had been for a long time, you know. You know, we were friends. I don't know what else to say.' The absence of language is of course an obstacle in many areas of lesbian existence where our experience is either not spoken of at all or is spoken of in negative or deficient terms. In striving to understand the possibilities of lesbian relations of care, we will need language for all sorts of unnamed and unendorsed patterns of commitment and closeness, and will need to be mindful that 'The language available to describe reality, particularly such a fundamental aspect of reality as relationships, serves as a method of social control. If we can't say it, it's hard to think it, and even harder to enact it.'[35]

Next, I further elaborate on two particular aspects of study participants' caregiving: first, the tension created when there is both a sense of obligation and an awareness of choice; and, related to this, the conditions or social structuring of caregiving that render it at one extreme an isolated, unshared responsibility, and at the other, a more public and shared activity.

Lesbian Relations of Care: Chosen or Coerced? Private or Public?

The feminist literature reveals how 'family care' is structured in a coercive fashion, in that women's obligation to care for relatives in need is exacted by the conventions of gendered kinship and by the dearth of publicly provided alternatives.[36] Responsibility for those in need of help with everyday survival, and the work involved in ensuring it, are thus pressed into the domestic sphere and rendered private, not public, matters. In accounts of lesbians caring for other lesbians we can also see surfacing the possibility of coercion and the privatizing of caregiving, though they appear in somewhat different guises than they do for heterosexual women. I explore their appearance here, keeping in mind the aspiration that caregiving be freely given and sufficiently shared, and that it not feel burdensome for either those caring or those being cared for.

In her discussion of lesbian ethics Sarah Hoagland addresses the 'freely given' aspect of this vision of caregiving, and further stirs our thinking about the tension between obligation and commitment to care identified by Vera, Natalie, and Amy.[37] Hoagland strives to articulate an unoppressed and unoppressive basis for responding to others' needs, one that is anchored in the realities of human interdependence and the details of everyday life: 'I make daily choices; at one time I may choose to help another, at another time not. But in choosing to help another, I am not thereby sacrificing myself. Instead, this is part of what I involve myself in. When we regard interacting with others as a sacrifice and not as an engagement, it is time to reassess the relationship.'[38] Choice as the basis for caring resists construing responsiveness to others' needs as a constraint on autonomy and leaves no room for obligation. In study participants' accounts, however, we can identify contextual forces that constrain the achievement of such uncompromised responses to others – forces that instead brought a sense of obligation and coercion to the fore.

Amy's account of the latter stages of caring for her partner illustrates some of these compromises and constraints. Her partner's depression and paranoia meant that she trusted few people, had alienated many, and was desperately afraid of being hospitalized because of a prior and very damaging period in an institution. 'I was doing too much in a way, but there was no one else to do it. And that's the trap that most of us get into. What do you do when someone else that you do love is in pain and there's no one else there?' Amy's sense of entrapment and lack of choice is reminiscent of the sense of 'inescapable necessity' experienced by women in heterosexual kinship ties when they know they are their relatives' last resort.[39] Her observation underscores how, for lesbians, the potential for injury in heterosexist institutions can generate a coercive basis for caregiving. Her partner's previous hospitalizations had illustrated not only the health care establishment's tendency to disrespect or negate lesbian relationships, but also its power to pathologize lesbianism itself. Fearing this, Amy strove to keep her partner out of hospital, at great cost to herself. Concerning lesbians growing older, the sparse literature suggests that a central concern is growing frailty and dependence, and the fear of being isolated and marginalized in oppressive institutions.[40] The even more sparse literature that has revealed the treatment of older lesbians in nursing homes and other kinds of formal service settings suggests that this fear is well founded.[41]

Lack of confidence in publicly provided care can thus press lesbians into caring for other lesbians, which in turn creates conditions of coercion and burden, for both those who care and those who must rely on them. This reality underscores the importance of challenging heterosexist institutions in this area, and educating service providers in antiheterosexist practices. The inadequacy of health and social services for lesbians also may represent a point of alliance with other groups marginalized by dominant institutions on the basis, for example, of race, age, or culture – groups who also find their entitlements as citizens compromised.

While the absence of supportive public care has emerged as one coercive element in the structuring of lesbian relations of care, the absence of informal options has emerged as another. Amy commented, for example, that there was 'no one else there' to respond to her partner's needs. Similarly, Natalie described how isolated she and her partner became over time, recalling an occasion when she herself was sick and had panicked at asking herself: 'if I don't function, who's going to look after us?' Such accounts of bearing exclusive responsibility for caregiving all came from lesbians describing caregiving for partners. Significantly, Amy recalled how, during a period of sickness some years before, a 'team' of friends had rallied round to sustain her with meals, household help, shopping, and company. However, she felt that had she been in a lesbian relationship at that time, these friends and acquaintances would have been much less engaged in helping her, and would have thought, 'She has someone; that person should be doing it.' This reflection on the impact of couple relationships on the possibilities of caregiving between lesbians brings into view the private-public conditions of caregiving relations.

Feminist analyses of caregiving in families have been organized around a central conceptual distinction between private and public care, where *private* signifies unpaid household/family care and *public* signifies the formal, paid care of strangers. Less well conceptualized is the terrain between these two spaces, in which a range of largely unseen voluntary and maintenance activities sustain people.[42] A number of participants in this study described caregiving in this ill-defined third arena – in community or friendship networks – and it may be here that lesbian caregiving contributes most to unsettling the confining images of family care and the family-state dichotomy. Along the public-private continuum represented in participants' experiences, we can identify some different tensions and possibilities.

Heterosexual spousal relations, the legitimate household form, represent a privatizing and narrowing of the site of intimacy, caring, and belonging. Amy articulated her reservations that lesbian couples duplicate this pattern: 'I think the model of living most of your adult lives as a, as part of a couple, as a pair, is I think very limiting and I don't know how ... I think there's a real need for that human intimacy, but how to integrate that into larger communities?' In effect, lesbian and gay legal battles for equality rights and relationship recognition reinforce this dominant patterning but cannot address Amy's broader concerns. Lesbians' achievements of, for example, insurance coverage for sick partners or access to partners' medical information, confirm the privileging of domestic partnerships and represent hard-won improvements in people's circumstances, even as they may also limit the transformative potential of lesbian relations of care.[43] As the state retreats from the provision of social programs of all kinds, it is easy to imagine that any kind of informal care will be put to use by health and social service institutions. For example, a lesbian willing to care for her partner at home, freeing up an expensive hospital bed (even if she is not accorded the respect given her heterosexual counterparts) represents an all-important saving of public money. In her discussion of the politics of lesbian and gay families Weston articulates this tension between 'assimilation and transformation,' and observes: 'From insurance companies to the courts, major institutions in the United States will find it easier to validate domestic partnerships, custody rights for lesbian and gay parents and the right to jointly adopt children, than to recognize gay families that span several households or families that include friends.'[44] To Weston's list of those not recognized, we can add the kinds of caregiving networks and connections described by Terry and Ann and exemplified in the Web.

Even as we acknowledge the contradictory implications of the quest for equality rights for domestic partnerships, we can identify some points raised by study participants and in the literature that suggest ways of resisting the coercive potential of caregiving in partner relations. First, some subjects clearly felt that their commitments to their partners, and hence their choices to provide needed care, were not taken seriously or respected by friends. The unhelpfulness of this response is captured in a passage in Rule's *Memory Board*.[45] Diana describes the limitations on her life resulting in her partner's cognitive decline: 'We rarely go out because the confusion of unfamiliar places can frighten Constance, and I don't go out without her, unless it's absolutely necessary. I suppose it sounds a terribly confining life, but it is one we've learned to live with with a good deal of contentment. It's as much for my own sake as for hers that I don't want it disturbed. I have had to cut off friends who have wanted to "rescue" me from it.'[46]

Rather than seeking 'rescue' from a chosen commitment, Natalie hoped for support but 'instead of being supportive, they were, like: "Why don't you get out?" Which wasn't the answer, or it certainly wasn't the answer I needed to hear. I was angry about that. My partner was, too. So, I suppose, instead of trying to make our situation clearer to our friends and asking for that support ... like, if it wasn't readily given, we just gradually cut them off.' That support was sometimes not forthcoming illuminates, again, the prizing of autonomy and independence in contemporary culture; others assumed that Diana and Natalie must have been unbearably constrained and weighed down by their partners' needs.

Such prizing of independence and individualism inevitably renders burdensome those who must depend on others to manage aspects of their everyday lives. Natalie and Diana did not use this diminishing imagery, however; rather, they described the positive aspects of their commitments. Diana speaks of her contentment and Natalie of the joy and fun in her relationship with her partner. The privileging of able bodies and health cannot, however, be underestimated and requires much deeper analysis. In describing how she lived with longstanding chronic illness, Nancy identified the need to expand our understanding of what it might mean to politicize caring, illness, and frailty. She observed that over time her friends gradually became less and less available to her and her partner. She noted that they all had extraordinarily busy and overextended work lives, and were, as she had been when able, engaged in a range of political activities. She felt, however, that their politics were 'out there' and seemed to have no place in her and her partner's closer, interpersonal worlds.

Janice Raymond articulates this tendency not to recognize our affective ties to women as the very basis of our politics and our community. She reverses the slogan, making it: 'The political is personal.'[47] This reversal jars us into recognizing the political character of our mundane conduct in our local worlds. It calls attention to the 'radical potential of daily life,' and to the political significance of working out our caring commitments, whether in partnerships or in wider networks, in innovative and conscious ways.[48]

Having experienced caregiving for her partner as a very isolating process for several years, Natalie was encouraged by Sandra Butler's and Barbara Rosenblum's account in *Cancer in Two Voices*[49]: 'I remember being the most impressed and moved by the extended family, the organization with which these women called up friends and organized a meeting ... "This is what's going on and we're going to need help with this, this and this." They *organized* to be there. And I just thought, "Wow, could it really be like this?"'

As we have seen, several participants in this study took part in caregiving groups that were not based in partner relationships and that spanned households. Thinking of the particular needs and demands of 'socially disabled' lesbians, Kitzinger and Perkins see the promise of wider networks of support and care, and call for just such collective responses: 'Helping or caring for someone who is very distressed, very disturbed is not easy. It is often more than any of us can handle alone. Therefore we need to think collectively about how to provide for the needs of such lesbians. At present we are sometimes able to achieve this for short periods, but only in a haphazard and not very safe way.'[50]

The small group that Terry mobilized for a few months to support her friend was perhaps just such a haphazard arrangement – haphazard in the sense that it was always fragile and very strained. Terry considered it as simply practical and necessary, if terribly taxing; she did not think about it in explicitly political terms at all. In contrast, the Web was self-consciously political for many of its members. Over the months that Chris Sinding documented the group's activities, she identified efforts to 'name, reframe and resist some of the more coercive and uncomfortable aspects of informal caregiving.'[51] Clearly, that the caregiving was shared among many was a significant element in minimizing its oppressive potential; if one Web member could not follow through on a commitment (e.g., to cook, to drive to a medical appointment), she knew, theoretically, how to find a substitute. The act of withdrawing from a commitment in this way proved difficult for some members, however, even in these well-supported and permissive circumstances. Members identified, too, the complexities and tensions involved in asking for help for women used to meeting others' needs and not themselves being burdensome.

Analysis of the Web and other caregiving groups illuminates two issues that significantly influence the positioning of such alternative caregiving relations on the coerced/chosen and private/public axes. First, the availability of resources (time, money, skill) shapes what can be accomplished. The caregiving group Terry described was small, its members had little time or flexibility in their lives, and they felt very stretched. In contrast, the larger Web includes women from a range of social backgrounds, some with the capacity to give time and money and some with particular political skills and institutional connections. The comparison between these two groups raises questions about the class-based character of such alternative caregiving forms; even if the affective and political commitment to such caregiving is present, material resources are essential to their operation. Caregiving innovations in response to HIV/AIDS clearly have some transferability to the situations of lesbians in need of care, at least in the sense that both lesbians and gay men experience illness in a heterosexist social context. The transferability of AIDS caregiving formations may, in other ways, be fairly limited however; the nature of the AIDS epidemic and the amount of support mobilized by gay men and by governments likely differentiates the resulting caregiving solutions from those possible among lesbians facing less obviously urgent, nontransmissible health problems with fewer resources.

In the experiences of the participants in this study, breast cancer was the health problem most akin to AIDS in the sense of its being politicized and life-threatening. Significantly, all three caregiving groups examined here emerged in response to lesbians with breast cancer. While these groups represent only one area of contemporary lesbian activity, it may be that breast cancer evokes particular concern and engagement. A number of study participants certainly identified ways in which the nature of an illness or disability and its duration shaped their own and others' caregiving responses. For example, Gail and Natalie reflected that their partners' conditions – chronic fatigue and migraine – are poorly understood, relatively invisible, and often treated sceptically. They felt that responses to them were often problematic: impatience, disbelief, and anger. Amy felt that her lesbian community responded poorly to women with mental health problems, the 'socially disabled' women of concern to Kitzinger and Perkins.[52] Understanding of illness and disability among lesbians may prove, in short, to be as conditional and qualified as those in our wider culture – a reality reflected in our slowness to talk about and politicize caring, illness, disability, and old age.

This project concerning lesbians and caregiving is ongoing, so that conclusions are less appropriate at this stage than some closing reflections and questions. Lesbians who have contributed thus far have identified some key issues and struggles that suggest arenas for action and challenge. In particular they illumi- nate the heterosexism of the institutions and services with which we must deal and to which we are entitled when sick, frail, or disabled, or when caring for someone who is. They also underscore the need to appreciate the privilege of being healthy, young, and able-bodied, and the manifestations of the politics of disability in our everyday lives and relationships.

Strategically, a focus on lesbians caring for other lesbians has the potential to disturb and challenge both fixed images of family care and a retreating state that foreclose the possibility of alternative care arrangements and of public support for them. The literature and study participants' accounts disrupt these images and assumptions to a certain extent. Accounts of the possibilities of alternative caregiving forms, worked out spontaneously in response to lesbians in need of support, certainly unsettle the dominant patterning of caregiving that offers only family care and the hollow 'rhetoric of community care.' As well, some participants identified politically conscious ways of working out unburdensome and positive care in partner relationships, ways which are rarely discussed in the literature on spousal caregiving. That lesbian relationships are not struc- tured around gender differences certainly does not eliminate issues of power, but it may create more flexible conditions in which the dynamics of caregiving and being cared for can unfold differently.

While for some participants the lesbian-ness of their connection to those they cared for represented an important basis of solidarity and motivation, some questioned the possibility of collectively organized caring arrangements and wondered whether it would take more than 'just being lesbians to bond us.'

This question brings to the fore debates about the meaning of community and lesbian community, and about whether both ideas are of significance for women with varying histories and experiences. In talking about the project with possible participants and in community settings, I have been struck by the interest – even urgency – with which it has been greeted by lesbians in their late fifties and sixties. This cohort of women who identify as lesbians (and my own, a decade behind) will face the possible frailties and caregiving demands as we age that to some degree previous generations of older women did not. Women in their fifties and sixties who identify themselves as lesbian have witnessed or taken part in unprecedented political mobilization around sexual identities, and are more likely to give words to the systemic heterosexism that surrounds them. Thus they may be more likely to anticipate the jeopardies of being frail and needing care – as lesbians – rather differently than their predecessors. These observations are only speculative, and the intersecting effects of ageism and ableism will shape the effects of sexual identity in older lesbians' lives. Nonetheless, these women's concerns lend this project some urgency and suggest the importance of lesbian identity as a focus for working towards change.

In continuing to explore lesbian relationships of caregiving, I am endeavouring to gather a more diverse range of experiences than those represented by these first study subjects, and to pursue the tensions and puzzles arising from them. Exploration of the everyday ways in which lesbians actually work out their responses to others' needs for care, and the ways in which class, race, and generation intersect with their experiences represents an important element in the larger political project of working towards unoppressive conditions of care that value and entitle both those in need of assistance and those who contribute to sustaining them.

Notes

1 Baines, Evans, and Neysmith, 'Caring,' 11.
2 Graham, 'Social Divisions in Caring,' 465.
3 See, for example: Finch, *Family Obligations*; Rapp, 'Toward a Nuclear Freeze?'; Yanagisako, 'Towards a Unified Analysis.'
4 Saraceno, 'Division of Family Labour,' 203.
5 Brown, 'New Voices, New Visions,' 451.
6 Laird, 'Lesbian Families,' 284.
7 Giddens, *The Transformation of Intimacy*, 135.
8 Aronson and Neysmith, 'Retreat of the State.'

9 For example, Ungerson, 'The Language of Care,' 13.
10 Weston, *Families We Choose*, 195–214.
11 Raymond, *A Passion for Friends*.
12 Weeks, 'Pretended Family Relationships,' 135.
13 Aronson, 'Lesbians in Social Work.'
14 Jane Rule, *Memory Board*.
15 Sinding, *Supporting a Lesbian*.
16 Thompson and Andrzejewski, *Why Can't Sharon Kowalski Come Home?*
17 Rockhill, 'And Still I Fight.'
18 Ibid., 98.
19 Butler and Rosenblum, *Cancer in Two Voices*.
20 Martindale, '(Lesbian) Breast Cancer Story.'
21 Finch, *Family Obligations*.
22 Epstein, 'Lesbian Parenting,' 61.
23 Thompson and Andrzejewski, *Why Can't Sharon Kowalski Come Home?*
24 Rockhill, 'And Still I Fight,' 95–6.
25 Aronson, 'Women's Sense of Responsibility,' 8–29.
26 Land and Rose, 'Compulsory Altruism.'
27 Hoagland, *Lesbian Ethics*, 144.
28 Allan, *Friendship*; Friedman, *What Are Friends For?*
29 Raymond, *A Passion for Friends*, 11.
30 Sinding, *Supporting a Lesbian*, 21–32.
31 Ibid., 58.
32 Ungerson, *Policy is Personal*, 86.
33 Opie, *There's Nobody There*. 112.
34 Ibid.
35 Hill, 'A Matter of Language,' 199.
36 See, for example, Aronson, 'Women's Sense of Responsibility'; Baines, Evans, and Neysmith, *Caring*; and Hooyman and Gonyea, *Feminist Perspectives*.
37 Hoagland, *Lesbian Ethics*.
38 Ibid., 92.
39 Saraceno, 'Division of Family Labour,' 199.
40 For example, Kehoe, *Lesbians Over 60 Speak*, 56.
41 For example: Timothy Diamond, 'Social Policy,' 47; Lesbian Information Service, *Old Lesbians*, 4–7.
42 Moore Milroy and Wismer, 'Communities, Work.'
43 Herman, *Rights of Passage*.
44 Weston, *Families We Choose*, 208.
45 Rule, *Memory Board*.

46 Ibid., 37.
47 Raymond, *A Passion for Friends*, 28.
48 Weiss, 'Feminist Reflections on Community,' 16.
49 Butler and Rosenblum, *Cancer in Two Voices*.
50 Kitzinger and Perkins, *Changing Our Minds*, 180.
51 Sinding, *Supporting a Lesbian*, iii.
52 Kitzinger and Perkins, *Changing Our Minds*.

9

Researching the Radical Right: Responses to Anti-Lesbian/Gay Initiatives

KRISTIN ESTERBERG AND JEFFREY LONGHOFER

At rallies and conferences, kitchen prayer gatherings and church services, noon luncheons and school board meetings, people are discussing and debating, even studying, homosexuality. They are probing religious documents, listening to radio commentary and television broadcasts, subscribing to newsletters and electronic bulletin boards, choosing candidates, donating money, and writing letters. They are storming the ballot boxes, running candidates for public office, conducting stealth campaigns, forming political action committees (PACs), amassing treasure chests, and building new constituencies. This disparate group of organizations and individuals is often called the new religious right. And with renewed zeal, its members are choosing to make homosexuality politically, culturally, and religiously problematic.

In this chapter, we explore the activities of the religious right in recent anti-gay and lesbian initiatives. First, we provide a brief historical sketch, focusing on the Christian dimension of the movement. Our purpose here is to provide background on some of the key activists and organizations currently devoting their resources to anti-lesbian/gay/bisexual projects. We discuss the emergence of these campaigns in three states – Colorado, Oregon, and Missouri – and examine anti-lesbian/gay/bisexual campaigns in light of the framing processes that structure conservative Christian activism.[1] We then examine several problems involved in conducting oppositional research, including the tensions between the activist and academic roles of opposition researchers, and issues of power and representation in doing this type of research.

Recent Theological Divisions: Church and State

In considering right-wing Christian activism we must understand several recent theological divisions and trends among American conservative churches. First, during this century most evangelical Christians (premillennialists) have believed it is impossible to undertake personal actions towards transformation of this world until after Jesus returns. For these believers, though there would be social chaos and cataclysm in the intervening period, only Christ could undertake the actions necessary to establish the millennium, a period of one thousand years during which Christ would reign on earth. Postmillennialists, on the other hand, imagine a world in which human action is not only necessary, but Christ's return will not lead to the establishment of the millennium *without* the deliberate and certain actions of Christian soldiers and political activists. Though these are few in number and often extreme in position, they often set the parameters for the wider debates among religious right activists and shift the discourse rightward.[2] When extremists such as R.J. Rushdoony (known as the father of the U.S. Christian reconstructionist and home schooling movements) advocate the death penalty for homosexuals, for example, laws to circumscribe lesbians, gays, and bisexuals' access to the political process seem, in comparison, relatively mild and reasonable.

At present these groups are setting aside their theological differences and have joined forces in a battle against the generalized threat of liberalism and secular humanism as represented by such disparate groups and popular icons as the American Civil Liberties Union and the talking purple dinosaur Barney. The issue of homosexuality is central to this coalition. In the view of traditionalists the increased visibility of lesbians, gays, and bisexuals and campaigns for gay/lesbian/bisexual rights represent the final assault on morality, the family, the economic order, the strength of the nation, and the masculinist conceptions of gender that sustain these institutions. The flowering of a queer social presence in the 1970s and the 1980s, combined with what traditionalists perceived as the breakdown of the family, signaled to some religious conservatives that the end of time was upon us. In these activists' eyes, the gains of the women's movement and the gay and lesbian rights movement were a clear sign of the need for action.

Religious conservatives have pioneered political mobilization at the grass roots level in many ways, and have formed impressive coalitions linking many formerly reticent Christians (those not likely in fairly recent times to embrace or condone participation in the affairs of the secular state) with others who have no such qualms, including those who would go beyond mere political participation to imagine a Christian theocracy. Some would argue that Richard Viguerie's now infamous direct mail campaigns to conservative Americans signaled the beginning of 'new right' efforts. Yet we argue that the longstanding organizational bases for mass mobilization such as church organizations, conventions, denominations, schools, newsletters, prayer and Bible study groups, and radio and television broadcast constituencies must be studied and analysed in their own right.

These grass-roots organizations have not received the scholarly attention they deserve. The lack of attention paid to this kind of research may, in part, result from the historic tendency to regard social movements as inevitably progressive in nature or based in some imagined working-class struggles.[3] It is also likely that our failure to focus on these issues results from a preoccupation with a kind of hagiographic writing of history, by liberal and right-wing scholars alike. See, for example, the unfortunate observation by Hixson, who argues that scholars have not paid sufficient attention to groups on the far right, partly 'because they have not proved particularly durable.'[4] It is especially important for those organizing the struggle against anti-lesbian/ gay/bisexual activities to recognize that these groups are not only durable, contrary to Hixson's observation, but that they often set the agendas for debates among moderate right-wing groups. And though specific organizations may ebb and flow, ideologically they endure, and remain powerfully persuasive and influential. Three groups that deserve special attention because they have played key roles in helping to strategize anti-gay and lesbian initiatives are the Traditional Values Coalition, the Christian Coalition, and Focus on the Family. We began studying these groups in 1994, when religious right groups in Missouri began collecting signatures for an anti-lesbian/gay ballot initiative. One of us was involved in the coordinating committee of the statewide group that formed to fight the initiative; the other was a founding member of an opposition research group affiliated with that effort.

Initially our attempts at opposition research were aimed at learning about right-wing groups nationally and those that were organizing in Missouri. We sought out publications by national organizations conducting opposition research, such as the Institute for First Amendment Studies, the National Gay and Lesbian Task Force, People for the American Way, and so forth.[5] Then we joined the mailing lists of a large number of national and regional right-wing groups. Along with other Missouri activists we sought out local and statewide right-wing Christian papers, publications, and flyers, as well as letters to the editor, paid advertisements, and articles in mainstream publications. Some activists sporadically monitored local Christian broadcast programming, and for a brief period one member of our research team attended a fundamentalist church we believed was active in the anti-lesbian/gay effort. Lesbian/bisexual/ gay activists openly attended public meetings held by Christian right groups.

As the immediate threat of a ballot initiative passed we began to focus less on local efforts and more on national debates and organizations. Through a donation to Focus on the Family, we were able to obtain several years of back issues of their publications, and through a personal contact at a local conservative church school we were able to obtain additional copies. More recently we have relied on right-wing writings available on the internet.

The Christian Coalition

As Sara Diamond's book *Spiritual Warfare* was going to press in 1989, Pat Robertson was busy forming what was to become one of the largest and most effective grass-roots political organizations in the history of Christian activism: the Christian Coalition. In a letter to new members Robertson writes, 'I founded the Christian Coalition as a pro-family citizen action organization to impact public policy on a local, state, and national level, to teach Christians effective citizenship, and to promote Christian values in government.' A Christian Coalition brochure lists as among the organization's stated objectives: (1) to provide 'America's 40 million Christian voters with the information and knowledge they need to make sure Christian voices are heard in government'; (2) to represent 'Christians before the U.S. Congress, state legislatures and local governing bodies'; (3) to register 'Christians to vote and make sure they cast ballots on Election Day'; and (4) to protest, 'unfair and biased treatment of Christians by the news media, the entertainment industry and officials in government.' The Coalition now boasts more than one million members, 900 local chapters in fifty U.S. states (with full-time staff in twenty states), thousands of precinct workers and church liaison leaders, and a $12 million annual budget (a figure that does not include money collected and spent at the local level). However, these figures cannot begin to capture the reach of Robertson's Christian empire. He controls, administers, or significantly influences the Christian Broadcasting Network, the 700 Club (founded in 1977), the Family Channel, Standard News, Regent University (complete with law and journalism schools), and the American Center for Law and Justice.

Perhaps the second best-known figure in the Christian Coalition is its youthful former executive director, Ralph Reed. Reed has attempted to soften the right's rhetoric by insisting that they are not attempting to impose Christian values, preach hate, or promote intolerance. In his book *Politically Incorrect* Reed outlines the strategies for the mainstreaming of Christian right agendas. Reed argues that evangelical Christians are concerned as much about the economy, taxes, and fiscal responsibility as they are with larger moral questions.

Like other religious right groups, the Coalition garners support for its anti-lesbian/gay agenda by promoting the converted Christian 'former homosexual,' and by depicting gays as recruiting children. For example, a recent 700 Club *Fact Sheet* (18 March 1994) announced that 'The importance of the battle over the homosexual agenda in our schools can be seen most clearly in the testimony of Marc Shelton, a former homosexual who was once a student at a school for homosexuals in New York City and is now HIV positive.' Speaking of gay activists, 'ex-gay' Shelton said, 'They're just targeting (children) at a very vulnerable point in their life, where these kids are actually believing that it's okay to be this way and to act this way. It happened with me. I'm a pure example of that fact, and my concern is for all the other kids out there in the world.'

To spread their message of 'Christian love' the Coalition helps local organizations by providing staff, advertising and media, and financial resources. Through their Congressional Scorecard they target supporters of welfare, abortion, and gay, lesbian, and bisexual rights. Through their television and radio networks, press service, newspapers and newsletters, direct mail, and vast network of grass-roots organizations, the Christian Coalition is able to mobilize millions of voters.[6]

Focus on the Family

Colorado Springs–based Focus on the Family, founded in 1977, is headed by licensed psychologist Dr James Dobson.[7] In their recruitment brochure *Helping You Build a Healthier Home* Dobson writes: 'At Focus on the Family, we believe that only a full-fledged return to biblical concepts of morality, fidelity and parental leadership in the home will halt the disintegration of the family. That is the message we bring to millions of homes across the continent each week.' And with a $78 million annual budget, a thousand employees, eight publications, and five different radio productions (aired on more than 1,600 stations around the world), Dobson's organization can claim to have enormous impact.

Focus on the Family has made significant inroads into Canada (as well as many other nations). Their Canadian association, headquartered in Vancouver, was established in 1983. Their radio broadcast is heard on 253 secular radio stations across Canada, and each month more than 130,000 households receive a copy of their magazine.[8]

The zeal with which Focus on the Family pursues the anti-gay and lesbian agenda differentiates them from other Christian right organizations and efforts, including the Christian Coalition. On this topic it is instructive to quote at length from one of their most widely circulated publications, *Citizen*, the magazine for Christian political activists.[9] *Citizen* regularly features 'scientific' findings, human interest stories, personal narratives, and political strategies focusing on homosexuality. Homosexuality is persistently referred to as a compulsive behavior disorder that is 'destructive to the individual' and likely to lead to death.[10] The following question and answer is typical. In response to the question 'Many great historical figures were gay?' *Citizen* responded, 'Men and women have been deviled with sins against nature throughout the ages. A number of historical figures have made contributions to society, in spite of their infidelity and afflictions. Just because a great man was syphilitic doesn't make the case for special rights for syphilitics.'[11]

Focus on the Family has been a leader in the anti-lesbian/gay ballot initiative campaigns, priding itself on providing materials for local groups and currying support in its columns and articles for Colorado's Amendment 2.[12] They were amply represented at a May 1994 national conference to discuss anti-gay strategies and tactics organized by Colorado for Family Values. Their research director was a keynote speaker at that conference.

Traditional Values Coalition

Perhaps the most active anti-gay and lesbian Christian right activist is Lou Sheldon, founder of the Traditional Values Coalition, based in Anaheim, California, and founded in 1983. Virulently anti-gay, Lou Sheldon has been quoted as saying that homosexuality 'is the most pernicious evil today. We must stop it before it spreads throughout the nation like a cancer.'[13] The Traditional Values Coalition has more than 25,000 affiliated churches in seventeen states (half in California). TVC sponsored an anti-lesbian/gay ballot initiative in Arizona in 1994, and helped organize similar efforts in Colorado, Washington, Oregon, and Missouri. One of the tools the TVC has used to garner support for its anti-gay/lesbian message is the video *Gay Rights, Special Rights*. In this video, which was distributed free to all members of the U.S. Congress, lesbians and gay men are depicted as affluent, decadent perverts. More insidiously, the film uses African-American spokespeople to discredit lesbians and gays' claims of discrimination.

Lou Sheldon made numerous visits to Missouri in 1994 to boost efforts to gather signatures for an anti-lesbian/gay amendment in that state and to rally support to repeal Springfield, Missouri's bias crimes legislation.[14] A Protect the Children Association advertisement for a Sheldon rally held on 7 February 1994 read, 'I hope the buildings will be packed and jammed as we pray our city back to God and out of the hands of a "city council" who will bring the wrath of God upon us by giving "Special Rights" to Sodomites. Christians, as well as good moral people from every ethnic group, must "vote"! [*sic*].' The Traditional Values Coalition is even more active in its home state of California, where it helped repeal lesbian/gay rights ordinances in the cities of Concord and Irvine, and was instrumental in persuading Governor Pete Wilson to veto a bill that would have prohibited job discrimination on the basis of sexual orientation.

The Campaigns: Colorado, Oregon, Missouri

The first successful statewide anti-lesbian/gay ballot initiatives appeared in Colorado and Oregon in 1992. Sponsored by the religious right groups, Colorado for Family Values and the Oregon Citizens Alliance, these initiatives were intended to amend state constitutions to prohibit state and local governments from passing any laws that would outlaw discrimination against lesbians, gays, and bisexuals. In addition, the initiatives would have repealed antidiscrimination ordinances that were already in effect, for example, in Denver, Boulder, and Aspen, in the state of Colorado. The 1992 Oregon initiative went even further than the Colorado effort. Oregon's Measure 9 would have required any organization that received government funding – including schools – to present homosexuality as 'abnormal, wrong, unnatural, and perverse.'

Oregon voters narrowly turned down Measure 9, with a 56 per cent majority. Yet much to the surprise of Colorado activists and pollsters, who predicted the initiative would lose by a wide margin, Amendment 2 was approved by 53 per cent of Colorado voters in November 1992. Colorado's amendment was never put into effect; it was declared unconstitutional by the Colorado Supreme Court in 1994 and by the U.S. Supreme Court in 1996. Still, the two ballot initiatives have had a major impact on religious right organizing tactics and strategies. Buoyed by their success in Colorado, and by their near-success in Oregon, where 44 per cent of the voters were willing to declare homosexuality abnormal and perverse, religious right groups were encouraged to try their initiatives in other states. The two test cases in Oregon and Colorado made clear that a large number of people were willing to mobilize and vote against lesbians and gays. Subsequently, in numerous communities, including Cincinnati, Ohio; Festus, Missouri; and many Oregon counties, religious right groups worked to pass local-level ballot initiatives and to repeal city and local-level civil rights protections for lesbians and gays. In 1994 religious right groups tried to introduce statewide ballot initiatives in eleven states: Missouri, Maine, Arizona, Florida, Idaho, Washington, Ohio, Michigan, Nevada, Texas, and (again) Oregon. In 1995 a statewide ballot initiative in Maine was narrowly defeated.

In Missouri the ballot initiative campaign was coordinated by a right-wing group called the Amendment Coalition, with substantial help from the California-based Traditional Values Coalition. Based initially in the Missouri capital, Jefferson City, and then subsequently in Springfield (which, with its numerous Bible colleges, is referred to by many Missourians as the 'buckle' of the Bible belt), Amendment Coalition activists were actively involved with the anti-abortion movement prior to spearheading their anti-lesbian/gay campaign. In Missouri, the Amendment Coalition used stealth techniques to gather signatures for their petitions: passing petitions around in churches, prayer meetings, and other small groups. In their flyers they preyed on people's economic fears, and portrayed themselves as 'patriots' who were working towards 'equal rights.' One flyer, for example, invited citizens of Kansas City to come to a 'speak out' on 'Gay Rights/Special Rights.' The flyer claimed that '"Gay rights" means a threat to your right to compete for employment and housing, but that "Equal rights" can be guaranteed with an amendment to our state constitution.' Ultimately the Amendment Coalition did not gather enough signatures to place its initiative on the November 1994 ballot.

Only two of the 1994 statewide measures (in Idaho and Oregon) were successful in getting on the ballot. Both of these were narrowly defeated, in the same election that saw the Republican Party take over the U.S. Senate and House of Representatives. But in the process of conducting these statewide efforts and collecting signatures for petitions, religious right groups mobilized thousands of conservative Christians and introduced a new tool to conservatives' repertoires of collective action: the constitutional amendment campaign.[15]

Analysis of these campaigns reveals that although the initiatives are, at least technically, statewide campaigns, they draw on and reflect the aims, priorities, resources, and organizing tactics of *national* religious right groups such as Lou Sheldon's Traditional Values Coalition, James Dobson's Focus on the Family, and Pat Robertson's Christian Coalition. Links between and among the statewide organizations are apparent. The language used in Colorado's 1992 constitutional amendment was virtually the same as that used in Missouri, Idaho, Michigan, and Washington.[16] In all of these states the wording of the anti-lesbian/gay ballot initiatives has been purposefully confusing, raising the specter of quotas, 'special rights' and 'minority status' for lesbians, gays, and bisexuals. In addition, the initiatives seem intentionally crafted to confuse voters. The wording contains double negatives, with a no vote indicating support for lesbian/gay/bisexual civil rights. In focus groups conducted in Missouri a number of participants could not understand the intent of the initiative even after it had been explained numerous times. A poll of 750 likely voters in the same state revealed that 69 per cent found it very or somewhat confusing to understand. Over one-third thought that the initiative, if passed, would provide *more* rights for lesbians and gays – and not, in effect, exclude lesbians and gays from the political process.

National activists were also present in the statewide campaigns. During the Missouri petition drive, TVC's Lou Sheldon, along with pseudoscientist Paul Cameron, made numerous visits to Missouri to mobilize conservative Christians.[17] Sheldon has also been linked to the Colorado initiative. In virtually all states facing these initiatives, the Christian Coalition has been active. The extent to which these anti-lesbian/gay campaigns reflect a national movement is amply reflected in the two national summit meetings, held in May 1993 and May 1994, which were convened by Colorado for Family Values to share strategies and resources and to forge a national anti-lesbian/gay agenda. The eight pages of strategies brainstormed at the 1994 conference, which was attended by representatives of various anti-lesbian/gay initiative groups, included the development of central computer networks and information clearing-houses as well as coordinated legislative and litigation strategies. Although some of the strategies may seem naïve, such as a call for an attack on the Kinsey studies of sexuality, as a whole they represent a fairly sophisticated effort to create a coordinated grass-roots movement, gain media attention positive to their anti-gay/lesbian/bisexual message, infiltrate political parties at the local and state levels, mobilize voters, and sway public opinion.

Framing Anti-Lesbian/Gay Activism

One might ask why these anti-lesbian and gay initiatives occurred when they did, and what motivates religious rightists to mobilize so vehemently around the issue of homosexuality. The influence of postmillennialist theology certainly provides a clue. Yet social movement theory also provides another piece of the puzzle. Like other identity-based social movements, the religious right can be characterized as a 'discursive community.'[18] The Christian right reinforces the identity claims of its constituents by portraying Christians as a beleaguered and righteous minority on the fringes of American society. They interpret American political and cultural life as deeply flawed and hostile to Christians, a position which they use to mobilize religious conservatives in the name of a 'pro-family' agenda.

Groups like Focus on the Family frame Christians as engaged in a 'civil war' between 'proponents of traditional family values and those who hold to a society based on godlessness and secular humanism.'[19] A recruitment brochure describes their only 'mission,' according to founder James Dobson, as being 'to strengthen the home' and to 'reconnect families with the ageless wisdom of Judeo-Christian values.' But doing so, writes Dobson in his March 1994 letter to the membership, involves 'hardship and persecution.' Thus Christian soldiers must remain ever vigilant for sources of moral decay, against which they must actively fight. As Dobson further explains: 'Flabby, overindulged, pampered Christians don't have the stamina to fight this battle. Thus, the Lord puts us on a spiritual treadmill every now and then to keep us in good fighting condition.'

At the same time as Christian activists are seen to be on a mission from God,

defending their homes and families, lesbians and gays are portrayed alterna-
tively as politically powerful, spiritually and emotionally weak, and woefully
degenerate. Lesbians and gays are portrayed as a privileged group that siphons
off social and political resources to the detriment of other groups, including
'deserving' Christian families. For example, in July 1993, in a response to a gay
critic, Dobson wrote, 'The average homosexual earns $59,000 per year, com-
pared with $32,000 for heterosexuals[20] ... Gays also have a much higher per-
centage of college degrees than the straight population. And when it comes to
political clout, how can they claim to be short-changed? Every objective of the
gay and lesbian community is being achieved today.' Dobson points to government funding for AIDS research as an example of gay political agendas
advanced 'because of the clout of homosexuals who turned their powerful gurus
on Congress and the White House.'[21] Gay activists are framed as 'hostile' to
psychologists and religious activists who are 'helping homosexuals to overcome their immoral conduct.'[22] Allies of lesbians and gays, like the American
Civil Liberties Union, are referred to as street gangs and thugs, 'the Crips and
Bloods of the legal Left.'[23]

In this way, framing processes serve to strengthen the boundaries between
Christian activists and lesbians and gays. Lesbians and gays are portrayed as
inherently unChristian, anti-family. One cannot be conservative, Christian, and
gay at the same time (although one may be Christian and *ex*-gay). At the same
time, Christians are portrayed as warm, family-oriented, and loving people
(though hating sin), and the only ones capable of saving America from its perilous decline. By bolstering participants' Christian identities and at the same time
reinforcing the notion that religious values are under attack, religious right
organizations mobilize individuals active in the prayer circles, church groups,
and other well-established social networks that the Christian right draws on to
fill its ranks.

Oppositional Research

The initiative campaigns and widespread organizing show the extraordinary
resources religious right groups are willing to commit to their anti-lesbian/gay/
bisexual agenda. Whether the religious right will ultimately prevail is uncertain.
Activists on both sides of the debate face a conflicted and divided electorate,
and the large mass of disgruntled voters in the mainstream like neither lesbians
and gays nor right wing extremists. (Bisexuals, conversely, are almost completely invisible.) On the other hand, the increasing mean-spiritedness with
which voters regard the poor, immigrants, and people of colour – and any government attempts to protect the rights of minority groups – seem inauspicious

for queer organizing. The increasingly sophisticated organizing of the religious right, and the strength of its grass-roots organizing networks, pose enormous challenges to those who seek a unified progressive movement.

Oppositional research is key to any such progressive movement. Yet critical issues arise for academics who become involved in opposition research.[24] First, the kinds of research and strategizing needed for the long range are very different from those needed in the thick of an initiative campaign. In the heat of such a campaign, opposition research tends to revolve around rooting out opponents' transgressions and deploying that information in strategic ways. In order to stir up progressive activists, an alarming picture of the right wing is often painted: it is all-powerful, uniformly wealthy, and always well organized. (Not surprisingly, the religious right uses the same tactics.) But this type of research and this framing of the issues, while they may be politically (and at times personally) satisfying, will not in the long range shift the debates about homosexuality onto a more fruitful terrain. To show that right-wing activists are "just as bad" as the rest of us fails to challenge the larger social structures of oppression.

Professional opposition researchers (see, for example, Zilliox's 1993 handbook)[25] of whatever political persuasion face a very different set of issues than academic researchers. Finding out that a spokesperson for a 'pro-family' group is a convicted child molester is just the kind of information activist groups can – and do – use in the short run. But in the longer run, oppositional researchers must take a much broader view. Oppositional research must help reframe the debates about sexuality, question the boundaries, and place the groups, organizations, and individuals involved in anti-lesbian/gay organizing in their broader social and political context. At the same time it must be useful for (and thus comprehensible to) grass-roots activists – a major shortcoming of much, though not all, queer and postmodernist theory. In our own research, we search for connections: How does this recent wave of right-wing activism connect to earlier waves? How do various right-wing groups work together – or not, and on what issues? How are the far right and the moderate right linked together? How does religious right activism reinforce the identity claims of its participants and serve to strengthen established boundaries? How are their identity claims deeply gendered?

A major strategy of the Christian right has been to argue that homosexuality is, essentially, a behaviour – and one that can be changed by sheer will or prayer. Thus, they argue, lesbians, gays, and bisexuals should not be protected against discrimination in employment, housing, access to the political process, or any other area of social life. Perverse behaviour, they argue, should not be protected. In the short run, political activists have tended to respond to these charges by falling back on the position that homosexuality is, instead, an essential and unchanging identity and style of life. We're not made this way, some activists argue, we're *born* gay.[26] Yet at the same time as many activists argue for the essential nature of lesbian/gay identity, queer theorists and other scholars have taken up a constructionist position.[27] In a perverse twist, religious rightists end up (unintentionally) as standard bearers for a constructionist view of sexuality, while many lesbian and gay activists tend to take up an essentialist position.

This contradiction poses thorny problems for oppositional researchers. Simply taking a strong constructionist position – that sexualities are fluid and evanescent – in the short range may pose problems for lesbian/gay/bisexual organizing. One of the ironies of identity-based movements, whatever their flaws, is that attempts to lessen the effects of discrimination and societal oppression serve to strengthen the identities themselves.[28] Deconstructing queer identities at the very moment that lesbians and gays have reached a certain political strength and face considerable backlash may seem at times more useful to those religious rightists who seek to eliminate queer bodies and behaviors than to grass-roots progressive activists. Yet, arguing that we 'can't help ourselves' is a peculiarly weak organizing platform – and certainly an unpalatable one for those of us who feel a certain fluidity about our sexuality. In the long range, activist researchers need to think strategically and creatively about this dilemma.[29] At the very least, an insistence that 'gay is good' – regardless of whether it is in our genes – might be a useful first step.

Power and Representation

At a very different level, oppositional researchers face a number of important methodological issues not faced by those engaged in more traditional forms of academic research. For those who take critiques of positivism seriously, another layer of complexity is added. A major theme in feminist methodology and critical approaches to social science, more generally is 'giving voice' to those whom one is studying.[30] In opposition to positivist models of social science, in which the omnipotent researcher is seen as privileged knower of the research subjects' reality, critical methodologists have struggled with the issue of power. Dorothy Smith[31] argues, for example, that social-science knowledge represents the world 'from a standpoint in the relations of ruling, not from the standpoint of those who are ruled.' Smith and others in this critical tradition argue for a radical restructuring of 'science as usual' in order to create a sociology by and for women and other dispossessed groups.

Critical researchers have thus struggled with issues of power and representation. Presenting the views and opinions of research participants in their own voices and allowing these voices to 'speak for themselves' is one way some critical researchers have solved the power issues involved in the relationship between researcher and researched.[32] Others have experimented with more participatory forms of research, giving those being studied more active roles in designing and carrying out the research.[33] But critical social scientists who have considered issues of power and representation typically consider the situation of those who study relatively powerless and disadvantaged groups. They have assumed by and large that researchers have power, and those being researched don't; they rarely consider the role of those who study 'up.' But this role poses thorny problems. What is the position of queer researchers studying right-wing activists? Who has power in this situation, and in what ways? In this situation it is not clear what studying up would mean – in terms of race? class? gender? sexuality? religion? Many grass-roots members involved in right-wing activities, for example, see themselves as economically dispossessed. In terms of access to professional privilege, they may indeed have less power than the researchers. Yet these very same individuals clearly have access to privilege based on sexuality and, sometimes, race and gender. Only if we think of power as unidimensional does the concept of studying up make sense.

Clearly, simply giving voice to the dispossessed and marginalized is not our major purpose in the oppositional research we conduct. The religious right, to our mind, clearly has a voice – often a fairly noxious one, at that. And although religious right activists tend to see themselves as politically and culturally disenfranchised, we probably wouldn't be studying them if they truly were. On the other hand, the kinds of distortions and tactics that a non-academic researcher might engage in during the course of a nasty political battle will not serve academic oppositional researchers well, either. As social scientists we have a commitment, not to a positivist conception of objectivity and truth but at least to a fairly accurate rendering of the world – at least as we see it. In studying right-wing activists it is important that we understand their world as best we can.

Researching from a queer activist/academic standpoint raises certain ethical questions, as well. Our participation in the political movement predated our decision to use the data we were collecting in an academic setting. In the later stages of our research, relying on published materials enabled us to avoid some of the sticky ethical issues involved in doing covert field research. As we moved out of the thick of the political campaign we increasingly came to use materials in the public domain. Perhaps we might have made different decisions about data collection had we begun the research as academics first; perhaps not. Still, ethical issues uneasily remain. To activists the issue of infiltration may seem substantially less problematic than it does to academics.[34] Faced with the prospect of losing one's civil rights, it is not a difficult decision to try to gain crucial tactical information through less than open means. As academics, however, the issue is far less easily resolved, and we ourselves do not always agree on the ethics involved in doing covert field research.[35]

On a practical level, there is no clear answer as to how to proceed. Our attempts to gain information are shaped by a host of political and ethical considerations, and different researchers will inevitably solve these dilemmas in different ways. Too, our representations of right-wing activists are, inevitably, shaped by our own social locations, just as right-wing representations of homosexuality are shaped by theirs. But these difficulties do not mean that progressive activists/academics must give up the attempt to understand the dimensions of right-wing activism – and the world views of activists themselves. Nor does it mean that we must fall back into what Jane Roland Martin (1996) calls the trap of 'aerial distance.'[36] Instead, we must move back and forth between academic and activist positions, always interrogating the ethical dilemmas and political impact of our work.

Notes

1 See Hunt, Benford, and Snow, 'Identity Fields', 185–208.
2 Sara Diamond argues that the postmillennialists are, in effect, a unifying ideological force in Christian right activism. Though many are not as extreme as Rushdoony (who advocates the death penalty for homosexuals), the Coalition on Revival clearly reflects the general concerns of Old Testament theocratic theologizing (Diamond, *Spiritual Warfare*).
3 See Brinkley 'Problem of American Conservatism,' 409–37; and Calhoun, '*Nationalism and Ethnicity*,' 211–39, for interesting discussions of these issues.
4 See Hixson, *American Right Wing*, xvi.
5 See Porteous and Clarkson, *Challenging the Christian Right*; People for the American Way, *Hostile Climate*; National Gay and Lesbian Task Force, *Fight the Right Action Kit*.
6 On 9 November 1994 Ralph Reed announced that the Christian Coalition made one million phone calls, mailed one million reminders to vote, and distributed thirty-three million score cards in the weeks preceding the November 1994 election.
7 Dobson was an associate clinical professor of pediatrics at the University of Southern California School of Medicine for fourteen years. He was commended by the Carter administration, served on the National Advisory Commission for Juvenile Justice in the Reagan administration, and sat on numerous governmental commis-

sions on pornography. In 1970 Dobson wrote a best-selling book about the importance of using physical punishment in the disciplining of children. *Dare to Discipline* continues to sell thousands of copies.

8 *Focus on the Family*, July 1994, 5.

9 Focus on the Family distributes 52 million pieces of literature each year and receives in excess of 200,000 letters every month. *Citizen* is sent to 300,000 subscribers.

10 *Citizen*, August 1988, 5.

11 Ibid., 18 March 1991, 8.

12 Ibid., 12 June 1991, 2; see also the July 1993 issue.

13 Porteous and Clarkson, *Challenging the Christian Right*.

14 Although the statewide initiative failed to gain enough signatures to be put on the November 1994 ballot, the Springfield initiative to repeal the bias crimes legislation was not only easily placed on the ballot but also passed by a wide margin.

15 Tarrow (1994). The 1996 U.S. Supreme Court decision that Colorado-style amendments are unconstitutional seems to have dealt only a temporary blow to right-wing activists, who have turned their attention to the issue of same-sex marriage.

16 The Missouri language read 'Shall the Constitution of Missouri be amended by adding a new Article which would prohibit the state of Missouri, through any of its branches, departments or agencies, and its political subdivisions, including counties, municipalities and school districts, from enacting, adopting or enforcing any statute, order, regulation, rule, ordinance, resolution or policy whereby homosexual, lesbian or bisexual activity, conduct or orientation shall entitle any person or class of persons to have or demand any minority status, protected status, quota preference, affirmative action or claim of discrimination?'

17 Paul Cameron, head of the Washington, D.C., Family Research Institute, is a psychologist who was expelled from the American Psychological Association and censured by the American Sociological Association. Although Cameron's studies are deeply flawed, he purports to show, among other things, 'scientific' evidence that the wages of sin are – literally – death. See his viciously anti-gay pamphlets *Medical Consequences of What Homosexuals Do, Child Molestation and Homosexuality*, and *The Psychology of Homosexuality*.

18 Tarrow, *Power in Movement*; see also Laranna, Johnson, and Gusfield, *New Social Movements*.

19 From a Focus on the Family catalogue description of a publication called *Children at Risk*, n.d.

20 These figures, much cited by the religious right, are based on marketing research done on gay magazine subscribers.

21 *Citizen*, July 1993, 6–7.

22 Ibid., 20 June 1994, 1.

23 Ibid., 15 November 1993, 7.

24 See Gottfried, *Feminism and Social Change*, for a useful set of essays by feminist activist/researchers.

25 Zilliox, *Opposition Research Handbook*.

26 Some gay academics, like Simon LeVay, have earnestly attempted to document a biological basis for homosexuality. Grass-roots lesbians and gays take a variety of stances. See Whisman *Queer by Choice*, and Esterberg, *Lesbian and Bisexual Identities*, for discussions of a variety of identity accounts.

27 See Stein, *Forms of Desire*, for a discussion of the constructionist/essentialist debates; also Esterberg, *Lesbian and Bisexual Identities*.

28 See Epstein, 'Gay Politics, Ethnic Identity,' for a fruitful discussion.

29 See Phelan, '(Be)Coming Out,' and Phelan, *Getting Specific*.

30 See, for example, Stringer, *Action Research*; Reinharz, *Feminist Methods*; Stanley and Wise, *Breaking Out*.

31 Smith, 'Contradictions' and *Everyday World as Problematic*.

32 See, for example, Gorelick, 'Contradictions,' for an interesting critique.

33 See, for example, Cancian, 'Participatory Research' and Naples with Clark, 'Feminist Participatory Research.'

34 We are fairly certain that our opposition research group was infiltrated by a member of the opposition.

35 One of us believes that covert field research is almost never justifiable in 'usual' research situations; the other is far more open. Yet both of us, as activists, agree that infiltration may be necessary for certain political fights, as for example when right-wing groups organize against lesbians, gays, people of color, and so forth.

36 Martin, 'Aerial Distance.'

10

Gay Identity Politics in Community-Based AIDS Organizations

ROY CAIN

Identity politics have always been a fundamental part of the community-based response to HIV. A central premise of AIDS organizing, like the gay and lesbian movement out of which it grew, is the idea that common experiences of oppression and marginalization lead to shared values and interests, and to the development of a shared identity. In the early years of the epidemic, gay men and lesbians mobilized when it was realized that gay men faced a common health threat to which most nongay 'others' were unprepared or unwilling to respond.[1] By representing a common threat to 'us,' AIDS also helped consolidate gay identities and sense of community.[2] Community-based AIDS organizations, at least in larger urban centres, were rooted in the assertive politics of gay and lesbian communities, which recognize the central role played by heterosexism and homophobia in shaping our lives and our relationships to gay and nongay others and to social institutions. To varying degrees, community-based AIDS organizations were explicitly established to challenge the homophobia and heterosexism that surround the epidemic. Many AIDS organizations have taken public positions on issues important to gay and lesbian communities, such as inclusion of sexual orientation in human rights legislation, and their very existence has promoted the mobilization of many gays and lesbians who otherwise might not have had much involvement in formal community activities. Community-based AIDS work can lead to interactions between gays and nongays, such as government agencies, in ways that had not previously been possible and that legitimated the gay and lesbian movement.[3]

Many community AIDS organizations recognize special ties to their local gay communities, although this association has often been an ambivalent one.[4] One of the more contentious issues concerning the epidemic has been whether HIV/AIDS is a 'gay disease.' Many people in the movement would argue that AIDS affects everyone and is therefore not a gay disease: anyone can become infected with HIV, and to associate it with gay sexuality is to reinforce the homophobia in our culture. But others disagree, arguing that gay men in North America are over-represented among those infected with and affected by HIV, and gays have been the principle target of those who would stigmatize the epidemic. Michael Callen, an American PLWA (Person living with AIDS) activist, bluntly asserted this view: 'AIDS is a gay disease. There. I said it. And I believe it. If I hear one more time that AIDS is not a gay disease, I shall vomit.'[5] When it comes to HIV/AIDS, identity and disease are intertwined in contradictory ways: in our heterosexist culture that often makes gays and lesbians invisible, failure to explicitly mention the needs of the gay community means that gays are easily ignored, but to recognize the gay community means, to many, that nongay others are excluded or unwelcomed. As well, organizations associated with the gay community can become vulnerable. As Epstein observes, 'By hardening a notion of group difference, identity politics presents a highly visible target.'[6]

Community-based AIDS service organizations (ASOs) and their politics ·have evolved to become considerably more complex over the past decade or more.[7] Earlier debates about the associations between HIV and gay communities are still unresolved, but now other self-conscious and politically active groups in Canada have increasingly come to recognize that they, like gay men, are affected by HIV. Women, gays and lesbians of colour, Native people, sex-trade workers, and injection drug users have come to assert that they have common interests and needs that can conflict with those of white gay men who tend to dominate the AIDS movement in North America. These other groups have, in turn, demanded more attention and appropriate services from AIDS organizations in their communities. The gay-male-dominated AIDS movement stirs up other tensions as well. For example, Beth Schneider describes how the 'financial and political energy directed towards gay men around AIDS has generated a heightened interest in lesbian health, particularly in the problem of breast cancer, and considerable resentment has surfaced.'[8] Gay identity politics also comes into play in the coalescing of a movement of people living with HIV and AIDS. As Gary Dowsett observed, 'the transference of terms – "coming out" as seropositive, the very notion of there being an HIV "identity" – borrows heavily from gay liberation tropes and political tactics.'[9] Self-identified PLWAs or PHAs (people living with HIV and AIDS) now demand that they be afforded more say in decisions that affect their lives and more influence in the planning and delivery of services; as Charles Roy described it, people living with HIV/ AIDS, despite numerous barriers, now play an increasingly important role in the Canadian AIDS movement.[10] Further complicating matters is a growing consciousness among many HIV-negative gay men that they share common experiences in relation to the epidemic and to the gay communities of which they are part. Many men experience multiple losses and survivor's guilt, and some feel marginalized by the high priority accorded the epidemic in the gay community. Some HIV-negative men do not feel that they have *really* come out as gay – as if an HIV diagnosis is an essential step in the coming out process in the 1990s.[11] HIV-negative workers are often unsure of whether they have a legitimate role and voice in the AIDS organizations to which they belong.[12] So while some people like to talk about the 'AIDS Community' – a phrase that suggests coherence and commonality of interests – the politics of recognizing and organizing around difference, marginality, and separateness from the majority now complicate AIDS organizing efforts. Ironically, the politics of identity that helped mobilize an effective response to the epidemic now challenges it.

The agenda of AIDS organizing goes beyond concerns with homophobia and heterosexism. Access to effective treatments at reasonable cost, the inclusion of people living with HIV in treatment decisions and in program development, and the reduction of international disparities with regard to prevention and treatment efforts are all important elements of the broader 'AIDS agenda.' Yet, despite the often-expressed desire to change the social context of the epidemic, translating political commitment into actual practice has not been easy for those working in ASOs. The political preoccupations of community-based AIDS workers have often been overshadowed by concerns about service provision. Understandably, community workers have priorized services over social change; instead of advocating for long-term social transformation, workers focus most of their attention on the more immediate needs for counselling, safer-sex education, support services, and the like.[13] Many people living with HIV are concerned that gay political issues compete against their need for services; at the same time, many people in the gay and lesbian movement have become concerned that AIDS consumes too much of their agenda. Finally, theoretical developments, and in particular the queer critiques of gay liberationist politics, challenge the wisdom of using identity as a central organizing principle, as it will inevitably exclude some people and privilege others.

In this chapter, I show how workers in Canadian AIDS service organizations attempt to negotiate the often contradictory political pressures that underlie their work.[14] I discuss how concerns about identity shape the kinds of services that are available, and the ability of ASOs to work towards progressive social change. I also examine how the context of identity politics in AIDS work has become more complex over the years. My intention in this examination is to highlight the dilemmas AIDS organizations and their workers face, not to criticize them. I write as a gay man concerned with the obstacles confronting AIDS service organizations in their efforts to address more seriously gay community concerns with regard to the epidemic. One of the aims of this study is to understand what happens to workers, many of whom are themselves gay, that leads them to become so cautious in dealing with the concerns and issues of the community. The chapter outlines how the contradictions in identity politics in community-based AIDS work leads to the unintentional reproduction of heterosexism, and it concludes with a discussion of the degree to which criticisms of identity politics by queer theorists and activists are reflected in and relevant to the day-to-day work of AIDS organizations.

Constructing Identity and Choosing Sides

In his essay examining the tensions between gay and AIDS politics, Eric Rofes asks, 'Are we [in the AIDS movement] a part of the gay and lesbian movement, or do we stand outside of it? ... There is no neutral position. Which side are we on?'[15] Indeed, most of the twelve groups that participated in this study have grappled with this question: Should a gay identity be embraced by the organization, given its historical roots in gay and lesbian organizing and by the current demographics of the HIV epidemic in Canada? This has been a particular debate in the large-city organizations. Virtually all respondents in this study recognized that the gay community in Canada has been the hardest hit by the epidemic, but agreement often seemed to end at this point. Questions revolved around whether organizational identification with the gay community would be helpful or harmful to the often vulnerable organizations, particularly as funding becomes more difficult to acquire. Would community support be diminished by such an identity? Would a gay identification communicate that nongays are not welcome as service users, volunteers, and staff? Might it scare away more covert gays and lesbians who would not be comfortable associating with a gay agency? Would efforts to reduce the stigma surrounding the epidemic be helped or undermined by asserting a gay identity? What would a gay identity mean for the work of ASOs in the long term, as the epidemic is expected to spread to an increasing number of nongay individuals?

Resolving these questions has been fraught with difficulty. One organization in this study has explicitly recognized that it is a part of the lesbian and gay community. This organization is located in a city that has a large network of AIDS service providers and a large and well-organized gay and lesbian community, features that help enable it to be more specialized in its focus. In describing this decision a volunteer stated,

We came out and said, we are a gay and lesbian community-based organization and I'm all for that. I think that was a great idea because that's where all of the blood, sweat, and tears have come from in this city. We've had to fight and fight and fight for everything. If [this organization] wasn't around God only knows what would be happening these days. And it is staffed by gay and lesbian people, and the majority of the volunteers are gay and lesbian. And the majority of the people in this city who are infected are gay men and I'm proud that we have said that we're not ashamed of who we are.

For many people, a gay organizational identity honors the history of the group, signals an openness and support for gays and lesbians, and provides a focus for many of its programs and services. Still, this identification has not been without costs and concerns. Some volunteers and service users have felt unwelcome, and a number of workers have expressed concern for what this kind of state- ment will mean for public support and funding. So even in a large city, where the group has its history in gay community organizing, the decision to identify with the community has generated tensions for years.

The vast majority of respondents in the other ASOs examined in this study rejected the idea that their organization should embrace a gay identity. Organi- zations in smaller cities, where there are often few, if any, other AIDS services, feel a pressure to 'be all things to all people.' Most have tried to nurture a more mainstream image as a professional service provision agency, believing that their associations with gay communities would be a liability. Many groups in Canada and elsewhere have undergone a process of 'degaying.'[16] A volunteer recalled some of the changes in the history of his organization in the following terms:

There was a period in this AIDS battle when everybody was working very hard to degay, or to de-emphasize the gay dimension in AIDS, because there was a real fear that if AIDS came to be seen as a gay disease, funding would dry up, research would stop, gov- ernment support would disappear, public sympathy would disappear. And on another level, people who should be hearing the prevention messages would tune them out, because they wouldn't see them as applying to them. So there was a lot of effort to degay AIDS.

Degaying was also justified in order to reach large segments of the gay commu- nity: some respondents believed that many relatively covert men would not risk coming to a gay organization. A lesbian board member noted that 'A lot of peo- ple who are gay are closeted, and they don't want to walk into a place that's known as a totally gay organization. It's funny because in my heart I want to believe that for most gay people this shift away [from the gay community] is not a positive thing. But a number of them would not go near a place that was gay or strongly gay-oriented. It saddens me because I want it to be the other way.' Moreover, many nongay people, such as family members of HIV-positive gay men, might not feel comfortable using their services if the organization asserted a strong gay identity. Identification with the gay community could undermine the often-cited assertion that people need to think about risk behaviours rather than risk groups. Since the late 1980s, the ideas that 'AIDS is not a gay disease' and 'AIDS is everyone's problem' have been promoted in an effort to destigmatize – and degay – the epidemic. While such efforts may have helped nongays to minimize their own risks of infection and to become more supportive of the aims of the AIDS movement, these messages implied that people were at equal risk of infection.

Some respondents were very strong in their views about the need to separate AIDS from issues of the gay community. A nongay board president was unequivocal about why he thought separation was necessary: 'There are only so many dollars, whether we want to admit it or not. If the organization gives off a gay image, politicians are just going to brush it to the side. That is the way that it is; they are homophobic and they just say, "They are just friggin' queers, let's let them all croak."' The concerns were not simply about homophobic politicians, and many respondents worried that a gay identity would affect their ability to raise private donations. An executive director noted: 'The homophobia thing, I fight it by putting an image out that people will give money, rather than putting out another image and they won't give.' As a result this respondent's organization consciously tried to change its image: 'The community out there, educated or not, tends to equate AIDS with gay. And as such, this agency has been seen in the community as being gay. The board wanted to change that. They realized that doors weren't opening to us because of that image.' Beyond concerns relating to funding, a number of respondents felt that their work would simply not be seen as credible or professional if their organization was viewed as gay.

While it avoids many of the problems associated with a gay organizational identity, a nongay image comes with costs of its own. It can undermine efforts to work in gay communities by communicating an unwillingness to take political risks in support of the community; organizational needs are seen to take priority over community needs. A gay staff member expressed his concern with an early decision in his group:

At our board/staff workshop, the board president talked about the founding of this organization and how there was a deliberate commitment by the fags and dykes that put this organization together to put themselves in a minority position [on the board] so that it would be credible in the community at large ... And then, from what I've seen, there is very little in terms of education for the gay community because they didn't want to be seen as a gay organization.'

To the extent that it reflects a discomfort with their gay roots and ongoing associations with gay communities, the decision to present a nongay image is seen by some respondents as heterosexist. A gay board member noted: 'People say we have to be careful, we don't want to be seen as a gay organization. My opinion is, Why not? I think that would be an excellent way to be seen as an organization, I think there is a lot to be proud of. Some hide behind the idea that it may jeopardize funding. I think that is crap.' For some people, efforts to degay AIDS implies that ASO workers believe that gay identification is something to be ashamed of. This runs counter to health-promotion efforts to build the self-esteem of gays, to promote the development of proud gay communities, and to confront the homophobic attitudes of others:

I think that the gay community deserves that openness. I think that they deserve the self-esteem and pride of an organization willing to put their money where their mouth is and say, This is what we are for, and this is what we are about, and we are proud to do this. And I think that is just as important to building self-esteem as creating programs. Not actually saying that you are really doing this, not making it terribly public, is probably doing more damage than admitting it would do. We spend so much energy trying to build self-esteem in the community, but this is where it really counts.

Ironically, there was a general recognition among respondents that most people assume that AIDS service agencies are gay organizations despite their assertions to the contrary. Given their history, the makeup of their staff and volunteer complements, and the number of gay service users, achieving a nongay identity requires active work. Groups may simply deny a close association with the gay community: 'We are not a gay organization. We are here for the entire community.' Others have consciously or unconsciously minimized their contact with local gay and lesbian communities. Some even try to choose their spokesperson carefully, to put forth the 'right' image: ' [If] you have someone who is obviously gay standing up saying this is not a gay agency, what are you going to think? What is the public going to think? They're not listening to the statement, they're looking at the person and they're listening to the way the person speaks.'

Most workers try to negotiate a middle ground by asserting a nongay identity while recognizing their gay roots. According to one long-time staff member: 'We never wanted to be publicly identified as a gay organization [but] We would never distance ourselves from the gay community. We presented ourselves as inclusive. Anyone who has concerns around HIV or AIDS is a concern for us ... But in our guiding principles that people have to subscribe to in order to become a member is that recognition of the leadership that the gay community has played in addressing the AIDS issue in Canada.' Workers in most (but not all) groups have actively tried to ensure that their organizations are welcoming of gays and lesbians. A gay staff member talked about the importance of creating a gay-friendly environment: 'Since this organization was founded by gay people, gay people are quite free to be completely themselves. So if a man wants to kiss his lover in the front office no one is going to say boo. And the language that's spoken and the visuals [e.g., posters] that are around are designed to make gay people feel comfortable.' In the current heterosexist social climate, ASO workers discover that a middle ground is difficult to find.

Educational posters are important symbols of organizational identity in AIDS work. The kinds of posters that appear on office walls play a symbolic role in representing what the agency is, and consequently they have been the centre of numerous and often acrimonious debates. For some, posters of explicit expressions of gay sexuality are essential to creating a welcoming setting for gay men. For others it can create an uncomfortable environment: 'A lot of the people who used to come in were parents who've just discovered their son's gay and he's dying of AIDS. And they come for some support and they're hit blatantly with these posters ... They've got enough adjusting going on in their lives, they don't really need that. So [let's have] a little empathy for the community at large.'

In response to these kinds of competing demands, posters targeted at gay men in some ASOs have not been entirely removed, but placed in specific offices, away from general view. Other organizations try to make sure that various groups get 'equal time' in terms of posters: 'We have posters of men engaging in same-gender sex all over the wall and we don't hide them. We say, "these men get AIDS." We have a picture of pregnant women right beside them. It is like we have them evenly divided, like "This is our same-gender sex wall, this our different-gender sex wall, and this is our hemophilia wall."' A volunteer in another group recalled the resolution to her group's struggle with the issue of posters: 'If we're going to have two gay males then we should also have two women, and we should also have a straight couple. That was the way we came around it. So if something's going to be up, then it's equal all the way across the board.' In these ways the physical appearance of the offices is nurtured so as to support the identification of the organizations as being gay-positive, but there for the entire community.

The difficulty for many is that when one looks at statistics with respect to those who are currently infected, things are not 'equal all the way across the board.' Gay men continue to represent the majority of HIV infections; and to the extent that the epidemic itself is represented, such poster displays can present a distorted image of who is at risk and who is currently affected.

Given the invisibility of gay culture, any recognition accorded to gays and lesbians will feel jarring to some; for others, anything less than an unequivocal association with the gay community would be inadequate. The ambivalence regarding gay identification results in a contradictory stance in most groups, where the ASO tries to appear gay-positive but not gay, and where many workers and volunteers work to distance themselves from gay communities at the same time as they try to reach out to them to provide culturally appropriate services and to confront homophobia and heterosexism.

Competing Identities, Competing Claims

Further compounding the efforts of workers in AIDS organizations is the reality that 'gay' is not a unitary concept: gay communities are as diverse as any other. When respondents did speak of the gay community, they typically referred to specific segments, most often to relatively young, urban, and white men. The kinds of images on the walls also represent 'the gay community' largely in these same terms. Older men, gays of colour, bisexual men and women, transgendered individuals, and lesbians tend not to be represented on AIDS education posters. Other groups also make claims on the organizations' commitments, energies, and resources: women, Native people, and members of various ethnocultural communities. Services, and particularly education programs, need to be focused in some way, but defining an 'appropriate' focus and determining how resources get allocated are contentious issues. As well, there are questions about who gets represented in, and by, the organizations. Identity politics, thus, continues to be a feature of community-based work.

AIDS organizing has benefited from the political analyses and contributions of women as well as gay men. Feminists in the movement, and particularly lesbian feminists, have contributed their analysis of the gendered basis of power. The experience of women has shown how health care institutions and professionals have been untrustworthy as benevolent caregivers. A worker noted: 'Women have really brought a knowledge of the health care system and how it fails you. A lot of gay men who had previously been healthy assumed the health care system would look after them when they got sick. Women already knew that wasn't true.' Feminist analyses have also contributed debates about how to structure AIDS service organizations, ensure greater representation from various constituencies, and more equitably distribute power and influence.

Interviews revealed many instances where issues of gender, race, and sexual preference overlapped and conflicted with each other. For example, a number of women respondents complained that the support and prevention needs of women were not receiving adequate priority. Some women in ASOs do not feel their work is valued, and a number of respondents have complained in their interviews of sexist behaviour on the part of gay men. A woman volunteer noted: 'Being a woman and being straight in that organization is almost like being invisible because people don't say anything around me.' Other women complained of various forms of sexism: 'Women speak differently, we have been more emotionally expressive within the organization, and that is not given credit at all. You have no points assigned to you, because if you're seen as emotional you're seen as hysterical, or just irrational.' One woman summed up her experience with sexism in AIDS work by saying, 'I am not coming into a gay organization to be a second-class citizen again.'

AIDS work also reveals overlaps in issues of sexual preference and race. Those respondents with backgrounds in working with ethnocultural communities brought analyses of how programs and services, to be effective, need to be culturally sensitive and involve community members. And, importantly, they drove home the point that the feminist and gay liberationist movements in North America typically reflect the needs and interests of white and middle-class people – and often marginalize those from different backgrounds. Respondents of colour often complained that the needs and interests of their communities were not taken seriously by white-dominated organizations: 'I think it's about people being uncomfortable with being challenged and their privilege being questioned, and I think that's happening for a lot of these gay men for the first time in their lives ... Even being gay and dealing with homophobia hasn't stopped many of them from getting employment; it hasn't stopped many of them from getting houses and having wonderful lives, and finding connections and friends in the community.'

Identity politics in Black communities is not the same as in many gay communities. For many Blacks race is a more salient reality than sexual preference: 'Gay Black men don't live their lives as gay Black men; they live their lives as Black men.' At the same time there are Black men who would rather go to a gay-identified AIDS organization. A Black respondent noted, 'You've got people [of colour] who are in different places around race and racial identity. For them Black is not a priority. They're very much assimilated into the dominant culture. Some people actually have even gone in the direction of, 'Black is in no way important to me. In fact, all my friends are white, all my relationships are white, that's not an issue for me. I want to see somebody white because I feel more comfortable that way.'

Respondents working in culturally specific AIDS organizations complained of the apparent reluctance of others in the movement to attend seriously to issues of racism and cultural difference. A Native worker expressed her frustration in going to First Nations conferences to experience homophobia, and to AIDS conferences to experience racism. Despite this, these conferences are sometimes useful in creating networks of people living with the same kind of marginalization:

All of these places gave me a chance to meet my peers and network and get support and offer strategies. For example, when we were at the second Aboriginal AIDS conference that was the first time that First Nations gays and lesbians across Canada actually sat down at one table and had a meal and talked and laughed and shared with each other. No one had ever heard of that happening before. We had a healing circle for two-spirited people, and it was a huge circle, and it when on for like five, six, seven hours. People just went around and talked, and that had never happened before'

Disagreements in priorities and strategies in ASOs were often understood in terms of identity politics. Such tensions were often more apparent in larger organizations, where there are enough people to organize into various subgroups of women, gay men, people of colour, and the like. When women complain that the ASO is not responsive to their needs, they were often seen by gay men to be homophobic; when gay men complain of the lack of attention to gay communities and how women's programs take a disproportionate amount of resources, some women view them as sexist. When discussing efforts to make her organization more appropriate for gay culture, another woman respondent stated, 'People there said that we were homophobic because we didn't want to look at that funny S&M poster, the guy with his cock and balls all tied up by the masked marauder. I don't want to look at that.'

Discussion of these issues is fraught with difficulty. Accusations (or fears of accusations) of racism, sexism, or homophobia often can contribute to an uncomfortable silence within groups on these difficult issues. For her part, a Jewish lesbian worker described the difficulty that can arise: 'It is no longer a question of being inclusive in terms of ensuring that you have representation, and ensuring that you have programming, or ensuring that you have whatever it takes to reach a bunch of people. If you don't agree with what a person of colour says is the way to go, well then you are racist. Period. And there is no dialogue beyond that.' Discussion about the overlapping nature of oppression sometimes feels like a ranking of which is more important to address. For example, some women have felt that sexism is a primary concern because homophobia is a function of men resisting the involvement and influence of women: 'we've had discussions about homophobia and sexism and homophobia being a tool of sexism. And it's really sexism that's the [bigger] issue, the dislike and discomfort of the feminine in our culture, that creates the homophobia.' For a number of people living with HIV, the AIDS agenda has been 'hijacked' by other political interests, and these people often expressed anger at the amount of time and the number of resources that can be consumed by such debates.

Competition for resources clearly comes into play. AIDS organizations are all small and poorly funded. Choosing to address the concerns of one group often means not having adequate resources to address others. A respondent spoke of the tension he saw among gay white men when they were asked to address the needs of people of colour:

Sometimes all the people who've lived their life dealing with homophobia, who are creating a space where they get some security and safety around making sure that gay men who are dying get help. And at that time, when they thought gay, they thought gay, white male. And actually gay, white male of a certain class ... So suddenly, when these other things [around race] came in, people were threatened, there was a sense of being threatened: What does this mean? Does this mean that we have less resources to do what I need to do, or does this mean that I'll have less time to go take care of this guy that I've known for ten years?

A Black respondent described the tension he sees in small and overstretched organizations: 'So you had the competition stuff around people who need resources for women, for people of colour, for people who were HIV positive. All that going on, and the question was: How does one organization do all this stuff.'

Statistics are an important resource in the competing claims for visibility and resources. Large numbers provide symbolic weight to claims that more attention needs to be paid to particular groups or issues.[17] While there is evidence to show a gradual spread of HIV to nongay populations, the vast majority of AIDS diagnoses in Canada (about 80 per cent) still occur among gay men. People have spoken for years of an impending spread of the epidemic beyond the groups currently most affected: gay men, and injection drug users, and their sexual partners. There is, however, a fair degree of uncertainty about the current demographics of those infected with HIV, and the speed at which HIV is spreading more broadly through the population, leaving considerable room for interpretation of the available data. Many people do not understand basic statistical concepts, and their confusion is compounded by features of the epidemic. For example, the long period of asymptomatic HIV infection means that many who are currently infected do not go for testing, so 'current' statistics may actually represent the epidemic several years earlier.

The lack of clarity about AIDS diagnoses versus HIV diagnoses, and differences in the rates of increase in new infections versus cumulative statistics, confuse many respondents. A volunteer stated: 'I must admit in my own brain I am very muddled because I have heard so many different statistics and ideas in terms of infected groups and high risk groups ... I have no idea right now which is accurate.' Some respondents clearly overstated the likelihood that AIDS is going to be seen among heterosexuals. One executive director, for example, noted in 1992: 'In five years' time there are going to be more people infected coming out of the heterosexual or mainstream community than the gay community. So we've got to make that switch [to become more mainstream] ... because heterosexual transmission is by far outnumbering gay transmission.'

There was particular concern – and uncertainty – among respondents about infection among women. A few respondents believed that the number of infected women outnumbered infected men in Canada, and that the relative decline in the rates of infection among gay men means that attention should be paid to other social groups. Even when there is agreement on the numbers, there can be great debate about their implications for service delivery. In discussing the debates about how resources should be allocated to women or gay men, a gay board member stated: 'Just because it has dropped from 80- something per cent to 70 per cent does not mean that we can now change our focus, and that everything is wonderful, and we can now move to another group.' Confusing matters further is the reality that the epidemiological pattern in Canada is different than in other countries. Globally, the epidemic is fairly evenly divided among men and women, and most of those infected are heterosexual. This provides workers with a rationale for focusing on the community-at-large rather than on gay communities. A volunteer, for instance, noted: 'We are always having people come up and say it's a gay disease, and we say, No it's not a gay disease. Primarily in the world it is a heterosexual disease.' This worker uses global statistics to discuss local issues, failing to attend to the differences between these two levels of analysis.

Conceptual Matters, Practical Consequences

The development of a position on organizational identity and its connections to issues such as heterosexism, sexism, and racism are not simply interesting academic questions. They have real-life implications. The heterosexism that characterizes the context of community-based AIDS work creates a situation in which many people are reluctant to recognize the degree to which gay men continue to be affected by HIV, and the likelihood that their communities will continue to be those at greatest risk of infection in the foreseeable future. There has been a relative lack of programming for gay men, despite the fact that they continue to be the largest group requiring support services and the most important group to receive targeted education. Some respondents expressed concern that gay men's programs are often quite marginal to the overall mission of the ASO, and that funds dedicated to gay men's programs are dwindling as other communities lobby for services and resources:

One of the things we are seeing and one of the things that we address is the ghettoization of issues with gay men within AIDS service organizations. This program is set up to deal with just gay men, and, if you look at us in terms of funding, we get a chunk of funding but compared to the entire agency and what is available for other concerns – women, children, ethnocultural groups – the amount devoted to gay men is less and less as you go along. So there is a real imbalance there. You sort of assume that gay men don't need to be educated any more, that the work is done and now we have to focus on women and ethnocultural groups.

The ambivalence about gay identity has had the result that many ASOs struggle with basic questions about whether they should provide *any* services targeted to gay men: AIDS, it is felt, is a health issue, and as such it has nothing to do with sexual identity. The organizations in this study have had relatively few gay-specific programs. When they do exist, specialized programs for gay men are typically time-limited projects that have relatively few resources. A staff member in a large city organization expressed his frustration at feeling marginalized in his gay-dominated ASO: 'We do need to address other communities, but let's not forget that AIDS is still killing predominantly gay men and the bulk of the people with AIDS are gay men. And most of the men, almost all of the men who work in this building, are gay. And we are the only gay-specific program, and there are only two staff people who work within this gay-specific program.'

The lack of targeted services for gay men is an increasing concern for a number of people within the AIDS movement in Canada.[18] Concern about targeted programming is not limited to ASO workers; a government worker complained that he receives grant applications from ASOs that do not mention the gay community. In referring to one such application, he recalled: 'They submitted a proposal to do an outreach campaign for youth during the summer last year, and nowhere in the proposal did it have the word gay at all. So I wrote back saying as much, and they revised their proposal. All they did was they used the word processor and used the insert function and whereever they put the word youth, they added "and gay youth." It was the same proposal with these gratuitous inclusions.'

Contributing to the relative invisibility of programs for gay communities is the terminology that describes such efforts as programs for men-who-have-sex-with-men rather than simply gay men. The more cumbersome term correctly recognizes that everyone who engages in homosexual behaviour does not identify as gay, yet we know that it is important to have programs that relate to individuals' self-identity and the norms of their community – it is one of the very reasons for establishing community-based groups in the first place.[19] Men who engage in same sex behaviour do not identify themselves as men-who-have-sex-with-men, but as gay, bisexual, or heterosexual. Self-identified gay men do not have programs that explicitly recognize them and their needs because the programs are identified in such a way as to reach straight- or bisexual-identified men who engage in homosexual behaviour.[20] In the end, gay-identified men are obscured from view, even in programs designed to reach out to them.

There are also problems with the content of prevention programs for gays. Gay men, but not heterosexuals, are told to use condoms or avoid penetrative sex, possibly for life. As Odets notes, we would never expect nongays to accept this state of affairs except as a very temporary measure, yet when gay men find this difficult they tend to be pathologized.[21] Their behaviour is often described in terms of relapse, complacency, poor skills, ignorance, or irresponsibility: 'Women need more negotiating techniques [and] straight men don't use condoms ... But straight men are not usually considered stupid for not using condoms. Gay men are considered stupid because we should know better. So that message is put out that we are dumb and that we are failures because it is supposedly easy, then if we are not doing it 100 per cent safe 100 per cent of the time ... then there is something wrong with you.' The context of homophobia has made it difficult to open up a discussion about prevention failures and ongoing unsafe sexual practices in gay communities.[22] The insistence on using a condom without fail has made it difficult to discuss the realities of what this means for many men. As the previous respondent noted, 'We have managed to create a secondary closet, there is already the first closet of being gay and now there is a second closet where you can't talk about unprotected sex.'

In resisting identification with gay communities and in distancing themselves from their gay political roots, many workers fail to appreciate basic tenets of gay liberation analysis: that understanding the epidemic requires an appreciation of the personal and social significance of sexuality and sexual identity. The history of community-based organizations is often rewritten so that the contributions of gay and lesbian activism, and the lessons to be learned from gay liberationist experiences, are quickly forgotten.[23] Many workers who do not come from the gay and lesbian political movement fail to understand the links between our sexual and nonsexual lives. A worker in Toronto noted: 'The straight people in the workshop, their comments were, "Why do you have to keep making this an issue about sexuality? Aren't we here to just work in AIDS. Why can't we just do this work, and why are you throwing your sexuality in my face, and why is it all so focused around that?"' This concern is, of course, not simply limited to nongays, as many gay workers and volunteers may not see a connection between gay political organizing and community-based AIDS work. A gay volunteer, for instance, asked; 'The issue is AIDS; why bring sexuality into it? Why can't we just be an AIDS organization and be straight, crocked, bent, or whatever. Does it really matter? It is not the issue.' For many people concerned about longer-term political change in the social context of HIV/AIDS, sexuality is indeed a central issue in understanding and responding to the epidemic.

Yet there are pressures within ASOs to focus on service provision in relative isolation from political concerns. Many respondents have felt that it is not the role of community-based AIDS organizations to engage in political work, but to provide services. In discussing the need for political activism, a board member noted: '[ASOs] must be gay-positive, but they shouldn't rub people's noses in it. Not at this particular point in history [...]Gay groups can do that. Gay Pride Day was great. I mean I loved the parade. We rubbed everybody's nose in it. That's fine, but not for a health organization sponsored by the government.' Several respondents have also expressed concern that workers not 'cloud' AIDS issues with gay political issues:

If somebody says something about faggots in front of a gay staff member, I don't want that person jumping at that question. If it has something to do with all AIDS patients being faggots, then they can jump at it. But they are jumping at it from an AIDS perspective, not from a gay one. You with me? Because if we were dealing with cancer, does lifestyle come into cancer? No, so why should it with this disease? ... We're here for AIDS. I don't care if you're gay or lesbian, a child molester, IV drug user, whatever you do. I really don't give a shit what you do. When you are out there you are just a person. I don't want any side.

Those workers asserting a professional identity bring to bear other kinds of pressures on AIDS service organizations. Professionals play an important role in ASOs, either as staff members, board members, or core volunteers. Several of the organizations in this study, particularly in the early years, made a conscious decision to recruit nongay professional board members to provide status and legitimacy. For many, professionalization means appearing and acting in particular ways, and in separating service interests from gay community concerns. This includes gay professionals:

It is ironic that you have got gay men running the agency but they don't have their gay hats on. They see it as they have different little hats to wear, and they have their professional hat on and that in not about them being gay ... Other people in the agency are trying to sort of professionalize themselves, or sanitize the epidemic and distance themselves although they themselves may well be gay. And they may not deny that they are in fact gay but they don't approach the issues as a member of the gay community ... I think that if you see professionalization as forgetting that you are gay, that is an expression of your internalized homophobia. To be a good corporate citizen or a good employee, you can no longer be a fag; that is an expression of internalized homophobia.

Respondents often failed to appreciate the more subtle and insidious forms that heterosexism can take. For instance, gay men's programs can be downplayed or overlooked. In one large-city ASO a worker in a gay outreach program – presumably a key program of the organization – complained that his work entirely ignored in a fund-raising brochure: 'It listed all the services and programs that we offer, and our program was left off the list. And we were up in arms about it. All the other programs got mentioned and not ours. And nowhere in the entire publication did it say the words gay or gay men or homosexual or gay community. Just a complete whitewash, and that was really indicative of the desire to sanitize the epidemic. The reality is that most of the people with HIV and AIDS are gay men and IV drug users.'

Confronting heterosexism requires a concerted and systematic effort on the part of organizations. Gays and nongays have been raised in a heterosexist culture, and most workers need support to begin challenging some of their taken-for-granted beliefs and values. AIDS organizations can assist in this process by supporting a process of consciousness-raising: helping their workers see the less visible forms and effects of heterosexist culture. Not surprisingly, given the ambivalent ties to their gay roots and the discomfort with tackling gay political issues, few ASOs provided much support to workers in analysing heterosexism. As political analysis is not nurtured, many respondents work as if they can separate HIV from its broader context, and conflict between workers who hold different political analyses is often generated. According to one support worker, many of her colleagues 'don't analyse in any kind of political or systemic way. So things are individual and we try to make it better on an individual basis.' Another support worker who was also concerned that many staff and volunteers underestimate how much heterosexism affects their work noted:

People could understand homophobia 'out there' someplace else in the world but when it came to services ... that became problematic for people. And they'd say things like, 'I'm not here to do politics; I'm here to get better services for people with HIV.' Like, there's a difference? Connect the dots. They just couldn't get that. If you're looking at HIV just as a simple infection, a disease, yes. If you want to be treated as a human being in the context of your gayness, that's highly political. There seems to be a difficulty in making that theoretical leap.

Identity in AIDS Work: Concluding Thoughts

Identity has had a central place in the history of the community-based AIDS movement. Groups were started by self-identified gay men and their allies, and identity has been an important focus of their activities. Even as the debates on the emphasis on gay communities has taken place over the years, they typically take the form of self-identified groups challenging the amount of attention or resources devoted to other groups. In an effort to manage these competing claims and to deal with the homophobic context that continues to surround the epidemic, workers have, in a number of ways, downplayed their associations with their gay communities. In the end many AIDS organizations end up working in ways very similar to traditional health and social service organizations. The needs and interests of gay communities are often overshadowed by other concerns, and the silences, uncertainties, and discomforts within these organizations mean that heterosexism is often recreated by the same workers who are attempting to respond effectively to the epidemic.

Queer and AIDS activists, among others, have come to appreciate the limitations of identity as an organizing principle. Categories such as gay or lesbian, it is argued, obscure the many differences that exist between people, and the use of such categories reinforces and helps render invisible pre-existing systems of privilege and power.[24] Identity-based movements have had difficulty recognizing the differences that exist between, and within, groups. Seidman, for example, argues that 'gay identity politics moves back and forth between a narrow single-interest-group politics and a view of coalition politics as the sum of separate identity communities, each locked into its own sexual, gender, class, or racial politic.'[25] Many criticize the ethnic/nationalist model of gay politics as white and middle class, and as the marginalizing of bisexual or transgendered people, among others. The category of queer is proposed as an alternative to traditional binary divisions of homo/heterosexuality, male/female. Queer and AIDS activists have embraced more transgressive, and sometimes offensive, political strategies.[26] We are challenged to recall the effectiveness of the political tactics employed by ACT-UP or AIDS Action Now!: the political gains of the AIDS movement in North American have been the result, in large measure, of such strategies. At a time when many activist groups like Queer Nation and ACT-UP appear to have self-destructed, and when many AIDS activists are now working as part of state-funded organizations, the warnings suggested by queer and postmodern theories may be particularly timely.

While usefully criticizing the limitations of identity, it is unclear how queer theory provides direction at the level of practical strategies to deal with the 'real' conditions of peoples lives.[27] There are those who are critical of the idea that the term queer is more inclusive than are gay or lesbian. Critics such as Anna Marie Smith note that the valuing and respect for difference in the new queer politics risk rendering lesbian sexuality invisible and often make any generalizations difficult.[28] In the words of David Thomas, 'Queer, whatever its appeal to other groups, may be just another male term masquerading as a comprehensive one.'[29] And, as Gamson has observed, there are fundamental tensions in rejecting identity categories when they are at the basis of community organization and solidarity.[30] The utility of these approaches is less clear when it comes to the organization of services. It is telling that respondents interviewed in this study did not talk in such terms, and did not seem to find this kind of analysis relevant to discussions of their work. Perhaps the practical concerns of these workers did not relate in obvious ways to the often abstract and theoretical nature of the queer challenges. To the extent that identity was raised as a concern, it was largely the debates about which identities were recognized or received services, rather than the degree which such identity-based groups are of utility in the movement. Queer critiques have not clearly outlined how to effectively organize a movement that does not rely on identity as a central organizing principle. Postmodernist critiques have also tended to focus on texts or discourse rather than on institutional analyses, which provides little direction for those concerned with the organizational realities of mounting an effective response to an epidemic. The new theories highlight interesting questions and contradictions, but they seem too removed and 'academic' to be very helpful when living with and responding to a very real epidemic.

The tensions associated with identity politics in AIDS work have not been resolved in the above discussion. Workers and their organizations are caught in a contradictory position of having identity as a central axis of their work. It seems that notwithstanding the queer critiques, identity-based politics – and the debates and disagreements they breed – are going to remain central to community-based AIDS work. Any identities that are embraced by AIDS organizations in order to focus their efforts are going to priorize some people and exclude others; that is both the advantage and the limitation of identity-based work. The trick will be to foster ongoing discussion and debates within groups to continue the struggle to more effectively respond to the epidemic within gay communities and elsewhere.

Notes

1 The history of the AIDS movement and its roots in gay and lesbian political organizing in North America has been described by authors such as Adam, *Rise of a Gay*;
   Altman, *Sex and the New Puritanism*; Patton, *Sex and Germs;* Perrow and Guillen,
   The AIDS Disaster; and Shilts, And *the Band Played On*. Aspects of the history of
   the AIDS movement in Canada are described by Kinsman, *The Regulation of Desire*,
   347–55; and Rayside and Lindquist, 'Canada: Community Activism,' 49–98.
2 Edwards, 'The AIDS Dialectics.'
3 Altman, 'Legitimation through Disaster,' 301–15.
4 For a discussion of some of the ambivalence, see Cain, 'Managing Impressions'; also
   see Rofes, 'Gay Lib,' 8–17.
5 Callen, 'AIDS a Gay Disease!' 42.
6 Epstein, 'Gay Politics, Ethnic Identity,' 292.
7 A network of community organizations, often called AIDS service organizations
   (ASOs), developed in Canada to respond to the needs created by the epidemic. ASOs
   typically provide a range of practical and support services for people affected by
   HIV: peer and professional counselling, practical care teams, food banks, emergency
   financial assistance, housing services, legal advice, support groups, and the like. As
   well, they provide education programs to the entire community and have targeted
   programs to specific communities of people at risk of infection.
8 Schneider, 'Lesbian Politics,' 164.
9 Dowsett, *Practicing Desire*.
10 Roy, *Living and Serving*.
11 Odets, *In the Shadow*, 99–105.
12 Rofes, *Reviving the Tribe*
13 A similar tension between the longer-term political goals and short-term service provision have also been discussed with regard to women's services. See, for example,
   Schecter, *Women and Male Violence*.
14 The chapter draws on data from a qualitative study of the development of AIDS service organizations in Canada. I interviewed respondents from twelve ASOs: AIDS
   New Brunswick; SIDA-AIDS Moncton; le Mouvement d'information et d'entraide
   dans la lutte contre le sida à Québec; le Comité SIDA aide de Montréal; the AIDS
   Committee of Toronto; the Hamilton AIDS Network; the AIDS Committee of Thun-
   der Bay; the AIDS Network of Edmonton; South Peace AIDS Council; AIDS Vancouver; Kelowna and Area AIDS Resources, Education, and Support; and AIDS
   Yukon Alliance. I invited these organizations to participate in the study to ensure
   representation from different regions of the country and from both large urban centres and smaller communities. I conducted in-depth interviews between 1990 and
   1994 with about 250 current and former staff members, board members, and volun-

teers. Interviews were also conducted with public health and hospital workers, provincial and federal civil servants, and gay and lesbian activists and workers in other community organizations. To help ensure that a broad range of perspectives was represented, respondents were also drawn from AIDS programs that specialize in providing services to women and specific ethnocultural communities. Interviews lasted from one to three hours, and were tape-recorded. The tapes were transcribed verbatim, and, using the grounded theory approach described by Glaser and Strauss in *The Discovery of Grounded Theory,* I coded the transcripts according to theoretical categories that emerged from the data. The discussion that follows draws extensively on quotes from interviews; quotes have sometimes been edited for clarity and to protect the identity of respondents.

15 Rofes, 'Gay Lib,' 10.
16 King, *Safety*, 169–232.
17 Best, 'Dark Figures.'
18 The Canadian AIDS Society has recently published a report on sustaining and evaluating 'men who have sex with men' programs in Canada: *Critical Work.*
19 King, *Safety in Numbers*, 53.
20 Ibid., 203–5.
21 Odets, 'AIDS Education,' 5.
22 See Rofes, *Reviving the Tribe*, 155–85.
23 Patton, *Inventing AIDS.* This observation parallels the history of services in the women's movement, where the activist history was also rewritten often, and where activists were replaced by workers with professional backgrounds who worked from more individualized, psychological models. (See Schecter, *Women and Male Violence;* and Walker, *Family Violence.*
24 Stein and Plummer, 'I Can't Even Think,' 181.
25 Seidman, 'Identity and Politics,' 105.
26 Aronowitz, 'Against the Liberal State,' 357–83.
27 Epstein, 'Gay Politics, Ethnic Identity' 243.
28 Anna Marie Smith, 'Resisting the Erasure,' 200–13; Meekosha, 'The Bodies Politic,' 180.
29 Thomas, 'The "Q" Word,' 75.
30 Gamson, 'Identity Movements,' 390–407.

11

The Anal-ytic Discourses of AIDS and Safer Sex

BLAINE MARK REHKOPF

Sex was not something one simply judged; it was a thing one administered. It was in the nature of a public potential; it called for management procedures; it had to be taken charge of by analytical discourses.

Michel Foucault, *The History of Sexuality*

[D]iscourse is not the majestically unfolding manifestation of a thinking, knowing, speaking subject, but, on the contrary, a totality, in which the dispersion of the subject, and his discontinuity with himself, may be determined.

Michel Foucault, *The Archaeology of Knowledge*

AIDS organizers and activists, especially, learned a hard lesson: it is difficult to predict the results of discursive battles.

Cindy Patton, *Fatal Advice*

Prevention and treatment of the opportunistic infections of AIDS continues to improve with the unprecedented production and exchange of information within and between scientific and activist communities. Vancouver's 1996 International Conference on AIDS, for example, was presented as an occasion for optimism concerning treatments for infections, perhaps the only time such widespread hope had been expressed publicly in the fifteen years since the first official report that a rare pneumonia had been found among gay men. Yet despite – or perhaps in light of – the tremendous increases in scientific knowl-edge concerning the structure and transmission of the human immunodeficiency virus (HIV), behavioural change correctly remains the primary focus of strategies for the prevention of new infections.

Early in the history of AIDS, during the so-called first wave of infections, behavioural change was often expected to follow directly from an understanding of the facts of HIV transmission and the course of HIV disease. Patterns of HIV risk-behaviour, it once seemed safe to presume, would follow what was thought to be a fairly typical epidemiological course. Risk-behaviour, wisdom had it, would vary inversely as a function of risk-behaviour knowledge. That is, it was common to suppose that 'health education and prevention are synonymous' and that 'by providing people with enough information about a health risk, behavior change will automatically follow.' As one prevention strategist writes, however, 'AIDS proves that view incorrect.'[1] From an ethical as well as a pedagogical perspective, I shall be arguing, that view is no less dangerous than it is naïve. That view underlies not only many ineffective safer-sex strategies, but also the judgmental moralism that *still* manages to find a place in the discourses of AIDS and safer sex.

Factual information, clearly, is a necessary element within a general strategy of prevention. But though necessary, such information cannot be considered sufficient. Safer-sex educational efforts focusing on behaviours and practices have facilitated the dissemination of information concerning the routes, relative risks, and methods of preventing HIV transmission. And yet, despite these efforts, evidence suggests a 'second wave' of new HIV infections is spreading among young gay men. I examine in this chapter the ethical and pedagogical implications of that apparent incongruity. That examination is warranted, in so far as the evidence that has emerged over the past years of the epidemic suggests, distressingly, that regular practice of safer sexual behaviours does not tend to correlate well with knowledge of the 'hard facts' of HIV transmission. Given the availability of factual information, many people understand these new infections to be the result of weakness or failure in both reason and morality. This understanding, I suggest, turns at a fundamental level on a liberal individualist conception of the self; I challenge that conception. My intention in writing this chapter is to loosen the grip of the moralistic and pedagogically ineffective discourses concerning AIDS and safer sex by calling into question the conceptions of the self and sexuality that produce and are produced within these very discourses.

Individualism places the individual subject before its social relations. All things being equal, that priority tends to favour autonomy, one's freedom to act in accordance with one's will. Thus it also tends to locate at the individual level responsibility for those actions freely performed. I will use the term *ethical individualism* to refer to the tendency to view as inseparable individual autonomy and moral responsibility. Ethical individualism is a predominant theme within general conceptions of modern Western selves; *a fortiori*, it is assumed within much of the discourse concerning AIDS and safer sex in Western societies. While preventative educational strategies are often imaginative and varied, they appear typically to presuppose as their ideal target a Rational Maximizer: 'a unified rational thinking subject, possessed of free will and the ability to choose life goals' in order 'to maximize [its] own self-interest.'[2] In this conception of the self, autonomy, freedom, and self-interest are closely bound. Assuming such an ontology of the self, educational efforts might be considered to be complete if they convey relevant information concerning the possible routes and relative risks of viral transmission.[3]

Pedagogically this sort of discourse might be termed reductive, for it reduces to a focus on specific and discrete practices, pointing out the dangers of higher-risk activities and urging their outright elimination or, as more realistic approaches stress, their substitution with lower-risk activities. These reductivist approaches are often taken to be sufficient, for they do indeed supply the raw facts necessary for autonomous and self-interested – *responsible* – behaviour. Risky behaviours are and tend to remain the focus here: consider the educational reminder-*cum-mantra* 'There are no high-risk groups, only high-risk practices.' For educationally pragmatic and political reasons, reductivist approaches emphasize that social-group membership implies neither viral immunity nor viral immanence. While I focus on the consequences for individual behaviour of stressing risk behaviours rather than risk groups, I do not deny that there are good reasons to worry about the latter focus: violence and discrimination often result from group stigmatization; group stigmatization might result in a sense of individual and collective fatalism; self-identity apparently involves more than simple sexual practices (witness the common classified ad: Straight man seeks same for casual sexual encounters); HIV really *doesn't* discriminate. All these reasons and others have been used to urge the presentation of safer-sex educational campaigns in identity-neutral, behaviourally reductive terms. Fuller discussions of these reasons can be found elsewhere.[4] Though I understand the reasoning behind these strategies, I am concerned with the perhaps less obvious yet still consequential ramifications of attempting such programmed interventions.

Reductivist strategies focus primarily, if not narrowly, on sexual activities themselves, often resisting the temptation to consider the deeper significance of those activities for identifiable social groups and their members. For example, the placing of various behaviours along a single axis constituting a 'risk continuum' is one common method of displaying the 'facts' necessary for risk reduction. Behaviours as diverse as shaking hands, sharing toothbrushes or razers, deep kissing, fellatio, and unprotected anal intercourse are casually, even blithely, portrayed as being on a continuum. On that continuum, a *quantitative* albeit notoriously vague modifier – 'riskiness' – is portrayed as the salient source of difference and similarity between each of the behaviours. No mention need ever be made concerning who one is, only what one does. And what one does on that continuum is a simple descriptive matter, not an evaluative one. That is, though the relative risk of each behaviour is carefully mapped out, the meaning(s) of each of those behaviours are left for each person to decide for himself or herself. The beauty of the continuum is that with such a tool in hand, educators, politicians, and citizens alike may remain, rather safely, on the shores of that murky swamp called personal identity.

Such approaches, which I am terming reductivist, do not serve the interests of educators and politicians alone, of course, for they are intended also, even primarily, to reduce the stigmatization of groups. The latter goal is a worthy one from both educational and political perspectives. The resulting focus is the individual: reductivist strategies serve to underscore individual responsibility to act safely. But urging individual responsibility for actions in turn yields moralistic condemnation when all the 'necessary' information is available and infection still occurs. That is, however unwittingly, reductivist approaches legitimate judgments of individual blame for engaging in those prohibited activities. Perhaps that tendency to judge is most troubling when it appears in those who themselves test positive for HIV. Consider Kevin, for example, a young gay man quoted in *The Advocate*: 'All I could think of was how I had done something wrong and thrown my life away, like all those nasty things conservatives have been saying about us were true. I remember my mom ... saying, "How could you have been so stupid?" I was asking myself the same question.'[5]

Despite one's sympathy for all the Kevins, the Rational Maximizer conception of the self tends to legitimate such blame: after all, if one has the necessary facts and the freedom to apply them, then it seems appropriate to judge their nonapplication as an individual's own ethical and even rational failures. But under what circumstances ought we to abandon that conception of the subject, and, by extension, the educational approaches and moral judgments that seem logically to stem from it? How much blame? How many lives? What empirical evidence would suffice to convince us that such a conception is misguided? I consider the following to be a starting point. A 1993 report from the San Francisco Health Commission states that 'almost 12% of 20- to 22-year-old gay men surveyed were HIV-positive, as were 4% of 17- to 19-year-olds.'[6] More recent studies are also finding that rates of infection are rising among young gay men.[7] Some health officials and AIDS educators have regarded this trend as a second wave of HIV infections among young gay men. The implications of these figures are sobering. Epidemiologically, the statistics suggest that if no significant intervention is made, 'the current generation of young urban gay men will have as high an infection rate by the time they reach their mid-thirties as middle-aged gay men are thought to have today.'[8] Seroprevalence studies indicate that present rates of HIV infection among middle-aged gay men are as high as 50 per cent in large cities.[9]

Because this second wave has occurred despite the tremendous increase in educational efforts since the early 1980s that have focused on behavioural change and risk reduction, difficult pedagogical and ethical questions must be raised. I believe that the second wave of HIV infections among knowledgeable young gay men complicates matters for (proponents of) the liberal individualist conception of the self.[10] I want to argue that it is time to reconsider the predominant conceptual presuppositions at work within this seemingly analytical discourse. Though the daunting nature of the task implied makes this sound pessimistic, only such a fundamental reconsideration can effect the significant intervention necessary to address the tidal wave of new HIV infections.

In place of the Rational Maximizer, or liberal individualist conception of the self, I want to draw from accounts of the subject that stress sociality over individuality. While this reconceptualization of subjectivity certainly has broader implications for both ethics and pedagogy, sexual behaviour provides fertile and important ground for a primary investigation. I agree with Stephen David Ross when he argues that '[t]he unmistakable and irresistible fact is that we cannot distinguish sexuality and love from sociality, not easily or clearly.'[11] And we cannot (any more, at least) distinguish sex from sexuality. We cannot separate what we do from who we are; or, to put it another way, in a homophobic culture we cannot separate *who* we do from *what* we are. As Foucault tells us, it would be a mistake to suppose that sex can be conceived of as autonomous from sexuality, or, importantly, from the deployments of *power* through which we are constituted as individual subjects: 'On the contrary, sex is the most speculative, most ideal, and most internal element in a deployment of sexuality organized by power in its grip on bodies and their materiality, their forces, energies, sensations, and pleasures.'[12] Foucault clearly is influential in this reconceptualization of subjectivity in light of his edifying work on sexuality. A reconsideration of subjectivity, therefore, begins with a consideration of the genesis of the 'modern' subject and the development of sexuality as a defining, disciplinary, subjectifying institution of modernity. The history of sexuality, then, is tantamount to a genealogy of modern selves.

In the first volume of *The History of Sexuality*, Foucault suggests that sexual science of the late 1800s began to concern itself 'primarily with aberrations, perversions, exceptional oddities, pathological abatements, and morbid aggravations.' This discursive obsession with aberration, this analytic science of discerning the normal from the abnormal, Foucault attributes to an 'inability or refusal to speak of sex itself.'[13] That science of evasion legitimated its own access to the most personal behaviours and desires of individuals by attributing social destructiveness to even 'the furtive customs of the timid, and the most solitary of petty manias ...; strange pleasures, it warned, would eventually result in nothing short of death: that of individuals, generations, the species itself.'[14] This evasive analysis specifically marked what it took to be abnormalities, and grounded such distinctions in the truth of scientific discourse. Given the assurance of concomitant destruction, that discourse might be understood as a sort of epistemic Darwinism. Predicated on the salvation of individuals, generations, and species, this science justified as its mandate the ability to delve into, and – where necessary – to correct the 'strange pleasures' it could locate. And it *always* seemed necessary. The primary discursive analytic tool was the separation of abnormal from normal, performed by aligning people along axes of identification. It was such axes of identification which could name and permit the scientific investigation of the destructive 'truth' of each individual, and, collectively, the destructive truths which could justify the various 'racisms of the state.'[15]

It is worth clarifying the notion of identification, then, since it is a central concept here. In *The Language of Psycho-Analysis* Laplanche and Pontalis define identification as the '[p]sychological process whereby the subject assimilates an aspect, property or attribute of the other and is transformed, wholly or partially, after the model the other provides. It is by means of a series of identifications that the personality is constituted and specified.'[16] The primary psychoanalytic sense of the term, then, is that of the '*identification of oneself with.*'[17] Importantly, identifications are not only the processes through which antecedently existent individuals are transformed; rather, they also comprise 'the operation itself whereby the human subject is *constituted.*'[18] The constitution of subjectivity itself as a result of the process of social interaction clearly has implications for the liberal individualist conception of the self, specifically the notion of rational maximization. On the understanding that identifications are constitutive (as opposed to merely augmentative) of subjectivity, the notion of maximization demands further specification. That is, given the array of possible identifications, 'demands coexist within an [agent] ... which are diverse, conflicting and disorderly.' Hence the agent, though autonomous in the sense of having an ability to choose by and for oneself, nevertheless 'is composed of identifications with cultural ideals that are not necessarily harmonious.'[19] This self, constituted *ex nihilo* from a series of social identifications, is not ideally unified, and any reference to maximization here necessarily evokes the further question: For *which aspect* of the self?

If Freudian psychoanalytic work had complicated the self by stressing identifications and by rejecting the idea of a unified core of subjectivity, Foucault's work further muddied the waters by positing the historical contingency of axes of possible social identifications. Rather than suppose transcultural or transhistorical axes of identification, Foucault's genealogies trace the production of contingent social identifications through institutional discourses and deployments of power. Thus, *inter alia*, Foucault's *Madness and Civilization* traces the production of insanity, within the medical and legal institutions, as a possible axis of identification; *Discipline and Punish* does the same for criminality; *The History of Sexuality, Volume I*, is a genealogy of sexuality and the plethora of identifications made possible as the result of medical, legal, and scientific discourses. For instance, in the last half of the 1800s, he suggests, it became possible for the first time to think of same-sex, or, indeed, opposite-sex sexual behaviours and desires, as evidence of fundamental and characteristic human differences.

It was during this time, then, that '[s]ex was driven out of hiding and constrained to lead a discursive existence.'[20] Now, same-sex behaviours had always existed, of course, as had opposite-sex behaviours. But Foucault's work suggests that it was only after the discursive production of sexuality as a possible axis of individual identification that such behaviours could be understood as evidence of the 'truth' of individual subjectivities. He suggests, for example, that it was during the late 1800s that the label *homosexual* came to describe persons, as opposed merely to naming deviant behaviours; that conceptual shift was accompanied by a general shift away from the conception of the sodomite as merely the 'juridical subject' of 'a category of forbidden acts.'[21] Thus, whereas '[t]he sodomite had been a temporary aberration,' writes Foucault, 'the homosexual was now [a member of] a species,' an individual for whom 'nothing that went into his total composition was unaffected by his sexuality. It was everywhere present in him: at the root of all his actions because it was their insidious and indefinitely active principle ... It was consubstantial with him, less as a habitual sin than as a singular nature.'[22]

Here, then, is the reason for my concern with reductivist discourses of AIDS, and, especially safer sex. Foucault's work stresses the cultural, conceptual shift *away* from sexual subjects as merely the performers of actions, and *toward* the notion of sexual subjects as produced by the actions and desires (or, more generally, though it would not be Foucault's term, by the identifications) made possible through the 'discursive existence' of sex. Yet, if I am correct, that conceptual shift is not typically accounted for within the reductive discourses of AIDS and safer sex. These reductive discourses tend to return the focus to collections of sexual behaviours in place of the constituted identities – especially sexual identities – of modern subjectivity. At best, these reductive discourses are anachronistic; at worst, they are contributorily deadly.

How did the discursive existence of sex come about? The discourses surrounding the workings of science are important to examine. While sexual science of the 1800s had to regard its results in terms of discovery, for Foucault the process must be understood as one of production. The mechanisms by which science forced sex to lead a discursive existence manifested necessarily at the constitutive level of the individual, the level of subjectivity itself. Power was and is implicated here, since for Foucault it is important to recognize the capriciousness of mere discovery. Science and State would not find simple random, aberrant behaviours to prevent; the insertions of power and the ability to discipline individuals (that is, very roughly, to guide their actions without apparent coercion, hence providing the semblance of freedom and autonomy) demanded more predictability. The identifications amalgamated under the banner of sexuality admitted (and continue to admit) the requisite sorts of predictability. Thus sexuality becomes a fundamental axis of individual psychology in the modern subject; in the words of David Halperin it becomes a conceptually 'autonomous system within the physiological and psychological economy of the human organism.'[23] According to Halperin, 'Before the scientific construction of "sexuality" as a positive, distinct, and constitutive feature of individual human beings ... a person's sexual *acts* could be individually evaluated and categorized, but there was no conceptual apparatus available for identifying a person's fixed and determinate sexual *orientation*, much less for assessing and classifying it.'[24] But if sexuality has become an orientation rather than a collection of acts – if it now describes a person rather than a person's behaviours – I suggest that this characterization is minimalized, if not ignored altogether, in the reductivism (that is, the tendency to reduce to descriptions of and cautions against individual risky behaviours) that characterizes much of the current discourse on AIDS and safer sex. This is not without repercussions. And in a homo-negating society, with a selective embargo against general cultural representations of same-sex sexuality, the impact of this reductivism is apparent in the behaviours of young gay men.

Foucault suggests that a main impetus for the proliferation of discourses focusing upon aberration was, ironically, the motivation to avoid speaking directly about sex itself. What took place instead, he describes as a 'screen-discourse' intent upon discovering the anomalies through painstaking procedures 'meant to evade the unbearable, too hazardous truth of sex.'[25] I want to suggest that the collective socially, politically, and scientifically sanctioned discourses of AIDS and safer sex should also be understood as a screen-discourse of sorts. The 'official' discourse legitimates its own existence by appealing to the otherwise disastrous consequences for individuals and society. Such discourse authorizes the production of and even the demand for intimate details about same-sex sexual activities while it simultaneously evades the 'unbearable, too hazardous truth' of same-sex sociality.

In light of this dynamic, I suggest, it is necessary to examine the concept of same-sex 'love,' or, better, emotional connection – as opposed to simply sexual behaviours per se – and to revise the discourses of AIDS and safer sex thereby. I must, however (and the need to provide this caveat is itself telling) preface that examination by making it explicit that my concern here is neither confined to nor particularly focused upon something like romantic love. The emotive, connective aspect of sexuality – what I am terming the *sociality* of sex – takes many different forms. A characteristically romantic sexual relationship certainly counts as one of these forms; but this sociality, this emotional connection, is present in far more discrete and/or brief encounters also. In any case, speaking of love, connection, or sociality conveys a central point I am trying to make: that sexual encounters in any context bear a self-affirming quality, not necessarily in an evaluative sense, but rather in a substantive, constitutive sense. Whether they take place in palaces or parks, sexual encounters bear a meaning beyond physical pleasure, and an importance beyond drive satisfaction. For modern subjects after the mid-1800s such encounters carry a self-constitutive quality, lined up as they now are along this axis of individual psychology called sexuality. This axis, as described above, is composed of the identifications made possible when sex was forced to lead a discursive existence. Given such a discursive existence and the identifications and thus the constitutions of subjectivity made possible thereby, the sociality of all sexual encounters must be considered when attempting programmed interventions.

The sociality of sex, then, may be thought of as the affirming and productive aspect of relational, sexual identifications. Sometimes we simplify, even attempt to 'purify,' this sociality by calling it love, but that name tends to be evaluative and exclusionary. The sociality of sex comes in many varieties, and it is an historical and political contingency that not all of them are equally accepted or valued. Nevertheless, what is important to recognize here is that there is a formative function to all sexual activity. It is a means through which we find for ourselves answers to the questions of who we are and what we are. As Ross puts it, for modern subjects sexuality 'not only shows who and what we are, as human beings, but it is a way of determining who we are.'[26] Sexual activity is not simply an expression of the modern subject; rather, via sociality, sexual behaviours are also constitutive of the modern subject. But that is a conception of sexual activity typically not accounted for within the reductive discourses of AIDS and safer sex.

In reductive discourses, actions are severed from concrete, located, individual subjects. The actions are then able to be described and evaluated within a nonspecific context of physical satisfaction as the discrete and select manifestations of a general sexual drive. But, clearly, the drive-satisfaction model underdetermines sexual activity. In other words, drive satisfaction is not congruent with sexual activity; or, put simply, a fuck is never just a fuck.[27] Thus the significance of sexual activity exceeds the activity proper, yet the reductive discourses of safer sex neglect this fact. Persons not only perform sexual acts; they are also constituted through the forms of sociality – not merely the sensual pleasures – permitted by those very acts.

In light of the second wave within the AIDS epidemic, we must consider what barriers to self-creation are put in place by discourses that attempt to save a self by rending from it the meanings of the actions by and through which it is constituted. We need to consider at which aspect(s) of the self such reductivist discourses are targeted, and, by corollary, which aspects of the self are immune to or even harmed by those same discourses. For in a culture that censors representations of the sociality of same-sex sexual activity, well-intentioned reductivist educational strategies serve iatrogenically to remove an essential means of self-constitution without simultaneously changing the impoverished background social conditions through which self-constitution is mediated. In practical terms, my point is that we cannot simply assume that 'protected' intercourse permits an adequate substitution for 'unprotected' intercourse within a sociopolitical environment that is not only disparately inhospitable to homosociality, but also thereby disparately infecund for homosubjectivity. What must be recognized, then, is that no matter how rational or reasonable such a programmed substitution of one degree of pleasure for another might seem, given a unified and constituting subject, that rationality and reasonability must be re-assessed in light of the dispersed and constituted subject-in-becoming that I am attempting to describe. In short, educators must focus upon meaning at least as much as they have focused upon moaning.

Reductivist safer-sex discourses tend to promote a very incomplete public representation of the significance of sexual activities, at least for certain people. These strategies are incomplete because they avoid the concepts of love and connection, of sociality.[28] The message that same-sex sexual behaviour is, can be, and/or ought to be distinguished from its constitutive effects takes (at least) three forms. First, mainstream culture carries the clear but false message that gays and lesbians can have only sex without love, caring, personal/emotional connection. (That culture fails to recognize the irony that accompanies the policies and attitudes it devises to attenuate the very connection it simultaneously supposes to be 'always already impossible.') Second, the 'counter-discourse' since the sixties has promoted the message that 'sex without love' is just fine; and so it is. Finally, the reductive discourse of safer sex carries the message that sexual behaviours can be isolated from the social meanings of sex vis-à-vis sexuality. Thus, the reductivist strategies of safer sex campaigns continue in the same vein as both the mainstream discourse and the counter-discourse. What all of these discourses tend to discount are the constitutive effects of sexual activity that occur through identification via the sociality of sexual activity.

Currently, it seems, the ideology of these discourses has run up against empirical behaviour. Neither the second wave of infection, nor indeed the first wave, can be explained sufficiently by grounding explanations in simple drive satisfaction. Sexual activity does not persist in the face of systemic discrimination, familial and social rejection, bashings, killings, and HIV simply because it *feels good*. Yet that myth seems to characterize many conceptions of (especially same-sex) sexual behaviours and desires. Rather, as Elizabeth Grosz notes, sexual drives 'are the consequence of the absorption of the drive by systems of cultural meaning, by representations.'[29] Such absorption, and thus the meanings of one's behaviours and desires, impacts disparately depending on – since I am suggesting the factors are inseparable – who one is, what one does and wants to do, and the sociopolitical context in which one lives. Pedagogically and ethically, then, information about sexual activity must be assessed through and against the cultural background; obviously, safer-sex discourse is not the sole source of sexual identity formation. Thus programs encouraging safer sex must be planned respective of the other potentially formative representations produced or prohibited within a society. Safer-sex programming has become a part of cultural production; it cannot be assumed to exist only incidentally in a culture that works so diligently to police all expressions of same-sex desire.

The fact that AIDS has become a cultural institution within many societies across the world is reflected in the work and writings of many artists and critical theorists. As James Miller points out in the introduction to one important collection of such work, *Fluid Exchanges: Artists and Critics in the AIDS Crisis*, 'other epidemics have affected the production of cultural objects and the construction of cultural history, and often deeply. But never so rapidly or so politically as AIDS.'[30] Miller is correct to explain this effect in terms of the political fertility of the artistic and critical-theory communities at the outset of the epidemic, as well as the fact that HIV had begun personally to affect the lives of many of those within these overlapping communities by the middle of the 1980s. The full story of the cultural inclusion of AIDS, of course, is one not only of cultural offerings – including the 'official' accounts and the attempts to call those accounts into question – but also of the social receptivity to those offerings. The psychosocial or psychosexual discourse of AIDS, then, is related to the ways in which sex has been made a political issue due to the historical 'proliferation of disciplinary technologies, targeting the body and legitimated in consenting identities.'[31] These 'consenting identities' are irretrievably inter-meshed with – since they are, dialectically, the result of and the condition for – the discourses surrounding sexuality, including of course the discourses of AIDS and safer sex.

In his contribution to *Fluid Exchanges*, Simon Watney convincingly argues that the effects of such official accounts of AIDS and safer sex can be analysed in terms related both to the individual and the society:

In Foucault's terms we may productively analyse *all* the various cultural and political practices generated in response to the epidemic in relation to two sets of historically given procedures of power, or *disciplines*. The first of these involves 'an anatomo-poli-tics of the human body' that centres on the body as if it were a machine, concerned with its productivity, its obedience, its recalcitrance, its *utility*. The second involves 'a biopol-itics of the population' that is effected through a multitude of regulatory controls, cen-tred on the body understood primarily as a participant in the life of the *species* ...'[32]

Watney argues, then, that Foucault's analysis of power can be applied 'to the types of disciplinary control exercised throughout "official" AIDS and safer-sex education campaigns.'[33] Thus, '[t]he meaning of the body that informs such campaigns may in turn be traced in other practices, from journalism and televi-sion coverage, to the protocols of clinical trials, the statements and policies of politicians, medical practice, and so on.'[34]

Watney's argument is important in that he recognizes the impact of such dis-courses and the counter-discourses they have spawned on the present and future of sexual – especially *gay* – identities. His concern revolves around the 'com-pliant identity of the "AIDS victim," who must totally and willingly acquiesce to the meanings that the coincidence of disease and sexuality have made his body speak.'[35] Watney rightly criticizes the official responses to the epidemic, pointing out that various political responses (for example, the Helms amend-ment to deny U.S. federal funding in the field of the arts for cultural products considered to be, *inter alia*, 'homoerotic,' and the British Parliament's endorse-ment of legislation forbidding 'the promotion of homosexuality' by any local government authority; to these I would add some of the seedier justifications offered more recently for the U.S. Defense of Marriage Act) can be interpreted, rightly, as an indication of 'the full extent to which sexual identity has now entered the foreground of ideological and political contestation in the West, and cannot be casually dismissed as "marginal." For what is ultimately at stake here is not only "sexual freedom," but the aggressive contemporary reassertion of the categories of sexuality as the exclusive legitimate means by which women and men are to be officially permitted to identify their erotic needs, individually or collectively.'[36] While I agree with his general assertion, I want to take another critical step by employing his insights concerning the discourses of AIDS in order to begin to analyse the safer-sex educational campaigns that have been developing in response to this foregrounding of sexual identity within the ideological and political contestations in the West.

Cultural representations must not be understood as benign, as merely decorative; they are functional. Thus if political contestations are taking place at the level of cultural representation, then it is important to examine which representations are – and which are not – authorized within a given society. Signification of the actual or idealized reality of heterosexual drives and desires is culturally ubiquitous; it is the normalized and naturalized assumption within cultural production. From our earliest storybooks, toys and games, fairly tales, nursery rhymes, cartoons, songs, and ceremonies to the immense bulk of what pass as adult expressions of 'our' ideals of human interconnection and love, heterosexuality is axiomatic, the *sine qua non* of culture and society. (From an *out*-side perspective, of course, the collective cultural offering seems little short of boy-meets-girl run amok.) If those heterosexual representations are absorbed and thereby integrated through cultural signification, it is doubtful that the same dynamic holds for same-sex drives and desires for deep interpersonal connection, conspicuous, to those who are looking, most typically by their absence or erasure. And if, as Lacan suggests, what has been foreclosed in the symbolic must return in the real, it is to be expected that the refusal to signify the constitutive results of same-sex sexuality demands the surfacing of the effects of that very refusal.

It is possible, though it often takes some searching, to find 'official' or widely condoned representations of same-sex desire. However, in these representations same-sex desire typically is simplified to mean the desire for same-sex sexual activity per se: that is, sexual activity void even of the possibility of connective and constitutive meanings typically not only associated, but also mistakenly *identified*, with heterosexual sexual activity. These simplified and reductive representations of same-sex sexual activity constitute the screen discourse I described above: they screen the possible interpretations of sexual activity that might actually represent the connective and constitutive result – the sociality – of same-sex sexual behaviours. And since it is sociality that permits the formation of subjectivity, the negation of representations of homosociality is tantamount to the denial of homosubjectivity. That erasure is a politically motivated denial of the significations and social conditions necessary for self-constitution. In this social context, then, far from an indication of some phylogenic or even ontogenic 'death drive,' educators and activists would do well to recognize the possibility that the seemingly irrational practice of risky sexual behaviours is at least occasionally and maybe typically a manifestation of something precisely the opposite – perhaps something like an existential will to subjectivity or self-creation.

It is not surprising, therefore, to recognize that while same-sex desire is occasionally acknowledged and represented within cultural discourse, it is and has been under the purview of sin and criminality that such representations take place. Yet these two 'institutions' notoriously reduce – at least 'officially' – to judgments of individual acts (or series of acts) rather than to judgments of identity. Thus it is possible to criminalize and punish sodomy as an isolated act, and to 'love the sinner but hate the sin.' This reductivism also serves, conveniently at times, to deny any deeper or more meaningful implications of young, drunken, or situational episodes of homosexual activity (for example, in prisons or single-sex schools). It is significant to note that virtually all sources of sexual information for young people emphasize that such behaviours are – paradoxically, to my mind – both extremely common and quite meaningless with respect to one's sexuality; of course the same is never said for similar heterosexual activities, no matter how young, how drunken, or how rare the chance that a member of the *same* sex might soon show up to *really* scratch that sexual itch.

Testament to this 'official' reductivism is the near-equation of homosexual activity with anal intercourse; that equation neatly determines a source of and a solution to the whole messy 'problem' of same-sex desire. And if sinful and/or criminal anal intercourse – sodomy – were the primary evidence for same-sex desire prior to AIDS discourse, the anus also gains particular prominence within AIDS discourse itself. As Cindy Patton notes, 'anal sex as a symbol of homosexual desire becomes an obsessive topic of interest in discussions about safe sex.'[37] There is little to be gained from disputing the supposition that unprotected anal intercourse is a relatively expedient means of viral transmission, and I would not pretend to deny that. But this 'fact' of transmission within safer-sex discourse has tended to subvert the possibility of considering what else might represent or indicate same-sex desire. Given a culture that officially authorizes the discourses of sin, criminality, and reductivist safer-sex education, and without a cultural background of alternative representations of same-sex desire, anal intercourse takes on a special meaning; it becomes one significant source of gay identity formation, accompanying transgression be damned. It is little wonder that, although heterosexuals are typically thought to be under-determined by their sexual activity, gay men and lesbians are typically thought to be overdetermined by theirs: there are so few representations of same-sex desire other than the drive satisfaction model that pervades our cultural milieu and memory. Surely, though, this has effects at the individual level, the psycho-sexual level, for self-constitution is mediated by and through this larger cultural representation.

Beyond sexual activity, I am arguing, same-sex desire must be represented as the desire to purposefully (that is, constitutively) connect at some deep level of social interconnection and cultural inscription, one man with another, or one woman with another. And again, what must be stressed is that this face of same-sex desire must be represented whether its expression is casual and anonymous sex in the park or the loving, sexual relations of monogamous gay or lesbian lovers celebrating a golden anniversary.

If the discourses of AIDS and safer sex appear to lay claim to a realm of simple, even objective (for who could/would dispute those 'facts' of transmission?) behavioural analysis, that apparent objectivity is exposed by discursive ruptures reflecting the differences between the cultural representations of heterosexuality on one hand, and lesbian and gay sexualities on the other. The focus on HIV in blood and blood products is one such rupture, and it has brought some important illustrations to light. Rochelle Pittman's husband, for one, apparently contracted HIV during surgery, and died of AIDS-related complications in 1990. Sadly, Rochelle Pittman subsequently tested positive for HIV. A *Toronto Star* article documented the Pittmans' struggle with AIDS, describing how Rochelle Pittman 'contracted HIV through making love with her husband.'[38] The Pittmans' ordeal was, indeed, a tragedy. But for those living and dying in this epidemic, the term *making love* foregrounds itself in this particular context. If public representation were the only evidence, the conclusion would have to be made that no gay man or lesbian has ever been infected with HIV by making love. If it is not simply assumed within an account of a gay man's infection with HIV, infection is nearly always referred to as having taken place through unprotected anal intercourse or by the more nebulous but less provocative 'sexual activity.' Making love, the accounts would have us believe, is not a means of transmission within the gay and lesbian communities. For unlike heterosexuality, with the general proscription against public representations of same-sex sexuality outside the discourses of AIDS, safer sex, criminality, and sin, the conclusion would have to be that no person has ever 'made love' with a partner of the same sex. Period.

If the clear message of AIDS and safer-sex discourses is that certain sexual behaviours are risky, typically there is no such message, for gay men or lesbians, that making love presents the same risk. And, arguably, those who identify as gay or lesbian do not consider their identifications to be based simply on their ability or desire merely to satiate drives, but rather to forge positive and healthy identifications, whether to love and/or to connect deeply with and through other people, to *become selves*. I suspect that it is this difference – that is, identifying through the connective and constitutive aspects of one's sexual desires and activities rather than simply finding one's identifications within the drive satisfaction that may result from those activities – that is at the base of a distinction Watney finds between gay identity and homosexual identity. He suggests that the 'official' responses to AIDS have attempted to reify a homosexual identity: 'The figure of "the homosexual" that has been widely established as the focal figure of AIDS commentary is thus constituted primarily in relation to an imagined repertoire of "sexual acts" from which both disease *and* identity are imagined to derive.'[39] But I would also point out that it is this homosexual identity that most easily coincides with the lack of constitutive interconnection that might be required for the emergence of that alternative, or gay, identity. And I would note that younger men typically identify with/as 'gay' rather than 'homosexual.'

Watney might not disagree with my chosen characterization of the difference between homosexual and gay identities. He apparently understands gay identity as arising within and giving rise to a counterdiscourse that rejects the simple derivation of identity from sexual acts; yet it is not clear, to me at least, just where gay men *do* derive sexual identity from within Watney's account. His account is, correctly, very political in its intent, and as such he describes refusals and rejections as beginning points for identifications. He highlights 'the strategic refusal of gay men to root an identity within the historically pre-given power relations of sexuality,' even though that strategy 'has little or no public acknowledgement.'[40] Watney also suggests that the 'emergence of gay identity in the course of the twentieth century provides an alternative structure of identity that proceeds from a collective refusal'[41] to 'accept derogatory classifications and to socialize in relation to them, even if, as seems likely, these terms of abuse took on ironic or counterdiscursive meanings for those whose identities were formed and lived out under the stigmatizing influence of such nomenclature.'[42] Thus Watney's account of emergent gay identity seems to focus on political strategies of refusal and resistance.

I agree with much, if not all, of Watney's account; yet I want to supplement his account by focusing on the positive/formative function of the connective aspect of same-sex desire. Doing so, however, leads me to problematize even nonofficial AIDS and safer-sex discourses more than Watney might do, at least more than he does in his article. I suggest, then, that counterdiscourses, when reductive, tend to emulate the screen discourse that erases gay sociality. And that emulation is deeply problematic.

Watney states that 'the gap that gay men feel between their perceptions of themselves and the constructions made of them in the mass media and popular culture continues to widen.'[43] That gap, or so I would argue, consists mainly in the failure to represent that connective and constitutive aspect of same-sex desire and sexuality that so pervades the cultural representations of heterosexuality. That lack is important, even if there was and still is a tendency to view same-sex sexual activity, especially prior to the epidemic, as a large, shallow party comprised mainly of anonymous and brief encounters, and detached from all interpersonal connection but the physical. In the wake of AIDS, same-sex sexuality is often retrospectively and occasionally still criticized for that (apparent) separation. In the words of one gay character from a Robert Chesley play, 'everyone's putting [that behaviour] down nowadays. "The party's over! The party's over!"'[44] Wisely, I think, Chesley's character, Bert, questions the validity of such judgments and condemnations of that most 'risky' expression of sexuality : 'Well, fuck it all *no! That wasn't just a party!* It was more: a *lot* more, at least to some of us, and it was *connected* to other parts of our lives, *deep* parts, *deep* connections ... For me, for a *lot* of guys, it was ... *living*; and it was *loving.* Yeah: *It was loving,* even if you didn't know whose cock it was in the dark, or whose asshole you were sucking.'[45] Bert's point ought not to be dismissed as mere fiction, either. Reflecting on his own early reaction to safer-sex information, HIV-positive columnist Michael Kealy writes: 'Clearly, safer-sex education had little effect on people like Andrew and me, people who didn't have enough self-respect to practice safer sex, people for whom a nice cock and a good fuck were more important than life itself. They were life.'[46]

They were *life.* It is not same-sex sexual activity per se, but rather these deep, life-making connections permitted by sexual activity and through which subjectivity itself is formed and transformed that are denied official sanction or even recognition, let alone representation, by the vast majority within this culture. It is this active avoidance, for example, that permitted the defeat in 1994 of the Province of Ontario's Bill 167 to ensure legal parity between opposite- and same-sex primary partnerships. For it is this active avoidance of the reality of homosociality that leads to the refusal to provide state recognition, let alone support, for the day-to-day relational connections of same-sex partnerships in a province at least legally committed to the prohibition of discrimination on the grounds of sexual orientation. That same refusal lurked at the base of arguments in opposition to Bill C-33 and the (ultimately successful) inclusion in 1996 of sexual orientation to the list of prohibited grounds of discrimination within the Canadian Human Rights Code. Too often, '[d]emands for the civil rights and cultural autonomy of lesbians and gay men are seen as "politicizing" AIDS or as manipulating AIDS policy for an unrelated gay rights agenda.'[47] But clearly that agenda is not unrelated to AIDS policy-making, for it is related to effective

strategies of education. The political demand for civil rights and cultural autonomy can be understood substantively and practically as the demand for cultural
representation of the realities of the lives and loves that include same-sex
desire. That demand is for access to nothing less than the very means of self-
constitution. And that is a political necessity, especially in the face of AIDS, if
ever there was one. We must be political. It is not a matter of choice so much as
survival, safer sex notwithstanding.

While education campaigns are obviously necessary for the dissemination of
information about AIDS and HIV, the simple facts are not enough. And we
must understand that the method of presentation is crucially important; what is
not represented is as important as what is represented. In a homo-negating society, and given the conception of subjectivity I argue for here, we must consider
the possibility that there is a qualitative and not simply a quantitative difference
between intercourse with and without a latex barrier. Departing from an understanding of sexual activity as mere drive satisfaction, it becomes plausible that
sex with and without barriers is different in type and not just in degree, just as
surely as sharing a toothbrush or razor is qualitatively different from – not
merely 'less risky' than – fucking even *with* a condom.

Safer-sex educational strategies are ineffective to the extent that they assume
the central function of sexual activity is pleasure maximization. This hedonist-
egoist calculus is insufficient because sex is not merely a matter of maximizing
pleasure any more than love is. We seem prepared to accept the fact that central
to love is the possibility – indeed, the probability – that intense pain may
accompany it, from arguments, through breakups, and even the loss or death of
a loved one. Love is not reducible to pleasure maximization, for it persists
sometimes even when the pain is unbearable. And this persistence is considered
to be not only a virtue, but also in some way a necessity. To lack such persistence is to be brutish, unfeeling, almost *inhuman*. We do not love simply
because we want to; we love because we need to. Must we assume that sex is so
different, despite the fact that it facilitates bodily contact and emotional connection that we encounter in no other context? I suggest not, so long as we also recognize that sociality does not necessarily imply traditional, romantic love. But
nor must it be represented as a political or personal act of simple hedonism, as
much as this has become a counter-discursive refrain: it was never true – not at
the deepest level of all, subjectivity itself.

Pedagogically and ethically, sex must not be understood as simple drive satisfaction, for this denies its formative role. Sex *makes* selves. Thus strategies to
decrease risky behaviours would benefit from a consideration of the ways in
which constitutive needs are both satisfied and produced by expressing one's
sexuality within a homophobic culture. In what ways might those needs be cir-

cumvented by participating in safer sex as opposed to higher-risk activities? What sorts of subjective bonds or connections are created or sustained through participation in higher-risk activities? Such questions suggest that a thorough educational strategy must focus on persons made whole within an extensive system of cultural and even counter-cultural representations. That consideration, of the subjectifying or formative aspect of sexual relations, would recognize the problem of reconstituting the same reductive discourses that contain traditional notions of homosexual (as opposed to gay) activity and identity that Watney and others[48] find at the heart of the 'official' accounts of AIDS and safer sex. Though I agree with Watney that those official accounts are problematic, I am less convinced than he seems to be that the 'gay counter-discourses' do not in specific ways provide some reconstitution of that rather impoverished version of identity. The task for current and future safer-sex educators and political activists will not be easy within a culture so distressed by the simple idea that same-sex love and emotional connection might actually serve as a primary source for the healthy constitution of subjectivity.

As Patton writes, the task will require people to 'risk articulating some other way of life in order to work together to reform sexual cultures that resist both disease and social oppression.'[49] The pedagogical task is both an ethical one and a political one, then. The articulation of that 'other way of life' involves working for the cultural representation of the sociality of same-sex relations, while at the same time resisting the temptation to, as Watney calls it, 'assimilate,' that is, resisting the temptation to structure the cultural representations of gay and lesbian relationships as indistinguishable from heterosexual relationships. Watney, for one, is highly critical of such assimilation, tempting as it may be when the alternative is presented, especially in an epidemic, as compliance in one's own annihilation. Watney is correct to point out that what is at risk here is the denial of the 'important point that [an] aggressive indifference to the lives of gay men is profoundly structured in the roles and relations that make up "heterosexuality."'[50]

Yet I'm unsure that Watney's entire conclusion should be granted. I am apparently more sceptical that self-constitution can be achieved by purely critical and reactive means, especially in light of my argument that the gay counter-discourses have often tended to reconstitute the divide between our sexual actions and our sexual identities. Watney and I regard things at least slightly differently, and I think it is the nature of the sociopolitical requirements for self-constitution on which our disagreement turns. For example, he argues that 'the gay movement needs to sustain its critique of sexuality, embodied *most precisely* in the institution of marriage, which should be our target, not our goal.'[51] I wonder, though, if Watney here gives enough weight to his own recognition that 'we should never expect the future of a gay identity to involve the constant reproduction of people like ourselves.'[52]

It is unclear to me why it might not be an important option for at least some gay men and lesbians to have as a goal a sexuality as it is embodied in the institution of marriage. But even beyond the possibility of finding room within 'traditional' marriage for same-sex relations, there is reason to reconsider the *a priori* jettisoning of marriage as a political goal. This is worth considering in light of the role that I have argued cultural representations play within self-constitution. Put simply, I'm unsure why the institution of marriage cannot serve both as a goal and a target. This can be accomplished in two ways. First, it is clear that obtaining a right and exercising a right are two different things. Obtaining the right to marriage could be the goal, while exercising the right could be the target; at least in such a case, the cultural representation of the connective possibilities of same-sex relationships would be instantiated formally. Second, for those same-sex participants who did choose to exercise the right, the substance or content of the marriage could remain a critical focus; surely there is much to be negotiated and improved within the institution. In sum, to have the right to marriage as a goal is not the same as to regard traditional marriage as a desirable destination, either formally or substantively.

Although I would urge consideration of the educational implications of accommodating at least some semblance of same-sex marriage within the broad political agenda of lesbians and gay men, I stress that the icon of heterosexuality must not be considered to be the only idealization of sociality. My point is that a worthy political agenda must accommodate goals that promote the production of a richly fertile cultural milieu in which the growth of healthy subjectivities – not the specification of proper modes of behaviour – is paramount. Thus, while same-sex marriage is not my focus in this chapter, it is one of the implications of my arguments that safer-sex education cannot be theorized, critiqued, or performed as though AIDS were isolable from this and other sociopolitical discourses. While I have turned the illustration on Watney's discussion of same-sex marriage, it should remain clear that Watney's general point about unthinking assimilationism is well taken. None the less, my intent here is to present a viewpoint that urges a rethinking of educational issues involving sex and sexuality as political in their broadest scope, and formative of individual subjectivities in their narrowest scope; that these goals are two sides of the same coin should be apparent. It is a viewpoint that centres concern for inchoate subjectivities rather than for always-already existent subjects, subjects I consider to be a type of political fiction. A broad but strategic implication of my view is that safer-sex educational campaigns must include general and specific procedures for encouraging and providing fertile cultural representations – both mundane and imaginative – of the connective possibilities of same-sex sexuality. This is an ambitious call, for many reasons, and its manifestations remain to be explored.

In the meantime, though, such a call suggests that what is minimally required of us at present is that we resist the temptation towards hard ethical individualism with respect to AIDS and the transmission of HIV. In the current social climate, such judgments simply are ethically inappropriate, and, apparently, pedagogically suspect. A culture-wide refusal to signify the connective sociality of same-sex relationships is a clear threat to (theoretically, ideologically, actually) equal members of that very culture. Such a culture cannot itself escape the scope of moral responsibility, even if that culture is composed of individually autonomous members. Each of those autonomous members rightly demands an appropriately hospitable and fecund culture, since each subject, each self, is constituted only through and within the social identifications made possible by that same culture.

We *must* recognize the significance of understanding the formative role of sexual interactions. Since I have called for cultural representations of this formative role, it seems appropriate to allow such representations to make the final case. Safer-sex educators and those who care about gay men and lesbians need to think hard about the implications, the real-life implications, of the following exchange, again, from the Chesley play. In a reflective moment, Bert is recounting to J.R. a brief, casual, anonymous, 'high-risk' sexual encounter, by all accounts one of many he has had:

BERT: ... and it felt warm and good, one of the most wonderful things I think I've ever felt, one of the most wonderful *connections* I think I've ever had with another person, one of the most beautiful acts of love I think I've ever known ... And that was all: we kissed and hugged and said goodbye ... *And it was love*, even if it was only for a few hours.
J.R.: Which is frequently best.
BERT: Yup. (*Laughs. Pause.*) Hey, thanks.
J.R.: For what?
BERT: For reminding me.
J.R.: Of what?
BERT: No: for getting me to remember – that it was love. And ... a virus can't change that: can't change that fact.[53]

And indeed a virus cannot change that fact of love, nor can moralistic judgments, nor can even well-intentioned educators. But what I am suggesting is that we should not to try to change or to forget that sexual fact of love, that loving fact of sex. That love and that sex is the reason lesbians and gay men exist. To be sure, now AIDS has confronted us with a challenging paradox: sex-as-life/sex-as-death. But it is a paradox only within current reductive discourses of AIDS and safer sex. We will do better to remember the fact of love than to try and deny it. We need to acknowledge it and thereby produce a discourse in which our sexualities are not understood paradoxically. To that end we will demand ethical representations of all of those social identifications, all of those formative intersubjective connections, and all of that love. Perhaps then we can talk – *responsibly* – about AIDS, safer sex, and ethical individualism. But perhaps *then* there will be no need to.[54]

Notes

1 Kelly, *Changing HIV Risk Behavior*, ix.
2 Ferguson, 'A Feminist Aspect Theory,' 94.
3 See, for example, Gagnon, 'Disease and Desire,' 47–77.
4 See, for example, a number of papers in Klusaček and Morrison, eds., *Leap in the Dark*.
5 Bull and Gallagher, 'The Lost Generation,' 36.
6 Ibid.
7 Nichols, 'Beating AIDS,' 38–43.
8 See note 5 above.
9 Kelly, *Changing HIV Risk Behavior*, 5. With Kelly it is worth noting that statistics are notoriously complicated owing to the fact that 'AIDS constitutes the endstage illness consequence of HIV infection and there is a long latency between initial infection and the development of AIDS.' While determining the current number of cases of AIDS is thought to be more accurate than estimating HIV infection rates, the former count essentially tracks nearly decade-old patterns of infection. Yet seroprevalence studies which assess the rates of HIV infection rather than cases of AIDS, though more accurately reflective of recent trends, are not without attendant problems. As a result, according to Kelly, 'estimations of seroprevalence are usually based on small select samples followed by a generous amount of extrapolation,' 5.
10 For the purposes of the present discussion, ensuring the existence of self-identified proponents of this view is less important than demonstrating that/how the dynamics of the discourse as a whole turn upon such a conception of the self.
11 Stephen Ross, 'The Limits of Sexuality,' 326.
12 Foucault, *The History of Sexuality*, vol. 1, 155.
13 Ibid., 53.
14 Ibid., 53–4.

15 Ibid., 54.
16 Laplanche and Pontalis, *Language of Psycho-Analysis*, 205.
17 Ibid.
18 Laplanche and Pontalis, *Language of Psycho-Analysis*, 206 [italics mine].
19 Ibid., 208.
20 Foucault, *The History of Sexuality*, vol. 1, 33.
21 Ibid., 43.
22 Ibid.
23 Halperin, 'Sex Before Sexuality,' 41.
24 Ibid.
25 Foucault, *The History of Sexuality*, vol. 1, 53.
26 Stephen Ross, 'The Limits of Sexuality,' 328.
27 The validity of this rather blunt assertion is demonstrated perhaps most clearly in liberal democratic societies, in the limited success of appeals to the harm principle and privacy doctrine – two basic tenets of liberal rhetoric – to mitigate ethical and legal discrimination against homosexuality. See, for example, Bowers v. Hardwick, 478 U.S. 186 (U.S. Supreme Court 1986), which upheld the constitutionality of the criminalization of 'consensual sodomy' (*contra* the harm principle) in the privacy of one's own home (*contra*, as Justice Harry Blackmun wrote in dissension, quoting a predecessor, ' "the most comprehensive of rights and the right most valued by civilized men," namely, "the right to be left alone" ').
28 It is important to note that some safer sex educational campaigns have emphasized a form of this connection. For example the AIDS Committee of Toronto – in a campaign titled 'Can We Relate?' – emphasizes the importance of considering safer-sex practises even within regular partnerships of those men who have sex with other men. Other campaigns have stressed the need to care generally for other members in one's 'community.' Such campaigns are important, of course. I am suggesting here, though, that a recognition of the formative function of sex requires a considerable revision of all educational efforts to consider sex outside of regular relationships in which one actually has genuine regard and sense of responsibility for one's partner(s). As I've been suggesting, the connective aspect or sociality of sex that I am thinking of is a broader concept than something like love or even care or regard for others. While one may genuinely care about the well-being of one's sexual partner(s), that is not, I think, a necessary requirement for fulfilling the self-constitutive or formative function of our sexual interactions.
29 Grosz, *Jacques Lacan*, 4.
30 Miller, 'Introduction,' *Fluid Exchanges*, 4.
31 Watney, 'The Possibilities of Permutation,' 357.
32 Ibid.
33 Ibid.

34 Ibid.

35 Ibid.

36 Watney, 'The Possibilities of Permutation, 334.

37 Patton, *Inventing AIDS*, 117.

38 Rebecca Bragg, 'Rochelle Pittman: Life Without Ken,' *Toronto Star*, 27 March 1994, 6. Richard Elliott brought this example to my attention.

39 Watney, 'Possibilities of Permutation,' 337.

40 Ibid.

41 Watney, 'The Possibilities of Permutation,' 354.

42 Ibid., 353–4.

43 Ibid., 337.

44 Chesley, 'Jerker, or Helping Hand.'

45 Ibid.

46 Kealy, 'Lurking in the Dark,' 23. Kealy himself moves from this point precisely to the opposite conclusion of the one for which I am arguing. He concludes his column: '... I see that we have missed much of the point – the issue of personal responsibility. I have ignored safer-sex guidelines, and that is not the fault of AIDS educators, bathhouses or bars – it's mine, and mine alone. Sadly I learned this lesson too late.' While I take Kealy's point about responsibility for one's own behaviour to be practically important, I obviously disagree with the implications of the word *fault* in this particular context.

47 Patton, *Inventing AIDS*, 111.

48 See, for example, Patton, *Fatal Advice*.

49 Patton, 'Designing Safer Sex,' 203.

50 Watney, 'Possibilities of Permutation,' 359.

51 Ibid., 346.

52 Ibid., 363.

53 Chesley, 'Jerker, or Helping Hand,' 482–3.

54 Many people have helped me formulate, reconsider, and revise my ideas on this topic, and I owe them all thanks. I especially thank the following people for their individual ways of helping me begin to think through this material: Nick Ashby, Andrea Austen, Deborah Britzman, Sue Campbell, Doug, Richard Elliott, Leslie Green, Craig Haid, Christine Overall, Janice Ristock, Catherine Taylor, Richard Teixeira, and Shelley Tremain.

12

'Explain It to Me like I'm a Six-Year-Old ...' The Pedagogy of Race, Sex, and Masculinity in *Philadelphia*

LEE EASTON

I was teaching report writing to police education students at a Metro Toronto community college when the film *Philadelphia* was released in 1993. These young, predominantly white, working- or middle-class males were renowned for their conservative and often homophobic tendencies. Imagine, then, my trepidation the day one student, Steve, exclaimed to his partner, 'Go ahead. Explain it to me like I'm a six-year-old.' I confess I had a moment where one recognizes, but cannot recall, information because the context seems so incongruous. Puzzled by my sudden aphasia I boldly queried Steve about the expression. Steve replied, 'It's from *Philadelphia*. Did you see it?'

For me, as a closeted gay teacher, the question was more loaded than I suspect Steve knew, although the epistemological questions surrounding *that* statement are problematic, revealing more about my own assumptions than necessarily about Steve's. Given the context, I tried to remain noncommittal in my response. I allowed that I had seen the movie and that *Philadelphia* was, in its way, a good movie. 'Did you cry?' asked Steve. Feeling all too acutely the pressures of a normative heterosexual masculinity, I was uncertain of what a 'correct' answer might be, particularly now that other class members were listening. Fortunately, Steve answered his own question, saying, 'I did. When Andy's young brother put his head on Andy's chest, I lost it.'

Even now, I admit, I remain unclear about the dynamics of what exactly was happening then. In retrospect the possiblities were many. Was this a moment in which Steve was trying to ascertain my orientation or signal his own? Had he assumed that we shared a certain kind of masculinity which an emotional response to the movie would either affirm or deny? Why did he focus on the brother as a defining moment? Indeed, what exactly did he mean by repeating the lines assigned to Joe Miller, the Black lawyer in the film? Certainly I continue to reflect on my assumptions about why a white, probably heterosexual young male would not only go to see *Philadelphia*, but also why he would want to discuss the film and his emotional reaction to it in a milieu where discussions of gay sexuality no doubt were deeply suspect. I understood my investments (as much as is possible, at any rate); Steve's were less clear.

But perhaps I should be less puzzled. If we consider that the movie is constructed for a heterosexual audience, not a specifically gay one, and if it constructs a white viewership rather than a Black one, then perhaps Steve's probings are quite in keeping with the film's audience and intentions. In other words, perhaps Steve's questions were not simply about notions of a normative heterosexuality but also about a specifically normative white male identity for which he sought affirmation. In this case I wondered how I might turn this unexpectedly queer moment into a moment of social action, a moment where Steve and I might take up the pedagogy of representation in popular culture and connect it to our notions around identities and their relative positions in society. In short, did this moment invite me to teach Steve about the pedagogies of popular film in exactly the fashion Andy teaches Joe about tolerance and love?

With these questions in mind, I have several goals for this chapter. First, since popular cultural representations work to secure a particular view of the world, I explore how the film *Philadelphia* operates in terms of its racialized representations, emphasizing its construction of whiteness in relation to gay sexuality. A film where a great many white bodies dominate the narrative space, *Philadelphia* provides a fertile ground for understanding how white identity functions, especially when it confronts Black and gay identities. Joe Miller (played by Denzel Washington) is a key figure here. Drawing on Toni Morrison's conceptualization of 'the white imagination'[1] I suggest that the representation of Joe's character, like that of Simon in Lawrence Kasdan's *Grand Canyon* (1992), is one that reflects more about whiteness than about Blackness in America. This leads to my second purpose: to answer the question 'How can unpacking the assumptions working here enable us to deploy this film in class settings to investigate the kinds of questions Steve raised for me?' I argue that by extending Morrison's conceptualization further, we can explore how whiteness operates in relation to the film's construction of gay male sexuality through postulating the existence of a heteronormative imagination, one that works to contain queer relations much in the way a white imagination works to contains Blackness.

Finally, central to both of these purposes, I want to suggest that *Philadelphia*'s box-office staying power and eventual Oscar success speaks directly to the way it framed its discussions of sexuality and race within ideologies which are intimately connected to its target audience. The film's popularity, I argue, is directly related to the manner in which it mobilizes discourses around love, liberty, and fraternity to contain its hegemonic constructions of Black, gay, and white bodies, and hence secure a white heterosexual viewpoint of society. Given that *Philadelphia* has what its star, Tom Hanks, calls 'a political bent [*sic*],'[2] this interrogation seems particularly urgent. If only because the film has been explicitly positioned as a 'teaching' movie, we, as cultural critics and educators, need to understand this political bent, its construction, and its potential effects so that we can (re)deploy them to our own ends.

Why *Philadelphia?*

The question is, Why undertake this analysis at all? Is this 'timid pioneer of a movie'[3] anything other than Hollywood's attempt to legitimate (and Hollywoodize) gay experience in mainstream terms? Certainly not according to some quarters of the gay community. For example, playwright and AIDS activist Larry Kramer denounced the film as ethically, medically, and politically incorrect, while comedian Scott Thompson (Kids in the Hall) felt that the film's portrayal of gay life was 'too polite, too ginger ... It's insulting to the public. It says they are so stupid that they wouldn't accept an honest portrayal.'[4] The effects of such representations are of course important. As Thompson quite rightly observed, 'If the public falls in love with gays, it is a false image they are in love with.'[5] And we all know what disillusioned lovers are like ...

Still, these reactions suggest that the film should have had something 'authentic' to say about being gay or having AIDS in the United States in the 1990s. One might even detect, if one were so inclined, hints of essentialism in those comments, as if there were some quintesssential gay truths that *Philadelphia* was not revealing. While I would not want to refute criticisms of the rather pristine, 'restrained' depiction of gay life in the movie, I would argue that of course these depictions are not about 'us' in any fundamental sense. On the contrary, it isn't so much what *Philadelphia* can tell us about being gay in the United States, but rather what the movie tells us about being straight. It is this turn which makes the film a potentially potent vehicle for social action. Precisely because it so successfully captured a (white heterosexual) American audience, these representations can tell us volumes about its intended audiences and the way they might perceive themselves in relation to the straight/gay divide.

Indeed, although the script itself is written by gay men, I would like to argue that while the film functions as a gay reading of what will 'pass' in middle America, its popular appeal lies in the straight, white imagination's embrace of the images of gays that the narrative constructs. In fact, this queer doubling makes *Philadelphia* a rich pedagogical resource for those interested in using popular culture for social action around issues of sexuality, race, and gender. From one perspective, for example, the film emphasizes the lengths gay/lesbian/bisexual folk go to 'pass' within a mainstream, white, heterosexual culture. Andrew leads a wonderful life until he can no longer pass, and indeed, his passing appears to be his central failing. But by the same token, the film's representations help us to limn out the contours of a straight imagination as it encounters and attempts to define its ideas about gays. Surely the snarling, raging, male partners of Wyant Wheeler are nothing so much as lions in winter roaring at their kingdom's invasion by gays, sensitive New Age men, Blacks, and other minorities. Given the overwhelming presence of men in the film – inasmuch as *Philadelphia* concerns itself specifically with homosexuality and AIDS – I suggest the film is equally about which view of masculinity should prevail in the late twentieth century.

Following these lines of logic, issues of race necessarily arise. Where else but in the Black body would white heterosexuals displace their own homophobia or white males debate their concepts of masculinity? As Hazel Carby notes, the Africanist presence has always been the body on which American national issues have been written.[6] This, then, is another reason why *Philadelphia* might interest us, especially given a critical tendency to dismiss the film's racial elements as 'resonant subtexts'[7] intended merely to underscore the central theme of homophobia. Such dismissals are themselves hardly new. They are analogous to the way white critics have traditionally downplayed the Africanist presence in American literature.[8] Still, if we follow Toni Morrison's assertion that freedom, the American Constitution, and American ideas of justice invariably invoke the Black presence in America,[9] how can any movie named after the site where the American Declaration of Independence was signed fail to be also directly and primarily about race? As Doug Stewart of Toronto's Black Coalition for AIDS Prevention observed, 'It's as if they set out to make a film and this other, stronger story kept glimmering through.'[10] I would argue, however, that the story is there.[11]

Following Morrison's work, my task is to analyse the constructions of race and sexuality in *Philadelphia*, first separately (insofar as that is ever possible) and then jointly. My aim is to explore how race and sexuality (and gender) are mutually inflected in and through each other. In doing this I locate this chapter squarely within a pedagogy of representation, one that Henry Giroux suggests is its starting point: 'the importance of illuminating the various ways in which representations are constructed as a means of comprehending the past through the present in order to legitimate and secure a particular view of the future.[12]

Through this analysis I explore the ways in which the conflicts in *Philadelphia*, which seem initially and primarily about (homo)sexuality, are equally about race. Indeed, race becomes a way to talk about sexuality, and sexuality becomes a means to address race. Undergirding both of these discourses lies a debate about masculinity. While it may not be new to say that Hollywood films are racist, ultimately *Philadelphia*'s success instructively underscores the manner in which its depictions of gays, whites, and Blacks alike are hegemonic representations – representations of what white, middle-class heterosexuals hope Blacks and gays not only *are*, but also what they *should be*.

Imagining Whiteness: Constructing Images of White Control

Whiteness as a category is rendered invisible as a symbol of ethnicity while simultaneously avowed as a major category to normalize definitions of class, race, gender, heterosexuality and nationality.[13]

Henry Giroux's comment offers a excellent entrée to discussions concerning race because it suggests that we first define what *whiteness* signifies in *Philadelphia*. The film's opening montage is helpful here. Beginning with an omniscient view of the city, the camera eventually brings us from the heights of the (white) elite to the heart of Philadelphia proper, and as we transit the city's urban spaces we are shown, documentary-style, its various sectors. In this montage, whiteness is linked to images of affluence and power or to hard work, while Blacknesss is linked exclusively either to images of poverty, unemployment, and disempowerment or to pictures of happy, dancing folk. The bleak Springsteen elegy, 'Streets of Philadelphia,' becomes, here, a mourning not only of the plight of AIDS victims ('Don't leave me alone like this,' 'Kiss me, lover') but also of the passing of the American Dream, as depicted in the murals prominently (albeit briefly) displayed in the opening montage. These apocalyptic spaces contrast with the safer suburban space inhabited by the Beckett family, and with those sites of white-identified affluence within the city. Indeed, if urban Philadelphia is the frontline of the wars the movie hints at, then surely the suburban Beckett home represents what is being fought for.

The opening also serves to construct significant aspects of Denzel Washington's character; it situates Joe Miller as a liminal character, a sort of cultural broker or border worker, who, in his role as lawyer, crosses daily the boundaries between race and class (and soon will traverse that of sexuality). The opening courtroom scene quickly establishes this liminality: as a neighborhood lawyer, Miller is very much a part of the Black community; yet in contrast to the images of poverty and unemployment associated with Blacks in the opening scenes, Miller is also positioned as different: industrious, ebullient, and canny. Joe Miller, just like Simon in Kasdan's *Grand Canyon*, is *of* the streets, without being *in* them. Indeed, Joe's humour links him with those 'happy' Blacks in the barber-shop, and with those dancing in the schoolyard while the 'other' Blacks conveniently disappear.

But whiteness is not as completely (homo)genized as the opening scenes might suggest. Indeed, the presence of the sexual deviant – the white homosexual Andrew Beckett, whose Karposi Sarcoma's lesions rupture the seemingly unified world of whiteness – divides the unified world of whiteness into two camps: one represented by the partners in the firm; the other represented by the Becketts. The former construction, exemplied by Charles Wheeler (played by Jason Robards), is homophobic, upper-middle class, and certainly Establishment. Wheeler's cartoonish, hopelessly outmoded character is unrepentantly masculinist – and probably Republican. (Significantly, Wheeler never develops much beyond his fanatical homophobia; the filmmakers rushed to rule out, I suspect, any possible audience identification that might occur by virtue of his whiteness.) Indeed, by making these characters corporate lawyers, they are, by Hollywood definitions, irredeemably venal. In contrast, Joanne Woodward's character, Mrs Beckett, epitomizes the film's alternative construction of whiteness. Looking ever so much like the woman who rode off into suburban bliss in *The Three Faces of Eve*, Woodward, only forty years later, plays the all-American mother of the nineties: AIDS-literate and accepting not only of sexual difference but also racial difference. (Miguel is, after all, Hispanic.) Although we are never sure exactly how the family afforded the large white suburban house, or how they sent Andy to law school and the other offspring to their (white) suburban fates, we can safely infer that it was all achieved through hard work and adherence to family values. We can be equally certain that the Becketts virtuously vote for Democrats and support the Rainbow Coalition.

Miguel, The (In)visible Homosexual

So whiteness appears polarized into stereotypes of either demonized homophobes or sanctified homophiles. Ironically, Miguel's presence as Andrew's lover works to undercut the latter construction even as it exemplifies again how matters sexual are inevitably expressed racially. Of course, casting Antonio Banderas as Tom Hanks's lover Miguel is, at first blush, a stroke of genius. As a Latino, Miguel's presence makes the Becketts appear even more inclusive, adding further lustre to their already-burnished (white) reputation. On a more pragmatic level, Banderas's European connections, especially his past filmic involvement with gay director Pedro Almodovar, lend a certain cultural legitimacy to the film's enterprise, while his sex-symbol status undoubtedly appeals to certain straight females and gay males. But most importantly, by

casting a Latino man who embodies 'an archetype of masculinity built for pleasure,'[14] the movie both employs and contests beliefs around masculinity and
homosexuality.

This is not to suggest, of course, that racial stereotypes surrounding Latinos
are not deployed throughout the movie to construct white identity. Hanks himself acknowledges that 'Antonio as Miguel is very passionate and he's foreign,
which is kind of adorable.'[15] Not surprisingly Miguel is depicted as emotional
and explosive in two of his biggest scenes, first at the hospital and then later at
the home he shares with Andrew. Both occasions show how Miguel's emotional and passionate (Latin) outbursts stand in contrast to Andrew's own
(white) analytical, restrained, but invariably correct, actions. The hospital scene
best illustrates the stereotype's deployment. When Miguel confronts the (white)
doctor, Andy coolly reestablishes control over the tense situation by apologiz-
ing for Miguel's behaviour, suggesting that his partner is upset. When Miguel
protests this assessment, Andy retracts the apology but leaves the adjective
upset in place, underscoring Latino excess while underlining the absolute
rational control of whites – even in these dire straits. Crucially, the racial and
sexual coding of emotional excess overlap here to produce an overdetermined
moment: both Miguel's Latin expressiveness and Andy's seething but WASP-
ishly restrained anger work with their gay sexuality to overdetermine their reactions. Finally, Hanks's comments also point to how the movie deploys
Banderas's status as a foreigner and 'the latest incarnation of the Latin Lover'[16]
to subtly boost Andy's own sexual status: ostensibly he's been able to maintain
a relationship with this exotic, 'adorable' dynamo for more than seven years.

As we have seen, Miguel's presence undercuts and hence makes apparent the
very constructions of whiteness the narrative posits, particularly during the seg-
ment where Miguel acts as the videographer for Andrew's return home. His
ascerbic comments about the mean streets of the Becketts' neighborhood undercuts Andy's pomposity, while linking us back to the streets of Philadelphia in
the opening. More importantly, Miguel's videography delivers the narrative
representation of whiteness to us, literally, as a construction. When he and
Andy visit the Beckett home for the parents' wedding anniversary, for example,
the entire family takes Andy into its (white) bosom while Miguel literally and
figuratively remains the outside observer (along with the viewer) who records
events for posterity. While Demme's strategy here may reinforce the documentary feel he promotes elsewhere in the film, using Miguel's perspective certainly emphasizes the constructedness of whiteness, and questions the
presentation of the family. (What are they really like when the cameras are off?)

More to the point, Miguel's isolation and marginalization are simultaneously
underscored. Miguel literally becomes the (in)visible homosexual whose status

as Andy's lover is barely recognized (except for a passing mention from *père* Beckett when he gives his benediction to Andy's cause). Miguel plays Boswell to Andy's Dr Johnson, and the extent to which this relationship mirrors (North) American/Third World relations demands to be noted. More important, erasing Miguel's presence, except when it becomes otherwise completely impossible to do so, effectively obliterates his relationship with Andy and the sexual identity it represents, even while appearing to work towards greater straight tolerance of gay relationships. In short, the 'tolerance' on offer here is a highly conditional offer that 'accepts' gay people even as it erases sexual differences.

Miguel's absence/presence is particularly powerful when he records Andy dancing with Mrs Beckett in the midst of the party. Miguel's cameramanship becomes the movie's alibi for not having the two racially mixed gays openly display their relationship in this supposedly safe space. This moment contrasts to the other dance scene where Andy and Miguel display the limited physical relationship that the film permits. Interestingly, in this scene both Andy and Miguel wear navy dress whites – a parodic moment, if only because the gesture seems to affirm Andy and Miguel's 'whiteness' in a sea of queerness while simultaneously acknowledging whiteness as a costume one wears. Or more likely it works to deracialize Miguel while foregrounding his sexual identity; Andy's whiteness is underlined, almost despite his gay identity.

In pedagogical terms Demme's framing of the family scenes is arguably an attempt to help the audience understand how gay relationships are marginalized in a heterosexual world, a feeling many gays are familiar with. From this perspective the family gathering only echoes more subtly the doctor's threat to exclude Miguel from the emergency ward. However, we need to counter this perspective with the racial one which illustrates the contradictions inherent in the strategy: Miguel, the racial other, looks on as the white family welcomes the prodigal son. What is so striking here is the way the narrative itself works to naturalize a coherent white hetersexual identity while simulatneously signaling the artifice of it. In *Philadelphia*, it seems, white identity can only be maintained when the racial (and sexual) other is marginalized.

But Why a Black Lawyer?

The contemplation of this Black presence is central to any understanding of [American] literature, and should not be permitted to hover at the margins of the literary imagination.[17]

Most critics and viewers acknowledge that *Philadelphia* raises questions of race, but racial aspects remain viewed primarily as subtexts. However, the question of race becomes pressing when we ask why Andy doesn't simply engage a white lawyer. Why cast a Black lawyer? What does it mean that the lawyer is Black? A number of reasons come to mind. First, Black audiences are increasingly important to box office success. To meet the demands of these demographics, top-billed white actors are being matched increasingly with top Black actors. *Philadelphia* simply mirrors this trend to ensure the widest possible market for the film. Second, thematically speaking a Black lawyer is also required. Who better to make impassioned plea for justice on behalf of gays than formerly enslaved Blacks? Indeed one cannot easily hear Joe Miller's impassioned defence of Andy except through Martin Luther King's 'I Have a Dream' speech (rather than through the words of Malcolm X, a more radical intertext). And given the generally accepted impression of Black homophobia (whether true or not), what better foil to Andy's white homosexuality than Joe's Black heterosexuality? One can imagine the gears cranking in the Hollywood casting offices as producers thought this one through.

But still, certainly at one level the body *must* be Black. Where else would all the fears of a white audience be placed except on a Black man, the body onto which, as Hazel Carby argues, all surplus fears are projected?[18] If a white viewer wants to retain the virtuous representation ascribed to him/her through Andy's family, homophobic impulses must be projected onto Joe Miller's Black body, which, like other African presences in American literature, becomes the site for 'talking about and ways of policing matters of class, sexual licence and repression, formations and exercises of power.'[19]

Toni Morrison's project of theorizing the white imagination becomes particularly helpful at this juncture. If Joe Miller is a construction of a white imagination, we can begin to see 'the ways in which a non-white, Africanlike (Africanist) presence or persona [is] constructed in the United States and the imaginative presence it serve[s].'[20] From this vantage point Joe's character arises exactly because there is no other place for homophobic impulses to be projected. Toni Morrison observes how Nancy in Willa Cather's *Sapphira and the Slave Girl* offers Cather an opportunity to meditate on the 'interdependent working of power, race and sexuality.'[21] Likewise, Joe Miller offers Demme (and his audience) an opportunity to dwell on the meaning of being white, heterosexual, and male in the 1990s. Just as director Lawrence Kasdan does with the Black bodies in *Grand Canyon*, so too does Demme employ Black bodies (in this case Joe's) to 'embody the anxieties of a white [male heterosexual] middle class ... [T]hese black bodies have to be acted upon, manipulated and made malleable'[22] so that white people can redefine and reinforce their own identities. As Jonathan Demme states, *Philadelphia* was 'made for people *like me* [italics mine]: people who aren't activists, who are afraid of AIDS, people who have been raised to look down on gays.'[23] One might add that the movie is also for people who are white, probably male, and presumably well off. Joe, therefore, is a safe stand-in for white audiences, whose homophobic impulses will in turn be, if not eradicated, at least remolded into tolerance – a tolerance which, as previously suggested, is based on heteronormative standards that operate to tolerate sexual difference on one hand and erase it on the other.

Given this pedagogical intent, then, it also seems not surprising that in a white imagination the Black body is the one requiring teaching. Since the white characters are either seeming paragons of heteronormative acceptance (the family and friends of Andrew and Miguel) or cartoonlike embodiments of homophobic prejudice (the partners of Wyant Wheeler), Joe, the safely contained Black man, becomes the person to be taught the necessary lessons about HIV infection and AIDS. Crucially, Joe, not Charles Wheeler, learns the lesson of heteronormative tolerance. The racial (and racist) implications of choosing a Black body for instruction are key here, the most important of which is the hierarchy of bodies implied: white bodies over Black ones. Significantly, it is possible to locate a counter-heirarchy at work here. Joe's transit from homophobic distaste to a bond with Beckett suggests that another pedogogical relationship operates here. Indeed, it might be expedient to encourage readings which foreground Joe's Black body as the one with the most to teach us 'rigid white folks' about how to overcome homophobia, making this counter-hierarchy a powerful tool within the film's pedagogical arsenal.

Finally, Joe Miller embodies an increasingly common figure in white-imagined films – the Black man who appears to assist the white man in distress. Just as Simon in Kasdan's *Grand Canyon* intervenes when Mack is in imminent peril, so too does Joe Miller intervene, first to help Andrew face down the AIDS-phobic clerk and then to take on his now-desperate case. Interestingly, by drawing on Hazel Carby's narrative genealogy of Simon we also can see how Joe fits into a broader field of white imaginative constructs where Blackness is carefully controlled. From this perspective Joe's frenetic, but often humorous, self-promotion works to make him less threatening to a white audience, for after all what is humour but a means of minimizing and controlling fear? Meanwhile, Joe's clearly middle-class life and successful law practice align him within a white belief of Black mobility. He is tough without being aggressive; he seldoms questions his own social position; he is a strong family man. In short, Joe Miller is a comforting figure for a white imagination because he makes no claims on its sympathy either by directly questioning white supremist capitalism or by suggesting anything other than a determination to succeed through hard work.

The opening sequences between Hanks and Washington in fact go to some length to convince us of the men's similarities, to underscore Demme's contention that Miller and Beckett are virtual mirror images, even to the point of belonging to minority groups. It is only later in the trial that the racial nature of their positions is fully exposed. As Joe chases ambulances and takes on cases for housing tenants, Andrew has been showered with all the privileges that whiteness can confer: a position at an Establishment law practice, a spacious loft condo, and a large staff of women at his command. The unspoken proposition, as Stewart Klewan correctly notes, is that Joe is a great lawyer whose race ensures he will never get a shot at such jobs.[24]

Even so, the narrative often strains to erase the difference between Blacks and whites. Note, for example, the implicit parallel between Joe's family at the hospital and Andy's at the anniversary party. And indeed, if anything, Joe's cockiness and entrepreneurial spirit serve as proof positive that middle-class professional Blacks are just like whites: hard-working and family-oriented. But, at the same time, these representations work to enable white people to view Black bodies as safe sites that can be molded, shaped, and saved through white interventions – in this case to learn about the nature of homophobia and AIDS discrimination from a sick, white gay. Even disempowered white gays, it seems, can still teach a Black person a thing or two.

Perhaps this aspect of *Philadelphia* is best illustrated in the now-classic opera scene, the film's pedagogical moment *par excellence*. Here Joe tries to assert his authority as Beckett's attorney in order to prepare him for trial the next day. But Andy, ostensibly still wound up after the party, keeps resisting Miller's attempts and interrupts constantly, drawing Joe's attention to the opera music. Most critics would see this scene, correctly, as a play on the now well-known connection between gays and opera: the opera queen. Since the moment is complex, such a connection is undoubtedly important, but at least part of Andrew's resistance must stem from the disruption of racial codes which Joe's professional demands for Andy's attention entails; that is, the Black man is the master here, the white man subservient. In order to circumvent Miller's professional authority, Andrew shifts the ground to one of high culture – opera – where Joe admits he is lost. This is an explicitly racial move: on this ground, that of high culture, which Isaac Julien has called 'the living dead of whiteness,'[25] Andrew re-establishes the authority Joe has tried to usurp. Shifting the ground to opera enables Andrew to display his superior (white) knowledge by translating the libretto into 'plain English' so that Joe can comprehend it. In effect Andy does what Joe so frequently demands: he explains it to him like he's a six-year-old. The lesson is simple: love conquers all; love me and you will be saved.

A cynic might suggest that the upshot of *Philadelphia* is that Andy dies leaving Joe a richer man for having known him, a fact symbolized by the bottle of

Dom Perignon which Joe could not earlier afford. Indeed, Joe's successful prosecution of Andy's case enables Miller to rise above his role of ambulance chaser to gain more legitimacy than he had prior to taking on Andy's case. By being a part of Andy's suffering, Joe too is sanctified and rewarded for his travails as well as for the aspersions cast upon his manhood. Fortunately, his reward also comes in the only thing that counts in late capitalism: cold, hard cash. That the film rises above this is a tribute to the work of both Washington and Hanks.

Before moving on to fuller consideration of the construction of sexuality in the movie, I would like to investigate the logic which dictates that if Joe is Black, by extension Andy must be white. Several explanations are apparent. First is a recognition that to most North Americans to be gay is to be white and middle class; the presence of gay identities beyond this narrow construction has only begun to be felt recently in representations within the gay imaginary, and even this statement demands a certain modesty. As Mark Nash has noted, 'A gay imaginary which is white and masculine dominates the gay lifestyle press of the major metropolitan cities of the overdeveloped world: London, New York, Los Angeles.'[26] Also, marketing dynamics must be factored in. Despite the growing weight of Black audiences, middle-class whites still buy the majority of movie tickets. To guarantee a financial success a white star is required – thus, Tom Hanks. As Jonathan Demme states, Hanks was cast because as 'a personality, Tom had the trust and confidence of America, which I felt would help us reach across to a mainstream audience.'[27] – a mainstream white audience, one might add. But ultimately, just as a white imagination demands a Black defender who must be taught his part, so too does it demand a white AIDS victim. Accepting a Black male AIDS victim means recognizing that person as a sexual being, and confronting white fears of black sexuality – straight, gay, or in-between – beyond white control. Note for example how quickly the young Black gay male is expelled from the narrative after his sexual advance on Joe, who ironically is buying diapers, a clear sign of heterosexuality. Miller's carefully modulated sexuality illustrates how Black sexuality must be strictly controlled in a white imaginary.

Finally, I suspect there is another possible linkage, one which is perhaps unconscious or at least unintentional. Perhaps the white homosexual AIDS victim affords a way to suggest that 'whites suffer, too.' The effect however is less ambiguous, especially given the well-intentioned appearance of the white woman who has contracted AIDS, notably through a blood transfusion. (Had it been through heterosexual contact, the movie's homo/hetero divide would have been undermined.)

Philadelphia racializes AIDS as a white disease, a move that elides the fact that AIDS is a global problem which in fact strikes hard, especially in the Third World. But again, raising these issues is problematic for the white, straight imagination. Doing so would remind viewers that AIDS in Africa and elsewhere is primarily a heterosexual disease, diminishing the sympathy that the film intends for Andy and his white family, and overtly dealing with the issue of race in a way this narrative is unprepared to do. Because the AIDS/homosexual/white conflation is so integral to the movie's structure, the movie must keep AIDS as a local, not global, disease in order to maintain its internal coherence.

Before closing this argument, it is important to question which conflicts and interests help to drive the representations *Philadelphia* constructs around race, especially around whiteness. First and foremost I think the film reflects a need to re-narrativize white identity around issues of control – even when control is impossible. Andy's characterization is key in this regard. His cool, rational, analytical behaviour, even in the face of the inevitable, shows the need for white control over emotion and circumstances. We wouldn't be far off the mark if we were to read Andy's 'fling' (just once, remember) as a loss of control for which he must now pay dearly. Apparently even death is finally under his control, when he tells Miguel, 'I'm ready.' Mother Beckett echoes this self-possession as she valiantly struggles to control her emotions throughout the movie. Given the *gravitas* of the film's presentation, it seems unlikely that these elements could be read easily as a parody of WASP repression. Notably it is this selfsame control which the 'bad' whites lack as our villians mutter and gnash their way to Hollywood perdition. Mary Steenbergen, on the other hand, gets to join the 'good' whites because she not only 'hates this case' but also drops her 'ice queen' composure long enough to tell us so. Now that we know just how much this control is costing her, she becomes aligned with all the other suffering 'good' whites.

Imagining Sexualities

Given the stereotypes surrounding the Black male body, casting a Black man in the main role begs the question of how this stereotype will be deployed within the framework of a white heteronormative imagination. To begin with, it is worth noting that the movie uses Black homophobia as the basis for the necessary pedagogy it delivers. This strategy is exemplified in Joe's visit to his physician. Joe's reaction to the suggestion of a blood test quickly outlines the nature of Black homophobia: his doctor doesn't want to know how he might have contracted the virus, and Joe immediately declines the test, a sign of marital hetero fidelity. (This Joe is one straight shooter!) Black homophobia is deployed then as a guarantee to the white (male) viewer that there will be no sexual interaction between the two main characters. Whatever the eventual nature of the relationship between Andy and Joe, the viewer can always see it as nonsexual, since 'Black men aren't gay.' Even when a gay Black man does approach Joe, Miller rebuffs him roundly, underlining the latter's heterosexual commitments. In order to support this guarantee further, his heterosexuality (and potent masculinity) are graphically affirmed early, when he participates in his daughter's birth. The child visibly proves Joe's masculine potency (which later of course will be challenged because of his association with Andrew), and inextricably ties him to heterosexuality in all its manifestations.

In order to understand fully the constructions of sexuality here, I extend Morrison's theoretical construct of a racial imagination to analyse the film's construction of a heterosexual's idea of gay sexuality, or, more precisely, the construction of a gay sexuality which passes in a heteronormative world. In other words Andy and Miguel are accurate depictions of gays as imagined by heterosexuals, a fact reflected most clearly in three scenes: the family discussion, the courtroom revelation of Andy's 'fling,' and of course the party at which Andy and Miguel finally dance.

The lack of physical intimacy between Andy and Miguel has been the subject of some discussion. Again, it is beyond the (liberal) heterosexual imagination to accept 'homo' sex (while *we* already know – from every movie made – all about 'het' sex). Even the film frame, which Andrew King has argued works to fetishize and consequently hold at bay any potential homosexual fears a straight male viewer might feel, seems unable to neutralize explicit depictions of gay relationships. The best a male heterosexual imagination can do (without losing its own liberal tolerance) is see two men dancing at a drag party, ironically in navy uniforms (a delightful political moment which resonates in light of the 1993 battle over gays in the American military). Hanks himself acknowledges this aspect of the film and normalizes it, a strategy he employs repeatedly in interviews. Speaking to *Advocate* interviewer Brad Gooch, Hanks explains, 'Andy married his best friend,' or 'This [the lifestyle in *Philadelphia*] is about making spaghetti with music in the background.'[28] While not wanting to further stereotypes of gays as eternally having sex, it is the omission, as we well know, that speaks loudest.

Perhaps it is simply that imagining male/male intimacy is the end-point of a heterosexual imagination. Indeed, the movie is quite clear on this point, in Joe's various reactions and discussions about homo sex practice. As Wheeler's speech shows, the problem with gays resides directly in straight men's inability to conceive (pardon the pun) of queer sex. Hanks's interview with *The Advocate* is most revealing here. For example, when reading Larry Kramer's *Faggots* – which Hanks says deals with the 'grittier details of gay life during the seventies (47) Hanks states, 'I read some stuff where I was like, "Whoa! Hey, you're kidding me!"' (45). But more interestingly, this material becomes the fodder for dinner conversations, where gay life is a spectacle for the others. Says Hanks, 'At dinner parties people would ask me what I was finding out. "Well, let me tell you ..."' (45).

In order for Hanks to make the connection between Andy and himself he resorts to what I call a heteronormative imagination. This imaginary, which effaces sexuality and reduces gay life to spaghetti dinners and two buddies marrying one another, enables Hanks to find the 'more relatable human details' (48) of Andrew's character, details that allow him to connect to the character of the sexual other by effacing the very traits which make Andy queer. Hanks says, 'I could see things in there that were exactly the same kind of stuff I'm into. Forget the sexuality. ... I remember feeling as bad ... at the same point in my life over the same things although obviously from different sides of the coin' (48). Or, in other words, 'it wasn't like shields dropped from my eyes. But I found the human connection' (49). Here, again, the heteronormative imagination works to elide difference, to appeal to some imagined common 'human' experience which transcends sexuality while simultaneously defuses the potentially upsetting elements of gay culture, a culture which has been, and remains at heart, a sexual one. In short, Hanks's interviews illustrate a strategy by which heteronormativity works to posit tolerance as a way of containing queer desires and maintaining the status quo.

Seeing Sexuality through Race: Inflections in *Philadelphia*

So far I have been dealing with race and sexuality as if they were analytically separable categories, two parallel constructions which only tangentially intersect. However, we need to be clear that bodies are never singularly marked; rather they are always severally and differentially marked in ways which are not equally enabling of all identities at the same time. The setting of *Philadelphia* itself illustrates how sexuality is viewed through race and vice versa. Although the movie is about Joe's lesson in 'brotherly love' – the literal translation of the name 'Philadelphia' – the title is also immediately refracted through the knowledge that the city was established as a space where slavery was abolished. In this sense, then, the setting is significant, for the city is one of the earliest white Utopias.

The question also arises with respect to how gay identity is cross-cut by markers of whiteness, or vice versa. As previously noted, the choice of a white gay male is already a racial inflection of sexuality. But I would also argue that gay identity functions as a disruption within a white imaginary, which Giroux describes as normalizing and naturalizing that which is neither normal nor natural. By resisting attempts to equate whiteness with a naturalized heterosexuality, gay identity disrupts monolithic images of whiteness as naturalized by exposing its strategies of containment. The Beckett family scenes in *Philadelphia* illustrate this operation concisely. While I have already noted how Miguel is marginalized to ensure that no disruptive intimacy between Andy and Miguel occurs, we might point to the family conference where Miguel and Andy discuss his impending lawsuit as evidence that gayness need not be disruptive. Here, as well as in the courtroom scenes, Miguel is clearly included within the family grouping. Others also might point correctly to how Andy's holding his infant nephew in his arms acts as a powerful antidote to and for those viewers who imagine all gays as pedophiles and perverts, one which demands acknowledgment.

But this transgressive moment, as crucial as it is, underscores exactly how heterosexual identity operates to erase sexual difference. First, at the very moment when Andy and Miguel finally appear as a couple, the presence of the baby effectively disavows their choice to live together, and implicates them in the reproductivist bias of family discourse (even as gays are institutionally barred from creating their own families). The image, admittedly a powerful one, especially for those for whom 'family' may be a language of exile,[29] seems to suggest however that whiteness can accept queerness only when it has been neutered and assimilated into a monolithic heteronormativity. In short, Andy and Miguel are accepted exactly to the extent that their relationship can been normalized as heterosexual. To quote Hanks again, 'Andy and Miguel have been together for eight years. He married his best friend.'[30] Tolerance cum acceptance becomes a means to recuperate queer identity within a heteronormative picture, one captured in the Beckett family conference scene.

Still, if the signs of sexual difference are on the one hand denied through a heterosexual imagination, we must also see the erasure as inspired by race on the other. Indeed, the erasure may be more a sign of racial solidarity than of accepting Andy and Miguel as part of one big happy (white) family. The observation of Joanne Woodward's character that she 'never taught [her] children to ride at the back of the bus' underlines how race works here. While emphatically endorsing 'rights' discourse, her comment also defines her children as 'not Black,' suggesting first that if Andy doesn't demand his rights he is going against what he was taught, that is, how to be white (to sit at the front of the bus). Being gay just gets in the way of the privileges accorded whites and is akin to being Black. In this context, then, the family gathers in racial solidarity to claim what should be Andy's, by virtue of being white, not necessarily by being gay.

But the converse is equally true from the other construction of whiteness. It is precisely Andy's orientation and now open contestation of presumed white heterosexuality that has brought him to the point where he must turn to Miller. Charles Wheeler's position is that Andy's orientation is a betrayal of all the ideals that white (male) culture holds dear: work, family, and money. If we still don't get the message, then the fact that Andy visits nine (presumably straight, presumably white) lawyers before he finds Joe should drive the point home. Interestingly, it is within the courtroom itself that Andy's whiteness ceases to matter, although the Beckett family's racial aspects, including Miguel's de facto whiteness, is still foregrounded. Here Andy's homosexual identity matters more than his colour, although even this is only partially true; after all, justice is blind, but not neuter. Andrew's queer identity is hauled into court, discussed, and gawked at, even while the narrative seeks to deny and minimize the most disruptive aspects of it: Beckett's casual sexual contacts.

Behind Andy's Door: Why Joe Can't Go Back

One of *Philadelphia*'s crucial moments occurs immediately after the opera scene. Suddenly grabbing his briefing material, Joe heads for the door and leaves. Then he pauses, goes back to the closed door, and then, shaking his head, he goes home to hold his child and crawl into bed with his wife. Why can't Joe go back? Simply put: because he *can't*. While one intepretation might posit that Andrew's impending death forces Miller back to his wife to affirm his own life and future, I would like to argue for another, less-benign reading.

Neither the narrative nor Joe (nor the film's heterosexual audience, for that matter) can tolerate, in imaginative terms, Joe's re-entering that room. Just as the white imagination cannot tolerate a fully free Jim in *Huckleberry Finn*,[31] neither can a heteronormative imagination tolerate a potentially queer Joe. Going back would be acknowledging that Andy has aroused 'something' more than just a client-client affection, a reaction which Joe cannot possibly acknowledge and which he fends off by fleeing home. There he disavows those emotions and reassures himself of his heterosexuality by holding his child and sleeping with his wife. Finally, the narrative itself could not bear Joe's return. In this fairy tale the prince cannot love his damsel in distress.

The scene is important in other ways, too. It scripts the way heterosexuality can exist only if there is an abjected homosexuality. As Judith Butler has pointed out, and this scene vividly shows, 'heterosexually sexed positions are themselves secured through repudiation of homosexual abjection and the assumption of a normative heterosexuality.'[32] To re-enter Andrew's room would necessarily end Joe's (and by extension the heterosexual audience's) definitions of heterosexuality. Consequently, just as freedom has no meaning for Huck without Jim in *Huckleberry Finn*, so too does heterosexuality have no meaning for Joe without Andy in *Philadelphia*. The symbols of Joe's own potent heterosexuality are meaningful only in relation to Andy and his barren homosexuality.

Unsurprisingly this crucial scene is also racially inflected. While I would argue that the scene itself represents the end-point of a heteronormative imagination, we need to see this imagination as an always-already white one, too. Hence the fact that Joe is Black reinforces the impossibility of his return to Andy simply because Joe is Black. Doing otherwise raises the possibility of interracial desire and fears of miscegenation (even if this is impossible within a gay context). More importantly, crossing that boundary would necessarily mean giving Joe a sexuality beyond the carefully controlled limits which the narrative has placed on him, raising impossible questions about that sexuality. As Isaac Julien has pointed out, this would create even more problems, since the maintenance of 'an essential Black identity is dependent upon active avoidance of the psychic reality of Black/white desire.'[33] Going back behind that door would throw into question not only the narrative's straight/gay definitions but also its constructions of essential Black and white identities, upon which the film rests. Little wonder then that Joe flees for home and clings to the symbols not just of his sexuality, but also of his masculine and racial identities.

This juncture does offer us an opportunity to intervene in the narrative in order to underscore how heterosexuality and homosexuality remain enmeshed in an unstable binary which requires immense efforts to maintain and has a high human cost. What would the story have been like if Joe had gone back? The movie dramatically underscores why we need to discuss how we remain connected to ancient fears and fantasies about difference around sexuality and eroticism. Here students might be invited to rewrite the story in other ways, opening up the movie to examine questions of cross-racial desire and same-sex desire, not only as they operate in the film but also in learners' lived experience. Using Joe's decision as an example, we as educators can encourage viewers to interrogate their own reactions and fears about AIDS and gay sexuality.

Framing the Discourses in *Philadelphia*

Finally, then, what makes this film so attractive to its audiences? Certainly the representations themselves are sympathetic to the imaginations of the intended audience, as we have discussed, but Demme also employs several key strategies to interpellate the viewer into the action. During the opening statements to the jury, for example, the actors speak directly to the camera, positioning viewers as jury members. The full impact of this positioning becomes apparent later, when, under Miller's questioning, Andy explains that he loves law because 'once in a while – not very often – justice prevails. And that feels good.' Consequently, the viewers qua jury members have the opportunity to be a part of justice being done. Finding the 'bad' white people guilty, the 'good' (white) viewers can be assured that in no way are they racist or homophobic. In this sense the movie becomes a dream of white redemption: by chastising those 'nasty' (Republican) white men, we can all go home assured of our virtue. By feeling that justice is served, the audience can be assured that the system works, even while the status quo remains intact. Indeed, the entire film has, to this point, shown how gay men and their relationships can be recuperated without disturbing society's white heterosexual normative basis. As Klewan caustically notes, Andy's testimony also functions as a whitewashing (quite literally) of the massive neglect and mismanagement that has characterized the AIDS epidemic.[34] Indeed, *Philadelphia* subtly suggests that, vindicated by the very people who would deny his existence, Andy can now die a rich queer – but a queer nonetheless.

This discourse of justice gives Washington's casting as Joe Miller added significance. Washington brings to the screen his past performances as the freed slave fighting for freedom in the Civil War in *Glory*, and as Malcolm X fighting for civil rights in the America of the sixties. This conflation of race and orientation as equal forms of discrimination is exemplified by Woodward's assertion: 'I never taught my kids to sit at the back of the bus.' The rhetorical strategy here demands skepticism, however, since it operates to link gay and lesbians into minoritizing discourses even while it makes the case for equal rights. As Warner points out, there is no reason to presuppose that there are natural, or even any, connections between racism, sexism, and homophobia.[35] *Philadelphia*, in contrast, suggests that race and sexuality are equal identities even as its very narrative illustrates how these two identities operate differentially in any given situation. As Warner states, 'race, ethnicity and sexuality may not be able to be used as four parallel bands of the Rainbow Coalition.'[36] In some contexts race may overwhelm and negate aspects of one identity while empowering others. Indeed, by reading against the grain, as I am attempting here, *Philadelphia* can be used a resource which illustrates how bodies are always marked in multiple and differing ways in a variety of contexts, some of which are empowering, some of which are not.

Certainly another powerful discourse that the movie mobilizes is that of love, and specifically familial love. While undoubtedly the discourse of family may be one with which some gays have at best an ambivalent relation, it is on these terms that this film is most powerful. Again the title and setting are key, first with respect to the implications of 'brotherly love' as a religious invocation, but also for the concomitant idea of equality envisioned as a 'brotherhood of men.' The religious invocations are directly in line with the image of Andy as the sanctified sufferer.(Indeed, the revelation of Andrew's Kaposi's Sarcoma lesions is framed precisely within Catholic iconography of the Revelation of the Sacred Heart.) Andy becomes a metaphoric Christ figure who will redeem past (political) sins, and from whose death we can benefit by becoming better (more loving) people.

Clearly Demme also uses the family as a powerful tool in the denouement, which shows Andy as a child to remind the audience (again eliding difference) that whatever they may think of gays, lesbians, and AIDS victims, the latter are members of someone's family. (This merely echoes the claims of gay and lesbian activists that everybody knows homosexuals, whether they are aware of it or not.) But by adding the demand for inclusion to its demand for justice, *Philadelphia* serves an important function. It reappropriates the discussion of family values from the religious Right and suggests that acceptance, compassion, and caring for others are necessary parts of that discourse. We should not lose sight of this formulation even as we point out that such acceptance, compassion, and caring is still provisional and limited, especially given that this construction tends to refuse aspects of identity which don't conform to heteronormative ideas around sexual behaviour. Still, one would imagine that it would take a considerable amount of manoeuvring by the 'new right' to articulate another vision.

The opera scene neatly encapsulates the various discourses which the movie deploys. First and foremost, it frames Andy not just within the discourse of love, but also by conflating Andy with the central character of Andrea Chenier – as the embodiment of Love itself. Beyond the Christ metaphor, which is clearly in play (underscored, for all the slow learners out there, with the lurid red lighting symbolizing life, blood, etc.), Demme recasts the question of homophobia as one of love, a potentially dangerous ground, especially for heterosexual men. There is equally no doubt that loving Andy becomes a means to everyone's salvation. This discourse, Andy himself feels, transcends difference and indeed death. While this is high romanticism indeed, it is a framing which at least momentarily flirts with finding a way through the power of homophobia. By invoking 'love,' particularly in the context of the pedagogical moment, the movie opens up 'the middle spot between knowledge and ignorance.'[37] Drawing on our shared yearnings to be loved and to love others, perhaps this moment offers another point where we can engage our students to find a way to not simply tolerate difference (*à la* Becketts) but to embrace it without completely knowing it.

Finally, the videotape of Andy's childhood is difficult to ignore for one last reason. While I do not wish to deny the power of those moments, I think we should be aware that the loss it evokes is also a nostalgia for a time that no longer exists: a time before sexualities made claims, before race mattered. In its elegiac quality, the video mourns and longs for an innocence which has, along with Andy, died. It is the innocence of whiteness in the 1950s, before it needed to contend with AIDS, poverty, and the homeless – or at least they were easier to ignore. At one level I feel we must approach any such nostalgia warily. The film's ending valourizes Andy's 'perfect' childhood while eliding the inevitable painful parts which that selfsame homophobic society has inflicted. Fortunately, the videotape functions in a similar manner as Miguel's early videography: it forcefully reminds us that this nostalgia remains a construction. However, I find that more optimism lies in the people that Andy's death brings together, not in suburban Philadelphia but, significantly, at Miguel and Andy's home. There all the different people of Andrew's life join together in mourning. One senses that Demme wants to posit at least the possibility of community with difference, which is, in and of itself, not bad. If anything good can come from the AIDS epidemic perhaps it can be that in our collective loss we can find ways to not just live together in heternormative silence, but love together acknowledging the downright queerness of all our lives without wanting to change the fact. Utopian, no doubt, but in discussing a movie this romantic, not out of place.

Conclusion

For all the foregoing I think it is important to note that being able to write about the issues involved in a mainstream production is in itself a progressive moment. In this sense *Philadelphia* can be viewed as both a progressive and yet paradoxically conservative production. More important, the film shows that homophobia results in a failure of imagination, one that ultimately has effects in the real world.

These observations, however, suggest a direction for intervention. We need to re-educate the heteronormative imagination, to make same-sex sex less 'creepy,' less unimaginable. The marked absence of gay sexuality as described above is a useful place to start this discussion if teachers will encourage learners to consider why this lacunae exists. Finally, we need to question heteronormative representations and to contest them by encouraging students to look critically at representations for heterosexist and heteronormative ideas. Perhaps we might also look for ways to have students discuss the ways in which they identify with Andy. Such identifications might be mined to bring out the audience's own queer moments.

Returning to Steve's questions, which began this chapter, I only ask that students locate the points which move them or make them uncomfortable. For example, I would invite Steve to explore his identification with Andy's younger brother, to understand how that identification engages his own location as a white male, and how he might relate to Andy both as a brother and as a gay man. Such an approach entails dealing directly and honestly about sexuality, a path replete with other dangers. Still, engaging students on this affective level avoids the more problematic features of 'rights' discourse which can often return us to the paralysis of identity politics. Personally, this chapter reaffirms that rather than closing the closet door Steve inadvertently opened, these are opportunities to have students work with popular culture and the representations it contains, challenging the sometimes oppressive, sometimes liberating pedagogies inherent in them. Of course, this conclusion suggests I would have to answer Steve's question 'Did you cry?' with 'Yes, Steve, I cried. We both cried. Now let's look at why.'

Notes

1 Morrison, *Playing in the Dark*, 6–9.
2 DeVries, 'When the Laughing Stops,' C1.
3 Corliss, 'Tidings of Job,' 52–54.
4 Corliss, 'The Gay Gauntlet,' 53.
5 Ibid.
6 Carby, 'Encoding White Resentment,' 236–47.
7 Kroll, 'Philadelphia,' 46.
8 Morrison, *Playing in the Dark*, 12.
9 Ibid., 65.
10 Val Ross, 'How Will It Play?' C1.
11 I need to note here the difficulties involved in finding information on Black reception to the movie. *Jet Magazine* devoted several issues in January 1994 to *Philadelphia* as did *Ebony*. Denzel Washington was interviewed in *Vanity Fair*. The problem here is finding libraries where back issues are supported. The Hamilton Public Library stocks issues of *Ebony*, but not past 1992 (ironic, given that Hamilton has a substantial Black population). Back issues of *Vanity Fair* are kept at the public library for only six months, and more academic libraries (OISE, McMaster) do not carry them either. The result, paradoxically, is that while I discuss race, a Black voice is suspiciously silent, a fact of which I am only too keenly aware.
12 Giroux, 'White Utopias,' 67–92.
13 Ibid., 82.

14 Verdecchia, *Fronteras Americanas*, 45.
15 Gooch, 'A Philadelphia Story,' 50.
16 Verdecchia, *Fronteras Americanas*, 43.
17 Morrison, *Playing in the Dark,* 5.
18 Carby, 'Encoding White Resentment,' 236.
19 Morrison, *Playing in the Dark*, 7.
20 Ibid., 8.
21 Ibid., 21.
22 Carby, 'Encoding White Resentment,' 245.
23 See note 4 above.
24 Klewans, 'Holiday Celluloid Wrap-up,' 32.
25 Julien, 'Confessions of Snow Queen,' 120–5.
26 Nash, 'Chronicles of a Death,' 97–104.
27 Gooch, 'A Philadelphia Story,' 47.
28 Ibid., 47.
29 Warner, 'Introduction.'
30 Ibid., 47.
31 Morrison, *Playing in the Dark,* 35.
32 Julien, 'Confessions of Snow Queen,' 125.
33 Ibid.
34 Kewans, 'Holiday Celluloid Wrap-up,' 53.
35 Warner, 'Introduction,' xix.
36 Ibid.
37 Serres, *The Parasite*, 220–5.

13

'Death Is Power's Limit': Sex and Politics in an Age of Epidemic

JEAN NOBLE

We recall the old saying: ... If you want to preserve peace, arm for war. It would be keeping with the times to alter it: ... If you want to endure life, prepare yourself for death.[1]

Sigmund Freud, 'Thoughts for the Times'

That death is so carefully evaded is linked less to a new anxiety which makes death unbearable for our societies than to the fact that the procedures of power have not ceased to turn away from death. In the passage from this world to the other, death was the manner in which a terrestrial sovereignty was relieved by another, singularly more powerful sovereignty; the pageantry that surrounded it was in the category of political ceremony. Now it is over life, throughout its unfolding, that power establishes its domination; death is power's limit, the moment that escapes it; death becomes the most secret aspect of existence, the most 'private.[2]

Michel Foucault, 'History of Sexuality'

Troubling Subjects

'"We have all the answers," Dostoevsky said, "It's the questions we do not know."'[3]

This chapter represents a series of tentative questions about the relationships between psychoanalysis, AIDS, and the reconfiguration of identity by queer theory. In a sense I will not attempt to offer answers to any of the questions I pose here, but rather, I want initially to foreground for myself both the conditions of the asking and the points of intersection between the questions in and of themselves. The context of these questions was a graduate student seminar in the faculty of education at York University, called Literature and AIDS. The course was structured around a set of problematics, the most important being

'What constitutes the subject of AIDS?' By the time our semester came to an end, the questions I consider here obstinately remained, demanding consideration and signalling the larger context and tensions within which our lives and work, both theoretical and political, occur. I remain struck, perhaps profoundly so, by Alexander Düttman's suggestion that 'thought must always think that which cannot be reduced to itself,'[4] a notion echoed brilliantly by Derek Jarman in his last film, *Blue*, as the difference between 'thinking blind, and becoming blind.'[5] This is not a tension that can be worked out in one short chapter, nor can it be resolved in a four-month graduate seminar. It is, however, a 'problematic' which structures the conditions of my questioning and writing here, and which needs to be acknowledged. Thus, for me, questions of sex, death, bodies, and the problematics loosely organized around the term *politics*, especially within the logic of epidemic, must constitute, at once, the always already unknowable and overdetermined.

To the degree that AIDS in the West was (and continues to be: read *Philadelphia*) represented originally as a 'gay cancer,' then meanings associated with it and its attendant losses are perceived by the so-called general population as of concern only to a primarily ('tragic,' inevitably 'guilty,' and otherwise fetishized) 'homosexual' minority.[6] However, as AIDS is a disease that does not differentiate between socially constructed identities, then clearly it is not only of concern to a homosexual and hence 'minoritized' population. Furthermore, given the overdetermined status of AIDS as a 'gay plague,' and given the clearly unconscious and panicked 'phobic' denial of gay sexual practices and 'identities,' the resistance to universalizing the immediacy and urgency of all high-risk sexual practices carries the full psychic brunt of unconscious disavowal, or the process where repressed trauma is both noticed and in the same gesture denied.[7] AIDS is a popular topic in mainstream discourse, however; that same discourse refuses its own perception of the realities of living with AIDS by partitioning its subjects into categories of 'general population' (i.e., 'good' or 'innocent' heterosexuals not at risk) and 'high-risk groups or communities' (the 'bad' or 'guilty' other, namely gay men).[8] As psychoanalysis suggests, it might be possible to name the fetishization of 'sick' and 'tragic' gay men as the moment where that negated repressed, the very real risk to all bodies posed by AIDS, returns in the compulsion to repeat that fetishization.[9]

I will also suggest here that the panicked legal and social climate surrounding the production of gay and lesbian sexual visibility within an 'epidemic' can be read as a melancholic form of pedagogy, and hence a displaced moral reproachment. The perceived link between sex and death has been displaced onto other more easily managed issues of 'life' and 'safety,' issues which, as Linda Singer notes, 'allow us to consider not only what is lost but also what is produced by the current organization of the sexual field which is itself a product of previous power deployments.'[10] Given the breadth of the theoretical argument I can only scratch the surface here. The risk of such theoretical discourse may be, as Dütt-man suggests, that 'there is no thought that [can] not be excessive and [can] not prove to be essentially impertinent.'[11] Nonetheless, my questions evolve around a set of problematics: If, as Freud writes, it is impossible to imagine our own death, then what kinds of disavowals are necessary to disavow death in an AIDS epidemic? And what do those disavowals look like, given that we live not only in a pandemic, but within the 'logic of an epidemic,' where 'the anxieties unleashed by the current epidemic are not limited to concerns about disease transmission. The recognition of this unhappy connection between sex and death has also prompted renewed concern about the production of life itself, about reproduction, fertility, and the family, which are also seen as threatened by current conditions.'[12]

Plagues or epidemics are never just medical problems; 'they are also world-transforming moments of ontological crisis which pervade the entire logic and fabric of a community existence by calling it into question in a funda-mental way, that is, within the currency of life and death.'[13] Furthermore, as Foucault notes, power is organized precisely by the operation of biopolitics that brings the processes of so-called life into relief, through a variety of diverse institutions '(the family and the army, schools and the police, individual medi-cine and the administration of collective bodies),' as well as through the deployment of sexuality.[14] Given such a foregrounding of 'life' in the operation of power within a logic of epidemic which is determined to disavow death, what is the full range of necessary disavowals? And what happens to questions of sex during such disavowals? Can we productively imagine its redeployment, in terms of panicked rulings like the Supreme Court of Canada's decision in *Butler* and Canada Customs' hysterical harassment of Vancouver's Little Sis-ter's Book and Art Emporium? In other words, can we read 'the establishment of a connection between epidemic and transgression [which have] allowed for the rapid transmission of the former to phenomena that are outside the sphere of disease' as panicked displacements from the disavowal of death onto the terrain of sex to justify regulation, surveillance, and body management?[15] While not all are of the opinion that the Butler case has proven to be a disaster for lesbians and gays, I concur with Cossman et al.[16] that Butler is, and has been to date, undeniably problematic. Finally, if it possible, as I suggest it is, to conceptual-ize the logic of epidemic as a form of pedagogy, then what counter-pedagogies might be available to resist the inscriptions and regulations ensuing from such displacements? It seems clear to me that any attempt to consider these questions must begin with an understanding of the relationships between death, the work of mourning, and the 'relation' of identity.

AIDS, Death and Psychoanalysis

'What will die with me when I die ...?'[17]

In his 1915 essay, 'Thoughts for the Times on War and Death,' Freud suggests that '[i]t is impossible to imagine our own death ... that in the unconscious every one of us is convinced of his own immortality.'[18] Freud compares attitudes towards death in so-called modern man and primaeval man, and puts forward two sets of overlapping propositions which directly interest me here. The first is that both experience two opposing attitudes towards death: 'the one which acknowledges it as the annihilation of life and the other which denies it as unreal.' The result of these opposing views lead to "then," (for primaeval man), 'the doctrine of the soul and to ethics,' and 'now,' (for modern man), 'neurosis, which affords us deep insight into normal mental life.'[19] It is precisely such neuroses which Freud explicates in his 1917 essay 'Mourning and Melancholia,' a discussion I will return to shortly. Secondly, Freud writes that conflicts of ambivalence, or the coupling of both love and hate, structure love relationships, and that it is in the death, or 'risk of death, of someone we love' that both of the opposing attitudes toward death collide and come into conflict.[20] In terms of the need to disavow death, Freud writes that this becomes most intense when the death of someone we love occurs: 'these loved ones are on the one hand an inner possession, components of our own ego, but on the other hand they are partly stranger, even enemies. With the exception of only a very few situations, there adheres to the tenderest and most intimate of our love-relations a small portion of hostility which can excite an unconscious death-wish' (298). The result is clear. '[O]ur unconscious is just as inaccessible to the idea of our own death, just as murderously inclined towards strangers, just as divided (that is, ambivalent) towards those we love, as was primaeval man' (299).

Both the opposing attitudes towards death, the one which acknowledges it as the end of another's life and the one which denies one's own death as unreal, and the conflict of ambivalence, remain in tension in 'Mourning and Melancholia.' Again, Freud writes that 'mourning is regularly the reaction to the loss of a loved person, or to the loss of some abstraction which has taken the place of one, such as fatherland, liberty, an ideal, and so on' (252).

Mourning, we are told, does involve 'grave departures from the normal attitude to life,' but is not a 'morbid condition,' and after a 'lapse of time' will be overcome as 'each single one of the memories and hopes which bound the libido to the object is brought up and hypercathected' (253). Melancholia, however, is characterized as somewhat different from mourning. With its shared features – 'a profoundly painful dejection, abrogation of interest in the outside world, loss of the capacity to love, inhibition of all activity' – melancholia is distinguished by one single quality: 'a fall in self-regard' (252).

Freud tells us that 'the occasions giving rise to melancholia for the most part extend beyond the clear case of a loss by death, and include all those situations of being wounded, hurt, neglected, out of favor, or disappointed, which can import opposite feelings of love and hate into the relationship or reinforce an already existing ambivalence' (260).

It is this conflict of already existing ambivalence that constitutes the fall in self-regard as the psyche displaces this love/hate ambivalence from the lost object onto their own egos, in order 'to avoid the necessity of openly expressing their hostility against the loved ones. Such self-reproachment subsequently prevents the termination of the work of mourning as ... the object-love, which cannot be given up, takes refuge in narcissistic identification, while the object itself is abandoned, [the] hate is expanded upon this new substitute-object ... [and] the sufferers usually succeed in the end in taking revenge by the circuitous path of self-punishment ...' (260). More specifically self-reproachment takes the form of moralizing self-reproachment and rigidity; as the subject 'represents his [*sic*] ego to us as worthless, incapable of any achievement, and morally despicable, he reproaches himself, vilifies himself, and expects to be cast out and punished' (244).

In other words, Freud constructs the complex of melancholia as the pathological 'interruptus' of the otherwise normal process of mourning a lost object or ideal. The work of mourning can and should come to an end; melancholia, which in effect, produces itself, cannot be resolved in quite the same way. Mourning is the testing of reality for the lost object, and the hypercathexis of memories upon confirmation of its absence. It is the normal, albeit painful, work of separation. Melancholia is the displacement of that painful and menacing ambivalence towards the lost object onto the narcissistic ego of the 'sufferer,' resulting in a profound loss of self-regard, pathological moral self-abasement, and the loss of ego boundaries.

The key factor in understanding melancholic ambivalence seems to be the process of psychic identification: the melancholic, as Freud suggests, 'takes refuge in narcissistic identification' in an effort to maintain the lost object and refuse the loss; hence, grief (260). Judith Butler suggests that it might be this very paradoxical process of identification that constitutes the psychic subject and 'its' identity to begin with.[21] Butler argues that the self only becomes a self on the condition that it has suffered a separation (grammar fails us here, for the 'it' only becomes differentiated through that separation), a loss which is suspended and provisionally resolved through a melancholic incorporation of some 'Other.' That 'Other' installed in the self thus establishes the permanent incapacity of that 'self' to achieve self-identity; it is as it were always already disrupted by that Other; the disruption of the Other at the heart of the self is the very condition of that self's possibility.[22]

Butler, following Lacan, is arguing here that Freud's notions of psychic ambivalence and identification, and hence loss and 'separation,' may be at the heart of what we commonly think of as identity. Such an identity, however, is no longer stable and coherent, but rather becomes inherently unstable, as it can now be read as a social relation rather than ontology: the self is constituted by the incorporation of the Other.[23]

A number of questions remain unanswered and troubling about Freud's work on mourning and melancholia. If love is constituted by ambivalence, or the coexistence of both love and hate, then why, or perhaps how, is it that any subject, suffering the trauma of loss, manages to avoid melancholia and complete the work of mourning at all? Kathleen Woodward has argued that Freud actually privileges separation or mourning over attachment, or melancholia.[24] Upon reconsideration of Freud's essay I am no longer sure that it reads as such. In fact, given the role that ambivalence (or ambivalences) play(s) in both mourning (the ability to complete the work of grieving the loss of a loved one, where love is always already marked by ambivalence) and melancholia (the inability or need to postpone that same loss by incorporating the lost object onto one's own ego as a function of ambivalence), it seems clear that separation may be the desirable condition; but it is, according to the terms of Freud's own argument, the almost unachievable condition. Given these considerations is it possible to argue that loss will be constituted as melancholic, unless one has engaged ambivalences to such as degree as to prevent identification, and hence allow for the work of mourning (and not melancholia) to occur? But, as Butler has outlined – I think convincingly – the production of the psychic subject is dependent upon the very identification and (paradoxically) incorporated 'separation' that induces melancholia. In a sense, then, melancholia, and proximity, seem to be the privileged or necessary condition for the production of subjectivity, not separation, as Woodward suggests. In fact, given the implications of Freud's essay for identity as I have very briefly sketched it here, all identity (as a social relation) is dependent upon imagined connection and proximity (as relation) and not separation (as it gestures toward ontology). Despite these questions I think it is possible to ask yet another: What are the tensions between constructions of

AIDS as a gay (and hence, minoritized 'disease,') and AIDS as a universaliz-able 'condition' with no social boundaries? Is it possible to read the panicked heterosexual disavowal of the AIDS crisis, its necessary phantasms of gay sex and/or identity (as the necessary Other at its centre), and, ultimately, its own risk of death, as melancholic? That is the question that I now consider.

Sex and Politics in the Age of Epidemic

Whatever else it may be, AIDS is a story, or multiple stories, read to a surprising extent from a text that does not exist: the body of the male homosexual. It is a text people so want – need – to read that they have gone so far as to write it themselves.[25]

The complicated overdetermination of AIDS as strictly a gay disease is well documented. AIDS has been primarily associated with a supposed essence in the particular social group in which it primarily appeared in the United States. Michel Foucault has provided a thorough history of the construction of the homosexual and its attendant 'truth' claims. In the *History of Sexuality* Foucault argues that the relationship between truth, knowledge, and sexuality is the product of a discursive machinery which has, since the eighteenth century, attempted to contain, regulate, and control sexuality by taking charge of men's [*sic*] existence as living bodies.[26] Medical, legal, and psychoanalytical dis-course sought to contain (but inevitably produced) so-called deviancy by con-structing definitive categories of sexually deviant and marginal personality types, thereby formulating and installing the uniform truth of sex.[27] In an often quoted passage, Foucault writes:

The nineteenth-century homosexual became a personage, a past, a case history, and a childhood, in addition to being a type of life, a life form, and a morphology, with an indiscreet anatomy and possibly a mysterious physiology. Nothing that went into his total composition was unaffected by his sexuality. It was everywhere present in him: at the root of all his actions because it was their insidious and indefinitely active principle, written immodestly on his face and his body because it was a secret that always gave itself away ... [t]he sodomite had been a temporary aberration, the homosexual was now a species.[28]

AIDS, in a sense, represents yet another mark of such a 'personage,' literally inscribing the host body, 'written immodestly on his face and body,' with its overdetermined text. A determination of AIDS came to be read as synonymous with an admission of homosexuality, and thus, guilt. And as Watney notes, echoing Singer, 'the dominant cultural agenda clearly invites us [*sic*] to regard

AIDS as both a well-deserved punishment and a justification for further puni-tive actions – the latter rationalized as defence mechanisms against its "spread."[29]

Watney cautions against collapsing what he identifies as the 'social and the psychic':

> the concept of 'homophobic' merely encourages us either to psychologize *all* aspects of homosexual stigmatization, or else to pathologize cultural and historical factors. It is highly unlikely that we shall ever be able to 'explain' the complex domain of attitudes to homosexuality by recourse to a single psychic mechanism. Above all, we must avoid the danger of collapsing together the workings of the social and the psychic.[30]

Later in the same essay, he does, however, concede the importance of psycho-analysis in understanding the overdetermined meanings associated with AIDS, and the pedagogies accompanying those meanings: 'An understanding of the kinds of germ theory that underpin lay perceptions of health and disease can hardly be clarified if we attribute them to the agency of the unconscious, though it should be said that we will not be able to understand how and why they are so widely taken up as sexualized metaphors without the aid of psychoanalysis.'[31]

I would agree that any understanding of the panic associated with AIDS needs to use as many diverse theoretical tools as possible. Linda Singer's work on sex politics in the age of epidemic provides us with a useful combination of both Foucauldian analyses of the deployment of power vis-a-vis sexuality, and psychoanalytic readings of intense psychic fear, anxiety, and disavowals, to understand how 'that which is consolidated by the term "sexuality" is also dis-placed and proliferated by that term.'[32] The widespread evidence of panicked disavowal makes clear that the struggle against sexual regulation is occurring in the context of psychological contributions to the logic of epidemic. Given this powerful pedagogy we need to acknowledge what our own queer pedagogies are up against when we try, for example to argue for less government control, or more autonomous funding.

As noted previously, Singer has suggested that within the framework of a logic of sexual epidemic, 'images of erotic access and mobility shift registers from those associated with freedom, surplus, choice, and recreation to those of anxiety, unregulated contact, and uncontrolled spread.'[33] Thus, sexual epidem-ics are particularly fruitful sites for conflicting political inscriptions, depending upon the perpetual revival of an anxiety it seeks to control, inciting a crisis of contagion that spreads to ever new fields of cultural life. In turn, epidemics 'jus-tify and necessitate specific regulatory apparatus which then compensate – materially and symbolically – for the crisis [they have] produced.'[44]

Thus, epidemic logic works through strategies of regulated production, exercising a kind of control through displaced incitements. Most importantly, Singer argues, regulated production works to isolate some phenomena which have reached quantitatively undesirable proportions, and then allay them by specific measures or larger strategies aimed at addressing the so-called problems thus named.[35] Epidemic inscription thus functions as a socially authoritative discourse, at once drawing upon and generating mechanisms for its own legitimation. It teaches that

in a climate induced by epidemic, it becomes reasonable to intervene into the bodies of others. In the name of protecting the health and well-being of the social body, it is only logical to try not only to close gay bathhouses and clubs, but also to test employees for drugs, athletes for steroids, [etc.] ... because epidemics justify and are in fact constructed in order to necessitate a complex system of surveillance and intervention, epidemic situations often provide occasions for the reinstitution for hegemonic lines of authority and control. With respect to this sexual epidemic in particular, there is much evidence that it has provided conservative forces with a unique opportunity to re-market their own rather specific and rigid social agendas.[36]

To anyone who has paid attention to the chilly Canadian legal climate over the past number of years, Singer's argument should be familiar. Although the numerous and detailed specifics of many of those legal decisions are beyond complex discussion here, a few brief examples are worth mentioning. The 1992 Canadian Supreme Court ruling known as the *Butler* decision serves as one initial example. In an attempt to provide a workable definition of 'obscenity' grounded in 'community standards' of tolerance, and to formulate a workable test to determine when the 'exploitation' of sex is undue, the Butler decision has to be read by its proponents, in theory, as an improvement over previous moral-based legislation. However, in the application of the decision, it is clear that primarily gay and lesbian materials are being regulated by Canadian Customs officials. Vancouver's Little Sister's Book and Art Emporium launched an effective challenge of that regulation (details are discussed more fully later). A prosecution of Glad Day Books, in which the court ruled 'Wunna My Fantasies,' a story in the lesbian magazine *Bad Attitude* was obscene under the Butler decision, serves as a second related example. Debate continues over the nature of such sexually explicit material within lesbian and feminist communities. However, the continued targeting of gay and lesbian books, magazines, and other materials suggests that decisions such as Butler function within very specific discursive economies which propound a view of gay and lesbian sex cultures as always already obscene, and now inherently deadly.

In addition, and by way of comparison, it is interesting to recall the recent Ontario court decision which defined table dancing in heterosexual clubs as not obscene under the same section of the Criminal Code of Canada considered in the Butler case. The irony of this particular ruling was its use of the community standards clause. The 'community,' defined as one of bar and club owners (and not necessarily the sex-trade workers themselves, many of whom have publicly criticized the decision), determined that table dancing did not violate its own sense of 'what is decent and what is not decent.'[37] However, the same community-standards test was not convincing enough in the Paris ruling. Crown prosecutors in that case evoked the feminist antipornography context as its 'community standard' and ruled against the lesbian magazine.[38]

The recent anti-child pornography legislation, Bill C-128, is yet another example of how legal decisions, in practice, regulate the production and dissemination of so-called dangerous gay and lesbian sexual practices. It has been touted in the *Toronto Star* as a law designed to protect children against predatory and dangerous pedaphiles and pornographers. In practice, at least in Toronto, the police have arrested primarily gay hookers and their tricks (who exchanged videos of two of those same young men having sex), and Eli Langer, who subsequently had charges against him, but not his art, dropped.[39] The 'art' was later acquitted.

There can be little doubt that each of these instances can be read as the displacement of anxieties from gay and (by association) lesbian sexual practices onto so-called epidemics of child abuse and pornography. When read against the backdrop of conservative political agendas, which not only incite the anxieties they seek to control but also promote the family as the supposedly exclusive site of safe sex, these examples clearly signal the shift of a regulatory and melancholic biopolitical apparatus from one site (anticontagion) to another (the justification of its right to intervene into the bodies of others it constructs as dangerous).[40] It might be important to underscore *melancholic* biopolitics here. If, as psychoanalysis has told us, the melancholic can be characterized by a moralizing self-reproachment, a certain rigidity in self-representation, an insistence on discourses of morality, and a disavowal of trauma, then it becomes possible to read many of these legal decisions and the social/political discursive economies which have produced them, as melancholic as well. The entire debate around pornography, for example, has been marked by rigidity, binarized moral equations, and at times a discourse of disparagement that cannot help but reflect a profound hatred of those necessary imaginary phantasms that same discourse produces. Likewise, the judicial discourse reflected in the legal decisions is informed by those same displacements and by moral panic. The pedagogical authority of jurisprudence is thus added to the already persuasive force of a logic for sexual repression rooted in psychic and social conditions.

Trials and Tribulations

MISS RADCLYFFE-HALL: I protest ...
THE MAGISTRATE: I must ask people not to interrupt the Court.
MISS RADCLYFFE-HALL: I am the author of this book.
THE MAGISTRATE: If you cannot behave yourself in Court I shall have you removed.
MISS RADCLYFFE-HALL: Shame! It is a shame!
... THE MAGISTRATE: This being the tenor of this book, I have no hesitation whatever in saying it is an obscene libel ... and I shall order it to be destroyed.[41]

What I have been foregrounding in this chapter is a set of theoretical questions organized around a set of problematics. I have been interrogating the relationships between Freud's work on death, mourning, and melancholia; Singer's epidemic logic vis-a-vis the subject of AIDS; and a shift in (queer) theory's configurations on identity from questions of ontology towards identity as social and psychic relations. It is clear that through the operations of a melancholic biopolitics, one premised on denials of death and displacements from the perceived, perhaps imagined, danger associated with death and sex, that danger is mapped onto sex itself. By way of further explication I want to shift theoretical gears and analyse what occurs when those social and psychic relations and their ensuing inscriptions and regulations collide with(in) the Canadian legal system; more specifically, with respect to the Little Sister's constitutional challenge of Canada Customs' interpretation and application of obscenity law. If what I am suggesting is true, that such judicial discourse as Judge John Smith's is imbricated with, perhaps overdetermined by, an epidemic logic and inscriptions and their attendant moral panics and regulations, then what can this trial and its outcome tell us about the practices, and, by implication, the pedagogies of juridical/discursive resistance, interruption, and disruption?

My interest in trials of this nature emerges after a longstanding fascination with Radclyffe Hall's novel *The Well of Loneliness*,[42] and its both successful and unsuccessful expeditions through British and American obscenity courts. *The Well* was banned outright in Britain shortly after publication, in 1928; various defendants, primarily publishers, were found guilty, then acquitted, in several American courtrooms in 1929. The lawyers defending the publishers of the novel in Britain (charges were not laid against the novel or Hall) attempted to use many of the same strategies the Little Sister's legal team deployed – they relied heavily on 'expert' testimony, arguing for context-specific interpretation or 'readings' of the text, evoking artistic or literary merit – but were not able to fend off the charge of obscenity successfully. While Canada in the 1990s and Britain in the late 1920s are unlikely comparable contexts, I remain intrigued by the moments of disruption afforded by these legal, sociopolitical, and discursively rich events.

This particular war waged by Canada Customs against queer culture has a long, ugly history. The most recent skirmish began in 1986 when Canada Customs detained a large shipment of books and magazines bound for Little Sister's Book and Art Emporium.[43] As reported by Still, Fuller, and Blackley, prior to its harassment of Little Sister's, Canada Customs held the Toronto gay and lesbian bookstore, Glad Day Books, in its panoptical gaze, banning *The Joy of Gay Sex* in 1985. The owners of Little Sister's initially mobilized artists, civil libertarians, and queer communities late in 1986 to protest book seizures, a mobilization which eventually brought the British Columbia Civil Liberties Association onside with a legal and financial commitment to mount a legal challenge to Canada Customs' powers (13–15). The publicity also brought with it threatening phone calls, harassment, and eventually, a series of bomb attacks on Little Sister's in 1987 and early 1988. However, on 7 June 1990, Little Sister's, the BCCLA, and the owners of the bookstore launched a massive attack on state censorship in Canada, an attack designed to challenge the constitutionality of Canada Customs practices (14, 15).

What I find remarkable about the Little Sister's court case is the fact that in addition to retaining a brilliant legal mind – Joe Arvay – to argue its case, many of the plaintiff's witnesses deployed *pedagogical* strategies within the courtroom to render intelligible that which is deemed not only unintelligible but always already obscene within the terms of legal discourse. There are many factors emerging from the trial which can account for the perceived success of the Little Sister's legal challenge. However, there is one that I foreground here: the pedagogical usefulness of queer theory, and by implication, its genealogical investigations and its methodologies of historicizing, contextualizing, and problematizing 'sex,' a use-value both legitimat*ing* a body of texts and, simultaneously, productively legitimat*ed* as a field of scholarly inquiry in the discursive and performative space of a courtroom. I then focus my attention on the decision rendered by Judge John Smith of the British Columbia Supreme Court.

The challenges faced in the courtroom by Little Sister's were enormous. Two years after launching the case the legal team for Little Sister's learned, as all of Canada did, that the 1959 obscenity law had been successfully challenged. The infamous Butler decision changed the measure of obscenity in Canada, changing it from antiquated notions of indecency and immorality to those of harm instead (40). Dividing pornography into three categories – explicit sex with violence, real or implied; explicit sex without violence, but which subjects people to treatment that is degrading and dehumanizing; and nonviolent, explicit sex that is neither degrading nor dehumanizing but which employs children in its production – the Butler decision constructs a three-stage test for obscenity. Courts consider whether the material is harmful according to community standards; according to whether the material exploits sex in a degrading or dehumanizing manner; and whether the material, though violent or degrading, is redeemed by a wider artistic, literary, or other similar purpose (41). All of the rather vague terms, such as *community, degrading, dehumanizing,* and *artistic,* are left undefined, and such vagueness has given enormous discretionary powers to judges. Moreover, the Supreme Court of Canada also has attempted to deal with the issue of consent. This is where the Butler decision becomes most treacherous. The Court says, 'In appreciation of whether material is degrading or dehumanizing, the appearance of consent is not necessarily determinative. Consent cannot save materials that otherwise contain degrading or dehumanizing scenes. Sometimes the very appearance of consent makes the depicted acts even more degrading or dehumanizing (42).' For obvious reasons, including those few examples I have already given, Blackley reiterates what the applications of the Butler decision have since demonstrated.

The Butler decision has so far been a 'disaster' for lesbians and gays (42). The strategies deployed in the courtroom to challenge Canada Customs needed to be as widespread and thorough as the applications of Butler have been. Joe Arvay's legal strategies were as eclectic pedagogically as they were diverse intellectually and politically, continually toggling between a facts-based pedagogical approach and a universalizing pedagogical approach, which argues that issues of sexuality, representation, and state regulation were of relevance to a much wider group of sexual and artistic communities. To a certain extent Arvay's task was to educate Judge Smith about the function of erotic materials in gay and lesbian cultures. To this end the defence saw its role as offering information about the 'other,' a minoritizing pedagogical method which attempts to win empathy and tolerance. At the same time Arvay drew upon strategies, especially those deployed by civil libertarians, to foreground the fact that heavy-handed state regulation should be the focus, not a particular sexual minority. Finally, Arvay drew upon the developing scholarly field of queer theory and sexuality studies with their accompanying pedagogies to demonstrate the complexities of sex, identities, and cultural texts.

To these ends Arvay had scheduled witnesses in various groups, bringing booksellers, book distributors, and librarians together to describe the economic, practical, and psychological burdens that Canada Customs' seizures imposed on the book industry (22). The next group of witnesses – artists, authors, and cultural critics – were called upon to instruct Judge Smith on the complexities of sexual identities by 'deconstruct[ing] gay and lesbian culture,' revealing 'the fluid, subjective, and historically complex nature of sexual images and text,' illustrating exactly how absurd it is to expect Customs officials to make such judgments about entire shipments of books (22). Social scientists, writers, and historians explained the meaning of lesbian and gay communities, and the significance of queer literature and culture to those communities. Moreover, this group examined how Canada Customs fit into a long tradition of state regulation of sexuality, and of homosexuality in particular, and also taught Judge Smith about the conventions and etiquette of gay and lesbian s/m, an enormous trigger for Canada Customs newly outfitted with the *carte blanche* of 'fake consent.' Finally, Arvay attacked the inconsistency of Canada Customs' internal procedures (22–3).

It was within the latter group of witnesses – social scientists, writers, and historians – that queer theory, albeit cloaked, made its appearance in the courtroom. A number of prominent American and Canadian scholars in the field of sexuality played key roles in historicizing, contextualizing, and denaturalizing 'sex' and the politics of representation. While the details of the arguments presented during the trial are remarkable, my concern here is more with the functionality of the 'scholar' as expert within the legal discourse. It is not my intention to hail these individuals solely as heroes, however important it is to acknowledge the courage and sophistication of their presence in the courtroom. Rather, I suggest that reading the testimony of these individuals as performative of a scholarly field is far more productive.

Carole Vance, one of the organizers of the infamous 1982 feminist conference on sexuality at Barnard College, New York, which ignited what has since become known as the 'sex wars,' presented an effective and important history not only of 'sexuality,' but of the displacements, investments, indeed, biomedical, theological, scientific, and psychological production of the sexed subject itself. Echoing precisely the biopolitical inscription I have been outlining here, Vance foregrounds the numerous and often contradictory and panicked discourses which collide around sexuality:

The focus ... is to examine the underlying history of sexuality ... [its perceived] dangers of mortality, of death, of health risks, of moral dissolution, of individual dissolution, notions of social decay, notions of great danger of pollution to particular social classes or groups, notions of moral impurity, and notions almost, in some cases, of disintegration and degeneration of the government and the society (51).

In that genealogical spirit, Becki Ross and Gary Kinsman, well-known and respected sociologists and queer activists, contextualized both the contemporary history of queer sexual representations and the attempted regulation of those images. Moreover, as social scientists, both challenged the questionable sociological 'evidence' presented by the Crown on issues of consent and perceived violence in queer pornography and s/m texts (100–7). Kinsman presented a 'history of the present' vis-a-vis gay legal and sociological history in Canada, while Ross not only defended but fiercely protected lesbian sexual pleasures during a hostile cross-examination. Finally, Lorraine Weir and Bart Testa escorted literary and critical theory into the courtroom to further challenge the supposed 'harm' of s/m imagery (83–6). Explicating the details and importance of hermeneutics, deconstruction, semiotics, and film theory to queer pornography, all of these scholars contextualized and defended the work of Pat Califia, John Preston, and others who had been continually seized and prohibited at the highest levels of the Customs' appeal process.

In his decision British Columbia Supreme Court Judge John Smith vindicates the efficacy of such queering pedagogical strategies within the Canadian judiciary. Described as a limited victory, Smith's judgment at once condemns Canada Customs' applications of its powers but upholds its mandate as authorized by the Customs Act and Customs Tariff, as well as by Section 163 of the Criminal Code: the 1992 *Butler* decision. Curiously, however, in the course of rendering his conclusions, Judge Smith makes a number of judicially unprecedented observations about queer sex, identities, and cultures, observations which, as I suggested earlier, are authorized by, and yet productively legitimate, the queer scholar and his/her field of inquiry.

However, these fruitful observations are not without unintended and problematical effects. Curiously, Judge Smith's construction of the young 'gay and lesbian reader' demonstrates the effectiveness of some of Arvay's strategies, in particular that which dangerously emphasizes empathy and toleration for the 'other.' Thus, this young gay and lesbian reading subject, constructed as one searching for 'self-affirmation and empowerment through expression,' one whose 'humanity' is 'distinguished from everyone else in society ... by their sexuality,' makes an ambiguous and troubling appearance in Judge Smith's courtroom.[44] He/she appears to be rescued from 'obscenity,' but the young gay and lesbian subject is always already produced by the terms of that same obscenity legislation and its accompanying regimes of truth. In other words (I return to this argument in more detail later) this innocent and searching subject is *not* obscene by virtue of his/her same-sex desires, but rather, *is* in need of even further protection from obscene literature which could conceivably cause undue harm to that innocence.

In his unexpected and bold conclusions leading up to his rather conservative 'remedy,' Judge Smith examines the functionality of both 'sex' and 'erotica' for 'homosexuals,' 'homosexuals as a group,' and 'homosexual culture.'[45] Deploying a curious mixture of language in a lengthy passage which at once ontologizes identity while claiming to be concerned with sexual practices, Judge Smith states that it is the latter which is constitutive of the former. I quote the passage at length to foreground the contradictory discourses overdetermining the intelligibility of same-sex desires:

The defining characteristic of homosexuals, the element that distinguishes them from everyone else in society is their sexuality. Naturally, their art and literature are extensively concerned with this central characteristic of their humanity. As attested by several of the plaintiffs' witnesses, erotica produced for heterosexual audiences performs largely an entertainment function, but homosexual erotica is far more important to homosexuals. These witnesses established that sexual text and imagery produced for homosexuals serves as an affirmation of their sexuality and as a socializing force; that it normalizes the sexual practices that the larger society has historically considered to be deviant; and that it organizes homosexuals as a group and enhances their political power. Because sexual practices are so integral to homosexual culture, any law proscribing representations of sexual practices will necessarily affect homosexuals to a greater extent than it will other groups in society, to whom representations of sexual practices are much less significant and for whom such representations play a relatively marginal role in art and literature.[46]

While Judge Smith's analysis of the relationship between culture, literature, and sexuality for (what he rather conservatively calls) 'homosexuals' is commendable and appears consistent with recent remappings of the terrain of sexualities, nonetheless it remains firmly rooted within the terms of an ontologizing, minoritizing discourse where questions of sexuality are considered to be of primary importance for a 'small, distinct, relatively fixed homosexual minority.'[47] It is possible to see the dangerous implications of this deployment of both identity and sexuality when Judge Smith addresses the 'unequal treatment before obscenity laws' claim that he himself vindicates in the last sentence of the passage.

   In attempting to deal with the claim that Little Sister's treatment by Canada Customs is unconstitutional, Judge Smith employed a concept argued in part by Arvay before the Supreme Court of Canada in the Egan and Nesbitt case. Jim Egan and Jack Nesbitt are an elderly gay couple who demanded equal treatment under the *Old Age Security Act*, which provides a pension benefit to spouses of old age security recipients, but only if the spouse is of the opposite sex.[48] The Supreme Court ruled that discrimination against gays and lesbians was prohibited under the Canadian Charter of Rights and Freedoms, and while they found that Section 15(1) of the Charter had been infringed, they also ruled that discrimination was justifiable, and denied the claim. In his efforts to decide whether Little Sister's was discriminated against directly by Canada Customs, Judge Smith quoted from the Egan and Nesbitt decision, which produced a distinction between direct discrimination and adverse effect discrimination: 'Direct discrimination involves a law, rule or practice which on its face discriminates on a prohibited ground. Adverse effect discrimination occurs when a law, rule or practice is facially neutral but has a disproportionate impact on a group because of a particular characteristic of that group.'[49]

Smith argued that the plaintiffs and 'other homosexuals' – sexualized and marked as an ontological category, while heterosexuality remains not only unmarked, but aggressively desexualized – have been *disadvantaged* by the obscenity laws and Canada Customs, but have not been *discriminated* against *directly*:

Sexuality is relevant because obscenity is defined in terms of sexual practices. Since homosexuals are defined by their homosexuality and their art and literature is permeated with representations of their sexual practices, it is inevitable that they will be disproportionately affected by a law proscribing the proliferation of obscene sexual representations ... The point is that homosexual obscenity is proscribed because it is obscene, not because it is homosexual. The disadvantageous effect on homosexuals is unavoidable ... [but] the unequal impact of the law on homosexuals has not been shown to be discriminatory.[50]

Smith does disentangle temporarily the knotted imbrication of 'homosexual' and 'obscene,' but as I will suggest in a moment, this separation only serves to reproduce and strengthen the perceived need for obscenity laws, and, by implication, the regulation of queer sexual imagery. Ironically, that very need is reconstituted by the judicial construction of the gay and lesbian reading subject.

There is a section in Judge Smith's judgment with the simple heading 'The Factual Background.'[51] Here, the history or background of the case, as Judge Smith perceives it, is laid out, and it is this particular set of facts that he is asked to adjudicate. What's remarkable about this particular section is the way it tells the history of the inception of Little Sister's bookstore vis-a-vis its owners' search for books, community, and context as young gay men. In other words Judge Smith tells a somewhat allegorical, meta-coming-out story, one in which three characters – James, Bruce, and Janine – quest to find and accept themselves as homosexuals, and are determined to maintain a bookstore that will provide other such 'homosexuals' with the 'homosexual' literature they need to adjust in a perceived hostile world. 'As a young man,' Judge Smith begins, the plaintiff James Deva was very confused by his homosexual feelings. After leaving university, he traveled to Vancouver to investigate 'the gay lifestyle' ... he was unable to find work ... [and] subsisted on welfare ... then he read 'The Joy of Gay Sex' and ... the book vitalized him. He and his partner, the plaintiff Bruce Smythe ... decided to open a bookstore specializing in homosexual literature. Mr. Deva ... believed the confusion and loneliness felt by homosexuals could be ameliorated by enabling individual homosexuals to obtain literature dealing with homosexuality. In this way, he believed, they would gain insight into their own lives and would come to realize, as he had, that there are other homosexuals experiencing similar difficulties coping with life in our society.[52]

Judge Smith continues telling the story of Little Sister's and eventually introduces the next character.

Mr. Deva and Mr. Smythe rely heavily on their manager, Janine Fuller, a lesbian ... like Mr. Deva, Ms. Fuller [experienced] difficulties as a young homosexual in a society she perceived to be hostile to homosexuals. Also like Mr. Deva, she attributes the 'validation' of her homosexuality to reading a book, 'Sapphistry,' ... the book encouraged her to understand the sexual feelings with which she was struggling, and to realize, as well, that she was not alone in those feelings. She overcame her fear of being known as a lesbian and 'came out.'[53]

Later, in his readings of expert testimony contextualizing the more hotly contested material – gay and lesbian s/m in literature by Pat Califia and John Preston – Judge Smith gave an insightful and seemingly encouraging analysis. Emphasizing the literary merit and utility of these works, he cites the expert evidence given by scholars Becki Ross, Thomas Waugh, and Bart Testa, and testimony by some of the writers themselves – Califia and Nino Ricci – that such works function much like *The Joy of Gay Sex* and *Sapphistry* in Judge Smith's own meta-coming-out narrative. In other words, as long as the 'work as a whole does not merely represent 'dirt for dirt's sake' but has a legitimate role when measured by the internal necessities' test – a test which determines 'genuine' artistic and literary merit, 'the serious-mindedness of the author,' and the quality of the work – then 'a society committed to the values underlying freedom of expression, as our society is, cannot defend the automatic prohibition of descriptions and depictions of homosexual sado-masochism.'[54] The moral of the story is this: Not only does the highly problematical coming-out narrative provide the only grid of intelligibility for juridical discourse here, its object – that ahistorical, renaturalized, ontological creature known as the homosexual (never the bisexual, or transgendered, or even gay, or lesbian, subject) – is reified and re/produced as a universal, normalized subject, now 'subjected' to even more regulatory mechanisms and technologies. In 'The Subject and Power' Foucault reminds us of the bind of subjectivity: 'There are two meanings of the word *subject*, subject to someone else by control and dependence, and tied to his [*sic*] own identity by a conscience or self-knowledge. Both meanings suggest a form of power which subjugates and makes subject to.'[55]

Furthermore, it is necessary to problematize the constructions and functionality of 'literature' as well. For upholders of literary tradition, and practitioners of 'great works by great authors' as well as periodization and genre methodologies, the judicial construction of the literary merit test resacralizes the literary text as an authentic object. Such an approach disavows the ways in which literature as the object of the discipline 'literary studies,' also functions as a discursive practice, equally invested and imbricated with dominant regimes of truth and power/ knowledge formations. Thus, in Judge Smith's decision literature functions as a pedagogue of universal truth and absolute morality, and as a mode of truth-telling, simply by unmasking naturalized truths about the human condition. Notions of literary merit and its presumptions of originality, authenticity, unity, and core selfhood – the central tenets of sacralized literature and criticism – cloak the power/knowledge machineries overdetermining truth, art, and value, investing one set of meanings at the expense of others.[56] The meanings invested in Judge Smith's decision 'fictions' a particular historical narrative that literature as a discipline invents and tells about itself as a self-generating, truth-telling regime. Moreover, such meanings beg the following questions: What exactly is this activity that consists of circulating fiction, poems, stories, etc. in a society? And why is it that a number of them are made to function as literature, while others are not?[57] The most disturbing part of Judge Smith's decision is that he authorizes Canada Customs officials to answer these queries: 'Modern society has come to rely on administrative decision-making as essential to proper government and to recognize that specialized tribunals and administrative decision-makers are particularly well-suited to deal with routine decisions requiring specialized knowledge. Customs officers can fill that role.'[58]

While it could be argued that Judge Smith's understanding of the difficult coming-out process, and of the importance of erotic and s/m 'literature,' is laudable and deserving of celebration, to be sure, on many levels, and especially from within a view of 'progress' it is important. But what emerges penultimately in his decision, especially in the constructions of pornography, or dirt for dirt's sake, and his defense of obscenity legislation, undermines such an argument. Judge Smith's judgment deploys and thus reproduces the distinctions between erotica and pornography. The deployment of this distinction indicates that sex continues to be a problem that needs to be known and governed, 'taken charge of, tracked down as it were, by a discourse that aimed to allow it no obscurity, no respite.'[59] 'Gay and lesbian literature is now reified and incited into discourse, into the field and operations of power itself, caused to speak itself through meticulous rules of self-examination, and account for itself as non-pornographic, or else.[60]

Moreover, the juridical deployment of sex uses this distinction to produce a gay or lesbian reading subject who innocently searches for equally innocent and valorized 'literature' that normalizes his/her identity. Thus, obscenity legislation is now needed more than ever to protect that very subject from dirt for dirt's sake material that will corrupt and expose that reader to harm. The separation of 'homosexual' from 'obscene' (recall Judge Smith's assertion: 'The point is that homosexual obscenity is proscribed because it is obscene, not because it is homosexual.'), while rhetorically important, further reifies obscenity as bad and dangerous sex ('Tomorrow sex will be good again.'),[61] vindicating both obscenity legislation and Canada Customs. In a performative and self-authorizing gesture, Judge Smith rehearses this mandate:

The legislation prohibiting the dissemination of obscenity is concerned with protecting individuals and groups who may suffer harm as a result of its production and utilization. The protection is extended not only to those who might suffer attitudinal and behavioural changes from exposure to obscenity, but to those persons and groups who might be harmed because of those changes and to vulnerable individuals and groups involved in its production. Their claims to protection must be balanced against the claims of importers and consumers of obscenity to free expression.[62]

What is at stake here is not a heartfelt and genuine concern for 'oppressed' peoples; neither are competing discourses of sexuality at stake. Rather, what is at stake are the imperatives for juridical discourse to reproduce and legitimate itself through the deployment, management, and regulation of sex. What crystalizes in this passage are the ways in which the judiciary mandates itself by deploying sex to construct/invent a flock of innocent subjects it is thusly authorized to protect. Once more the gay and lesbian (again, never bisexual or transgendered) subject is now included within this flock, seemingly freed from but now subjected to obscenity laws, and protected from harmful dirt for dirt's sake.[63]

'What Is to Be Done?'

A country that cannot protect its borders is not a country. Ronald Reagan

It is important to acknowledge the enormous challenges facing the Little Sister's legal team and its witnesses. Many of Judge Smith's most hopeful and pro-gressive views expressed in his decision can be credited to the sophistication and determination of those involved in the case. And as Blackley and Fuller note, it is not over yet. My own interest in the Little Sister's case, as I have indi-cated already, circulates around the ways in which various larger political, social, and psychic relations and operations collide in and around the bookstore itself, as well as in Judge Smith's courtroom. In addition I have been attempting to discern the ways in which pedagogical strategies, methodologies, and genea-logical investigations loosely organized under the rubric of Queer Theory hold up outside the university. The inside/outside distinction, of course, is com-pletely arbitrary as the subject of queer theory is queer culture itself, fed in part by much of the material scrutinized by Canada Customs at the Canada-United States border. While many of the pedagogical strategies used in Judge Smith's courtroom were successful, albeit limited, my reading of his decision suggests that they are not without unintended consequences. One of the pedagogical strategies which proved most effective both inside and outside the courtroom/ classroom is to continue thinking that which thinks it can't be thought. White-ness, masculinities, nation, heterosexuality, death, sex, et al. are constituted by the very fact of their supposed natural existence. In the text of his decision Judge Smith demonstrates that he was indeed 'educated' by the testimonies of Vance, Ross, and Kinsman in his courtroom, reminding us that politically invested scholarship must continue to probe the phantasmagoric scaffolding of those so-called facts.

Recall, too, Alexander Düttman: 'Thought must always think that which can-not be reduced to itself.' I am struck by the absolute necessity of the white sexed subject to think beyond itself. For instance Judge Smith repeatedly emphasizes other hysterias overdetermining his decision, especially those troubling questions of nationhood and national [read white, Anglo-Saxon] identities:

People entering Canada have an even lower expectation of privacy than in most other sit-uations ... people do not expect to be able to cross international borders free from scru-tiny. It is commonly accepted that sovereign states have the right to control both who and what enters their boundaries. *For the general welfare of the nation the state is expected to perform this role.* Without the ability to establish that all persons who seek to cross its borders and their goods are legally entitled to enter the country, the state would be precluded from performing this crucially important function.[64]

An overwhelming anxiety about borders and the necessity of policing them cir-culates throughout Judge Smith's text, suggesting that it is through such ideological and performative 'customs' that a nation identifies itself as a nation. The identity-based discourse employed by witnesses in court perhaps played into this massive social/legal orientation of western culture to police borders:

Comfort for the conclusion that the infringement created on freedom of expression by the impugned legislation may be found in the fact that many other free and democratic societies employ similar schemes of customs control over obscenity. The Canadian scheme does not criminalize the importation of obscenity and does not subject the importer to the possibility of conviction for importing obscenity as in the case of several other countries ... In that respect *we* differ from Australia, Bermuda, Germany, New Zealand, Singapore, Hong Kong and France where the importation of obscene articles is a criminal offence ... The objective is to restrain the proliferation of obscenity and that objective is founded on the notion that obscenity diminishes fundamental values of society.[65]

By way of comparison, consider this similar, although far more explicit, admission of anxiety from Judge Chartres Biron, the British magistrate who banned *The Well of Loneliness* in 1928:

Obscenity is to be judged by the standards of the laws of this realm ... You might get a native of another race, be it a white race or a yellow race or a black race, accustomed to practices which are not merely tolerated but which are part of a religious ritual, and who might theoretically produce a book in this country which would not be obscene in their land, be it Africa or any other land ... in this country we have standards laid down by the law ... if not ... it is obvious that every nation would be exposed to influences which it would be powerless to destroy.[66]

By way of conclusion, and in an effort to address the question that the editors of this collection want to foreground ('What Is to Be Done?'), my reading of the Little Sister's case suggests the following: a close reading of Judge Smith's decision through discourses and anxieties of nationalisms reveals stakes which a lens of sexuality will miss. In explaining why he refused to declare the Customs Act and Custom Tariffs unconstitutional, Judge Smith makes the following remarkable declaration about the '*business* of the nation,' unwittingly gesturing towards a counter-discourse of resistance as well:

Parliament has tailored a system of customs regulations which gives an importer the right to seek judicial review of administrative decisions if aggrieved while preventing the legitimate and important business of customs administration from being brought to a standstill. *Given the volume of importations in Canada at the various points of entry each year no other practical alternative can be envisioned ... It must be remembered that the business of government is a practical one.*[67]

Thus it seems that the deployment of sex is merely one biopolitical operation through which a juridico-nation-state constitutes itself. It seems quite unlikely that any judge will eliminate legislation such as the Customs Act and Customs Tariff, legislation which not only facilitates the 'business of the nation' but which is constitutive of the very nation itself. It seems that future legal challenges of Canada Customs and their seizure of gay and lesbian cultural materials must think and *teach* questions of nationhood, nationalisms, *and* identities to be effective. In failing to force sexuality *and* nationhood to 'think themselves together,' as Düttman suggests, thought, politics, and pedagogy all risk profound impertinence.

Cases

Little Sisters v *Canada* (1996), 131 Dominion Law Reports (4th series) 486 (British Columbia Supreme Court).
R. v *Butler*, [1992] 1, Supreme Court Reports 452 (Supreme Court of Canada).

Notes

1 Freud, 'Thoughts for the Times,' 289.
2 Foucault, *History of Sexuality*, vol. 1, *An Introduction*, trans. Robert Hurley (New York: Pantheon, 1978), 138.
3 Quoted in Felman and Laub, *Testimony*, xiii.
4 Düttman, *What Will*, 111.
5 Jarman, *Blue* (movie, 1993).
6 Grover, '*AIDS: Keywords*,' 23–30.
7 Wright, *Feminism and Psychoanalysis*, 70.
8 Grover, '*AIDS: Keywords*,' 23–8.
9 Wright, *Feminism and Psychoanalysis*, 70–1.
10 Singer, *Erotic Welfare*, 121.
11 Duttman, *What Will*, 111–12.
12 Singer, *Erotic Welfare*, 114.
13 Ibid., 119.
14 Foucault, *History of Sexuality*, 139.
15 Singer, *Erotic Welfare*, 118.

16 Cossman et al., *Bad Attitude/s on Trial.*
17 Felman and Laub, *Testimony.*
18 Freud, 'Thoughts for the Times,' 289.
19 Ibid., 298.
20 Freud, 'Mourning and Melancholia.'
21 Judith Butler, *Inside/Out*, 25.
22 Ibid., 27.
23 Ibid.
24 Woodward, 'Freud and Barthes.'
25 Treichler, '*AIDS, Homophobia*,' 42.
26 Foucault, *History of Sexuality*, 89.
27 Ibid., 35.
28 Ibid., 43.
29 Watney, 'The Subject of AIDS,' 68.
30 Ibid., 71.
31 Ibid.
32 Singer, *Erotic Welfare*, 28.
33 Ibid.
34 Ibid., 29.
35 Ibid.
36 Singer, *Erotic Welfare*, 30–1.
37 R. v *Butler.*
38 Ross, 'Wunna His Fantasies,' 41.
39 Sex Workers Alliance of Toronto, press release.
40 Singer, *Erotic Welfare*, 30.
41 *The Queen* v *Jonathan Cape and Leopold Hill*, 6–7.
42 Radclyffe Hall, *The Well of Loneliness.*
43 Fuller and Blackley, *Restricted Entry*, 8.
44 All further quotations can be found in Smith's judgment under *Little Sisters* v *Canada*, 614–15.
45 *Little Sisters* v *Canada*, para. 128.
46 Ibid., para. 128
47 Sedgwick, *Epistemology of the Closet*, 1.
48 Fuller and Blackley, *Restricted Entry*, 107.
49 Ibid., 190.
50 *Little Sisters* v *Canada*, paras. 135–6.
51 Ibid., paras. 88–119.
52 Ibid., paras. 88–9.
53 Ibid., para. 92.
54 Ibid., paras. 225–30.

55 Foucault, 'The Subject and Power,' 212.
56 Quinby, *Genealogy and Literature*, xvi.
57 Foucault, 'The Functions of Literature,' 4.
58 *Little Sisters* v *Canada*, para. 243.
59 Foucault, *The History of Sexuality*, 20.
60 Ibid., 18–19.
61 Ibid., 7.
62 *Little Sisters* v *Canada*, para. 213.
63 See Cossman, 'Feminist Fashion,' in Cossman et al., *Bad Attitude/s*.
64 *Little Sisters* v *Canada*, para. 176.
65 Ibid., paras. 240–6.
66 *Queen v Jonathan Cape*, 20–1.
67 *Little Sisters* v *Canada*, paras. 214–15.

14

Representing Lesbians and Gays in Law

DIANA MAJURY

In thinking about what I wanted to do in this chapter, which the editors had described as discussing how sexual identities are represented in Canadian law,[1] I initially thought I would focus my discussion on the recent (May 1995) Supreme Court of Canada decision in the case of Egan and Nesbit.[2] John Norris Nesbit, a gay man, had applied for and been denied the spousal allowance provided for by the *Old Age Security Act*,[3] because being in a gay relationship, he did not meet the statutory definition of *spouse* and was therefore considered not to qualify for the allowance. Nesbit and his partner, James Egan, challenged the definition of spouse as discriminating against them on the basis of sexual orientation. They were unsuccessful at every level of court, including the Supreme Court of Canada. The case is important, because despite the fact that a number of cases raising sexual orientation issues have been before the Supreme Court, Egan and Nesbit is the first case in which this court was actually forced to address directly the issue of sexual orientation as a prohibited ground of discrimination and make a decision on this basis. It is a decision that it is binding on all other courts in this country. As such, while it is certainly only a single legal representation, and a representation that, like all others, will change and be changed over time, it is at this point in time a significant representation for lesbians and gays in Canada.

On rereading the case with a view to writing this chapter, however, I found that I did not have much to say about it. The case is quite legalistic and really says very little, and certainly nothing new, about lesbians and gays. In fact it doesn't say anything about lesbians, except to the extent that we are included in the term *homosexual*, which of course we are even though we may not want to be. But then my assumption is that Egan and Nesbit may not have wanted to be referred to as homosexual either. I have no doubt that the decision would have been the same if it had been a lesbian couple instead of a gay male couple, and the case will apply to lesbians as it will to gay men, but there is no representation of lesbians in the case. I am not sure that there is really any representation of gay men in the case either, beyond a brief description of the relationship of the two gay men who brought the case to court.

There have been a large number of cases and a huge amount of legal academic writing on the question of whether lesbians and gays are, or can be, or want to be, considered spouses under the law; whether we are, or can be, or want to be, considered family under the law. The Egan and Nesbit case does not add anything to these discussions except the temporary final judicial word on the question of whether we are or whether we can be spouses for the purposes of spousal allowances under the *Old Age Security Act*. Four judges said we are not and cannot be; four judges said we are and can be; one judge said it is premature to require government to recognize us as such. So five to four say we aren't and can't be – for now.

The case was disappointing, not only in its outcome, but in its analysis.[4] So when I thought about spending my time writing at length about it and readers spending their time reading at length about it, I felt a little depressed and a little bored – for all of us. Then when I was reading, or rereading, some of the current legal literature on lesbians and gays to help me think about Egan and Nesbit, I felt energized and excited and challenged; I felt the possibilities of and for change. There has been a recent explosion of writing on legal issues pertaining to lesbians and gays. There are major debates going on in that literature about who we are, and if and how and for what purposes we should represent ourselves in law. There is vitality and questioning and exploration going on in and through that literature – lots of it. Clearly, then, this is what I should be writing about as representations of sexual identities in Canadian law. However, I find myself unable totally to abandon Egan and Nesbit, given its significance at this moment as the principal legal representation to be addressed/undressed/downdressed/redressed/re-addressed. So, I am going to do a little on the literature and then a very little on Egan and Nesbit.

Keeping the case at the centre, or perhaps at the perimeter, or perhaps as a sounding-board for my discussion, provides me with a basis for selection from what really is a large literature on lesbian and gay legal issues. And it provides me with a structure for presenting the discussion. Given that Egan and Nesbit is a Charter equality/discrimination case challenging legal definitions of spouse and family, I will examine some of the current lesbian and gay legal literature on equality theorizing and on family theorizing. I will focus, but not exclusively, on Canadian literature and work by Canadians. Even so restricted, I will not cover all of the recent publications; there is too much material even in these two areas[5] to be able to do it justice in the confines of this chapter. My choice of the articles I discuss is somewhat idiosyncratic, a reflection of what I have read, and, within that, what I have found most interesting and challenging and relevant with respect to the exploration I want to undertake here. I want to use this valuable and divergent material to help me investigate and assess Egan and Nesbit as a legal strategy for, and as a legal representation of, lesbians and gays in Canada.

In referring to legal representation I simply mean representations made in a legal context. In these circumstances the term *representation* has no particular legal meaning or significance. It is, however, a term with lots of meaning(s) that resonate in the legal context. For instance, one 'represents,' that is acts on behalf of, a client. There are numerous and ongoing discussions among lawyers and among clients, and between the two, about the nature of that representation – how much re-presentation is involved, and the distortions and misrepresentations that occur in the process. I discuss this issue in relation to the representation of lesbian and gay clients further on in this chapter. Legal cases and decisions re-present people's lives and concerns as rules and rulings; the people are often barely referred to in the decision itself; they are no longer represented in the case. In addition there is the matter of the law itself as representation: that is, the question of who and what we are talking about when we talk about 'the law' and what is being hidden by the invocation of something called the law. The law stands in for, and in so doing provides a front for, the 'state,' for government, for society, for dominant interests, for control, for order. The representation of the law as an entity in itself protects the actors who make up, enforce, and benefit from the law or a law, as well as neutralizes the critiques of those who are subordinated and circumscribed by the law or a law.

In exploring these legal representations I am, in a sense, exploring the pedagogical role of law. Law as representor is law as teacher and law as enforcer. The law tends to be a rigid and powerful teacher which seeks to bring and keep its unruly students in line. But engaging in and with the law is a learning experience that can have repercussions far beyond the individuals involved and the lessons directly laid down by the law. The challenge is felt even though the teacher drones on; the classroom dynamic and discourse shift, if only a little.

Theorizing (Lesbian/Gay) Equality

Sexual Orientation as an (Un)protected Human Right

In her article entitled, 'Lesbians, Gays and the Struggle for Equality Rights: Reversing the Progressive Hypothesis,'[6] Mary Eaton challenges what she perceives as the widely accepted narrative of 'the relentless emancipatory progress of human rights law, and the textual grounding of sexual orientation as an out-lawed form of discrimination.'[7] This is the progressive hypothesis she refers to in her title. She argues that while the law has moved forward positively in terms of recognizing and providing protection for 'homosexual'[8] 'orientation,' that is the status of being 'homosexual,' the law has, at the same time, tried to contain us by denying protection to 'homosexual' practices, thereby dividing who we are from what we do. In protecting the passive status but not the active practice of being lesbian or gay, the law denies the sex in our sexuality.[9] Given this legal de-sexing, Mary Eaton[10] argues that as a strategy of resistance it is 'not simply that "homosexual" sex should be spoken of – although I do think it should – but rather that law's continuing circumscription of "homosexual" sex should be put squarely in issue.'[11]

Mary Eaton traces the judicially created and enforced status/conduct distinction from its roots in the first lesbian/gay human rights cases in the mid-1970s in which the fear and abhorrence of 'homosexual' sex felt by the judges were at times visceral,[12] to its more recent manifestations in domestic partnership and other constitutional and human rights claims, in both Canada and the United States. And, she argues, the terms in which most litigants have constructed their claims have supported, rather than challenged, the bifurcation. In the hope of succeeding in their cases, complainants have tended to deny the 'difference' of their sexual selves and to assert the 'sameness' of their non-sexual selves, a strategy that has only sometimes actually met with success.

Although Mary Eaton sees the status/conduct distinction as pretty firmly entrenched in the law, she ends her article on a note of promise, introduced by the decision in the Andrews case.[13] She heralds the Supreme Court of Canada's first decision on the meaning of equality in s.15 of the Charter, that is the Andrews decision, as effecting 'a paradigmatic shift from the sameness/difference approach'[14] to an approach rooted in the recognition of the subordinated position and experiences of some groups in our society. Eaton suggests that this shift offers the possibility of a similar shift from the status-same/conduct-different approach to sexual orientation to an approach that would recognize the ascribed 'difference' of 'homosexuality' as the sign of inequality. She argues that

Andrews has made possible a critical evaluation of 'homosexual' inequality because, in recognizing that it is through the discourse of difference that inequality is put into play and immunized from critique, it has created the jurisprudential space to analyze 'homosexual' sex, not as a site of difference but as a site of dominance. Within that analysis neither assumed problems with 'homosexual' sex nor the standard objections to it – that it is abnormal, unhealthy, immoral, the outward symptom of arrested psychic development – suffice to rationalize discrimination; grounded as they are in discriminatory notions themselves, such rationales serve to reinforce domination.[15]

The potential that Mary Eaton saw in the Andrews decision for a significant reformulation of equality analysis generally, and for putting lesbian and gay sex at the centre of sexual orientation equality analysis, has not since been borne out by lower courts or even by the Supreme Court itself.[16] Andrews is still a leading Charter equality decision, and is quoted and applied extensively. However, instead of providing a springboard for an expansive approach to equality based on a dominance model of equality, Andrews has largely been restrained, contained, and even regressed. As well as its potential for inducing a paradigmatic shift, Andrews contained the seeds for its own constraint,[17] and this tension plays itself out between majority and dissenting opinions in many of the post-Andrews equality cases and across the (in)equality spectrum. The tension is apparent in the Supreme Court of Canada decision in Egan and Nesbit[18] in which, as will be discussed below, the majority of the Court engaged in a very traditional same/different equality analysis which focused on reproduction as the critical site of difference, while the dissenting judges focused on issues of inequality.

The analysis that Mary Eaton presents in this article on lesbians' and gays' struggle for equality rights is, I think, extremely important, both pragmatically and theoretically. She raises, explicitly and implicitly, critical questions about the extent to which lesbian and gay litigants frame and/or distort their claims in order to accord with the dominant discourse and dominant characterizations of lesbians and gays, and the extent to which they thereby re-enforce these characterizations. This risk may, to a large extent, inhere in the move into the legal arena, and is an issue I investigate further in this chapter through the perspectives of others writing on this issue and in my discussion of the Egan and Nesbit case.

The analysis of the judicial responses to lesbian and gay human rights claims in terms of a status/conduct split provides a useful tool for exploring the goals, strategies, and underlying assumptions at work in these cases. However, there is some debate as to whether a judicially imposed distinction between status and conduct operates in lesbian and gay cases. Jane Schacter in her article, 'The Civil Rights Debate in the States: Decoding the Discourse of Equivalents,'[19] argues that this distinction that operates in human rights law generally has been collapsed with respect to lesbians and gays so as to deny them any human rights protection: 'Because sexual behaviour is seen as the defining aspect of gay and lesbian life, homosexuality is all "doing" and no "being." Because civil rights laws protect people only for who they "are" and not for what they "do," homosexuality is not entitled to civil rights protection.'[20]

While Schacter's claim may be based on U.S. cases,[21] there are some Canadian cases that provide support for this position. In at least some of the Canadian cases in which the claim would seem fairly clearly to constitute a status claim, the court nonetheless makes reference to homosexual sexual activity in the process of denying the claim.[22] However, these cases do not lead me to conclude that the orientation/practice distinction collapses in all lesbian/gay cases. If that were the situation, then either there would have been no successful claims – which is not the case – or lesbians and gays would have been recognized and treated as sexually active beings in the cases that have been successful – which may sometimes be, but certainly is not always, the case. The distinction between status and conduct and the related fear of 'homosexual sex' are, I think, operating in most if not all the lesbian/gay cases, but not necessarily in as definitive a way as some authors portray. While the distinction provides a useful construct for analysing the cases and the courts' resistance to lesbian/gay claims to human rights, it cannot be relied upon as the sole explanatory model for the decisions in the cases.

Another question that the status/conduct analysis raises for me relates to the assertion that the lesbian/gay conduct that is denied is sex, that sex is the divide between status and conduct. While I do think sex is a big part of the denial and rejection of us, I think there is more to it. To focus exclusively on sex as the site of our ascribed difference is to focus too narrowly.[23] Such an analysis runs the risk of re-inscribing us as only about sex and in so doing of de-politicizing our sex. I think for most decision-makers the question of whether or not to extend human rights protection to us relates to our assimilation and our assimilatability, of which sex is only a part. In this context some perceive all lesbians and gays as, by definition unassimilatable because of 'homosexual sex'; but for others it is not because of our sexual practices per se that we do not deserve protection. Our words, our actions, for some of us our very appearance, can challenge and threaten in ways that have little or nothing to do with sex.[24] In this regard I find Lynne Pearlman's notion of the continuum of outness extremely helpful.[25] She describes the 'lesbian continuum' in the following terms:

It is about how lesbian-identified one is willing to be publicly; it is about how much heterosexual privilege one is willing to renounce; it is about how many traditional vestiges of femininity one chooses to carry; it is about how much energy one invests in males (be they gay or straight friends, ex-lovers, fathers, brothers, cousins, nephews or sons); it is about how vocal or activist one is about what it means to be lesbian-identified; it is about the extent to which one is willing to challenge heteropatriarchal norms and principles.[26]

Within this analytic framework, the further one is along the lesbian continuum the less likely it is that one's claim to human rights protection would be recognized.[27] In some ways Lynne's approach could be seen as elongating the status/ conduct split, transforming the dichotomy into a continuum. Because it is more complex I think the continuum offers more scope for analysing the sexual orientation cases, but I see it as building on rather than rejecting the bifurcation analysis put forward by Mary Eaton and others.[28]

The status/conduct split imposed by law is readily apparent in some areas; for example, the history of lesbian custody cases clearly demonstrates the distinction in operation.[29] Lesbian mothers separating from heterosexual partners were initially denied custody of their children when they went before the courts and were 'exposed' as lesbians. Gradually lesbian mothers were granted custody, but only if they were not 'practising' lesbians; that is, sexually active, or otherwise 'flaunting' their lesbianism. More recently, lesbian mothers who are in a sexual relationship have been granted custody when that relationship is seen to be monogamous and stable. While it has been a major struggle for lesbian mothers to be 'allowed' to be in a lesbian relationship – that is, a sexual relationship – and still keep their children, while there still are serious limitations on the willingness of most judges to see a sexually active lesbian as a good mother, sex is not the only factor that has concerned the courts in their scrutiny of lesbian mothers. The courts continue to express concerns about lesbians flaunting their lesbianism, about politically active lesbians, about 'bad' lesbians; courts continue to deny these lesbians custody of their children. A lesbian mother's right to mother is at greater risk the further she is along the continuum of outness.

The status/conduct distinction and the continuum of outness are both constructs that one can recognize as operating in the cases, and are useful tools to employ in analysing the cases.

Interactive Discriminations

Mary Eaton, in her article 'Homosexual Unmodified: Speculations on Law's Discourse, Race and the Construction of Sexual Identity,'[30] presents a compelling argument that 'homosexuality has been legally coded as white.'[31] Lesbians and gays who come before the law are seen by the court as 'raceless.' In the context of white supremacy this means that they are seen and read as white, regardless of their actual skin colour and regardless of how they would define their own racial identity. According to Mary Eaton this white encoding happens because 'the very notion of homosexual as an outsider class requires the erasure of race.'[32] In order to maintain the strict divide between heterosexual and homosexual the law requires that the distinction be kept 'pure,' uncomplicated by other sites of oppression that might confuse or compound the basis for and/ or the meaning of the ascribed difference of homosexuality.

This need for homogeneity within a prohibited ground of discrimination is a function of the strict compartmentalization upon which our human rights laws are premised.[33] The law requires that those within a protected group be the same, so that their difference from the dominant group is clear and can be assessed as to whether or not it constitutes a legitimate basis for discrimination.[34] Differences within a protected group and the recognition of individuals within that group as sites of intersecting positions of dominance and subordination would make the assessment of specifically sited, ground-based discrimination complex if not impossible. Rather than accept the challenge of dealing with interactive oppressions and intersecting sites of dominance and subordination, our human rights system continues to insist on applying single and unidimensional categories. The best that the law has been able to do to date, if one can consider it better, is to recognize that a person may be situated in more than one unidimensional category.

To help her explore interactive discrimination as it applies in relation to race and sexual orientation, Mary Eaton turns to the work of women of colour who have analysed how the law has 'fragment[ed] women of colour into their constituent race-d and gender-ed parts.'[35] Black women have had to choose to base their claims on either race or sex, because the law did not recognize a race/sex category. The discrimination experienced by Black women was then assessed in conjunction with, rather than in opposition to, the experiences of Black men with respect to race and the experiences of white women with respect to sex. The experiences of Black men and of white women were seen as the defining experiences of race and sex discrimination respectively. Mary Eaton's argument is that this fragmentation has not occurred with respect to sexual orientation. Instead, sexual orientation is treated as a category incompatible with other categories. Nonwhites who claim sexual orientation discrimination are not forced to decide between race and sexual orientation, but are de-raced and treated as white. Rather than being fragmented into their constituent parts, sexual orientation claimants are reduced to a single isolated part, their sexual orientation; the other parts of themselves are simply erased. This is done in order to maintain and solidify the demarcation between 'heterosexual normalcy' and 'homosexual otherness.'

Mary Eaton's analysis is well supported by the two U.S. cases that she examines.[36] These were the only two lesbian/gay equality cases that she located in which 'the race of the plaintiff surfaced to the level of the text.'[37] The plaintiff in each case was an African-American gay man. In one case the claim was based on race discrimination. The court rejected the claim, implying that if any discrimination had occurred, it had been based on sexual orientation which was not a protected ground under the applicable legislation. The court failed to credit that the thing that set his treatment apart from that of his coworkers, both gay and straight white men, was race.

The plaintiff in the second case was successful in his claim of sexual orientation discrimination in relation to his dismissal from the U.S. army. However, not only was race not considered a factor in the selectively negative treatment of this gay man, but the court's analysis was premised on the assumption that race (that is nonwhite) and sexual identity (that is nonheterosexual) cannot coexist. The decision is riddled with comparisons and analogies between sexual orientation discrimination and race discrimination, as if the two are mutually exclusive. The Court seems oblivious to the fact that the person before it is subject to both, and that for him they are not separated points of comparison but integrated sites of interactive discrimination.

Mary Eaton seems to imply that the reductive unifocused approach in sexual orientation claims is different from the fragmented treatment of race/sex discrimination claims because there is a greater perceived need to demarcate and protect the sexual orientation boundary than the gender or race boundary.[38] My thought is that the differences in treatment may have more to do with the stage in the legal histories of each of these types of claims than with fundamental differences in response to the claims themselves. It is my understanding that in their early claims, women of colour were either de-raced or de-sexed, depending on the basis and nature of their claim, and that in fact this still happens with respect to some claims.[39] The fragmented approach came about because women of colour challenged and critiqued the reductive approach.[40] The same may occur with respect to sexual orientation/race claims as the result of the work of Mary Eaton and others on these issues.

It is critical to racialize sexual identity and our analysis of sexual identity, because it is inaccurate and oppressive not to. Also, Mary Eaton argues that the racialization of sexual identity will disrupt the rigid demarcation between heterosexuality and homosexuality that the law has been so desperately protecting; that it provides a way of challenging and resisting both the categories and the dominant/subordinate dichotomy the categories embody. 'Re-racializing the homosexual is thus not only a matter of the feel-good politics of inclusivity, it is crucial to the deconstruction of the category "homosexual."'[41]

The legal construction of the heterosexual/homosexual dichotomy erases all differences, not just racial ones. Mary Eaton addresses the question of other sites of oppression as potential disrupters of the sexuality boundary, but she asserts the primacy of race as a uniquely disruptive force. Mary Eaton argues that there are 'differences in the way the courts exclude differences from the category of sexual orientation'[42] in order fully to contain the homosexual other. She uses sex as an example to explore these differences. Gender has been excluded from sexual orientation, and the separation of sex discrimination claims from sexual-orientation discrimination claims has been rigorously enforced. Nonetheless, the terms in which the sex/sexual orientation distinction is announced implicitly recognize a connection between the two even while explicitly and vehemently denying the existence of any such connection: 'Whereas sex and sexual orientation are first configured together in order to set them apart, the means by which the wedge between race and sexual identity is driven is distinct. Race enters the discourse of sexual identity only analogically and never derivatively. This suggests that, although race and sex ultimately may share the same fate, expulsions from the realm of sexual orientation have been effected differently.'[43]

I accept Mary Eaton's point that differences are excluded differently. The points of intersection, that is the connections between sexual identity and other axes of oppression, are different; the contexts of denial are different, that is racism is different from sexism; thus the effects of racializing sexual identity will be different from those of gendering sexual identity. However, I do not accept what I understand to be Mary Eaton's conclusion that 're-racializing' is somehow uniquely situated as a strategy of disruption. It seems to me that gender has a similar, but different, potential significantly to disrupt the security of the sexual orientation boundary. Other oppressive constructs, such as disability and class, offer similarly upsetting potential. For example, AIDS discrimination may provide a context for exploring the erasure of sexual identity in a context in which underlying stereotypes would clearly dictate its inclusion.[44] And of course there is the additionally confusing potential of multiple, not just dual, intersections. Race may not be the only disrupter of sexual orientation in operation. All points of intersection are important; all warrant exploration – as strategy, as theory, as necessitated by a politics of inclusion.[45] Our discussions of sexual orientation cases should be racializing, gendering, classing, (dis)abling the sexual orientation analysis.

Sexual Orientation Discrimination as Sex Discrimination

In terms of exploring the gender dimensions of sexual orientation discrimination, a number of people,[46] myself among them, have put forward an analysis of sexual orientation discrimination as a form of sex discrimination. The conventional argument that has been put forward in this regard is that 'sexual orientation is "literally" sex discrimination because it involves sex distinctions that are different for each sex.'[47] This is the 'but for sex' argument, according to which, but for one's sex or but for the sex of one's partner one would not be denied the benefit at issue, or otherwise be treated disadvantageously. While this argument is probably fairly accurate at a descriptive level, it does not address the underlying roots of this discrimination; and, in failing to do so it becomes an argument of assimilation.

Andrew Koppelman and I both argue that sexual orientation discrimination is at its root about the preservation of gender polarity and the enforcement of ascribed gender roles premised on the subordination of women. Sexual orientation discrimination is about sustaining sexual inequality.[48] 'Sex equality is dangerous; it will reduce men to the level of women; thus, maintaining the boundary between the sexes is a terribly important undertaking.'[49]

Gender reenforcement through the oppression of lesbians and gays works in a multitude of ways: stereotypes of 'mannish' lesbians and of 'effeminate' gay men, the hierarchy implicit in the sex act of penetration and the related horror and fear generated by the spectre of a man being reduced to the status of a woman through that sex act, the inconceivability of 'sex' between two women, the use of 'homosexuality' as 'a metaphor for failing to live up to the norms of one's gender.'[50] If sex discrimination is about protecting the divide between women and men, and keeping women subordinated, then sexual orientation discrimination is a particularly virulent form of sex discrimination because it tries to cement the divide through extreme censure and scare tactics. A statement quoted by Robert Wintemute and made by 'conservative writer William Gairdner' captures the interrelationship most succinctly:

[H]omosexuality ... thrives when male/female role distinctions are discouraged. Cultures that want to guard against the threat of homosexuality must therefor drive a cultural wedge down hard between maleness and femaleness, for it is no simple coincidence that homosexuality is flourishing in a time of feminism. They go together like the two sides of a coin. The attempt of the state to neutralize male and female differences is manifest in its effort to 'normalize' homosexuality, marketing it to us in its agencies and schools as a 'value-free' matter of 'sexual orientation.'[51]

Cynthia Petersen and others[52] have critiqued this analysis on the basis that collapsing sexual orientation discrimination into sex discrimination hierarchizes oppressions, putting gender at the top and ignoring other equally significant potential intersections of oppressions, such as race. This would be gendering sexual oppression to the exclusion of racializing, (dis)abling, and classing it. This is a serious criticism and one that continues to plague me and challenge me to rethink my analysis. However, I repeat here, still with a lot of questions and uncertainty, what I said on this subject in my article:

I ... wonder if, in my analysis of the limitations of sexual orientation, I am privileging gender and downplaying other forms of oppression that give rise to differences and power imbalances among lesbians and gays ... [But] I am not arguing that gender is an oppression that we experience simultaneously with sexual identity oppression and that thereby transforms the experience of both oppressions, but rather, at least for lesbians, sexual identity oppression is gender oppression. If my doubts about collapsing lesbian inequality into gender inequality have grounding, then my fear that I am privileging gender has grounding too. However, if lesbian oppression is a form of gender oppression, then I am only privileging gender to the extent that focusing on one form of oppression means that one is, to some extent, downplaying other forms of oppression.[53]

It seems to me that collapsing sexual orientation discrimination into sexuality discrimination, as many writers do, is much more problematic and more limited in analytic scope. As Andrew Koppelman points out, 'Everyone understands "sexual preference" or "sexual orientation" to refer to the gender of one's object-choice [*sic*]. Why, given the immense number of axes along which human sexuality varies, is *this* presumed to be the one that matters most, the one that is defining?[54]

The 'sexual orientation discrimination is sex discrimination' position raises questions of both strategy and analysis. In my discussion of Egan and Nesbit, I try to explore, at least on a preliminary basis, how the issues in the case might look different if analysed in terms of sex discrimination.

The Questionable Pursuit of Rights

In the work I have discussed to this point, most of the authors have taken lesbian and gay engagement with law as a given. However, there are many writers who express fundamental concerns about trying to use law as a vehicle for social change. These questions and strategic differences are often framed in terms of a debate over the usefulness of rights claims. Didi Herman, in her book *Rights of Passage: Struggles for Lesbian and Gay Legal Equality*,[55] enters into 'the rights debate' to question lesbian/gay human rights litigation as a strategy. As a strategy for what? Are the claims being made to try to solve individual inequities experienced by lesbians and gays? Are they about lesbians and gays seeking social recognition and acceptance? Or are they about challenging heterosexuality and ascribed gender roles? And how effective are they or can they be in doing any of these? Didi Herman avoids simplistic analysis of the pursuit of rights as either good or bad, right or wrong. She explores the issues in all of their complexity and contradictions, to come to the following conclusion:

More often than not, right-claims are neither inherently radical rearticulations nor dangerous and diversionary; occasionally, they may be both. To say that rights are difficult, complicated tools for social change does not mean that the struggle for their acquisition is doomed or that 'real issues' are being obscured. At the same time, an unreflexive seeking of rights and yet more rights may not bring about the changes to social relations many of us would like to see.[56]

Didi Herman describes the early human rights cases as rooted primarily in a psychological model of homosexuality. The very early cases carried traces of the by then waning perception of homosexuals as dangerous sexual predators who should be feared and contained, if not eradicated.[57] But by the time human rights claims were starting to be pursued by gays (and lesbians),[58] that is, in the mid-1970s, the medical discourse was shifting 'from an approach which feared and pathologized the homosexual to one which advocated empathy and tolerance.'[59] This new construction of homosexuals as 'abnormal but harmless' corresponds quite closely to the liberal equality model of minority rights which underlies our human rights laws. Homosexuals are seen as an homogeneous group that possesses an immutable characteristic that renders its members 'different' and implicitly lesser, but who are not thereby to be considered appropriate objects of prejudice or discrimination. According to the liberal human rights paradigm, they/we [homosexuals] are to be accorded tolerance and compassion, while the 'status quo dominance' of heterosexuality remains unchallenged and unexamined.

In the very recent cases, a sociological approach has been advocated by at least some of the claimants and adopted by some of the decision-makers. Didi Herman considers this approach more promising than the psychological medical model in that sociology deals 'with group relations and structural inequalities.' However, Didi Herman's assessment of the cases discloses that the sociological analysis being put forward has been largely assimilationist and directed towards acceptance of lesbians and gays, rather than towards dismantling heterosexuality and its underlying gender constructs. Sociology has been used largely to deny 'the difference,' not to dismantle the difference construct.

As litigants and as lobbyists, gays and lesbians have 'generally adopted the dominant discourse and represented themselves as nonthreatening and easily assimilatable.'[60] While Didi Herman recognizes the limitations and problems inherent in such an approach, she is not as dismissive of the strategy as many of its critics. She refers to a number of positive changes which are probably, at least in part, attributable to lesbian and gay human rights litigation: the public discourse on lesbian/gay issues has opened up considerably; lesbians and gays are more publicly evident; overtly lesbian- and gay-hating speech and conduct seem to be less publicly condoned; 'the articulation of principles such as "equality" together with "lesbian and gay" has, to some extent, caused cracks in the firmament of "universal" heterosexuality.'[61] The activists interviewed by Didi Herman who had participated in these strategies had done so consciously and self-reflectively, and often with goals other than displacing heterosexual dominance. Some saw these strategies as a means of mobilizing and politicizing their communities; some had an incrementalist approach to social change; some were focused on short-term pragmatic goals; and some did frame their arguments in ways that challenged heterosexuality.[62] Additionally, Didi Herman points to the potential for even a liberal assertion of lesbian and gay rights to 'trouble' the dominant heterosexual norm.[63]

Didi Herman also analyses the positioning and strategies of a number of groups within the new Christian right (NCR) which have actively opposed lesbian/gay human rights claims and have intervened in some of the cases to put their views before the courts.[64] She finds that, like the lesbian and gay organizations, these extreme right-wing organizations have muted their language and their position to fit within the liberal paradigm and to dress themselves suitably for presentation to the court. While the in-house literature of these organizations is replete with detailed and hateful depictions of 'homosexual disease and depravity,' Didi Herman found that none of this venom appeared in their factum or in their argument before the court in the Mossop case, a gay familial bereavement-leave case in which a coalition of NCR groups intervened. 'The homosexuals who "eat and rub themselves with faeces," "defecate on their partners," and "drink urine" are nowhere to be found'[65] in the sanitized-for-judicial-consumption NCR presentation. What is put before the court by these organizations is a flat, dry recitation of previous cases and bland legal argument in support of the exclusivity of the traditional family and of heterosexual marriage. According to Didi Herman, 'What is interesting about this process are the specific ways in which legal discourse compels the adoption of a particular pragmatic politics (liberal legalism) and that it appears to affect social movements on either side of the political spectrum.'[66]

Didi Herman's analysis provides a number of interesting and important tools for exploring the effect and effectiveness of a case such as Egan and Nesbit. The questions she asks in terms of the articulation of rights claims and the goals being pursued are questions we should be asking of all lesbian/gay cases that are coming forward. Similarly, the respect she shows both for the lesbians and gay men who have been willing to put forward these challenges at great personal cost, and for the activists who have supported them, is a vital component of doing this critical work.

Picking up on themes developed by Mary Eaton in 'Homosexual Unmodified' and by Didi Herman in *Rights of Passage*, as well as by others writing on these issues, Carl Stychin is more unqualifiedly critical of the human rights model and seems to be more pessimistic about its potential for social change.[67] He explores two related concepts upon which our human rights laws are premised – categorical thinking and immutability – and considers their implications in the analysis of lesbian and gay human rights claims. Categorical thinking, that is the focus on categories of discrimination, assumes that the categories constructed as prohibited grounds of discrimination are homogeneous and clearly divisible. Differences within categories are ignored and individuals are required to identify themselves along a single 'axis of oppression.'[68]

Relatedly, categorical thinking 'gives rise to rigid binary classification – the norm (heterosexuality) and the exception (homosexuality) – into which individuals can be "slotted." ... In creating this division, the norm remains invisible and unproblematic.'[69] The requirement that these categories be 'immutable,' that is, 'not within the control of the individual,' is a function of the need to ensure that the categories are fixed and static so that they can be clearly recognized when an individual falls within a category of difference. Within this essentialist context '[h]omosexuality becomes defined as an innate inability to realize the heterosexual norm,'[70] and homosexuals are seen as people who should be granted protection because they cannot help being 'not heterosexual.'

Carl Stychin points out that this essentialist sexual orientation argument may be more attractive to white, able-bodied gay men in that, on the basis of this argument, presented in a human rights context, they may be able to gain access to the 'trappings of male gender privilege.' However, Carl Stychin acknowledges that while the characterization of sexual orientation as immutable is exceedingly problematic, the counteranalysis of sexual orientation as socially constructed and thereby an open and fluid category has been employed in the United States to deny protection and benefits to lesbians and gays. If lesbians and gays 'choose' to be 'homosexual,' then they can also choose not to be; there is no need to protect an 'illegitimate' choice. Thus, the human rights model can be seen as presenting a catch-22: to assert ourselves as we see ourselves is to be kept out; to be let in is (at least for some of us) to falsify ourselves. The human rights model regulates and contains us by means of the categories it inscribes, while at the same time tantalizing us with the promise of protection and even benefit by means of those same categories. Carl Stychin describes this as a process of 'normalization,' and he turns to queer theory and queer social practices as a means to resist and disrupt that process: 'Rather than constituting an identity category itself, queerness highlights the contingency of all boundaries of social practice and identity, including its own. It represents a subversion of categorical thinking so that "queer" as a term is capable of constant reworking to serve new political purposes. Queer theory, then, is closely related to the critical approaches of deconstruction and post-structuralism.'[71]

I agree with Carl Stychin's critique of the human rights model, and I see the concerns that he raises clearly playing themselves out in judicial decisions like that in Egan and Nesbit. His call for 'a greater degree of of self-reflexivity about identities, an awareness of their intersected character, and their social contingency and mutability,'[72] and his warnings of the constraining power of categories, are all matters which I support and think are consistent with much of the writing I am exploring in this chapter. However, his invocation of queer theory makes me nervous. I, too, am drawn to its language of disruption and subversion and its refusal to be constrained or bounded. I see queer theory as somewhat like a game – enticing and alluring and fun. It is the place where the 'bad' girls and boys[73] are hanging out, and part of me wants to be one of them. But I fear that it is a game enjoyed by the relatively privileged. The critiques of elitism and apoliticization that have been made of Queer Nation's 'theoretical wing' – deconstruction and poststructuralism – would similarly apply to queer theory.[74]

From a queer point of view, any representation of categories of identity is false. At the level of the question of the accuracy of these representations in terms of the people they are meant to describe, I would agree that the categories are false. However, on the level of politics and strategy I do not think it is helpful simply to deny the categories. I regard the categories as problematic, incomplete, rigidly circumscribed, and oppressive, but these are the things that make these categories very real as constructions of and for subordination. While boundaries and categories need to be challenged and contested, they do provide a position from which it is possible to name and resist oppression and dominance. I am not sure that subverting that position is a good place to start. If we deny the category, in fact all categories, how can we challenge the dominance and subordination that are inscribed into and represented by those categories? What would the denial of categories mean in the context, for example, of human rights claims? What are the implications, for example, of denying the existence of the sexual orientation category for a claim like that made by Egan and Nesbit? These questions are further explored in my discussion of the case.

Theorizing the [Lesbian/Gay?] Family

Given that the majority of the recent lesbian/gay human rights cases in Canada have involved claims to some form of spousal or family benefit, it is not surprising that the majority of the recent Canadian writing on lesbian/gay legal issues has been in this area. This itself is arguably a form of (self-)/(legal-) constraint in that this area provides only a narrow and moderate focus for lesbian and gay legal analysis and presents a limited vision of lesbian/gay interaction with law.[75]

I do not intend here to provide a comprehensive review of all, or even some, of the articles on this subject. Instead, I try to canvass some of the varied arguments and positions put forward by the authors.

A primary question that underlies all of the articles relates to the implications for lesbians and gays of claims for inclusion within legal meanings of spouse and/or family. The arguments tend to fall along a spectrum which at one end rejects these strategies as inherently and unredeemably assimilationist, and at the other end accepts these strategies either as a means to gain some benefits and some acceptance for some lesbians and gays on a pragmatic incremental basis and/or as a means to challenge and disrupt the categories of spouse and family. However, even in describing the issue in terms of a spectrum, I have oversimplified and dichotomized it in much the same way that the law does, with all of the same problems that derive from such dichotomization. The two ends of the spectrum are not necessarily mutually exclusive, and one can simultaneously hold variants on positions from each end of the spectrum. This is the point Brenda Cossman makes in her article 'Family Inside/Out':

My own concern is with the effect that this increasing legalization of lesbian and gay struggles is having on us. For our legal strategies, we have to argue that we are, or are not, family. And the more we translate our position into legal language – the more that we argue that we are or we are not family on law's terrain – the more entrenched we become in our positions. The increasing legalization is further entrenching the dichotomization of the debate. We increasingly find ourselves having to decide whether we believe that we are family, or not. We have to take a side. The choice is constructed as one between two mutually exclusive categories – between family and its opposition, not family.[76]

While I agree with Brenda Cossman's analysis of the dichotomizing effects of law and the need to recognize and work with issues in all of their complexity and with all of their apparent contradictions, I am nervous about where this position leads in terms of participation in legal claims that are brought forward. I fear that having recognized the complexity and contradictions we will feel required to support, or at least not publicly challenge, the simplified and contradiction-purged versions of the debate as they are presented in legal forums. To me this raises the spectre of liberal pluralism and liberal tolerance, with the attendant risks of reenforcement and preservation of the status quo. I would agree with Brenda Cosman that '[w]e must be able to pursue these multiple and contradictory strategies at the same time, for it is the only way that we will be able to challenge the multiple and contradictory discourses that construct us,'[77] but only if each strategy, on its own, is clearly multiple and contradictory. I will explore this question of ambiguity with respect to the strategy reflected in and by the Egan and Nesbit case.

In her article 'Expanding the "Family" in Family Law: Recent Ontario Proposals on Same-Sex Relationships,' Susan Boyd explores the question of the expansion of family law to include lesbian and gay relationships.[78] None of the proposals that she examines – Ontario Bill 167, the Ontario Law Reform Commission Report on the Rights and Responsibilities of Cohabitants under the Family Law Act, and the background research paper on which that report was based[79] – fully addresses the general and fundamental critiques of family law made by feminists and other progressive social critics. These include concerns relating to the privileging of apparently monogamous sexual relationships,[80] the choice of the family as a 'unit of social policy determination,'[81] concerns 'that family law operates mainly to the benefit of those who are wealthy, at least in terms of property laws, and that support law operates mainly as a mechanism to diminish the burden on the social welfare system.'[82] Accordingly, the expansion of conventional family law to include lesbian and gay relationships would simply subject those relationships to the same 'two-tiered, class-based system of "family" law.'[83]

The class-based implications of this system are a concern that Shelley Gavigan addresses at length in her article 'Paradise Lost, Paradox Revisited: the Implications of Familial Ideology for Feminist, Lesbian and Gay Engagement to Law,'[84] and are the basis for her rejection of the family based model. The prospect that low-income lesbians, particularly sole-support lesbian mothers, may have their access to social assistance denied or curtailed as a result of an expanded definition of *spouse* should perhaps be enough to stop 'progressive' reformers in their tracks. On the other hand, and however critical one may be of the policy, family law is expected to make up for the inadequacies of the social welfare system. As Susan Boyd points out, denying lesbians, particularly lesbian mothers, access to legally mandated and enforced support from their former partner may be consigning them to the inadequacies of welfare.

Each critique of the family as it is constructed in and by law provides only a single piece in the complex and multifaceted dilemma presented by the possibility of legal recognition of lesbian and gay families. And, as with the social assistance example, most issues have contradictory implications. The recognition that white feminist critiques of the family have been exposed as race, class, and nondisabled specific has been used as an argument both for and against attempts to expand the legal definition of family. For Shelley Gavigan '[t]he struggles of people who can never fit into the ideal of the nuclear family illuminate, rather than negate, what some feminists identify as the oppressive *implications* of the idealization and *romanticization* of the nuclear family.'[85] However, according to Susan Boyd, 'because "family" ... has been used as a mode of resistance against oppression, notably by people of colour – it may be unrealistic to move away from it altogether.'[86]

Similarly, the potential for assimilation and for disruption is operating simultaneously in and through claims for family recognition or spousal benefits. The strength and vehemence of the resistance to these claims, put forward under the banner of family values, are testament to the threat that these claims represent. And yet, almost no matter how disruptive a claim one is trying to make, it almost inevitably becomes framed in terms of those same 'family values': monogamy,[87] stability, economic (inter)dependence, and often the care and nurturing of children.[88] In making a claim to family, one is still inscribing a line between family and not-family, or spouses and not-spouses, and defining who falls on which side of that line. The fulcrum – the conventional nuclear family – remains constant; movement, the possibility for change, is only ever on the periphery.

It may be impossible or at least impractical to try to eradicate the boundary; perhaps the best one can do is disrupt, challenge, shift the boundary. But then does this leave the conventional nuclear family safely rooted in the centre of the maelstrom, largely unchanged, even unshaken? Are we conceding too much in accepting that family should have legal meaning and legally sanctioned power? Are strategies designed to expand the legal meaning of family mutually exclusive from strategies designed to explode family as a legal category, or can these strategies be envisioned as mutually supportive? Is strategic ambiguity part of the disruption? Are expansionist strategies incremental strategies, or can they be? Or is this just rationalization? Do we ultimately have to choose and if so, what is it we are choosing?

Jody Freeman has written an article in which she provides a thoughtful and detailed account of the participatory process of drafting an intervenor's factum (the document outlining the legal argument to be presented to the court) in the case of *Mossop v. DSS*.[89] The group that participated in this process struggled with the types of questions I have just listed, in their attempt to frame an argument that accepted the legal category 'family' while retaining a fluid, context-specific approach to the legal meaning to be ascribed to family. In so doing the group clearly positioned itself on the expand-the-concept-of-family end of the spectrum. Yet in so doing they were apparently trying to expand the meaning to a point with no fixed boundaries to contain the meaning. They may have been trying to transform what I have described, problematically, as a spectrum into a circle where expansion and explosion perhaps converge. However successful they actually were in capturing and articulating this contradiction in a factum,[90] I am inspired and encouraged by Jody Freedman's description of the process. I am also reminded of the multiple, but largely unapparent, potential impacts and benefits of a particular case being litigated, impacts that may have much larger significance than the decision in the case itself.[91]

The majority of those writing on this issue take a position similar to that put forward by Jody Freeman: that we can and should support the inclusion of lesbian and gay relationships within the legal meaning of family, while at the same time decentring the family as a primary unit for social and economic organization and challenging sexual relationships as a vehicle for the distribution of economic benefits. Most writers would be positioned, therefore, somewhere along the (non-) spectrum, but not clearly at one end of the spectrum.[92] Ambivalence and contradiction are defining features of much of the legal writing in this area.

In contrast to this embraced ambiguity Ruthann Robson clearly positions herself at the 'not-family' end of the spectrum. She is perhaps one of the most clear and unequivocal voices in her censure of attempts to redefine the legal category, family, to include lesbians: 'While such a redefinition has practical benefits in particular circumstances, I nevertheless want to posit a theoretical challenge to the inclusion of lesbians in any family, redefined or otherwise, and to challenge further conceptualizations of lesbian relations as correlated – either by inclusion or exclusion – to the family.'[93] Ruthann Robson argues that 'the legal notion of family domesticates lesbians through its strategies of demarcation, assimilation, coercion, indoctrination and arrogation.'[94] She is troubled by the romanticized rhetoric of the family which emanates from the privatized and individualized lived experience of trying to recreate the myth of the family, lesbian-style. This is the myth which presents the family as a harmonious, safe haven; this is the myth of the family of which feminists have been so critical.

Ruthann Robson is concerned by the decontextualization and depoliticization of the family such that lesbians fail to recognize it as a legal construct that regulates those who fall outside of its definitional boundaries, as well as those captured within. She explores the confrontation over the meaning of family that is taking place in the courts and in the law more generally. This is the confrontation between the conservative, formalist, essentialist definition of the family and the liberal, functional approach to defining the family. But despite the confrontation, Ruthann argues that the difference is pretty minimal, that the functional approach simply mimics the essentialist definition. She argues that the goals of challenge and disruption cannot be met by a strategy for inclusion: '[T]he functional criteria used to determine whether relationships are under the rubric of family guarantee exclusion of the very relationships that might transform the functions.'[95]

Ruthann Robson's critique of the family is not dissimilar to the critiques of the other authors whose work I have reviewed in this chapter. And there are strong connections here between the critiques of the family and the critiques of human rights categories in the earlier argument with respect to equality theorizing. Concerns with essentialism and containment-by-category permeate all of this writing; all of the writers seek, to varying degrees, to contest the categories inscribed by law. Where Ruthann Robson departs from most of the others is in her refusal to be tempted by the concrete benefits and protection that would be made available to at least some lesbians brought into the family fold. Nor does she believe it is possible to collapse the 'family-not-family' spectrum; in so doing, one would still be operating within the confines of the family. Instead she argues for the unnaming of the family as a strategy of resistance, a strategy that would encourage us to reconceptualize ourselves and our relationships. This would mean the rejection altogether of the family as a legal construct, to be replaced by other, more accurate, non-heterosexist, more varied descriptions of interpersonal relationships better targeted to their requirements for legal recognition. Personally, I have much less discomfort rejecting the legal category of the family than I have rejecting the human rights categories that Carl Stychin arguably wants to jettison. Although the arguments are in many ways similar, to me family as a legal category is one of dominance, not one that provides a position from which to acknowledge and challenge dominance.

The (Not) Family Case[96]

As indicated at the outset, I do not, in the context of this chapter and this book, want to get embroiled in a detailed legal analysis of the decision in Egan and Nesbit. Instead, I now briefly raise some questions and make some observations about the case and the decision, following from the issues raised and the analysis provided in the material that has just been reviewed. Egan and Nesbit were claiming to be spouses for the purposes of the *Old Age Security Act* in order for John Nesbit to qualify for the spousal allowance provided for under that Act. *Spouse* is defined in the Act exclusively in terms of opposite-sex relationships. Egan and Nesbit were challenging that definition and its restrictive application on the ground that it discriminated against them as gay men and denied them their s.15 Charter equality rights. In making this claim it would appear that Egan and Nesbit were asserting what would be, at its core, a status claim: that is, they were claiming the status of spouses. However, this case may be an example of where the status/conduct distinction explored by Mary Eaton breaks down. While 'spouse' presumably is a 'status,' it is a status that signals certain 'conduct.' The conduct in this case would be the 'homosexual sex' that Mary Eaton warned that judges are so loathe to condone, even to acknowledge. So it is in this case: the majority of the Supreme Court of Canada judges who heard the case deny the claim to spousal status and in so doing deny the sex that lurks beneath the claim.

As was done by the majority in the court below, Justice La Forest, writing for the majority of the members of the Supreme Court of Canada,[97] clearly desexed the 'homosexual couple' by grouping them with other non-spousal couples: 'The singling out of legally married and common law couples as the recipients of benefits necessarily excludes all sorts of other couples living together such as brothers and sisters or other relatives, regardless of sex, and others who are not related, whatever reasons these other couples may have for doing so and whatever their sexual orientation.'[98] In his attempt to desex the homosexual couple, Justice La Forest 'couples' these other cohabiting relationships. These are relationships that are not usually referred to as couples precisely because the term *couple* has a sexual implication.[99] Sex is the great unspoken, but the sex is irrepressible and speaks volumes through its denial.

Justice La Forest goes on to present his rationale for the spousal allowance. He describes the allowance as a necessary and justified support for married couples. He then rationalizes the extension of the allowance to nonmarried couples because they too need and deserve support. And, according to Justice La Forest, the bottom-line reason that this social support is needed is children. It does seem a bit of a leap to base a spousal-pension claim – where one member of the couple is over sixty-five and the other over sixty – on the rationale of supporting children, but let me try to trace the (il)logic of it. Justice La Forest first finds the distinction between heterosexual married and common law couples, on the one hand, and all other, 'couples' on the other, 'both obvious and deeply rooted in our fundamental values and traditions.'[100] To the extent that this is heterosexism we are talking about, I tend to agree with this characterization; heterosexism is deeply rooted in traditional values. In the name of these discriminatory values, then, the spousal allowance is seen as intended 'to accord support to married couples who were aged and elderly.'[101]

It is because marriage is 'fundamental to the stability and well-being of the family' that it is seen as deserving and needful of this special support. And the stability and well-being of the family are all about ensuring that children are born and raised within a heterosexual, two-parent household. After all, according to Justice La Forest, 'children brought up by single parents more often end up in poverty and impose greater burdens on society.'[102] The solution to keeping heterosexual couples and their children together is state support for the institution of marriage:

[M]arriage has from time immemorial been firmly grounded in our legal tradition, one that is itself a reflection of long-standing philosophical and religious traditions. But its ultimate *raison d'etre* transcends all of these and is firmly anchored in the biological and social realities that heterosexual couples have the unique ability to procreate, that most children are the product of these relationships, and that they are generally cared for and nurtured by those who live in that relationship. In this sense, marriage is by nature heterosexual.[103]

And because common-law heterosexual couples also perform 'this critical task which is of benefit to all society,' they too have need for state support in the form of access to a spousal pension allowance. But lesbians and gays apparently do not raise children and therefore do not deserve state support in the form of an old age pension spousal allowance:

None of the couples excluded from benefits under the Act are capable of meeting the fundamental social objectives thereby sought to be promoted by Parliament. These couples undoubtedly provide mutual support for one another, and that, no doubt, is of some benefit to society. They may, it is true, occasionally adopt or bring up children, but this is exceptional and in no way affects the general picture. I fail to see how homosexuals differ from other excluded couples in terms of the fundamental social reasons for which Parliament has sought to favour heterosexuals who live as married couples. Homosexual couples, it is true, differ from other excluded couples in that their relationships include a sexual aspect. But this sexual aspect has nothing to do with the social objectives for which Parliament affords a measure of support to married couples and those who live in a common law relationship.[104]

Finally, in this excerpt, we are acknowledged to have a 'sexual aspect,' but because our sex is not procreative sex, it is not supportable. Not that we would want 'support' for our sex, but this surely is the point: sex does not warrant state support. Children do need and deserve state support, but the maritally institutionalized sex that creates (some of) them surely does not need state support. Despite the fact that Justice La Forest denies the importance of sex as a defining feature, the only basis for the heterosexual/homosexual distinction he is drawing is that heterosexual sex may 'produce' a child while lesbian or gay sex will not; neither will nonsexual 'couples' 'produce' a child. But couples and noncouples, and other relationship combinations, can and do care for and nurture children, if that is really what this is about.

Just as lesbian and gay sex is dismissed as irrelevant, so too is the childlessness of many heterosexual couples. If the rationale for the pension benefit rests on support for children, then why not restrict the benefit to couples who have children, although it is hard to think why, if this is the basis, one would delay the benefit until the parents are sixty and sixty-five? But the distinction is clearly not based on actually having children, because lesbians and gays who have children are dismissed as exceptional and are denied the pension, while heterosexual couples who don't have children are dismissed and given the pension in the interests of avoiding 'meticulous line drawing,' as well as 'unnecessarily intrusive' and difficult administration.

None of the promise for 'a critical evaluation of homosexual inequality' that Mary Eaton saw in the Andrews decision is borne out in the majority judgment in Egan and Nesbit. There is in this decision a reluctance even to admit of homosexual sex, no matter about analysing it as a site of oppression. There is no recognition of inequality. The difference that the decision constructs between heterosexual couples and all other couples is transparent in its attempt to rationalize the fear and self-protectiveness that permeate the judgment.

While at one level sex is clearly at the core of the distinction being made by Justice La Forest, I am not sure that sex is the critical issue. I think it is more about who is considered to deserve benefits and to deserve state support. I read the denial of benefits to lesbians and gays as more than a denial of 'homosexual sex' and of our sexuality, and more than a denial of our reproductive capacities. It is more fundamentally a rejection of who we are and of our places as contributing members to our society. And in this case the rejection takes place on the family front, a site where biology and prejudice converge to exclude lesbians and gays. The majority decision is clear; there is no hint of a shift or a crack or even a serious challenge to the centrality and exclusivity of the conventional heterosexual nuclear family.

A number of progressive groups intervened in this case: Equality for Gays and Lesbians Everywhere (EGALE), the Metropolitan Community Church of Toronto, and the Canadian Labour Congress. I have not read the factums submitted by any of these groups; I do not know if they struggled with the types of questions Jody Freeman described the intervenors in Mossop to be working on. If they did, and if they tried to present those struggles and contradictions to the court, it is not apparent from any of the judgments. The radical challenge does not appear to have been made. In this case it is not Egan and Nesbit, it is not the progressive intervenors; instead it is the Canadian government, in defending its restrictive legislation, that asserts that Egan and Nesbit 'are requesting the Court "to change fundamentally the essential meaning of the societal concept of marriage."'[105] Justice Cory, writing for three of the dissenting judges, reassures us that marriage is safe: 'This case cannot be taken as constituting a challenge to either the traditional common law or statutory concepts of marriage.'[106] Justice Cory is willing to extend the benefit but not to question its underpinnings.

If this case, or cases like it, are intended as more than simply claims to the benefits now accorded to heterosexual couples, then it would seem, at least in the judgment context, that it is hard to make them appear so. As many of the authors have said, the temptation exists for all participants, including the judges, to frame their argument in the most nonthreatening terms possible in the hope of being persuasive. This clearly stifles the radical potential of these kinds of actions. Aside from Justice L'Heureux-Dubé's dissent in this case, in which she shifts the equality focus away from the grounds and onto the impact of discrimination, there is not much disruption going on in, or through, this case. The three other dissenting judges are willing to give lesbians and gays the spousal pension allowance as long as they meet the same criteria as heterosexual common-law couples. But at least these judges recognize the problem of holding lesbians and gays to more stringent criteria. They reject the functionalist approach that would hold gays and lesbians to a higher standard of compliance with the myth of the nuclear family than that imposed on heterosexual couples: 'In this case, a great deal of time was spent demonstrating the nature of the warm, compassionate, caring relationship that very evidently existed between the appellants. ... It is not necessary that the evidence demonstrate that a homosexual relationship bears all the features of an ideal heterosexual relationship for the relationship of many heterosexual couples is sometimes far from ideal.'[107]

It is not unusual, in discrimination cases, that oppressed persons are expected to demonstrate that they are more of what they are not; that is, more like the dominant group than the dominant group itself. So, this statement of Justice Cory's is a tiny step forward, even though it does not contain even an inkling of a challenge to the dominance of heterosexuality.

According to a number of the authors writing on these issues, expounding sexual orientation from the perspective of interactive oppressions would be a much more unsettling process. Certainly in this case there is no disruption of the homosexual category. Egan and Nesbit are seen as unidimensional. Race is not mentioned in the decision. In this absence it would seem that Egan and Nesbit have been legally coded white, regardless of their actual skin colour or racial identity, and race is thereby read out of the case. Similarly, disability is read out, even though John Nesbit apparently has a disability. Nesbit's disability is raised in the context of the argument that he should not be awarded the spousal pension because he is receiving provincial 'disability income assistance owing to a degenerative back condition which had precluded him from working.' As both programs have income ceilings, he would not have been able to collect both benefits. In an attempt not to allow his disability income to be used against him, the court considers his disability irrelevant. John Nesbit and James Egan are legally coded nondisabled.

While there is quite a lot of discussion about gender in the case, Egan and Nesbit are not seen as gendered and there is no gender analysis. The gender concern in this case is the argument that the spousal allowance was created for dependent women and therefore was not intended to apply to 'homosexuals.' Lesbians do not even seem to be contemplated as falling within the parameters of this discussion, despite the fact that they clearly could fall into the 'dependant woman' category. The same rules are assumed to apply to lesbians as to gay men without any recognition of gender as a 'complicating' factor. Again the potential for disruption of the categories is not pursued, or perhaps even noticed. It may be an overstatement to say that there is an assumption of the same rules applying to lesbians as to gay men; it is more likely that the court did not give lesbians a moment of thought in the context of this case, nor does it appear that lesbians were brought to the court's attention.

A full gender analysis of this 'spousal allowance' might have helped to explode the categories in this case. While the argument that this allowance was created for 'dependant women' is not accepted by the court as the purpose of the legislation, I have no doubt that it was the underlying premise of the spousal allowance. The assumption behind the legislation was that it would be [heterosexual] women who would need and who would apply for the allowance. It was an allowance that recognized and reenforced women's dependency on heterosexuality and on men, and as such constitutes sex discrimination as well as 'sexual orientation' discrimination. If the allowance is sex discriminatory per se, then extending it to lesbians and gay men does not necessarily address the discrimination. A sex discrimination analysis would lead into an analysis of the benefit structure and its underlying premises and goals, and to the question concerning why benefits are disseminated on the basis of sexual relationships. If benefits are about supporting children or adults in need, then what does sex have to do with it? This may then lead into the family/ not-family discussion, and may create the space for the position of ambivalence that so many of the authors endorsed, or it may lead to arguments for the rejection of family as a legally relevant category. This analysis would be complicated and enriched by race and (dis)ability analyses, which would provide additional concerns with respect to the basis on which benefits are transmitted, and through whom.

In terms of strategy an interactive discrimination approach might mean that claims like the one put forward by Egan and Nesbit would be more disruptive, and would present a more fundamental challenge to heterosexuality[108] if they were brought by a variety of different groups, including lesbians and gays, but not necessarily limited to lesbians and gays. In addition to facilitating challenges to 'the family' as a relevant legal category, at least for the purpose of the distribution of government benefits, such a strategy, rooted in an understanding of discrimination as interactive, would disrupt the strict and legally inscribed boundaries between the protected grounds of discrimination. This might go some way towards addressing the concerns of categorical thinking and immutability raised by Carl Stychin and others, while at the same time addressing my concern not to abandon these categories of oppression altogether.

Immutability did play a central role in the decision of the majority in Egan and Nesbit that sexual orientation is a protected ground under s.15 of the Charter: 'I have no difficulty accepting the appellant's contention that whether or not sexual orientation is based on biological or physiological factors, which may be a matter of some controversy, it is a deeply personal characteristic that is either unchangeable or changeable only at unacceptable personal costs and so falls within the ambit of s.15 protection ...'[109]

This ascription of immutability or near-immutability carries with it all of the problems of false universalism, biologism, essentialism, privatization, paternalism, and subordination that several authors warned of. And the fears of what these problems mean in practical terms are borne out in the majority judgment with its focus on biologically based reproduction. The three dissenting judges moved away from the criterion of immutability by focusing on the 'historic disadvantages suffered by homosexual persons.' This analysis has the potential to expose the heterosexual/homosexual boundary as one of dominance and subordination, not simply one of 'difference,' and in so doing upset the boundary itself, along with its heterosexist and lesbian/ gay-hating underpinnings. However, the analysis is tamed in the judgment of the three dissenting judges, and serves only to open the door to treating homosexual couples the same as heterosexual couples.

Madam Justice L'Heureux-Dubé, in her dissent, focuses on the impact rather than on the ground of discrimination. In so doing she is de-emphasizing the categories and arguably introducing the potential for a more flexible and complex analysis that would be less prone to stereotype and essentialism and would more easily accommodate interactive discrimination. This approach may respond to many of the concerns raised by the authors. However, it also has the potential to individualize the discrimination and undermine a power-based analysis of discrimination as largely a function and exercise of dominance.

While the split decision[110] and much of the analysis in Egan and Nesbit were fairly predictable, the different approaches taken by the judges in Egan and Nesbit do provide food for thought, as does the meaning and significance of the final result. A decision that Egan and Nesbit are not spouses does not trouble me; a decision that Egan and Nesbit are not eligible for an allowance made available to other 'couples' troubles me slightly; a decision that leaves intact a government program of spousal benefits, allegedly in the name of supporting marriage and children, troubles me greatly. As a representation of [lesbians and] gay men in law, the decision in Egan and Nesbit offers a very limited image. However, as a reflection of the strategic and ideological issues that face us as lesbians and gays seeking our human rights, the case is full and complex. The decisions in the case do, explicitly or implicitly, pick up on all of the issues raised by the writers in this field whom I canvassed for this chapter. While it would be a mistake to look to the law for answers to our dilemmas of self-representation, legal cases do provide a mirror in which to see those representations reflected back. While the reflections are often distorted and sometimes unrecognizable, it seems to me that such is the risk of engaging in the legal forum, a risk to be seriously weighed in the assessment of these cases. Cases such as Egan and Nesbit provide us with the opportunity to raise new questions and re-examine old questions about who 'we' are, if there is a we, and if and how we want to define ourselves, both in legal contexts and for ourselves.

Cases, Statutes, and Legal References

Andrews v. *Law Society of British Columbia,* [1989] 1 S.C.R. 143.
Egan v. *Canada,* [1995] 2 S.C.R. 143
Gay Alliance Toward Equality v. *Vancouver Sun* (1977), 77 D.L.R. (3d) 487 (B.C.C.A.)
Index to Canadian Legal Periodical Literature. Montreal, 1995.
Old Age Security Act. R.S.C/ 1985, c.O–9.
Thwaites v. *Canadian Armed Forces* (1994), 19 C.H.R.R. D/259.
Watkins v. *U.S. Army* 847 F.2d 1329 (9th Cir. 1987).
Williamson v. *A.G. Edwards & Sons Inc.* 876 F.2d 56 (8th Cir. 1989).

Notes

1 Perhaps I could obviate the need even to write a chapter here by simply pointing to what I consider an extremely telling representation of sexual identities in Canadian law: the representation that is put forward by the *Index to Canadian Legal Periodical Literature* (Montreal 1995), in which there is no subject heading of lesbian and gay, or sexual orientation, or heterosexuality, only of *homosexuality* which, after the listings is followed by 'See also sex crimes.' While I am certainly not the first to note this egregious reference, it is such a revealing representation that I wanted to draw attention to it here.
2 *Egan* v. *Canada,* [1995] 2 S.C.R. 143.

3 R.S.C., 1985, c. O–9.

4 By far the most interesting, thought-provoking, and promising piece of the judgment was the dissenting decision of Madam Justice L'Heureux-Dubé, in which she suggested a new way to approach s.15 of the Charter that would focus on the impact of the discrimination rather than on the prohibited ground of discrimination. This chapter is not the place for me to fully explore and try to assess this new approach. It is a general approach to equality analysis, and does not address the specifics of lesbian and gay inequalities. I am not at this point quite sure even what I think of Madam Justice L'Heureux-Dubé's analysis, but I am keen to get back into it and start thinking about it. Regardless of where I end up in my thinking on this approach in terms of what it says about (in)equality and what it might mean in terms of addressing inequalities, I loved this part of the decision – because it is new and exciting and promising, but most of all because Justice L'Heureux-Dubé is really trying to make equality work.

5 Admittedly the bulk of the recent writing on lesbian and gay legal issues is in these two areas of equality theorizing and family theorizing. This correlates with the fact that the bulk of current lesbian- and gay-issue cases are in these two areas. Often, as in Egan and Nesbit, a case involves both areas simultaneously. Similarly, many of the articles straddle the two areas. Earlier cases and legal writing involving lesbians were largely about lesbian custody, while the writing and cases involving gay men were largely related to the criminalization of gay male sex. Other areas of law addressed in recent writing on lesbian and gay issues include: tax (see Young, 'Taxing Times,' 534ff); lesbian abuse (see Ristock, 'And Justice for All?' 415–30; teaching (see Petersen, 'Living Dangerously,' 318ff; pornography (see Scales, 'Avoiding Constitutional Depression,' 349ff); and sadomasochism (see Stychin, 'Unmanly Diversions,' 503ff).

6 Eaton, 'Lesbians, Gays,' 130ff.

7 Ibid., 131.

8 I, like Mary Eaton and many others writing on these issues, put homosexual as well as similar and related words in quotation marks because, given their repressive origins and histories, they are not words that I would use to describe myself or other lesbians or gay men. There is a serious risk in writing about law and using the language of the law and of legal decisions that one re-enforces, at least to some extent, the very oppressions that one is trying to challenge. This risk is of course not limited to legal writing but is endemic to writing and speaking, and is a function of the hegemonic limitations of language.

9 The status/conduct distinction being made in law may reflect the pervasive social response: 'I don't care if you are a lesbian; it's none of my business. I just don't want to hear about it.'

10 I am always in a quandary about how to refer to authors. Last names alone seem so

distant and institutional, both names so cumbersome, Mr/Ms so formal, and first names so familiar. And each of these options has gender and cultural implications. But one has to choose one of them. I wanted to use first names in this chapter because I feel some connection with all of the authors; I know many of them personally and some are friends. And even though our differences are many I wanted to reflect a sense of community, of alliance. However, I did worry that in so doing I might be being presumptuous, facile, or hypocritical. Regardless, my deliberations and angst were for nought. I have been required to choose between using first and last names together and last names only in order to avoid confusion in following the references.

11 Eaton, 'Reversing the Progressive Hypothesis,' 134.

12 See for example the following comment made by Mr Justice Branca of the British Columbia Court of Appeal in *Gay Alliance Toward Equality* v. *Vancouver Sun* (1977), 77 D.L.R.(3d) 487 (B.C.C.A.): 'If one bases a bias against homosexuals because they are persons who engage in unnatural sexual activity, which may make them guilty of a serious crime in certain circumstances and because they are forbidden to enter Canada as undesirables, can one say that such a bias, if it is arrived at for those reasons, is unreasonable?' 495. The discrimination complaint in this case arose because the *Vancouver Sun* refused to publish an advertisement for the complainant's publication, *Gay Tide*.

13 *Andrews* v. *Law Society of British Columbia*, [1989] 1 S.C.R. 143.

14 Eaton, 'Reversing the Progressive Hypothesis,' 182.

15 Ibid., 184.

16 See for example David Lepofsky, 'The Canadian Judicial Approach,' 315.

17 For a more critical assessment of Andrews see Diana Majury, 'Equality and Discrimination,' 407.

18 The same tension is similarly apparent in the Federal Court of Appeal decision in *Egan* v. *Canada*, from which the claimants appealed to the Supreme Court of Canada.

19 Others, in addition to Mary Eaton, have written about and analysed this bifurcation of 'being' and 'doing,' in human rights law generally, and as it has been applied specifically in the context of lesbian and gay claims. See for example Schacter, 'Gay Civil Rights Debate,' 283.

20 Ibid., 294.

21 Schacter's claim is not true with respect to all U.S. cases. Some sexual orientation discrimination claims in the United States have been successful.

22 For an example, see note 12 above.

23 Koppelman, in 'Why Discrimination,' 197, argues that a focus on homosexual sex 'misdescribes most anti-gay prejudice, which focuses on gay identity rather than homosexual conduct' (260). While I agree with Koppelman's locating identity as the

target, I think his attempt to separate identity from [sexual] conduct is problematic. As his own analysis earlier in the same article so clearly demonstrates, lesbian and gay identities are inextricably bound up in lesbian and gay sex. See also Blaine Rehkopf's chapter in this volume.

24 They may instead have everything to do with gender constructs, or heterosexual dominance, or racialized stereotypes, or ablist discomfort.

25 Pearlman, 'Theorizing Lesbian Oppression,' 454.

26 Ibid., 462.

27 Cynthia Petersen, in her article 'Envisioning a Lesbian Equality Jurisprudence,' 118–37, criticizes Lynne's continuum of outness on two grounds. Cynthia's first criticism is that Lynne's analysis does not address the oppression of 'invisibility' experienced by unassimilated lesbians, who, because of white solipsism or ablist solipsism, may be denied their appropriate place on the continuum. Cynthia's second criticism is that the framework of the continuum obscures or even denies the unique forms of oppression experienced by lesbians who are closeted.

28 Some people may see a continuum analysis as contradicting or undermining a bifurcation analysis because it obfuscates the clarity of the divide between what it is about lesbians and gays that the courts are willing to protect and what it is that they are not willing to protect. It is because I don't think that the divide is so clear that I prefer the nuances of the continuum.

29 See for example Arnup and Boyd, 'Familial Disputes? Sperm Donors, Lesbian Mothers and Legal Parenthood,' in Herman and Stychin, eds. *Legal Inversions*, 77–101.

30 Eaton, 'Homosexual Unmodified,' in Herman and Stychin, eds., *Legal Inversions,* 46–73.

31 Ibid., 46.

32 Ibid., 69.

33 A number of authors have explored this problem and the distortions, difficulties, and denials faced by those who experience interactive oppressions and seek redress through our human rights system. See for example, Crenshaw, 'Demarginalizing the Intersection,' 139; Nitya Iyer, 'Disappearing Women,' 25; and 'Categorical Denials' and Emily Carasco, 'Case Of Double Jeopardy,' 142.

34 The requirement of homogeneity within a protected ground is rife with potential for essentialist and universalist analysis and the creation and perpetuation of stereotypes.

35 Eaton, 'Homosexual Unmodified,' 51.

36 *Williamson* v. *A.G. Edwards & Sons Inc.* 876 F.2d 56 (8th Cir. 1989) and *Watkins* v. *U.S. Army* 847 F.2d 1329 (9th Cir. 1987).

37 Eaton, 'Homosexual Unmodified,' 48.

38 Mary Eaton makes these comparisons recognizing the risks and oversimplifications to which comparisons inevitably give rise. She offers her 'suggestions' in order to promote thinking and analysis, not to provide definitive answers. Ibid., 73, n. 49.

39 See Carasco, 'Case of Double Jeopardy.'

40 This is not to imply that the fragmented approach is a positive approach, only that it is probably preferable to the reductive approach, and that it may be a stage in the evolution to an integrated approach.

41 Eaton, 'Homosexual Unmodified,' 68.

42 Ibid., 67.

43 Ibid., 68.

44 I am thinking here of the case of *Thwaites* v. *Canadian Armed Forces* (1994), 19 C.H.R.R. D/259. Simon Thwaites is a gay man in the armed forces whom the armed forces clearly wants rid of because he is gay; he was 'released' because he was HIV-positive. A human rights tribunal found that he was discriminated against on the basis of disability. While the tribunal does acknowledge the striking overlap between the special investigation into Thwaites's homosexuality and the failure of the medical review board to properly assess Thwaites's medical condition, they go on to find that the armed forces acted in good faith in dismissing Thwaites. In other words, the tribunal found that the clear anti-gay animus of the armed forces against Thwaites did not affect, either intentionally or unconsciously, their decision to fire him. Me – I don't think so.

45 Hopefully this politics of inclusion is taking place not just at the feel-good level to which Mary Eaton alludes. In fact, if truly being practised, a politics of inclusion would not be about feeling good, but about challenge, discomfort, and self-questioning, at least, or primarily for members of dominant groups. I am, as I write this, acutely aware of Elizabeth Spelman's critique of the term *inclusion* when used in this context. Inclusion clearly denotes the power to include, and, implicitly, the power also to exclude. In so doing the term re-enforces the dominance and assimilation model of 'equality.' This is, I assume, the feel-goodism to which Mary Eaton refers. See Spelman, *Inessential Woman* 1988. I use the term here due to lack of imagination.

46 See Koppelman, 'Why Discrimination'; Diana Majury, 'Refashioning the Unfashionable,' 286; and Robert Wintemute, 'Sexual Orientation Discrimination,' 429.

47 Wintemute, 'Sexual Orientation Discrimination,' 469–70. Although he does make brief reference to the sexual subordination/sex discrimination analysis, Wintemute is advancing the traditional 'but for sex' argument in his article.

48 Apparently Evelyn Gigantes, the Ontario Government NDP minister responsible for introducing the amendment that led to the inclusion of sexual orientation as a prohibited ground of discrimination under the Ontario Human Rights Code, also saw this issue as one that at its root was about sex equality. In her speech to the House on the proposed amendment, she made the following statement: 'It is the maleness of economic and social domination of our society that is threatened by this reform; not the

womaness or the childness, but the maleness that so profits by its domination through being male ... it is my humble opinion that the hatred and victimization of homosexual people is part of a male-dominated system, dealing with men who do not join as if they were traitors.' (As quoted by Didi Herman in *Rights of Passage*, 41–2.)

49 Koppelman, 'Why Discrimination,' 249.

50 Ibid., 235. Most of the examples I use in this sentence are taken from Koppelman's article.

51 Wintemute, 'Sexual Orientation Discrimination,' 471–2. Note the violent phallic import of this statement.

52 Petersen, 'Envisioning a Lesbian Jurisprudence'; see also references in Koppelman, 'Why Discrimination,' 202, n. 16.

53 Majury, 'Refashioning the Unfashionable,' 316. While I am troubled by and made to think because of Cynthia's gently but strongly put critique of my analysis, I am still not fully persuaded by it. This may be simply resistance on my part; it may be that I am stuck in the dominance of my own white gender analysis. But I am not sure that Cynthia got my point that I am not arguing that sexual orientation overlaps with or intersects with sex discrimination; I am arguing that sexual orientation is sex discrimination.

54 See Koppelman, 'Why Discrimination,' 239, in which a few of the manifold variations in sexuality are enumerated.

55 Herman, *Rights of Passage*. Didi Herman explores a number of related issues and themes in her book. I do not in any way, in this short section, try to discuss even most of them. I draw from her book what I consider to be the most relevant to the issues I am exploring in this chapter.

56 Ibid., 149.

57 See note 12 above. This perception is, of course, still very prevalent, particularly among the new Christian right (see Herman, *Rights of Passage*, 77–127), but it no longer appears to be the dominant understanding informing human rights cases.

58 I put *lesbians* in brackets here because all of the early cases were brought by gay men or gay organizations. Given my gender analysis (see Majury, 'Refashioning the Unfashionable') I think this is significant in terms of the arguments being put forward and the decisions being made.

59 Herman, *Rights of Passage*, 29. This shift from pathologization to tolerance has been far from comprehensive in legal, medical, or public discourses, as evidenced with respect to legal discourse, for example, by the 'see also sex crimes' reference under 'homosexuality' in the *Index to Canadian Legal Periodical Literature* (see note 1 above). It may even be questionable whether such a shift has actually taken place. It may be more accurate to look at this in terms of the addition of new discourses that

compete with, but do not necessarily replace, the old. See Stychin, 'Unmanly Diversions.'

60 Mary Eaton raises a similar concern in the context of her discussion of the status/conduct distinction. Eaton, 'Reversing the Progressive Hypothesis.'

61 Herman, *Rights of Passage*, 8.

62 See Jody Freeman, 'Defining the Family,' 41; and Gwen Brodsky, 'Out of the Closet,' 523.

63 Here Didi Herman is drawing from the work of Judith Butler in *Gender Trouble.*

64 A group called Inter-Faith Coalition on Marriage and the Family intervened in the Egan and Nesbit case. While this is not one of the organizations discussed by Didi Herman in her book, I assume from its name that it may also be associated with the new Christian right. However, names are sufficiently ambiguous that I may be wrong in this assumption.

65 Herman, *Rights of Passage,* 114; reference omitted.

66 Ibid., 115.

67 Carl Stychin, 'Essential Rights,' 49.

68 This is the critique that Mary Eaton develops with respect to race in 'Homosexual Unmodified.'

69 Stychin, 'Essential Rights,' 54. My only concern with what Carl says here is the implication that the human rights approach creates these classifications rather than reflects socially inscribed categories already in existence.

70 Ibid., 57.

71 Ibid., 61.

72 Ibid., 65.

73 I fear, but do not know for sure, that it is mostly 'boys.' I fear, but I do not know for sure, that it is mostly white, nondisabled academics.

74 See Crenshaw, 'Demarginalizing the Intersection'; Nancy Hartsock, 'Foucault on Power,' Tania Modleski, *Feminism Without Women* and 'State of the Art,' 23, in which Patricia Hill Collins, Mae Henderson, June Jordan, and Nellie McKay are interviewed.

75 My statement here refers to the body of literature as a whole and the focus of that literature, not to the content of individual articles within the literature, many of which are wide-ranging and radical in their analysis. Further to this point, Ruthann Robson criticizes feminists and feminist legal theory for arrogating lesbianism to familialism, Robson, 'Resisting the Family,' 975, 990–91. This is a critique that I think we might consider with respect to our own arrogations. Needless to say, this is also a self-critique in terms of my choice of what I am writing about in this article.

76 Cossman, 'Family Inside/Out,' 1, 2–3.

77 Ibid., 39.

78 Boyd, 'Expanding the 'Family,' 545.

79 Cossman and Ryder, *Gay, Lesbian*
80 Actually, the Ontario Law Reform Commission proposed a model, Registered Domestic Partnership, which was restricted to the registration of two people but did not require that they be in a sexual relationship. See Boyd, 'Expanding the "Family,"' 550.
81 Ibid., 549.
82 Ibid., 555.
83 Ibid.
84 Shelley Gavigan, 'Paradise Lost, Paradox Revisited,' 589.
85 Ibid., 606.
86 Boyd, 'Expanding the "Family,"' 561–2.
87 Robson, 'Resisting the Family,' 987, critiques the requirement of sexual exclusivity as demonstrating a property-based model of relationships.
88 Freeman, 'Defining the Family,' and Brodsky, 'Out of the Closet.'
89 Ibid., for the view that the framing is not inevitably in these conventional terms. The Mossop case involved a challenge to a family-based bereavement-leave policy.
90 I have not read the factum, but Jody discusses the constraints of the 'factum' concept as a vehicle for making a complex, open-ended argument. Factum: the name alone provides ample indication of the form's resistance to ambiguity and fluidity. And even without the constraints of the legal document, it is difficult, deliberately and effectively, to articulate a contradictory argument.
91 In conventional terms of 'success' in the legal context, Mossop was not successful; he lost before the Supreme Court of Canada. However, the decision was a five to four split. Madam Justice L'Heureux-Dubé wrote a strong dissent in which she referred extensively to a wide range of lesbian feminist writing. My heart sings when I read the list of authorities for this decision, and when I think that Audre Lorde and Adrienne Rich are required reading for our Supreme Court judges, and hopefully increasingly for the lawyers who appear before them. I can only think that this is in large part thanks to the factum put before the court by the intervenors. There are many meanings of success. From interviews that she conducted with Brian Mossop and his partner, Ken Popert, Didi Herman is able to show us why they regarded their litigation as largely 'successful,' even though they 'lost' in court. For them the public exposure, 'the ability to ... gain access to the media to talk about homosexuality, was the whole point of the action.' Herman, *Rights of Passage,* 60.
92 I would say that this is not true of most activists, who much more clearly position themselves at one end of the spectrum or the other and often resent the academic water-muddying. It is interesting and important to think about and question this tension between activists and academics, especially for those of us who aspire to be both. Didi Herman offers some thoughtful self-reflections on this issue in the introduction to *Rights of Passage,* 11–17.

93 Robson, 'Resisting the Family,' 975.

94 Ibid., 976.

95 Ibid., 989.

96 Technically the Egan and Nesbit case was about spousal status, not family status, but in this context I am using the more general term to include spouse. The term *spouse* has all the same problems I have outlined with respect to family, but in a significantly more entrenched and definitive way. To me, spouse is irredeemably heterosexist.

97 Referring to Justice La Forest as writing for the majority is a bit of a misnomer. There were four different judgments written in this case, two of which were dissents. One of the dissents was written by Justice L'Heureux-Dubé and the other written jointly by Justices Cory and Iacobucci and joined by Justice Mclachlin. La Forest was joined by Justices LaMer, Gonthier, and Major. The swing vote was Justice Sopinka, who held that the definition of spouse in the Act was a breach of gays' and lesbians' s.15 Charter rights, but that such a breach was reasonable because our time has just not yet come in the evolving expansion of the intended recipients of benefits.

98 Egan and Nesbit, 535.

99 One of the meanings of the verb *to couple* is 'to copulate.' The (hetero)sex of the term is clear.

100 Egan and Nesbit, 535.

101 Ibid.

102 Ibid., 537. This is simply a statement that La Forest makes; he offers no support for it. There is of course no mention here that 'children brought up by single parents,' that is, by single mothers, are often brought up in poverty because of inadequate child support, pay inequity, and/or inadequate social assistance; nor is there is any mention, in the course of this discussion about the need to support children, of the serious problem of child sexual and physical abuse within the heterosexual nuclear family.

103 Ibid., 536.

104 Ibid., 538–9.

105 Ibid., 583.

106 Ibid.

107 Egan and Nesbitt, 599.

108 I recognize and respect that disruption and challenge to heterosexuality may not have been goals of Egan and Nesbit, and I do not wish to impose my political agenda on them nor critique them for perhaps not sharing my political agenda. But their case in some ways stands separate and apart from them, and I am exploring their case for its potential to raise the kinds of challenges that I and the authors whose work I am drawing from might seek.

109 Egan and Nesbit, 528. This is an argument put forward by the lawyer for Egan and Nesbit, which raises the question asked by Didi Herman and by Mary Eaton concerning the extent to which the claimants are, or feel, compelled to present their case in the terms set by the dominant legal discourse.

110 Although I must confess I thought the split would be the other way and that Egan and Nesbit would win their case. I continue to think that this is an issue that will be won, and that what matters most are the terms on which it is won.

Bibliography

Abelove, Henry, Michele Aina Barale, and David M. Halperin, eds. *The Lesbian and Gay Studies Reader*. New York and London: Routledge, 1993.

Adam, Barry. *The Rise of a Gay and Lesbian Movement*. Rev. ed. New York: Twayne Publishers, 1995.

Adams, Mary Louise. 'Thoughts on Heterosexism, Queerness and Outlaws.' In *Resist: Essays against Homophobic Culture*, ed. Mona Oikawa, Dionne Falconer, and Ann Decter, 36–43. Toronto: Women's Press, 1994.

Agamben, Giorgio. *The Coming Community*. Trans. Michael Hardt. Minneapolis: University of Minnesota Press, 1993.

Allan, Graham. *Friendship: Developing a Sociological Perspective*. Boulder: Westview Press, 1989.

Altman, Dennis. *Homosexual Oppression and Liberation*. New York: Outerbridge and Dienstfrey, 1971.

– *Sex and the New Puritanism*. London: Pluto Press, 1986.

– 'Legitimation through Disaster.' In *AIDS: The Burdens of History*, ed. Elizabeth Fee and Daniel Fox, 301–15. Berkeley: University of California Press, 1988.

Ang-Lygate, Magdalene. 'Waking from a Dream of Chinese Shadows.' *Feminism & Psychology* 6, no. 1 (1996): 56–60.

Anzaldua, Gloria. '*La Conciencia de la Mestiza: Towards a New Consciousness.*' In *Making Face, Making Soul*, ed. Gloria Anzaldua, 377–90. San Francisco: Aunt Lute Books, 1990.

Arnup, Katherine, and Susan Boyd. 'Familial Disputes? Sperm Donors, Lesbian Mothers, and Legal Parenthood.' In *Legal Inversions*, ed. Didi Herman and Carl Stychin. Philadelphia: Temple University Press, 1995.

Aronowitz, Stanley. 'Against the Liberal State: ACT-UP and the Emergence of Post-Modern Politics,' In *Social Post-Modernism: Beyond Identity Politics*, edited by Linda Nicholson and Steven Seidman, 357–83. Cambridge: Cambridge University Press, 1995.

Aronson, Jane. 'Women's Sense of Responsibility for the Care of Old People: "But Who Else Is Going to Do It?"' *Gender and Society* 6 (1992): 8–29.

– 'Lesbians in Social Work Education: Processes and Puzzles in Claiming Visibility.' *Journal of Progressive Services* 6 (1995): 5–27.

Aronson, Jane, and Sheila Neysmith. 'The Retreat of the State and Long–Term Care Provision: Implications for Frail Elderly People, Unpaid Family Carers, and Paid Home Care Workers.' *Studies in Political Economy.* Forthcoming.

Atkinson, Paul. *The Ethnographic Imagination: Textual Constructions of Reality.* New York: Routledge, 1990.

Bahktin, Mikhail. *The Dialogic Imagination.* Austin: University of Texas Press, 1981.

Baines, Carol T., Patricia M. Evans, and Sheila M. Neysmith, eds. *Women's Caring: Feminist Perspectives on Social Welfare.* Toronto: McClelland and Stewart, 1991.

Balan, Angie, Rhonda Chorney, and Janice L. Ristock. *Training and Education Project for Responding to Abuse in Lesbian Relationships.* Final report 4887-07-93-011. Ottawa: Health Canada, 1995.

Benjamin, Jessica. *Like Subjects, Love Objects: Essays on Recognition and Sexual Difference.* New Haven: Yale University Press, 1995.

Best, Joel. 'Dark Figures and Child Victims: Statistical Claims about Missing Children.' In *Images of Issues: Typifying Contemporary Social Problems*, ed. Joel Best, 21–37. New York: Aldine, 1989.

Blumenfeld, Warren, J. *Homophobia: How We All Pay the Price.* Boston: Beacon Press, 1992.

Boffin, Tessa, and Sunil Gupta, eds. *Ecstatic Antibodies: Resisting the AIDS Mythology.* London: Rivers Oram, 1990.

Bogdan, Deanne. 'When Is a Singing School (Not) a Chorus?' In *The Education Feminism Reader*, ed. Lynda Stone. New York: Routledge, 1994.

Boles, Jacqueline, and Kirk Elfison, 'Sexual Identity and HIV: The Male Prostitute.' *Journal of Sex Research* 31, no. 1 (February 1994): 39–46.

Borch-Jacobsen, Mikkel. *The Freudian Subject.* Trans. by Catherine Porter. Stanford: Stanford University Press, 1982.

Boyd, Susan. 'Expanding the "Family" in Family Law: Recent Ontario Proposals on Same–Sex Relationships.' *Canadian Journal of Women and the Law* 7 (1994): 545–563.

Brinkley, Allen. 'The Problem of American Conservatism.' *American Historical Review*, 99 (April 1994): 409–37.

Briskin, Linda. *Feminist Pedagogy: Teaching and Learning Liberation.* CRIAW Feminist Perspective Series No. 19. Ottawa: Canadian Research Institute for the Advancement of Women, 1990.

Briskin, Linda, and Rebecca Priegart Coulter. 'Feminist Pedagogy: Challenging the Normative.' *Canadian Journal of Education* 17, no. 3 (1992): 247–63.

Britzman, Deborah. 'Beyond Rolling Models: Gender and Multicultural Education.' In *Gender and Education*, ed. Sari Knopp Biklen and Diane Pollard. Chicago: University of Chicago Press, 1993.

– 'The Ordeal of Knowledge: Rethinking the Possibilities of Multicultural Education.' *Review of Education* 15 (1993): 123–35.

– 'Is There a Queer Pedagogy? Or, Stop Reading Straight.' *Educational Theory* 45, no. 2 (Spring 1995): 151–65.

– *Lost Subjects, Contested Objects: Toward a Psychoanalytic Inquiry of Learning.* Albany: SUNY Press, 1998.

Britzman, Deborah, and Alice Pitt. 'Pedagogy and Transference: 'Casting the Past of Learning into the Presence of Teaching.' *Theory into Practice* 35, no. 2 (1996): 117–23.

Britzman, Deborah, Kelvin Santiago-Valles, Gladys Jimenez-Munoz, and Laura Lamash. 'Slips That Show and Tell: Fashioning Multiculture as a Problem of Representation.' In *Race, Identity, and Representation in Education*, ed. Cameron McCarthy and Warren Crichlow. New York: Routledge, 1993.

Brodkey, Linda, and Michelle Fine. 'Presence of Mind and Absence of Body.' *Journal of Education* 170, no. 3 (1988): 84–99.

Brodsky, Gwen. 'Out of the Closet and into a Wedding Dress? Struggles for Lesbian and Gay Legal Equality.' *Canadian Journal of Women and the Law* 7 (1994): 523.

Bromley, Hank. 'Identity Politics and Critical Pedagogy.' *Educational Theory* 39, no. 3 (1989): 207–21.

Brown, Catrina. 'Feminist Postmodernism and the Challenge of Diversity.' In *Essays on Postmodernism and Social Work*, ed. Adrienne Chambon and Allan Irving, 35–49. Toronto: Canadian Scholars' Press, 1994.

Brown, Judith. 'Lesbian Sexuality in Medieval and Early Modern Europe.' In *Hidden from History: Reclaiming the Gay and Lesbian Past*, ed. Martin Duberman, Martha Vicinus, and George Chauncey, 67–75. New York: Basic Books, 1990.

Brown, Laura. 'New Voices, New Visions: Towards a Lesbian and Gay Paradigm for Psychology.' *Psychology of Women Quarterly* 13 (1989): 445–58.

Bryson, Mary, and Suzanne de Castell. 'Queer Pedagogy: Praxis Makes Im/Perfect.' *Canadian Journal of Education* 18, no. 3 (Summer 1993): 285–305.

Bull, Chris, and John Gallagher. 'The Lost Generation.' *The Advocate*, 31 May 1994.

Butler, Judith. *Gender Trouble: Feminism and the Subversion of Identity.* New York: Routledge, 1990.

– 'Imitation and Gender Insubordination.' In *Inside/Out: Lesbian Theories, Gay Theories*, edited by Diana Fuss, 13–31. New York: Routledge, 1991.

– 'Sexual Inversions.' In *Discourses of Sexuality: From Aristotle to AIDS*, ed. Donna Stanton, 344–61. Ann Arbor: University of Michigan Press, 1992.

– *Bodies That Matter: On the Discursive Limits of 'Sex.'* New York: Routledge, 1993.

Butler, Sandra, and Barbara Rosenblum. *Cancer in Two Voices*. San Francisco: Spinsters Book Company, 1991.

Cain, Roy. 'Managing Impressions of an AIDS Service Organization: Into the Main-stream or Out of the Closet.' *Qualitative Sociology* 17 (1994): 43–61.

Calhoun, Craig. 'Naturalism and Ethnicity.' *Annual Review of Sociology*, 19 (1993): 211–39.

Callen, Michael. 'AIDS Is a Gay Disease!' *PWA Coalition Newsline* 42 (March 1989).

Campbell, Marie, and Ann Manicom, eds. *Knowledge, Experience, and Ruling Relations: Studies in the Social Organization of Knowledge*. Toronto: University of Toronto Press, 1995.

Cancian, Francesca. 'Participatory Research and Alternative Strategies for Activist Sociology.' In *Feminism and Social Change: Bridging Theory and Practice*, ed. Heidi Gottfried, 187–205. Urbana and Chicago: University of Illinois Press, 1996.

Carasco, Emily. 'A Case Of Double Jeopardy: Race and Gender.' *Canadian Journal of Women and the Law*, 6 (1995): 142–52.

Carby, Hazel. 'Encoding White Resentment: Grand Canyon – A Narrative for Our Time.' In *Race, Identity, and Representation in Education*, ed. Cameron McCarthy and Warren Crichlow, 236–47. New York: Routledge, 1993.

Cather, Willa. *Sapphira and the Slave Girl*. New York: Random House, 1975.

Chafetz, Janet Saltzman. *Gender Equity: An Integrated Theory of Stability and Change*. London: Sage, 1990.

Champagne, John. *The Ethics of Marginality: A New Approach to Gay Studies*. Minneapolis: University of Minnesota Press, 1995.

Chauncey, George. *Gay New York: Gender, Urban Culture and the Making of the Gay Male World, 1890–1940*. New York: Basic Books, 1994.

Chesley, Robert. 'Jerker, or the Helping Hand: A Pornographic Elegy with Redeeming Social Value and a Hymn to the Queer Men of San Francisco in Twenty Telephone Calls, Many of Them Dirty.' In *Out Front: Contemporary Gay and Lesbian Plays*, ed. Don Shewey, 449–91. New York: Grove Press, 1988.

Clifford, James. *The Predicament of Culture*. Cambridge: Harvard University Press, 1988.

Clough, Patricia Ticineto. *Feminist Thought*. Oxford: Blackwell, 1994.

Cohen, Ed. 'Who Are "We"? Gay "Identity" as Political (E)motion.' In *Inside/Out: Lesbian Theories, Gay Theories*, ed. Diana Fuss, 71–92. New York: Routledge, 1991.

Copjec, Joan. 'Cutting Up.' In *Between Feminism and Psychoanalysis*, ed. Teresa Brennan, 227–46. New York: Routledge, 1989.

Corliss, Richard. 'Tidings of Job: Nothing to Cheer about This Movie Season,' *Time*, 27 December 1993.

– 'The Gay Gauntlet!' *Time*, 7 February 1994.

Cossman, Brenda. 'Family Inside/Out.' *University of Toronto Law Journal* 44 (1994): 1–39.

Cossman, Brenda, and Bruce Ryder. '*Gay, Lesbian and Unmarried Heterosexual Couples and the Family Law Act; Accommodating a Diversity of Family Forms.*' Research paper, Ontario Law Reform Commission, 1993.

Cossman, Brenda, Shannon Bell, Lise Gotell, and Becki L. Ross. *Bad Attitude/s on Trial: Pornography, Feminism, and the* Butler *Decision*. Toronto: University of Toronto Press, 1997.

Crenshaw, Kim. 'Demarginalizing the Intersection of Race and Sex: A Black Feminist Critique of Antidiscrimination Doctrine, Feminist Theory and Antiracist Politics.' *University of Chicago Legal Forum*, 139–67. 1989.

Crimp, Douglas. 'Hey, Girlfriend!' *Social Text* 33 (1992): 2–18.

Cruikshank, Margaret. *Lesbian Studies: Present and Past*. New York: The Feminine Press, 1982.

Davis, Katherine Bement. *Factors in the Sex Life of Twenty-Two Hundred Women*. [1929]. New York: Arno Press, 1972.

de Castell, Suzanne, and Tom Walker. 'Identity, Metamorphosis, and Ethnographic Research.' *Anthropology and Education Quarterly* 21 (1991): 3–22.

de Certeau, Michel. *The Practice of Everyday Life*. Berkeley: University of California Press, 1984.

de Lauretis, Teresa. 'Queer Theory: Lesbian and Gay Sexualities, An Introduction.' *Differences* 3, no. 2 (1991): iii–xviii.

d'Emilio, John. *Sexual Politics, Sexual Communities*. Chicago: University of Chicago Press, 1983.

– *Making Trouble: Essays on Gay History, Politics, and the University*. New York and London: Routledge, 1992.

de Sade, Marquis. *The 120 Days of Sodom and Other Writings*. Translated by Austryn Wainhouse and Richard Seaver. New York: Grove Press. 1966.

Degler, Carl. 'What Ought to Be and What Was: Women's Sexuality in the Nineteenth Century.' *American History Review* 79 (December 1974).

Delany, Samuel. 'Street Talk/Straight Talk.' *Differences: A Journal of Feminist Cultural Studies* 5, no. 2 (1991): 21–38.

Derrida, Jacques. *De la Grammatologie*. Paris: Minuit, 1967.

de Vries, Hillary. 'When the Laughing Stops.' *Globe and Mail* (Toronto), 4 January 1994.

Diamond, Sara. *Spiritual Warfare: The Politics of the Christian Right*. Boston: South End Press, 1989.

Diamond, Timothy. 'Social Policy and Everyday Life in Nursing Homes: A Critical Ethnography.' In *The Worth of Women's Work: A Qualitative Synthesis*, ed. Anne Statham. Albany: SUNY Press, 1988.

Dowsett, Gary W. *Practicing Desire: Homosexual Sex in the Era of AIDS*. Stanford: Stanford University Press, 1996.

DuBois, W.E.B. *A W.E.B. DuBois Reader*, ed. Andrew G. Paschal. New York: Macmillan, 1971.

– *The Souls of Black Folk* (1903). In *DuBois: Writings*, ed. Nathan Huggins, 357–547. New York: Viking, 1986.

Duggan, Lisa, and Nan Hunter. *Sex Wars: Sexual Dissent and Political Culture*. New York and London: Routledge, 1995.

du Plessis. 'Blatantly Bisexual of Unthinking Queer Theory.' In *RePresenting Bisexualities: Subjects and Cultures of Fluid Desire*, ed. Donald Hall and Maria Pramaggiore, 19–54. New York: New York University Press, 1996.

Duttman, Alexander Garcia. 'What Will Have Been Said about AIDS: Some Remarks in Disorder.' *Public* 7 (1993): 95–115.

Earl, William. 'Married Men and Same-Sex Activity: A Field Study on HIV Risk among Men Who Do Not Identify as Gay or Bisexual,' *Journal of Sex and Marital Therapy* 16, no. 4 (winter 1990): 251–7.

Eaton, Mary. 'Lesbians, Gays and the Struggle for Equality Rights: Reversing the Progressive Hypothesis.' *Dalhousie Law Journal* 17 (1994): 130–86.

– 'Homosexual Unmodified: Speculation on Laws, Discourse, Race and the Construction of Sexual Identity.' In *Legal Inversions*, ed. Didi Herman and Carl Stychin. Philadelphia: Temple University Press, 1995.

Edelman, Lee. 'The Plague of Discourse: Politics, Literary Theory and AIDS.' *South Atlantic Quarterly* 88, no. 1 (Winter 1989): 301–17.

– *Homographesis: Essays in Gay Literary and Cultural Theory*. New York: Routledge, 1994.

Edgerton, Susan Huddelston. 'Toni Morrison Teaching the Interminable.' In *Race, Identity and Representation in Education*, ed. Cameron McCarthy and Warren Crichlow. New York: Routledge, 1993.

Edwards, Tim. 'The AIDS Dialectics: Awareness, Identity, Death, and Sexual Politics.' In *Modern Homosexualities: Fragments of Lesbian and Gay Experience*, ed. Ken Plummer, 151–9. New York: Routledge, 1992.

Eisen, Vitka, and Irene Hall, eds. 'Lesbian, Gay, Bisexual, Transgender People and Education.' Special Issue of *Harvard Educational Review* 66, no. 2 (Summer 1996).

Elliot, Pam. 'Shattering Illusion: Same-sex Domestic Violence.' In *Violence in Gay and Lesbian Domestic Partnerships*, ed. Claire Renzetti and Charles Harvey Miley, 1–9. New York: Haworth Press, 1995.

Ellsworth, Elizabeth. 'Teaching to Support Unassimilated Difference.' *Radical Teacher* 42 (1991): 4–9.

– 'Why Doesn't This Feel Empowering? Working through the Repressive Myths of Critical Pedagogy.' In *Feminisms and Critical Pedagogy*, ed. Carmen Luke and Jennifer Gore, 90–119. New York: Routledge, 1992.

– 'Situated Response-ability to Student Papers.' *Theory into Practice* 35, no. 2 (1996): 138–43.

Epstein, Rachel. 'Lesbian Parenting: Grounding Our Theory.' *Canadian Woman Studies* 16 (1996): 60–4.

Epstein, Steven. 'Gay Politics, Ethnic Identity: The Limits of Social Constructionism.' *Socialist Review* 93/94 (1987): 9–54.

– 'Gay Politics, Ethnic Identity: The Limits of Social Constructionism.' In *Forms of Desire: Sexual Orientation and the Social Constructionist Controversy*, ed. Edward Stein, 239–93. New York: Routledge, 1992.

Escoffier, Jeffrey. 'Generations and Paradigms: Mainstreams in Lesbian and Gay Studies,' *Journal of Homosexuality* 24, nos. 1/2 (1992): 7–26.

Esterberg, Kristin. *Lesbian and Bisexual Identities: Constructing Communities, Constructing Selves*. Philadelphia: Temple University Press. 1997.

Faderman, Lillian. *Surpassing the Love of Men: Romantic Friendship and Love between Women from the Renaissance to the Present*. New York: Quill William Morrow, 1981.

– *Odd Girls and Twilight Lovers: A History of Lesbian Life in Twentieth-Century America*. New York: Penguin, 1991.

Fay, Brian. *Social Theory and Political Practice*. London: George Allen and Unwin, 1975.

Feinberg, Leslie. *Stone Butch Blues: A Novel*. Ithaca, NY: Firebrand Books, 1993.

Felman, Shoshana. *Jacques Lacan and the Adventure of Insight: Psychoanalysis in Contemporary Culture*. Cambridge: Harvard University Press, 1987.

Felman, Shoshana, and Dori Laub. *Testimony: Crises of Witnessing in Literature, Psychoanalysis and History*. New York: Routledge, Chapman and Hall, 1992.

Ferguson, Ann. 'A Feminist Aspect Theory of the Self.' In *Women, Knowledge, and Reality: Explorations in Feminist Philosophy*, ed. Ann Garry and Marilyn Pearsall, 93–107. New York: Routledge, 1992.

Fernie, Lynne. *School's Out*. 25 min. Coproduced by Great Jane Productions and the National Film Board of Canada, 1996. Videocassette.

Finch, Janet. *Family Obligations and Social Change*. Cambridge: Polity Press, 1989.

Flax, Jane. *Disputed Subjects: Essays on Psychoanalysis, Politics and Philosophy*. New York: Routledge, 1993.

Fonow, Mary Margaret, and Debian Marty.'The Shift from Identity Politics to the Politics of Identity: Lesbian Panels in the Women's Studies Classroom.' *NWSA Journal* 3, no. 3 (1991): 402–13.

Foster, Thomas, Carol Seigel, and Ellen E. Berry. eds. *The Gay '90s: Disciplinary and Interdisciplinary Formations in Queer Studies*. Special issue of *Genders* 26 (1997).

Foucault, Michel. *Madness and Civilization: A History of Insanity in the Age of Reason*. Trans. by Richard Howard. New York: Random House, 1965.

- *The Archaeology of Knowledge and The Discourse on Language.* Trans. by A.M. Sheridan Smith. New York: Pantheon, 1972.
- *The Birth of the Clinic: An Archaeology of Medical Perception.* Trans. A.M. Sheridan Smith. New York: Pantheon, 1973.
- 'The Functions of Literature.' In *Genealogy and Literature.* ed. Lee Quinby, 3–8. Minneapolis: University of Minneapolis Press, 1975.
- *Histoire de la sexualite,* vol. 1. *La volonte de savoir.* Paris: Gallimard, 1976.
- 'What Is an Author?' In *Language, Counter-Memory, Practice: Selected Essays and Interviews by Michel Foucault,* ed. Donald F. Bouchard, 113–38. Ithaca: Cornell University Press, 1977.
- *Discipline and Punish: The Birth of the Prison.* Translated by Alan Sheridan. New York: Random-Vintage, 1979.
- *Power/Knowledge: Selected Interviews and Other Writings, 1972–1977.* Ed. Colin Gordon. New York: Pantheon Books, 1980.
- 'The Subject and Power.' In *Michel Foucault: Beyond Structuralism and Hermeneutics,* ed. Hubert L. Dreyfus and Paul Rabinow, 208–26. Sussex: Harvester Press Limited, 1982.
- 'On the Genealogy of Ethics: An Overview of a Work in Progress.' In *The Foucault Reader,* ed. Paul Rabinow, 340–72. New York: Pantheon, 1984.
- *The History of Sexuality: An Introduction.* Vol. 1. New York: Pantheon Books, 1991.
- Frank, Blye. 'Queer Selves/Queer in Schools: Young Men and Sexualities.' In *Sex in Schools: Canadian Education and Sexual Regulation,* ed. Susan Prentice, 44–59. Toronto: Our Schools/Ourselves, 1994.
- Freeman, Jody. 'Defining the Family in *Mossop* v. *D.S.S.*: The Challenge of Anti-Discrimination Essentialism and Interactive Discrimination for Human Rights Litigation.' *University of Toronto Law Journal* 41 (1994): 41–96.
- Freud, Sigmund. 'Negation.' In *The Complete Psychological Works of Sigmund Freud.* Vol. 19 (1923–1925), 235–9. Trans. James Strachey. London: Hogarth Press, 1925.
- 'Thoughts for the Times on War and Death' (1915). In *The Complete Psychological Works of Sigmund Freud.* Vol. 14, 275–302. Trans. James Strachey. London: Hogarth Press, 1957.
- *Civilization and Its Discontents.* Trans. Joan Riviere. London: Hogarth Press, 1975.
- 'Mourning and Melancholia.' (1915/1917). In *On Metapsychology: The Theory of Psychoanalysis,* 251–67. Trans. James Strachey. New York: Penguin, 1984.
- Friedman, Marilyn. *What Are Friends For? Feminist Perspectives on Personal Relationships and Moral Theory.* Ithaca: Cornell University Press, 1993.
- Fuller, Janine, and Stuart Blackley. *Restricted Entry: Censorship on Trial.* 2nd ed. Vancouver: Press Gang Publishers, 1995.
- Fuss, Diana. *Essentially Speaking: Feminism, Nature, and Difference.* New York: Routledge, 1989.

– ed. *Inside/Out: Lesbian Theories, Gay Theories.* New York: Routledge, 1991.

– *Identification Papers.* New York: Routledge, 1995.

Gagnon, John. 'Disease and Desire.' *Daedalus* 118 (Summer 1989): 47–77.

Gamson, Josh. 'Must Identity Movements Self-Destruct?: A Queer Dilemma.' *Social Problems* 42 (1995): 390–407.

Garber, Linda, ed. *Tilting the Tower: Lesbians Teaching Queer Subjects.* New York: Routledge, 1994.

Gates, Henry Louis, Jr. 'Beyond the Culture Wars: Identities in Dialogue.' *MLA Profession* 93 (1993): 6–11.

Gavey, Nicola. 'Feminist Poststructuralism and Discourse Analysis: Contributions to Feminist Psychology.' *Psychology of Women Quarterly* 13 (1989): 459–75.

Gavigan, Shelley. 'Paradise Lost, Paradox Revisited: the Implications of Familial Ideology for Feminist, Lesbian and Gay Engagement to Law.' *Osgoode Hall Law Journal,* 31 (1993): 589–624.

Giddens, Anthony. *The Transformation of Intimacy: Sexuality, Love and Eroticism in Modern Society.* Stanford: Stanford University Press, 1992.

Gilroy, Paul. 'Cultural Studies and Ethnic Absolutism.' In *Cultural Studies,* ed. Lawrence Grossberg, Cary Nelson, and Paula Treichler, 187–98. New York: Routledge, 1992.

Giroux, Henry. 'White Utopias and Nightmare Realities: Film and the New Cultural Racism.' In *Disturbing Pleasures: Learning Popular Culture,* ed. Henry Giroux, 67–92. New York: Routledge, 1994.

– 'Disturbing the Piece: Writing in the Cultural Studies Classroom.' Paper, Pennsylvania State University, n.d.

Glaser, Barney, and Anselm Strauss, *The Discovery of Grounded Theory: Strategies for Qualitative Research.* Chicago: Aldine, 1967.

Goldberg, David. *Racist Culture: Philosophy and the Politics of Meaning.* Oxford: Blackwell, 1993.

Golding, Sue. 'Sexual Manners.' *Public* 8 (1993): 161–8.

Goldstein, Richard. 'Go the Way Your Blood Beats: An Interview with James Baldwin.' In *James Baldwin: The Legacy,* ed. Quincy Troupe, 173–85. New York: A Touchstone Book, 1989.

Gooch, Brad. 'A Philadelphia Story.' *Advocate* 14 (December 1993).

Gore, Jennifer. *The Struggle for Pedagogies: Critical and Feminist Discourses as Regimes of Truth.* New York: Routledge, 1993.

Gorelick, Sherry. 'Contradictions of Feminist Methodology.' In *Feminism and Social Change: Bridging Theory and Practice,* ed. Heidi Gottfreid, 24–45. Urbana and Chicago: University of Illinois Press, 1996.

Gottfried, Heidi. *Feminism and Social Change: Bridging Theory and Practice.* Urbana and Chicago: University of Illinois Press, 1996.

Graham, Hilary. 'Social Divisions in Caring.' *Women's Studies International Forum* 16 (1993): 461–70.

Grosz, Elizabeth. *Jacques Lacan: A Feminist Introduction*. New York: Routledge, 1990.

Grover, Jan Zita. 'AIDS: Keywords.' In *AIDS: Cultural Analysis/Cultural Activism*, ed. Douglas Crimp, 17–30. Cambridge: MIT Press, 1988.

Habermas, Jurgen. *Communication and the Evolution of Society*. Boston: Beacon Press, 1979.

Haggerty, George E., and Bonnie Zimmerman, eds. *Professions of Desire: Lesbian and Gay Studies in Literature*. New York: MLA, 1995.

Hall, Donald, and Maria Pramaggiore, eds. *Representing Bisexualities: Subjects and Cultures of Fluid Desire*. New York: New York University Press, 1996.

Hall, Radclyffe. *The Well of Loneliness*. London: Virago, 1982.

Halley, Janet E. 'The Construction of Heterosexuality.' In *Fear of a Queer Planet: Queer Politics and Social Theory*, ed. M. Warner, 82–102. Minneapolis: University of Minnesota Press, 1993.

Halperin, David. 'Sex Before Sexuality: Pederasty, Politics, and Power in Classical Athens.' In *Hidden from History: Reclaiming the Gay and Lesbian Past*, ed. Martin Duberman, Martha Vicinus, and George Chauncey, Jr., 67–75. New York: Basic Books, 1990.

Hammersley, Martyn. *What's Wrong with Ethnography?* New York: Routledge, 1992.

Haraway, Donna. 'Situated Knowledges: The Science Question in Feminism and the Privilege of Partial Perspectives.' *Feminist Studies* 14 (1988) 575–99.

Hartsock, Nancy. 'Foucault on Power: A Theory for Theory.' In *Feminism/Postmodernism*, ed. Linda Nicholson, 157–75. New York: Routledge, 1990.

Haug, Frigga. *Female Sexualization: A Collective Work of Memory*. London: Verso, 1987.

Haver, William. 'Thinking the Thought of That Which Is Strictly Speaking Unthinkable: On the Thematization of Alterity in Nishida-Philosophy.' *Human Studies* 16 (1993): 177–92.

Henriques, Julian, Wendy Hollway, Cathy Urwin, Venn Couze, and Valerie Walkerdine. *Changing the Subject: Psychology, Social Regulation and Subjectivity*. London: Methuen, 1984.

Herman, Didi. *Rights of Passage: Struggles for Lesbian and Gay Legal Equality*. Toronto: University of Toronto Press, 1994.

Herman, Didi, and Carl Stychin, eds. *Legal Inversions: Lesbians, Gay Men and the Politics of Law*. Philadelphia: Temple University Press, 1995.

Hernandez-Leon, Ruben, et al. eds. Special issue of *Critical Sociology* 20, no. 3 (1994).

Hill, Marcia. 'A Matter of Language.' In *Boston Marriages: Romantic but Asexual Relationships among Contemporary Lesbians*, ed. Esther D. Rothblum and Kathleen A. Brehony. Amherst: University of Massachusetts Press, 1993.

Hixson, W.B.J. *Search for the American Right Wing: An Analysis of the Social Science Record, 1955–1987*. Princeton: Princeton University Press, 1992.

Hoagland, Sarah L. *Lesbian Ethics: Towards New Values*. Palo Alto: Institute of Lesbian Studies, 1988.

Honeychurch, Kenn Gardner. 'Researching Dissident Subjectivities; Queering the Grounds of Theory and Practice.' *Harvard Educational Review* 66, no. 2 (1996): 339–55.

hooks, bell. *Talking Back*. Boston: South End Press, 1989.

– *Yearning: Race, Gender, and Cultural Politics*, Boston: South End Press, 1990.

– *Teaching to Transgress: Education as the Practice of Freedom*. NYC: Routledge, 1994.

Hooyman, Nancy R., and Judith Gonyea. *Feminist Perspectives on Family Care: Policies for Gender Justice*. Thousand Oaks, CA: Sage, 1995.

Hughes, Holly. 'Identity Crisis: Queer Politics in the Age of Possibilities.' Interview by Alisa Soloman. In *Village Voice*, 30 June 1992.

Hunt, Scott A., Robert D. Benford, and Daniel A. Snow. 'Identity Fields: Framing Processes and the Social Construction of Movement Identities.' In *New Social Movements: From Ideology to Identity, ed.* Enrique Laraña, Hand Johnston, and Joseph R. Gusfield, 185–208. Philadelphia: Temple University Press, 1994.

Hutchins, Loraine, and Lani Ka'ahumanu, eds. *B: Any Other Name: Bisexual People Speak Out*. Boston: Alyson, 1991.

Indigenous Queers. 'Preaching to the Perverted, OR Fluid Desire.' Document produced for the Bisexual Caucus at the American Association of Physicians for Human Rights/ National HIV Prevention/Education Seminar, Dallas, 1994. Reprinted in *Anything That Moves* 9 (1995): 38.

Irvine, Janice. *Disorders of Desire: Sex and Gender in Modern American Sexology*. Philadelphia: Temple University Press, 1990.

– 'Lesbian Battering: The Search for Shelter.' In *Confronting Lesbian Battering*, ed. Pamela Elliot, 25–30. St. Paul: Minnesota Coalition for Battered Women, 1990.

Iyer, Nitya. 'Categorical Denials: Equality Rights and the Shaping of Social Identity.' *Queen's Law Journal* 1 (1993): 179–207.

– (also publishs as Nitya Duclos). 'Disappearing Women: Racial Minority Women in Human Rights Cases.' *Canadian Journal of Women and the Law*, 6 (1993): 25–51.

Jacobs, A.J. 'Out?' *Entertainment Weekly*, 4 October 1996, 18–25.

Jay, Karla, and Edith Benkov, eds. 'Queer Theory, Queer Concerns.' Special issue of *Concerns* 23, no. 3 (Fall 1993).

Jeffreys, Sheila. 'Does It Matter If They Did It?' In *Not a Passing Phase: Reclaiming Lesbians in History, 1840–1985*, ed. Lesbian History Group, 158–187. London: The Women's Press, 1989.

Jennings, Kevin, ed. *One Teacher in 10: Gay and Lesbian Educators Tell Their Stories.* Boston: Alyson Publications, 1994.

Johnston, Susan. 'Not for Queers Only: Pedagogy and Postmodernism.' *NWSA Journal* 7, no. 1 (1995): 109–21.

Julian, Isaac. 'Confessions of Snow Queen: Notes on the Making of the Attendant.' *Critical Quarterly* 36, no. 1: 120–5.

Kader, Cheryl, and Piontek, Thomas. 'Not a Safe Place: Feminist Pedagogy and Queer Theory in the Classroom.' *Concerns* 23, no. 3 (Fall 1993): 25–36.

Katz, Jonathan Ned. *Gay American History: Lesbians and Gay Men in the U.S.A.; A Documentary History.* New York: Cromwell, 1976.

– *The Invention of Heterosexuality.* New York: Penguin, 1995.

Kaye/Kantrowitz. *The Issue Is Power.* San Francisco: Aunt Lute Books, 1992.

Kealy, Michael. 'Lurking in the Dark: Are Backrooms an Antidote to or a Denial of Safer Sex?' *Xtra!* Toronto edition, no. 275 (1995), 23.

Kehoe, Monika. *Lesbians over 60 Speak for Themselves.* New York: Harrington Park Press, 1989.

Kelly, Jeffrey. *Changing HIV Risk Behavior: Practical Strategies.* New York: Guilford Press, 1995.

Kennedy, Elizabeth Lapovsky, and Madeline Davis. *Boots of Leather, Slippers of Gold: The History of a Lesbian Community.* New York: Penguin Books, 1994.

Khayatt, Didi. 'Legalized Invisibility: The Effects of Bill 7 on Lesbian Teachers.' *Women's Studies International Forum* 13, no. 3 (1990): 185–93.

– *Lesbian Teachers: An Invisible Presence.* Albany: State University of New York Press, 1992.

– 'In and Out: Experiences in the Academy.' In *Resist! Essays against a Homophobic Culture,* ed. Mona Oikawa, Dionne Falconer, and Ann Decter, 210–17. Toronto: Women's Press, 1994.

King, Edward. *Safety in Numbers: Safer Sex and Gay Men.* New York: Routledge, 1993.

Kinsman, Gary. 'Social Constructionism and Its Discontents.' Presentation at La Ville en Rose: First Quebec Lesbian and Gay Studies Conference, Montreal, November 1992.

– *The Regulation of Desire: Homo and Hetero Sexualities.* 2d ed. Montreal: Black Rose Books, 1996.

Kirby, Sandy, and Kate McKenna. *Experience, Research, Social Change: Methods from the Margins.* Toronto: Garamond Press, 1989.

Kitzinger, Celia. *The Social Construction of Lesbianism.* London: Sage, 1990.

Kitzinger, Celia, and Rachel Perkins. *Changing Our Minds: Lesbian Feminism and Psychology.* London: Onlywomen Press, 1993.

Klewans, Stuart. 'Holiday Celluloid Wrap-up.' *Nation* 3 (January 1994).

Klusáček, Allan, and Ken Morrison, eds. *A Leap in the Dark: AIDS, Art and Contemporary Cultures.* Artexte Edition. Montreal: Véhicule Press, 1993.

Koppelman, Andrew. 'Why Discrimination against Lesbians and Gay Men Is Sex Discrimination.' *New York University Law Review* 69 (1994): 197.

Kroll, Jack. '*Philadelphia*.' *Newsweek*, 27 December 1993.

Laird, Joan. 'Lesbian Families: A Cultural Perspective.' *Smith College Studies in Social Work* 64 (1994): 263–96.

Land, Hilary, and Hilary Rose. 'Compulsory Altruism for Some or an Altruistic Society for All?' In *In Defence of Welfare*, ed. Philip Bean, John Ferris, and David Whynes. London: Tavistock, 1985.

Laplanche, Jean. *Life and Death in Psychoanalysis*. Trans. Jeffrey Mehlman. Baltimore: Johns Hopkins Press, 1990.

Laplanche, Jean, and Jean Bertrand Pontalis. *The Language of Psycho Analysis*. Trans. Donald Nicholson Smith. New York: W.W. Norton, 1973.

– *The Language of Psycho-Analysis*. London: Hogarth Press, 1983.

Laraña, Enrique, Hank Johnston, and Joseph Gusfield. *New Social Movements: From Ideology to Identity*. Philadelphia: Temple University Press, 1994.

Lather, Patti. *Getting Smart: Feminist Research and Pedagogy With/In the Postmodern*. New York: Routledge, 1991.

– 'Critical Frames in Educational Research: Feminist and Post-structural Perspectives.' *Theory into Practice* 21, no. 2 (1992): 87–99.

Lather, Patti, and Elizabeth Ellsworth. Introduction, 'Situated Pedagogies' issue. *Theory into Practice* 35, no. 2 (1996): 70–1.

Lepofsky, David. 'The Canadian Judicial Approach to Equality Rights: Freedom Ride or Rollercoaster?' *National Journal of Constitutional Law* 1 (1992): 315.

Lesbian Information Service. *Old Lesbians: Resource List*. Todmorden: Lesbian Information Service, 1994.

Lorde, Audre. *Zami: A New Spelling of My Name*. Trumansburg. New York Crossing Press, 1982.

Lucas, J.R. 'The Lesbian Rule.' *Philosophy* 30 (1955): 195–213.

Maguire, Patricia. *Doing Participatory Research: A Feminist Approach*. Amherst: Center for International Education, School of Education, University of Massachusetts, 1987.

Majury, Diana. 'Strategizing (In)Equality.' *Wisconsin Women's Law Journal* 3 (1987): 169–87.

– 'Inequality and Discrimination according to the Supreme Court of Canada.' *Canadian Journal of Women and the Law* 4 (1991): 407–39.

– 'Refashioning the Unfashionable: Claiming Lesbian Identities in the Legal Context.' *Canadian Journal of Women and the Law* 7, no. 2 (1994): 286–317.

Manicom, Ann. 'Feminist Pedagogy: Transformations, Standpoints, and Politics.' *Canadian Journal of Education*, 17, no. 3 (1992): 365–89.

Martin, J.R. 'Aerial Distance, Esotericism, and Other Closely Related Traps.' *Signs* 21 (1994): 584–614.

Martindale, Kathleen. 'Theorizing Autobiography and Materialist Feminist Pedagogy.' *Canadian Journal of Education* 17, no. 3 (1992): 321–40.
– 'My (Lesbian) Breast Cancer Story: Can I Get a Witness?' In *Resist! Essays against a Homophobic Culture*, ed. Mona Oikawa, Dionne Falconer, and Ann Decter, 137–50. Toronto: Women's Press, 1994.
Maynard, Steven. 'Desperately Seeking a Discourse: Queer Theory and the Social Historians.' Presentation at La Ville en Rose: First Quebec Lesbian and Gay Studies Conference, Montreal, November 1992.
– 'In Search of Sodom North: The Writing of Lesbian and Gay History in English Canada, 1970–1990,' *Canadian Review of Comparative Literature* (March–June 1994): 117–32.
McLaren, Angus. *Our Own Master Race: Eugenics in Canada, 1885–1945*. Toronto: McClelland and Stewart, 1990.
Meekosha, Helen. 'The Bodies Politic – Equality, Difference and Community Practice.' In *Community and Public Policy*, ed. Hugh Butcher et al., 171–93. London: Pluto Press, 1993.
Mercer, Kobena. *Welcome to the Jungle*. New York and London: Routledge, 1994.
Merck, Mandy. *Perversions: Deviant Readings*. London: Verso, 1993.
Miller, D.A. *Bringing Out Roland Barthes*. Berkeley: University of California Press, 1992.
Miller, James. 'Introduction.' *Fluid Exchanges: Artists and Critics in the AIDS Crisis*, ed. James Miller, 3–22. Toronto: University of Toronto Press, 1992.
Minton, Henry, ed. *Gay and Lesbian Studies*. New York: Haworth, 1992.
Mittler, Mary L., and Amy Blumenthal. 'On Being a Change Agent: Teacher as Text, Homophobia as Context.' In *Tilting the Tower: Lesbians, Teaching, Queer Subjects*, ed. Linda Garber, 3–10. New York: Routledge, 1994.
Modleski, Tania. 'The State of the Art.' *Women's Review of Books* 8 (1981): 23.
– *Feminism without Women: Culture and Criticism in a 'Postfeminist' Age*. New York: Routledge, 1991.
Money, Janet. 'Oxford, London School Board Bigots?' *Xtra!* 288 (10 November 1995).
Moore Milroy, Beth, and Susan Wismer. 'Communities, Work and Public/Private Sphere Models.' *Gender, Place and Culture* 1 (1994): 71–90.
Morales, Edward. 'HIV Infection and Hispanic Gay and Bisexual Men.' *Hispanic Journal of Behavioural Sciences* 12, no. 2 (1990): 212–22.
Morrison, Toni. *Playing in the Dark: Whiteness and the Literary Imagination*. Cambridge: Harvard University, 1992.
Morton, Donald. 'The Politics of Queer Theory in the (Post)Modern Moment,' *Genders* 17 (Fall 1993): 121–50.
Myers, Ted, Dan Allman, Ed Jackson, and Kevin Orr. 'Variation in Sexual Orientations

among Men Who Have Sex with Men, and Their Current Sexual Practices.' *Canadian Journal of Public Health* 86, no. 6 (November–December 1995): 384–88.

Myers, Ted, Gaston Godin, Liviana Calzacara, Jean Lambert, and David Locker. *L'enquête Canadienne sur L'infection à Vih Menée auprès des Hommes Gais et Bisexuels: Au Masculin.* Société Canadienne du Sida: Ottawa, 1993.

Namaste, Ki. 'The Politics of Inside/Out: Queer Theory, Poststructuralism, and a Sociological Approach to Sexuality,' *Sociological Inquiry* 12, no. 2 (July 1994): 220–31.

– '"Tragic Misreadings": Queer Theory's Erasure of Transgender Subjectivity.' In *Queer Studies: A Lesbian, Gay, Bisexual, and Transgender Anthology*, ed. Brett Beemyn and Mickey Eliason, 183–203. New York: New York University Press, 1996.

Naples, Nancy A., and Emily Clark. 'Feminist Participatory Research and Empowerment: Going Public as Survivors Of Childhood Sexual Abuse.' In *Feminism and Social Change: Bridging Theory and Practice*, ed. by Heidi Gottfried, 160–183. Urbana and Chicago: University Of Illinois Press, 1996.

Nash, Brad. 'Chronicles of a Death Foretold: Notes Apropos of Les Muits Fauves,' *Critical Quarterly* 36, no. 1 (1994): 97–104.

National Gay and Lesbian Task Force. *Fight the Right Action Kit.* Washington, D.C.: National Gay and Lesbian Task Force, n.d.

Newton, Ester. *Mother Camp: Female Impersonators in America.* Englewood Cliffs: Prentice-Hall, 1972.

– 'The Mythic Mannish Lesbian: Radclyffe Hall and The New Woman.' In *Hidden from History: Reclaiming the Gay and Lesbian Past*, ed. Martin Duberman, Martha Vicinus, and George Chauncey, 281–93. New York: Basic Books, 1990.

Nichols, Mark. 'Beating AIDS : A "Cocktail" Treatment of Several Drugs Offers Hope.' *Maclean's* (15 July 1996): 38–43.

Nussbaum, Martha. *Love's Knowledge.* New York: Oxford University Press, 1990.

O'Connor, Patricia. 'Introduction: Discourse Of Violence.' *Discourse & Society* 6, no. 3 (1995), 309–19.

Odets, Walt. 'AIDS Education and Harm Reduction for Gay Men: Psychological Approaches for the 21st Century.' *AIDS and Public Policy* 9 (1995): 3–15.

– *In the Shadow of the Epidemic: Being HIV-Negative in the Age of AIDS.* Durham: Duke University Press, 1995.

Opie, Anne. *There's Nobody There: Community Care of Confused Older People.* Philadelphia: University of Pennsylvania Press, 1992.

Orner, Mimi. 'Teaching for the Moment: Intervention Projects as Situated Pedagogy.' *Theory into Practice* 35, no. 2 (1996): 72–8.

Ornstein, Michael. *AIDS in Canada: Knowledge, Behaviour and Attitudes of Adults.* Toronto: University of Toronto Press, 1989.

Padgug, Robert. 'Sexual Matters: On Conceptualizing Sexuality in History.' In *Passion and Power: Sexuality in History*, ed. K. Peiss and C. Simmons, 14–31. Philadelphia: Temple University Press, 1989.

Parker, Richard G., and John H. Gagnon, eds. *Conceiving Sexuality: Approaches to Sex Research in a Postmodern World*. New York and London: Routledge, 1995.

Patton, Cindy. *Sex and Germs*. Montreal: Black Rose, 1986.

– *Inventing AIDS*. New York: Routledge, 1990.

– 'Visualizing Safe Sex: When Pedagogy and Pornography Collide.' In *Inside/Out*, ed. Diana Fuss, 373–86. New York and London: Routledge, 1992.

– 'Designing Safer Sex: Pornography as Vernacular.' In *A Leap in the Dark: AIDS, Art and Contemporary Cultures*, ed. Allan Klusacek and Ken Morrison. Montreal: Véhicule, 1993.

– *Fatal Advice: How Safe-Sex Education Went Wrong*. Durham: Duke University Press, 1996.

Pearlman, Lynne. 'Theorizing Lesbian Oppression and the Politics of Outness in the Case of *Waterman* v. *National Life Assurance*: A Beginning in Lesbian Human Rights/Equality Jurisprudence.' *Canadian Journal Of Women and The Law* 7, no. 2 (1994): 454–508.

Peiss, Kathy, and Christina Simmons. 'Passion and Power: An Introduction.' In *Passion and Power: Sexuality in History*, ed. Kathy Peiss and Christina Simmons, 3–13. Philadelphia: Temple University Press, 1989.

People for the American Way. *Hostile Climate: A State by State Report on Anti-Gay Activity*. Washington, D.C.: People for the American Way, 1993.

Perrow, Charles, and Mauro Guillen. *The AIDS Disaster: The Failure Of Organizations in New York and the Nation*. New Haven: Yale University Press. 1990.

Petersen, Cynthia. 'Living Dangerously: Speaking Lesbian, Teaching Law.' *Canadian Journal of Women and the Law* 7, no. 2 (1994): 318–48.

Phelan, Peggy. *Unmarked: The Politics of Performance*. London: Routledge, 1993.

Phelan, Shane. '(Be)Coming Out: Lesbian Identity and Politics.' *Signs* 18, no. 4 (1993): 765–90.

– *Getting Specific: Postmodern Lesbian Politics*. Minneapolis: University of Minnesota Press, 1994.

Porteous, F., and S. Clarkson. *Challenging the Christian Right: The Activist's Handbook*. Great Barrington: Institute for First Amendment Studies, 1993.

Pratt, Minnie Bruce. *S/He*. Ithaca: Firebrand Books, 1995.

Queen, Carol. 'The Queer in Me.' In *Bi Any Other Name: Bisexual People Speak Out*, ed. Loraine Hutchins and Lani Ka'ahumanu, 17–21. Boston: Alyson, 1991.

Quinby, Lee, ed. *Genealogy and Literature*. Minneapolis: University Of Minneapolis Press, 1995.

Rabinow, Paul. 'Representations Are Social Facts.' In *Writing Culture: The Poetics and Politics of Ethnography*, eds. James Clifford and George E. Marcus. Berkeley: University of California Press, 1986.

Rapp, Rayna. 'Toward a Nuclear Freeze? The Gender Politics of Euro-American Kinship Analysis.' In *Gender and Kinship: Essays toward a Unified Analysis*, ed. Jane Fishburne Collier and Sylvia Junko Yangisako. Stanford: Stanford University Press, 1987.

Rapp, Rayna, and Ellen Ross. 'The Twenties Backlash: Compulsory Heterosexuality, the Consumer Family, and the Waning of Feminism.' In *Class, Race and Sex: The Dynamics of Control,* ed. Amy Swerdlow and Hanna Lessinger, Boston: G.K. Hall Publishers, 1983.

Raymond, Janice. *A Passion for Friends: Towards a Philosophy of Female Affection.* Boston: Beacon Press, 1986.

Rayside, David, and Evert Lindquist. 'Canada: Community Activism, Federalism, and the New Politics of Disease.' In *AIDS in the Industrialized Democracies: Passions, Politics, and Policies*, ed. David Kirp and Ronald Bayer, 49–98. Montreal: McGill-Queen's University Press, 1992.

Reed, Ralph. *Politically Incorrect.* Ingram Book Company, 1994.

Reinharz, Shulamit. *Feminist Methods in Social Research.* New York: Oxford University Press, 1992.

Renzetti, Claire M. 'Building a Second Closet: Third Party Responses to Victims of Lesbian Partner Abuse.' *Family Relations* 38 (1989): 157–63.

– *Violent Betrayal.* Newbury Park: Sage, 1992.

– 'Studying Partner Abuse in Lesbian Relationships: A Case for the Feminist Participatory Research Model.' In *Lesbian Social Services: Research Issues*, ed. Carol Tully, 29–42. New York: Haworth, 1995.

Rich, Adrienne. *On Lies, Secrets, and Silence.* New York: Norton, 1979.

Riley, Denise. *Am I That Name? Feminism and the Category of Women in History.* Minneapolis: University Of Minnesota Press, 1988.

Ristock, Janice L. 'Beyond Ideologies: Understanding Abuse in Lesbian Relationships.' *Canadian Woman Studies* 12, no. 1 (1991): 74–9.

– '"And Justice for All" ... Legal Responses to Abuse in Lesbian Relationships.' *Canadian Journal Of Women and The Law* 7, no. 2 (1994): 415–30

– 'The Cultural Politics of Abuse in Lesbian Relationships: Challenges for Community Action.' In *Subtle Sexism*, ed. Nijole Benokraitis. Newbury Park: Sage Publications, 1997.

Ristock, Janice L., and Joan Pennell. *Community Research as Empowerment: Feminist Links, Postmodern Interruptions.* Toronto: Oxford University Press, 1996.

Robson, Ruthann. 'Resisting the Family: Repositioning Lesbians in Legal Theory.' *Signs: Journal of Women in Culture and Society* 19 (1994): 975–996.

Rockhill, Kathy. 'And Still I Fight.' *Canadian Woman Studies Journal* 16 (1996): 93–8.

Rofes, Eric. 'Gay Lib vs. AIDS': Averting a Civil War in the 1990s.' *Out/Look* 2 (1990): 8–17.

– *Reviving the Tribe.* New York: Harrington Press, 1996.

Roof, Judith. *Come as You Are: Sexuality and Narrative.* New York: Columbia University Press, 1996.

Roof, Judith, and Robyn Wiegman, eds. *Who Can Speak? Authority and Critical Identity.* Chicago: University Of Illinois Press, 1995.

Rose, Daniel. *Living the Ethnographic Life.* London: Sage, 1990.

Rosenau, Pauline. *Insights, Inroads, Intrusions: Postmodernism and the Social Sciences.* Princeton, NJ: Princeton University Press, 1992.

Rosenberg, Rosalind. *Beyond Separate Spheres: Intellectual Roots of Modern Feminism.* New Haven: Yale University Press, 1982.

Ross, Becki. 'Wunna His Fantasies: The State/D Indefensibility of Lesbian Smut.' In *Fireweed* 2, no. 38 (Spring 1993): 38–47.

– *The House That Jill Built: A Lesbian Nation in Formation.* Toronto: University of Toronto Press, 1996.

Ross, Michael, A. Wodak, J. Gold, and M.E. Miller, 'Differences across Sexual Orientation on HIV Risk Behaviours in Injecting Drug Users.' *AIDS Care* 4, no. 2 (1992): 139–48.

Ross, Stephen. 'The Limits of Sexuality.' *Philosophy and Social Criticism* 9, no. 3–4 (1982): 320–36.

Ross, Val. 'How Will It Play in Peoria?' *Globe and Mail,* 14 January 1994.

Roy, Charles. *Living and Serving: Persons with HIV in the Canadian AIDS Movement.* Ottawa: Canadian AIDS Society, 1996.

Rule, Jane. *Memory Board.* Toronto: Macmillan, 1987.

Sacks, Oliver. *An Anthropologist on Mars.* Toronto: Random House, 1996.

Saraceno, Chiara. 'Division of Family Labour and Gender Identity.' In *Women and the State,* ed. Anne Showstack Sassoon. London: Unwin Hyman, 1987.

Scales, Ann. 'Avoiding Constitutional Depression: Bad Attitudes and the Fate of Butler.' *Canadian Journal of Women and the Law* 7 (1994): 349–92.

Schacter, Jane. 'The Gay Civil Rights Debate in the United States: Decoding the Discourse of Equivalents.' *Harvard Civil Rights–Civil Liberties Law Review* 29 (1994): 283–317.

Schechter, Susan. *Women and Male Violence: The Visions and Struggles of the Battered Women's Movement.* Boston: South End, 1982.

Schneider, Beth. 'Lesbian Politics and AIDS Work.' In *Modern Homosexualities: Fragments of Lesbian and Gay Experience,* ed. Ken Plummer, 160–74. New York: Routledge, 1992.

Scott, Joan. 'Experience.' In *Feminists Theorize the Political,* ed. Judith Butler and Joan Scott, 22–40. London: Routledge, 1992.

Sedgwick, Eve Kosofsky. *Between Men: English Literature and Male Homosocial Desire.* New York: Columbia University Press, 1985.

– *Epistemology of the Closet.* Berkeley and Los Angeles: University Of California Press, 1990.

– 'White Glasses.' *Yale Journal of Criticism* 53, no. 3 (1992): 193–208.
– 'Queer Performativity: Henry James's *The Art of the Novel.*' In *GLQ* 1, no. 1 (1993): 1–16.
Seidman, Steven. 'Identity and Politics in a "Postmodern" Gay Culture: Some Historical and Conceptual Notes.' In *Fear of a Queer Planet: Queer Politics and Social Theory,* ed. Michael Warner, 105–42. Minneapolis: University of Minnesota Press, 1993.
– 'Queer Theory/Sociology: A Symposium,' *Sociological Theory* 12, no. 2, (July 1994).
Serres, Michel. *The Parasite.* Baltimore, MD: Johns Hopkins University Press, 1982.
Sex Workers' Alliance of Toronto. Press release, September 1992.
Shilts, Randy. *And the Band Played On.* New York: St Martin's, 1987.
Shrewsbury, Carolyn. 'What Is Feminist Pedagogy?' *Women's Studies Quarterly* 21, no. 3/4 (1993): 8–16.
Silin, Jonathan. *Sex, Death and the Education of Children: Our Passion for Ignorance in the Age of AIDS.* New York: Teachers College Press, Columbia University, 1995.
Simon, Roger. *Teaching against the Grain: Texts for a Pedagogy of Possibility.* Toronto: OISE Press, 1992.
Sinding, Chris. 'Supporting a Lesbian with Breast Cancer: Weaving Care outside "Family."' MSW research report, McMaster University, 1994.
Singer, Linda. *Erotic Welfare: Sexual Theory and Politics in the Age of Epidemic.* New York: Routledge, Chapman, and Hall, 1993.
Smith, Anna Marie. 'Resisting the Erasure of Lesbian Sexuality: A Challenge for Queer Activism.' In *Modern Homosexualities: Fragments of Lesbian and Gay Experience,* ed. Ken Plummer, 200–13. New York: Routledge, 1992.
Smith, Dorothy. *The Everyday World as Problematic.* Toronto: University of Toronto Press, 1987.
– *The Conceptual Practices of Power: A Feminist Sociology of Knowledge.* Toronto: University of Toronto Press, 1990.
– 'Contradictions for Feminist Social Scientists.' In *Feminism and Social Change: Bridging Theory and Practice,* ed. Heidi Gottfried, 46–59. Urbana and Chicago: University of Illinois Press, 1996.
Smith, George. 'Political Activist as Ethnographer.' *Social Problems* 37, no. 4 (November): 629–48.
Smith-Rosenberg, Carroll. *Disorderly Conduct: Visions of Gender in Victorian America.* New York: Oxford University Press, 1985.
Spelman, Elizabeth. *Inessential Woman: Problems of Exclusion in Feminist Thought.* Boston: Beacon, 1988.
Spivak, Gayatri Chakravorty. The Post-Colonial Critic: Interviews, Strategies, Dialogues, ed. Sara Harasym. New York: Routledge, 1990.
– 'Acting Bits/Identity Talk.' *Critical Inquiry* 18, no. 4 (1992): 770–803.
– *Outside in the Teaching Machine.* New York: Routledge, 1993.

348   Bibliography

Stanley, Liz, and Sue Wise. *Breaking Out: Feminist Consciousness and Feminist Research*. London: Routledge and Kegan Paul, 1983.

Stein, Arlene, and Ken Plummer, '"I Can't Even Think Straight": "Queer" Theory and the Missing Sexual Revolution in Sociology.' *Sociological Theory* 12 (1994): 178–87.

Stein, Edward, ed. *Forms of Desire: Sexual Orientation and the Social Constructionist Controversy*. New York: Routledge, 1992.

Stone, Sharon, ed. *Lesbians in Canada*. Toronto: Between the Lines, 1991.

Stringer, Ernest. *Action Research*. Newbury Park: Sage, 1996.

Stychin, Carl. 'Unmanly Diversions: The Construction of Homosexual Body (Politic) in English Law.' *Osgoode Hall Law Journal* 32 (1994): 503–536.

– 'Essential Rights and Contested Identities: Sexual Orientation and Equality Rights Jurisprudence in Canada.' *Canadian Journal Of Law and Jurisprudence* 8 (1995): 49–66.

Sumpter, Sharon. 'Myths/Realities of Bisexuality,' In *Bi Any Other Name: Bisexual People Speak Out*, ed. Loraine Hutchins and Lani Ka'ahumanu, 12–13. Boston: Alyson, 1991.

Tancred–Shriff, Peta, ed. *Feminist Research: Prospect and Retrospect/Recherche Féministe: Bilan et Perspectives d'avenir*. Kingston and Montreal: McGill-Queen's University Press, 1988.

Tarrow, Sidney. *Power in Movement*. New York: Cambridge University Press, 1994.

Terry, Jennifer. 'Theorizing Deviant Historiography.' *Differences* 3, no. 2 (Summer 1991): 55–74.

Thomas, David. 'The "Q" Word.' *Socialist Review* (1995): 69–93.

Thompson, Karen, and Julie Andrzejewski. *Why Can't Sharon Kowalski Come Home?* San Francisco: Spinsters/Aunt Lute, 1988.

Tielman, Rob, ed. *Bisexuality and HIV/AIDS: A Global Perspective*. Buffalo: Prometheus Books, 1991.

Tielman, Rob, Manuel Carballo, and Art Hendriks, eds. *Bisexuality and HIV/AIDS: A Global Perspective*. Buffalo: Prometheus Books, 1991.

Toronto Centre for Lesbian and Gay Studies. *Lesbian, Gay, Bisexual, Transgender Studies in Canada: A Directory of Courses*. Toronto: TCLGS, 1995.

Trebilcot, Joyce. 'Dyke Methods.' *Hypatia* 3, no. 2 (1988): 1–13.

Treichler, Paula A. 'AIDS, Gender, and Biomedical Discourse: Current Contests for Meaning.' In *AIDS: The Burdens of History*, ed. Elizabeth Fee and Daniel Fox, 190–266. Berkeley: University of California Press, 1988.

– 'AIDS, Homophobia, and Biomedical Discourse: An Epidemic of Signification.' In *AIDS: Cultural Analysis/Cultural Activism*, ed. Douglas Crimp, 31–70. Cambridge, MA: MIT Press, 1988.

Tsing, Anna Lowenhaupt. *In the Realm of the Diamond Queen*. Princeton: Princeton University Press, 1993.

Turner, Bryam. *Descent into Discourse: The Reification of Language and the Writing of Social History.* Philadelphia: Temple University Press, 1990.

Udis-Kessler, Amanda. 'Present Tense: Biphobia as a Crisis of Meaning.' In *Bi Any Other Name: Bisexual People Speak Out*, ed. Loraine Hutchins and Lani Ka'ahumanu, 350–8. Boston: Alyson, 1991.

Ungerson, Clare. *Policy Is Personal: Sex, Gender and Informal Care.* London: Tavistock, 1987.

– 'The Language of Care: Crossing the Boundaries.' In *Gender and Caring: Work and Welfare in Britain and Scandinavia.* New York: Harvester Wheatsheaf, 1990.

Uribe, Virginia, and Karen M. Harbeck. 'Addressing the Needs of Lesbian, Gay, and Bisexual Youth: The Origins of PROJECT 10 and School-Based Intervention.' In *Coming out of the Classroom Closet*, ed. Karen M. Harbeck, 9–28. New York: Harrington Park Press, 1992.

Valverde, Mariana. 'As If Subjects Existed: Analyzing Social Discourse,' *Canadian Review of Sociology and Anthropology* 28, no. 2 (May 1991): 173–87.

– *'The Age of Light, Soap and Water': Moral Reform in English Canada, 1885–1925.* Toronto: McClelland and Stewart, 1991.

Van Maanen, John. *Tales of the Field: On Writing Ethnography.* Chicago: University of Chicago Press, 1988.

Verdecchia, Guillermo. *Fronteras Americanas: American Borders.* Toronto: Coach House, 1992.

Visweswaran, Kamala. *Fictions of Feminist Ethnography.* Minneapolis: University of Minnesota Press, 1994.

Walker, Gillian. *Family Violence and the Women's Movement: The Conceptual Politics of Struggle.* Toronto: University of Toronto Press, 1990.

Walsh-Bowers, Richard and Sydney Parlour. 'Researcher-Participant Relationships in Journal Reports on Gay Men and Lesbian Women.' *Journal of Homosexuality* 23, no. 4 (1992): 93–113.

Walters, Suzanna Danuta. 'From Here to Queer: Radical Feminism, Postmodernism, and the Lesbian Menace.' *Signs* 21, no. 4 (1996): 831–69.

Warner, Michael, ed. *Fear of a Queer Planet: Queer Politics and Social Theory.* Minneapolis: University of Minnesota Press, 1993.

– 'Something Queer about the Nation State.' *Alphabet City* 3 (1993): 14–17.

Watney, Simon. 'School's Out.' In *Inside/Out*, ed. Diana Fuss, 387–404. New York and London: Routledge, 1992.

– 'The Possibilities of Permutation: Pleasure, Proliferation, and the Politics of Gay Identity in the Age of AIDS.' In *Fluid Exchanges: Artists and Critics in the AIDS Crisis*, ed. James Miller, 329–68. Toronto: University of Toronto Press, 1992.

– 'The Subject of AIDS.' In *AIDS: Social Representations, Social Practices*, ed. Peter Aggleton, Graham Hart, and Peter Davies, 64–73. New York: Falmer, 1989.

Weeks, Jeffrey. *Sexuality and Its Discontents: Meanings, Myths and Modern Sexualities.* London: Routledge, 1985.
– 'Post-Modern AIDS?' In *Ecstatic Antibodies: Resisting the AIDS Mythology,* ed. Tessa Boffin and Sunil Gupta. London: Rivers Oram, 1990.
– 'Pretended Family Relationships.' In *Against Nature: Essays on History, Sexuality and Identity.* London: Rivers Oram Press, 1991.
Weinberg, Martin, Colin Williams, and Douglas Pryor. *Dual Attraction: Understanding Bisexuality.* New York: Oxford University Press, 1994.
Weiss, Penny A. 'Feminist Reflections on Community.' In *Feminism and Community,* ed. Penny A. Weiss and Marilyn Friedman, 3–20. Philadelphia: Temple University Press, 1995.
West, Cornel. 'Cornel West on Heterosexism and Transformation: An Interview.' *Harvard Educational Review* 66, no. 2 (1996): 356–67.
Weston, Kath. *Families We Choose: Lesbians, Gays, Kinship.* New York: Columbia University Press, 1991.
Whisman, Vera. *Queer by Choice.* New York: Routledge, 1996.
White, Barbara, ed. Special issue on sexual orientation. *NWSA Journal* 7, no. 1 (Spring 1995).
Wickham, Gary, and William Haver. 'Come Out, Come Out, Wherever You Are: A Guide for the Homoerotically Disadvantaged.' Unpublished Paper, 1992.
Williams, Barbara J. 'Inadmissible Teaching Identities: Subjects of Sexuality.' *Review of Education/Pedagogy/Cultural Studies* 16, no. 2 (1994): 153–61.
Williams, Diane. 'Who's That Teacher? The Problem of Being a Lesbian Teacher of Colour.' In *Resist! Essays against a Homophobic Culture,* ed. Mona Oikawa, Diane Falconer, and Ann Decter, 65–9. Toronto: Women's Press, 1994.
Williams, Raymond. *Keywords: A Vocabulary of Culture and Society.* London: Fontana Press, 1983.
Wilton, Tamsin. *Lesbian Studies: Setting an Agenda.* London and New York: Routledge, 1995.
Wintemute, Robert. 'Sexual Orientation Discrimination as Sex Discrimination: Same-Sex Couples and the *Charter.* In *Mossop, Egan, and Layland.*' *McGill Law Journal* 39 (1994): 429–478.
Wolff, Robert Paul. *Beyond Tolerance.* Boston: Beacon Press, 1965.
Woodward, Kathleen. 'Freud and Barthes: Theorizing Mourning, Sustaining Grief.' *Discourse* 13, no. 1 (Fall–Winter 1990–1): 93–110.
– 'Grief-Work in Contemporary American Cultural Criticism.' *Discourse* 15, no. 2 (Winter 1992–3): 94–112.
Woog, Dan. *School's Out: The Impact of Gay and Lesbian Teaching Issues on America's Schools.* Boston: Alyson Publications, 1995.

Wright, Elizabeth, ed. *Feminism and Psychoanalysis: A Critical Dictionary*. Massachusetts: Basil Blackwell, 1992.

Yanagisako, S.J. 'Towards a Unified Analysis of Gender and Kinship.' In *Gender and Kinship: Essays toward a Unified Analysis*, ed. Jane Fishburne Collier and Sylvia Junko Yangisako. Stanford: Stanford University Press, 1987.

Young, Claire. 'Taxing Times for Lesbians and Gay Men: Equality at What Cost?' *Dalhousie Law Journal* 17 (1995): 534–559.

Zilliox, L., Jr. *The Opposition Research Handbook: Guide to Political Investigations*. McLean: Investigative Research Specialists, 1993.

Zimmerman, Bonnie, and Toni A.H. McNaron, eds. *The New Lesbian Studies: Into the Twenty-First Century*. New York: Feminist Press, City University of New York, 1966.

Zita Grover, Jan. 'AIDS: Keywords.' In *AIDS: Cultural Analysis, Cultural Activism*, ed. Douglas Crimp, 17–30. Cambridge: MIT Press, 1988.

– 'Activism, Federalism, and the New Politics Of Disease.' In *AIDS in the Industrialized Democracies: Passions, Politics, and Policies*, ed. David Kirp and Ronald Bayer, 49–98. Montreal and Kingston: McGill-Queen's University Press, 1992.

Contributors

Jane Aronson is an associate professor in the School of Social Work at McMaster University in Hamilton. In her teaching and in her participation in the Hamilton Lesbian and Gay Social Work Group, she is interested in challenging heterosexism and homophobia in social work and social welfare, and in working towards anti-oppressive practice and policy. Her research and writing focuses on women's paid and unpaid caring labour, the positioning of elderly women receiving care, and underlying constructions of family, need, and entitlement to public support and resources.

Deborah P. Britzman is an associate professor in the Faculty of Education at York University in Toronto. She is the author of *Practice Makes Practice: A Critical Study of Learning to Teach* (1991) and *Lost Subjects, Contested Objects: Toward a Psychoanalytic Inquiry of Learning* (1998), both from the State University Press of New York, in Albany.

Mary Bryson teaches in the Faculty of Education at the University of British Columbia. Her work is in the areas of queer pedagogy and queer ethnography.

Roy Cain is an associate professor of social work at McMaster University. His previous publications examine the evolution of community-based AIDS organizations in Canada, complementary-therapy use among people living with HIV/AIDS, disclosure and secrecy among gay men, and confronting heterosexism in social-work education. He has recently begun a study of the role of community choirs in the development of social networks of gay men and lesbians.

Suzanne de Castell teaches in the Faculty of Education at Simon Fraser University in Burnaby, B.C. She continues to work in the areas of queer pedagogy and queer ethnography.

Lee Easton teaches communications theory and composition in the Department of English at Mount Royal College in Calgary. He is currently researching the impact of new technologies on the teaching of English for his doctoral dissertation at the Ontario Institute for Studies in Education/University of Toronto (OISE–UT). In addition to an interest in representations of sexuality in popular culture, he is working on issues arising from the intersection of technology, the body, and sexuality in cyberspace.

Kristin Esterberg is an assistant professor of sociology at the University of Massachusetts-Lowell. In addition to her work on the religious right, her research focuses on the construction of sexual identities and sexual communities. Her book *Lesbian and Bisexual Identities: Constructing Communities, Constructing Selves* was published in 1997 by Temple University Press.

Margot Francis is a doctoral candidate in the Department of History and Philosophy at OISE–UT, and is a teaching assistant at the University of Toronto. She continues to queer(y) antihomophobia education with youth.

Didi Khayatt is an associate professor in the Faculty of Education, at York University. She is the author of *Lesbian Teachers: An Invisible Presence* (SUNY Press, 1992) and related articles in a number of publications. She works in the areas of feminist pedagogy, lesbian and gay studies, and critical theories.

Jeffrey Longhofer is associate professor and chair of the anthropology department at the University of North Texas. He has published widely in the area of sectarian religious communities. More recently his work has concentrated on religious and political extremism and agrarian populism.

Diana Majury is a white, nondisabled lesbian feminist. She teaches in the Department of Law at Carleton University in Ottawa.

Ki Namaste currently researches HIV/AIDS and health care issues for transgendered people in Québec. Her book on these questions is forthcoming from the University of Chicago Press.

Jean Noble is a PhD student in the graduate program in English at York University, and is currently exploring the pleasures and perils of female masculinity in the twentieth century.

Blaine Mark Rehkopf is a doctoral student in the Department of Philosophy at York University. He works primarily on topics in the philosophy of gender and sexuality. His dissertation examines the possibility and implications of sexual perversion as a philosophical concept.

Janice L. Ristock is an associate professor and coordinator of women's studies at the University of Manitoba. She coauthored, with Joan Pennell, *Community Research as Empowerment: Feminist Links, Postmodern Interruptions* (Oxford University Press, 1996). She is past-president and a founding member of the Canadian Lesbian and Gay Studies Association. She continues to do antiheteronormative work with feminist and lesbian community groups.

Catherine G. Taylor teaches in the Centre for Academic Writing at the University of Winnipeg. She is completing her doctoral dissertation at OISE/University of Toronto on the emergence of lesbian studies into the discourse of the liberal arts. She was a founding member of the Canadian Lesbian and Gay Studies Association and has served as the lesbian caucus representative on the executive of the Canadian Women's Studies Association. She and Janice Ristock are co-editing a special issue of *Atlantis* on the theme of "Sexualities and Feminism."

Index

abuse, 108, 138, 141; heterosexual, 145; in lesbian relationships, 148; racialized, 147; violence, 138, 150
academic activism, 4
ACT-UP (AIDS Action Now), 216
Adams, Mary Louise, 7
affirmation, 17
African-American, 188, 299–300
African-Canadian community, 127
Afro-American studies, 16
Agamben, Giorgio, 63
AIDS, 6, 62, 90, 114–15, 122, 127, 178, 201, 204, 206–7, 210–11, 214, 220, 226, 228, 230, 234–5, 239–41, 253, 255, 268, 273–4; activism, 7, 113, 200, 216; ACT-UP (AIDS Action Now), 216; agenda, 201; Committee of Toronto, 131; bisexual activism in, 125, 127; Black Coalition for AIDS Prevention, 127, 131, 247; Black identity and response, 208, 210; Canadian AIDS Society, 122, 125; caregiving, 178; community-based organizations, 199; community based work, 217; education, 7, 58, 65, 118, 122–3, 126–9, 132, 158, 206; feminist analysis, 207; First Nations/Native people, 200, 207, 209;

homophobic response, 209; identity politics in AIDS work, 217; identity issues in, 216; IV drug users, 215; movement in Canada, 212; movement in North America, 200–2; not a gay disease, 204; person living with AIDS (PLWA), 200; person living with HIV and AIDS (PHA), 200; policy-making, 236; program funding, 212; psychosexual discourse of, 230–1; psychosocial discourse of, 230–1; racism in AIDS work, 209; research, 122; San Francisco Health Commission, 223; second wave, 229; service organizations, 126, 158, 200–1, 203, 205–6, 212, 214; service providers, 202; sexism in AIDS work, 208–9; women and, 211
Altman, Dennis, 111
Amendment 2 (Colorado), 188
American Civil Liberties Union, 184, 192
American Constitution, 247
American Declaration of Independence, 247
Andrews decision, 295–6
Anglo-American: social scientists, 117; scholarship, 117

Christian right (NCR), 305; Oregon Citizens Alliance, 189; postmillennialist theology, 184, 191; Reed, Ralph, 186; Regent University, 186; religious right, 6, 158, 183, 185, 191, 263, 305; Robertson, Pat, 186; 700 Club, 186; Sheldon, Lou, 188, 190; Traditional Values Coalition, 185, 190
Renzetti, Claire, 140
representation, 17, 250; legal, 294
research, 13; as empowerment, 140; community-based, 13, 139–40; ethnographic, 104, 137; feminist, 8, 149; historical, 13, 79-81; historiographic, 78; participatory, 139; social action, 137
research theory, 3, 6
Ricci, Nino, 284
Rich, Adrienne, 105
Rights of Passage: Struggles for Lesbian and Gay Legal Equality (Herman), 303, 306
Riley, Denise, 76
Ristock, Janice, 5, 13, 157
Robertson, Pat, 186
Robson, Ruthann, 311–12
Rockhill, Kathy, 164
Rofes, Eric, 202
role models, 16–17, 32, 37, 40–1
Rose, Dan, 99
Rosenberg, Rosalind, 79
Rosenblum, Barbara, 164, 177
Ross, Becki, 280–1, 284, 287
Ross, Stephen David, 224
Rotundo, Anthony, 85–6
Rule, Jane, 163, 176
Rushdoony, R.J., 184

Sacks, Oliver, 97
sadomasochism, 147–8, 209, 281, 284

safer sex, 7, 90–1, 221, 226–8, 230–1, 234, 241; education, 7, 221, 233, 237; reductivist discourse, 229–30, 233
same-sex: desire, 233; experience, 83; love, 238; partnerships, 171–2; relationships, 80, 83, 240; sexuality, 236, 240
San Francisco Model, 122
Sapphistry, 284
Schacter, Jane, 296–7
Schneider, Beth, 200
scholarship: Anglo-American, 117; anti-racist, 78; ethnographic, 98; gay, 111; feminist, 78; lesbian, 111; queer, 78
Scott, Joan, 4, 72, 77–8
Sedgwick, Eve Kosofsky, 21, 35–6, 38, 45, 58, 61–3, 81
Seidman, Steven, 89, 277
sexologists, 88
sexuality, 78–9; as power, 8; class and, 79, 84; historical discourse on, 87; in movies, 245, 247; labelling, 73; language of, 87; race and, 79, 84, 90–1; same-sex, 236, 240; studies, 279; women's, 73
sexual orientation, 31–2, 72, 149, 188, 294–5, 299, 301, 303, 318
Sheldon, Lou, 188, 190
Shelton, Marc, 187
Shrewsbury, Carolyn, 19
Siegel, Carol, 4
Silin, Jonathon, 34, 42, 45
Simon, Roger, 20
Sinding, Chris, 164, 178
Singer, Linda, 268–9, 273–4, 277
Smith, Anna-Marie, 217
Smith, Dorothy, 100, 113, 130, 137, 194
Smith, George, 113–14
Smith, Judge John, 278, 280–8
Smith-Rosenberg, Caroll, 87–8

DATE DUE

AUG 2 9 2000			
NOV 1 3 2000			
NOV 1 3 2000			
DEC 1 1 2000			
DEC 1 1 2000			
DEC 1 8 2002			
JA 02 03			
MAR 1 6 2004			
APR 2 1 2004			
AP 16 '04			
DEC 1 4 2004			
APR 0 5 2007			
GAYLORD			PRINTED IN U.S.A.